EDWARD GREER

# BLACK LIBERATION POLITICS: A READER

**Black Liberation Politics**
A Reader

# Black Liberation Politics
## A Reader

Edited by

**Edward Greer**
WHEATON COLLEGE, Massachusetts

**ALLYN AND BACON, INC., Boston**

*To the leaders of the American revolution,*
Huey P. Newton and Bobby Seale

# Contents

# Black Liberation Politics
A Reader

# 1 | Introduction*

The problem of the twentieth century is the problem of the
color line.                    —W.E.B. Du Bois (1903)

Black liberation politics is the most vital force in
American life. In its struggle to overcome the centuries
of oppression of black people in America, it represents the
most serious and consistent mass attempt to realize the
democratic, egalitarian impulses of American society.
It fosters an atmosphere conducive to the flourishing of
American culture—in art, music, literature, and philosophy.

The oppression of black Americans is simultaneously a
*class* oppression and a *national* oppression. Black Americans
have undergone experiences of exploitation in common
with all the working people of America—in the workshops
and offices, in the urban slums, as matériel for the military
machine. Hence they suffer, along with nonblack workers,
from the nature of a political economy in which those
few who control production control as well the quality
of life for everyone.

Yet black Americans have faced a further historic
oppression on the basis of race. As a people they have
been subjected to chattel slavery, then to southern peonage
as sharecroppers; and finally they have undergone
urbanization as the most oppressed sector of the industrial
working-class and as a sub-proletariat restricted to

* The editor gratefully acknowledges the invaluable assistance of
Miss Fran White of Wheaton College in the preparation of this
manuscript; and Mr. Stewart Pollack in the preparation of the
introductory materials.

marginal service jobs. These experiences common to black
Americans, singled out for massive and systematic
discrimination, have resulted in the development of a
common cultural identity: black nationhood.

The black liberation movement addresses itself to both
the class and the national aspects of black oppression.
Thus, the struggle for the liberation of black America is,
on the one hand, part of the worldwide struggle of
oppressed nationalities for national liberation—the
anti-imperialist struggle; and on the other hand, it is
part of the struggle of those subject to the dehumanization
of the capitalist work process to gain control over the
fruits of their labor—the class struggle. In the modern
world, these two struggles largely coincide in practice,
for the battle against imperialism is simultaneously the
battle against capitalism and the fight for socialism.

This is the position of revolutionary forces throughout
the world. It is the position taken by the Black Panther
Party, the vanguard of the black liberation movement in
the United States. The American government has left no
question open regarding its policy toward the Black
Panther Party—toward the goal of eliminating the Panther
as a political force, the government has fabricated
frame-up trials and permitted the murder of Party
members by local police forces. Such violent repression
bears testimony to the potential danger that the Party,
and the black liberation movement as a whole, holds
for the existing social order.

The major unanswered question before this country is
whether the mass of the white working population will
unite with the black people of America in their struggle
against imperialism; or whether whites will stand aside,
blinded by the racism engendered in them by centuries
of relative privilege within the system, while those who
rule the country resort to mass extra-legal violence to
contain the black liberation struggle. The fate of America,
and perhaps the world, lies in the balance.

This *Reader* does not address itself to that question.
Its task is rather to explicate the rise of black liberation
politics, in particular the rise of black nationalism, and
to explore the dialectic within the black community

regarding the strategic direction which the struggle for
liberation should take. The *Reader* does not pretend to
be more than an introduction to the subject, incomplete
in many respects, and more useful as a guide to the
development of black politics than as a treatment of black
history or a discourse on America's political and
social order.*

The format of the *Reader* is uncomplicated. Following
this introduction, the book is divided into four sections,
each with a preface by the editor. Section II, *The
Structural Basis of Black Oppression*, attempts to give a
brief summary of the nature and magnitude of the
oppression which black America experiences.

Section III, *The Forging of a Black Nation in America*,
attempts to describe and analyze some of the forces and
events which account for the growing conviction of black
Americans that their unique cultural life amounts to a
separate national identity. This section offers articles on
the legacy of slavery; on the role of religion in the black
community and the relation of religion to political life;
and on some aspects of black politics during this century,
particularly in the late thirties and the forties. This
thesis on the emergence of a black nation, still controversial,
is implicit in the materials in this section—materials
which discuss the character of black religious organizations
and their special role in shaping political consciousness,
and articles on radical black political activities prior to
the flourishing of the civil rights movement.

Section IV, *A Case Study of Gary, Indiana*, undertakes
a dual task. First, it makes use of the city as a concrete
example to examine the milieu surrounding the emergence
of black political consciousness, the obstacles to black
power, and the manner in which the black citizens of
Gary have achieved enough effective power to elect a
mayor. Second, Section IV attempts to indicate what
the election has really produced and what it implies
for future political efforts.

---

* Readers are referred to the works of Eugene Genovese, and to
Paul Baran and Paul Sweezy, *Monopoly Capital* (New York: Monthly
Review Press, 1966), for a good place to begin learning about
such matters.

Section V, *The Struggle for Black Political Power,* is by
far the longest and most important part of the book.
This final section contrasts the high degree of black
participation in the formal political process with the
relatively small share of actual power which blacks possess.
It indicates that the direction and content of black politics
is increasingly determined by the grass-roots activities
of local black militants. Section V presents the views of
black politicians and intellectuals concerning the process
of ferment within the black community; and it suggests
something about the roots and the implications of the rise
of a revolutionary component within black America—one
which demands the radical reconstitution of American
society.

This summary perhaps grants the various readings more
unity and cohesion than is actually the case. Indeed,
what is most striking about current black liberation
politics is its fluidity. Although the problems remain
almost intractable, black political activitists and intellectuals
formulate their approaches, goals, strategies, and tactics
with remarkable mobility and energy.

# II | The Structural Basis of National Oppression

Throughout the history of our nation, black Americans have been subjected to an *institutional structure of racism.* Institutional racism remains the single most important fact in the life of black America.

The institutional structure of racism exists independently of the opinions and intentions of the American people. It rests on the character of American social institutions: in the distribution of property and power. It manifests itself in every sphere of life: in employment and income distribution; in educational opportunity; in commerce and industry; in scientific endeavor; in the trade unions and churches; in the media and cultural apparatus.

This structure of racism also provides the basis in human experiences for the existence and perpetuation of racial prejudice, for it divides black and white Americans into two separate, and unequal, worlds.

Despite the wishful thinking of many white people, recent years have not seen a significant breakdown of the institutional structure which supports racism. Although there are some areas in which blacks have made important gains, such as the destruction of jim crow, there are others in which the trends have been adverse, such as the increase of *de facto* school segregation since 1954. On balance, it is unlikely that the relative position of the mass of black Americans has been significantly improved since the end of World War II.*

---

* The best short summary of the social and economic situation of black Americans is Thomas Mayer, "The Position and Progress of Black America," readily available in David Mermelstein (ed.),

The two articles in this section are intended as illustrations of the position of black Americans within the institutional structures of the society. Conclusions similar to those drawn from these articles follow an examination of black America's place in virtually every sector of American life. For instance, it is now notorious that the American legal system, from police behavior to jury selection, from court sentencing patterns to chances of parole, sharply discriminates against blacks.† Likewise the college where the editor teaches has fewer than 2 percent black students and does not have a single black faculty member, administrator, or trustee.

"The Enduring Ghetto," by Gilbert Osofsky demonstrates that in New York City—with America's largest concentration of blacks—the major slum problems of housing discrimination, poverty, inadequate employment opportunity, etc., remain as pressing as ever. Professor Osofsky, a white American historian, has written an excellent historical monograph on Harlem, *Harlem: The Making of a Ghetto* (New York: Harper and Row, 1966), which has many additional details about the formation of the Manhattan ghetto.

It is worth noting that the gloomy picture of Harlem is typical for black urban communities. Although Osofsky devotes himself mainly to social and economic indicators, the problem of housing segregation lies near the heart of the matter. All available evidence indicates that housing segregation has been on the rise throughout the country in recent times.‡

In "Black Powerlessness in Chicago," Harold M. Baron and his co-authors focus on the economic and political decision-making power wielded by black Chicagoans.

---

*Economics: Mainstream Readings and Radical Critiques* (New York: Random House, 1970), pp. 297–307. More generally, see *The Report of the National Advisory Commission on Civil Disorders* (Washington, D.C.: U.S. Government Printing Office, 1968).

  † A good introduction is Haywood Burns, "Can a Black Man Get a Fair Trial in This Country?," *The New York Times Magazine* (12 July 1970): 5ff.

  ‡ See, for instance, Karl E. Taeuber, "Residential Segregation," *Scientific American* (August 1965): 12–19, for a nontechnical discussion of this phenomenon.

Their careful scrutiny of the available evidence leads
them to the conclusion that although blacks make up
almost 30 percent of Chicago's population, they hold less
than 1 percent of the power. Though one may question
whether such matters can really be accurately quantified,
there is no doubt that black Chicago dwellers are grossly
underrepresented in positions of authority and power.
Chicago undoubtedly possesses one of the most powerful,
wealthy, and cohesive black communities in America.
The Chicago black community was well formed at least
a decade earlier than most other major northern ghettoes;
and it developed an internal political structure and business
class of some size even prior to the First World War.
See Allan H. Spear, *Black Chicago: The Making of a
Negro Ghetto, 1890–1920* (Chicago: University of Chicago
Press, 1967). The relative powerlessness of black Chicago
stands for an equivalent weakness in other northern
ghettoes, and in southern urban and rural areas as well.

The constant tendency to understate the extent and
depth of the institutional structures of racism in American
life is not surprising; for to acknowledge it is to indict
America's political economy. And moreover, it is to point
toward a political strategy for black power which has as its
objective the dismantling of those institutional structures
which support racism—a task of considerable magnitude.
But a clear recognition of the obstacles to the advancement
of the black community in America is the prerequisite
of any serious effort to overcome them.

# 1 | The Enduring Ghetto*

## Gilbert Osofsky

There were two passengers on board the Atlantic when I returned from Europe who had rode with me on the same car from London to Liverpool, and we enjoyed the same privileges on board the steamer. They were foreigners, and I a American; and when they landed in this country, they were boasting that they had arrived at a land of liberty, where they could enjoy religious and political freedom. I, too, might have rejoiced, had I not been a colored man, at my return to my native land. But I knew what treatment I had to expect from my countrymen— that it would not be even such as was meted out to those foreigners, and I rejoiced only to meet my anti-slavery friends. We all started to walk up the streets of Philadelphia together; we hailed an omnibus; the two foreigners got in; I was told that "niggers" were not allowed to ride. Foreigners, mere adventurers, perhaps, in this country, are treated as equals, while I, an American born, whose grandfather fought in the Revolution, am not permitted to ride in one of your fourth-rate omnibuses. The foreigner has a right, after five years' residence, to say who shall be President, as far as his vote goes, even though he cannot read your Constitution nor write his name, while 600,000 free colored people are disenfranchised. And then you talk about equality and liberty, the land of the free and the home of the brave, the asylum of the oppressed, the cradle of liberty!

William Wells Brown, 1854

This essay will discuss what I consider the most important generalization that emerges from a study of Negro life in New York City from

Reprinted from *Journal of American History* LV (September 1968): 243–255. By permission of the Organization of American Historians.

* The term "ghetto" is most commonly applied to racially restrictive housing patterns. It is meant to have broader connotations in this essay: as an impressionistic and interpretive phrase which meaningfully summarizes the social, economic and psychological positions of black people in the city in the nineteenth and twentieth centuries and also symbolizes the tone of urban race relations in these years.

the early nineteenth century to the present.[1] At first glance the worlds seem hardly comparable. The most obvious distinctions appear to be the radical changes in Negro status and in race relations that have taken place between the Jacksonian era and the America of Watts, Newark and Detroit. It is my thesis, however, that despite seeming transformations, some of which I shall describe, the essential structure and nature of the Negro ghetto has remained remarkably durable since the demise of slavery in the North. There is an unending and tragic sameness about black life in the metropolis over the two centuries.

Some of the most obvious differences should be noted within this dominant pattern of continuity. The most striking relate to the size and origins of the Negro population. When slavery ended in New York in 1827 some 13,000 black people, the majority of whom had been born within the state, resided in Manhattan. They represented 1.5 percent of the city's population on the eve of the Civil War as, at the same time, more than half the residents of the metropolis were foreign born. The Negro population remained relatively stable from the 1850's through the 1870's as the city literally became "Gotham," with Manhattan's population exceeding a million in 1875. Between 1860 and 1890 Negroes never represented more than 1.6 percent of the city's increasingly heterogeneous population.[2] They were indeed "invisible" to all but a small group of abolitionists in the antebellum period and the handful of religious and charity workers in the late nineteenth century.

Mass migration since the 1890's reshaped the Negro community. By 1900, for the first time in the city's history, more than half the black population had migrated from other states. In 1920 more Negroes lived in New York City than in any other American urban area. The present black community, exceeding a million, represents the largest concentration of blacks in any metropolitan area in American history. The status of a formerly "invisible" minority ("It is a . . . whole stratum of society . . . of whose very existence most of us are wholly unaware") has been transformed into one of the principal concerns of contemporary society. The burgeoning growth of the Negro population has also laid the foundations for the important shift in ghetto militancy and mood that have characterized America's urban areas since Harlem's riot of 1964. And it has also permitted the emergence of a modicum of black political power—a force that was almost totally absent from nineteenth century life.[3]

Another difference, one most commonly pointed to, deals with the physical location of the black population. There were no Harlems in the nineteenth century. Although Negroes were usually more concentrated in one single area than in others—early in the century in Five Points, later in the Tenderloin and San Juan Hill districts—these neighborhoods were small enough to be bordered by and interspersed with streets occupied by whites. Occasionally, especially among the lower classes, some whites lived in the same tenements as Negroes.[4] A more general dispersion was caused by the number of Negro domestics who resided in the homes of their white employers. When the Quakers of Philadelphia attempted to estimate the size of the black population in 1837 and 1847, for example, they found it necessary to add 4000 to 5000 people to their calculations to account for "servants living in."[5] In 1835, six Manhattan wards had more than 1000 Negro residents; in 1860 and 1875 four wards had a similar number of inhabitants; in 1890 there were again six wards of heavy Negro concentration, each inhabited by 2000 to 4000 black people.[6]

Dr. Robert C. Weaver has used this apparent dispersion of Negro residences in the nineteenth century city to argue that black people were "concentrated but not always separated" then. "Few Americans realize that widespread, enforced residential segregation on the basis of color is relatively new in the North," Weaver writes. ". . . Negroes, themselves, though better informed than the general public, sometimes forget that their ancestors and older friends were not always hemmed into too little space. . . . The Negro ghetto in northern cities is of recent origin. . . ."[7] The implications of Weaver's interpretation are obvious (and are analogous to other well known historical restoration themes dealing with slavery and race relations): If America had once permitted greater residential mobility to Negroes, present advocates of racially-free occupancy in the city are attempting to reclaim an older tradition that was lost under the pressure of the great migrations of the twentieth century; they are not establishing a new one. History in this view becomes a useful weapon for the socially conscious city planner, a tool for the housing reformer. The danger, however, is that in attempting to destroy the racial myths of our past, new ones, in turn, may be advanced.

No one can question the basic facts of nineteenth century human geography, but one may ask about their meaning. Did the wider dispersion of Negro residences imply a more enlightened racial view of housing then? Was there any substantive differences between a small group of densely populated ghettos and one, two or three large ones? Were the small ghettos of the nineteenth century more liveable, healthful and wholesome than those of the twentieth? Might black youngsters in the nineteenth century have a more hopeful vision of their future than those in recent times?

Whatever evidence we have points to an emphatic "no" for all of these questions. The sections of the city where the races had closest contact were also those traditionally subject to periodic violence. The brutal frenzy, mutilations, lynchings and burnings that accompanied the Draft Riots of 1863 occurred in the sections of lower and midtown Manhattan where Negroes and whites—especially but not only the Irish—lived in close proximity to one another. The Tenderloin and San Juan Hill sections were the centers of a serious race riot in 1900 and a lesser confrontation in 1905. San Juan Hill itself was named as a parody on the interracial conflicts that took place on a steep upgrade leading to the Negro section.[8] The checkerboard housing patterns that permitted a closer contact of people were as likely to breed trouble as brotherhood. They were not symbols of viably integrated communities.

And conditions within the ghettos for other than the small black middle class were as appalling in the nineteenth century as they have remained in the twentieth. Charles Dickens visited some lower-class Negro homes in Five Points in 1842 and described them as "leprous houses," "hideous tenements," "cramped hutches." They lacked minimal comforts, were dingy, dark, and surrounded by alleys "paved with mud knee-deep." "Where dogs would howl to lie, women and men . . . slink off to sleep, forcing the dislodged rats to move away," Dickens wrote.[9] Other contemporaries found lower-class Negroes living in cellars, rickety shanties and in the "Old Brewery"—a beer factory ingeniously transformed into a tenement house. What was probably America's first model tenement was constructed for the city's black population in 1855; an obvious sign of their need for improved housing then.[10] A Committee of Merchants formed to aid victims of the Draft Riots found one old man lying in a small room. It was, they recorded, "the kitchen, sitting-room, bedroom and garret of four grown persons and five children." The Committee, which provided financial assistance to practically every black family in Manhattan in 1863 (aid was received by 12,782 Negroes), referred to typical Negro homes as "humble tenements."[11]

The lengthiest description of an antebellum Northern ghetto that has yet come to light depicts a Negro slum of Philadelphia in 1847. An investigating group of Quakers, careful to point out that this was the *worst* Negro neighborhood in the city, was shocked by the "dismal abodes of human wretchedness" they uncovered. The following is a section of their report:

> We followed through a dirty passage, so narrow, a stout man would have found it tight work to have threaded it. Looking before us, the yard seemed unusually dark. This we found was occasioned by a long range of two story pens, with a projecting boarded walk above the lower tier, for the inhabitants of the second story to get to the doors of their apartments. This covered nearly all the narrow yard, and served to exclude light from the dwellings below. We looked in every one of these dismal abodes of human wretchedness. Here were dark, damp holes, six feet square, without a bed in any of them, and generally without furniture, occupied by one or two families: apartments where privacy of any kind was unknown—where comfort never appeared. We endeavoured with the aid of as much light as at mid-day could find access through the open door, to see into the dark corners of these contracted abodes; and as we became impressed with their utter desolateness, the absence of bedding, and of ought to rest on but a bit of old matting on a wet floor, we felt sick and oppressed. Disagreeable odours of many kinds were ever arising; and with no ventilation but the open door, and the foot square hole in the front of the pen, we could scarcely think it possible that life could be supported, when winter compelled them to have fire in charcoal furnaces. . . . Some of these six by six holes, had six and even eight persons in them, but more generally two to four. . . . It is not in the power of language to convey an adequate impression of the scene of this property.[12]

Similar reports have issued from the offices of investigating agencies ever since. Social reformers in the 1880's and 1890's, for instance, concluded that New York City Negroes paid more money for housing and received less adequate accommodations in return than any other ethnic group in the metropolis. "The present housing conditions of the vast majority of colored families in New York can only be characterized as disgraceful," a late-nineteenth century survey maintained.[13] Black sociologists Ira deAugustine Reid and E. Franklin Frazier found the same to be true in the 1920's; contemporary students have uncovered similar conditions today.[14] Statisticians in 1960 could not find a single census tract in Harlem in which more than 45 percent of the housing was considered adequate. In one tract 91 percent of the homes were classified as slums.[15] And, although some people were shocked to learn of Harlem's current population density,[16] it should be recognized that New York's predominantly Negro neighborhoods have been the most congested residential areas of the city at least since the early twentieth century. The studies have droned on but the conditions have endured.

Nor are there marked differences in the economic status of Negro New Yorkers over the two centuries. To come to a fair estimate of antebellum economic conditions in the city, one must first evaluate the rhetoric that pervaded the debate over slavery and freedom in the 1830's, 1840's and 1850's. Defenders of slavery were anxious to prove that Negroes could not survive as free men. As one contemporary put it, racists "attempted to prove that freedom made the black man insane, blind, . . . deaf and dumb. . . ."[17] Black and white abolitionists, on the other hand, regularly responded to the attack by emphasizing the benefits of freedom and the great progress that had been made by free Negroes in the North, in spite of handicaps. They customarily compiled biographical sketches of successful black businessmen and professionals or totalled the *aggregate* wealth of the Negro community to illustrate that economic progress had been made in the North.[18] Neither side presented a representative view of the economic status of the free Negro majority.

Although some free Negroes were permitted to work as craftsmen and a small, militant, middle class of teachers, businessmen, caterers and journalists existed in New York City, and in other Northern cities,[19] the majority of the antebellum Negro population lived in poverty and worked as domestics ("day's work women"), unskilled laborers, or in some service occupation. In 1855, the New York State Census recorded a hundred or more city Negroes engaged in the following occupations: dressmakers, cooks, waiters, laundresses, laborers, porters and coachmen. The largest occupational grouping, the only one in which more than a thousand Negroes were employed, was domestic service. There was one Negro lawyer and six Negro physicians in Manhattan's black population of 11,840. At no time between 1825 and 1865 did more than two percent of the city's Negro population own the $250 worth of property that would have qualified them to vote; in 1855, 91 percent paid no taxes.[20] This is obviously a description of a predominantly lower-class community: a "hard working, honest, humble people," "the great body are of the laboring class."[21]

Individuals who somehow acquired skills were often not permitted to use them or, if allowed to do so, often remained mired in the same type of job throughout their entire careers. The traditional routes to upwardly mobile economic positions were generally blocked by race prejudice; what the leading black abolitionist and emigrationist Samuel

Ringgold Ward called "the ever-present, ever-crushing Negro-hate." Ward, who grew up in New York City in the Jacksonian era, illustrated this theme in his autobiography by describing the career of W. L. Jeffers, a black clerk. "I never knew but one colored clerk in a mercantile house," Ward recalled. "Mr. W. L. Jeffers was the lowest clerk in a house well known in Broad Street, New York; but he never was advanced a single grade, while numerous white lads have since passed up by him, and over him, to be members of the firm. Poor Jeffers, till the day of his death, was but one remove above the porter."[22] Black abolitionists repeatedly offered similar illustrations at antislavery meetings and black protest conventions and urged white allies to help them break through these economic barriers.

Data over the last hundred years obviously vary. In the last quarter century there has been a meaningful increase in the number of Negro women who work in clerical positions in the city, a reflection of some general progress of the black middle class in the nation.[23] When such advances are measured against areas of increasing technological unemployment, economic stagnation and economic retrogression, however, their significance is muted. Over the decades one finds an essentially similar pattern: a relatively small, though presently growing, urban Negro middle class, and an overwhelmingly working-class or semi-skilled Negro majority employed in marginal occupations. In unending repetition the largest number of city Negroes work as domestics, janitors, porters, servants, cooks, waiters, chauffeurs, longshoremen, laundry operatives, messengers, elevator operators, general factory help of some kind and lower-level clerks. The traditional Negro entrepreneur has been and still is the owner of a small store in the ghetto who supplies the community with a few standard services: grocers, hair stylists, undertakers, restaurant and bar owners. Two-thirds of the men and three-fourths of the women in Central Harlem today continue to work in service and unskilled positions. Only 7 percent of Harlem men are employed in professional or managerial occupations, and half of the community's families earn less than $4000 annually. "The roots of the pathology of ghetto communities lie in the menial, low-income jobs held by most ghetto residents," Kenneth B. Clark writes of present-day Harlem. "The Negro has been left out of the swelling prosperity and social progress of the nation as a whole. He is in danger of becoming a permanent economic proletariat."[24] Professor Clark's analysis in the 1960's echoes the views of New York City's newspaper the *Colored American* in the 1830's, those of black abolitionists Theodore S. Wright, Charles L. Reason, Frederick Douglass, Charles Lenox Remond, W. C.

Nell and dozens of others in the 1840's and 1850's, the published reports of the New York Mission in the 1870's, 1880's and 1890's, and the innumerable articles and treatises that have analyzed the status of the city's Negro population throughout the twentieth century. All complained of the poverty, discouragement and loss of pride that resulted from enforced Negro economic and social immobility over the centuries. As a New Yorker wrote in 1830: "We adopt a system towards them, which is directly calculated to debase and brutalize the human character; and then condemn them for the . . . desolation which this system produced."[25]

And the same might be said about popular racial attitudes of the white majority over the two centuries, although the question is quite complex and deserves intensive analysis. Many immigrant groups that settled in the metropolis acquired a racist position in the very process of assimilation; one way to adopt the values of the dominant culture, one way to become "American," was to be anti-Negro. The dignified and sensitive black abolitionist, Charles Lenox Remond, pointed to this phenomenon in 1854. On a stroll through State Street in Boston he ran into a hale of vile epithets tossed at him by Boston's Irish immigrants who, among other things, told him to leave the country. "I cannot but settle down in the conviction, that were it not for this spirit of negro hate, we should not hear them say these things," Remond commented.[26]

Such ethnic-racial antagonisms were always most intense when they coincide with concrete situations—economic competition on the docks in the 1850's and 1860's, residential succession in Harlem in the early twentieth century, the recent fight over a New York City Civilian Review Board—but they were never absent from city life. Black leaders in all generations noted this ethnic and racial pecking order and wrote about it with bitterness. "It is quite remarkable how easily . . . foreigners catch on to the notion . . . to treat Afro-Americans disdainfully and contemptuously," the Negro *New York Age* commented in 1905. "Pat O'Flannagan does not have the least thing in the world against Jim from Dixie," a black school principal said at the first meeting of the NAACP, "but it didn't take Pat long after passing the Statue of Liberty to learn that it is popular to give Jim a whack."[27] A *Newsweek* survey in the summer of 1966 uncovered an inordinate amount of blue-collar racism in Northern areas throughout the country. It disclosed a surprising number of people who continue to believe in the ancient racial myths and stereotypes.[28]

The endurance of a popular folklore of racism, especially among working-class ethnic groups, has itself been countered by a tradition of nativism in the black community. Negroes in the city, and elsewhere—conservatives, moderates, radicals—have often been disheartened by the eventual acceptance accorded white immigrant groups over the years while Negroes, as native Americans, have remained alienated. Bishop Richard Allen, a prominent early nineteenth century Negro clergyman, pointed to this problem as early as 1827. Rejecting the lures of the American Colonization Society, Allen said: "Why should they send us into a far country to die? See the thousands of foreigners emigrating to America every year: and if there be ground sufficient for them to cultivate, and bread for them to eat, why would they wish to send the *first tillers* of the land away?"[29] A prominent New York physician and Liberty Party politician, James McCune Smith, wrote an essay on "The German Invasion" in 1859. "And we, sharp witted American sovereigns, will not wake up to the importance and thoroughness of this German invasion," Smith said, "until some 4th day of March, a man shall uncover his head on the Capital steps and deliver an Inaugural in good *High Dutch* . . . and merchant marts on Broadway, shall hang out signs declaring "English spoken here.""[30]

Black novelist and Garrisonian, William Wells Brown, described the hostility he felt when he returned from an extended visit to England in the 1850's. Two foreigners, "mere adventurers," readily boarded the bus at the dock but "I was told that 'niggers' were not allowed to ride." "They were foreigners, and I an American," Brown wrote, "and when they landed in this country, they were boasting that they had arrived at a land of liberty, where [they] could enjoy religious and political freedom. I, too, might have rejoiced, had I not been a colored man, at my return to my native land. But I knew what treatment I had to expect from my countryman—that it would not be even such as was meted out to those foreigners. . . ."[31]

Disparaging remarks about immigrants traditionally ran through speeches delivered at the many state and national black conventions of the antebellum years. They are especially evident in discussions of the suffrage. A New York City minister denounced restrictions on the Negro vote while the franchise was "granted to European paupers, blacklegs and Burglars! ! !"[32] Frederick Douglass said that if the Negro knew "as much sober as an Irishman knows when drunk, he knows enough to vote." An 1864 Negro convention issued an "Address to the People of the United States" which stressed the importance of the vote as the key protective weapon in a democracy. "In a republican country where general suffrage is the rule, without the ballot personal liberty and . . . other . . . rights become mere privileges held at the option of others," their statement insisted. "What gives the newly arrived immigrants special consequence?; not their virtue, because they are often depraved; not their knowledge, because they are often ignorant; not their wealth, because they are often poor."[33]

Shortly before his death Malcolm X demonstrated that this abrasive theme has endured in black thought. "If you and I were Americans, there'd be no problem," Malcolm said. "Those Hunkies that just got off the boat, they're already Americans; Polacks are already Americans; the Italian refugees are already Americans. Everything that came out of Europe . . . is already an American. And as long as you and I have been here, we aren't Americans yet."[34] The anti-Semitism that has recently flourished in America's ghettos is most obviously directed at Jewish businessmen in these neighborhoods but, in perspective, seems also rooted in an historical tradition of more ancient vintage.

This is not to suggest that there were *no* changes in racial attitudes or conditions in the North over these many years,[35] but it is to say that whatever positive modifications occurred were short-lived or secondary in importance to the broader truth: the continuance of an enervating and destructive racism; the institutionalization, in thought and action, of second-class citizenship for black people. In the 1870's and 1880's, a barrage of legislative reforms cracked patterns of racial discrimination which had remained intact since the city was settled by the Dutch. Negroes were legally guaranteed equal access to public transportation facilities, theaters, restaurants and cemeteries. The officially segregated public schools were transformed into ward schools and Negro teachers after the 1890's were permitted to take jobs throughout the city. Especially since World War II New York has been the most progressive state in the nation in legislating against job and housing discrimination. Social workers and urban reformers from the Progressive era to the present have attempted to alleviate the myriad social and medical problems that inundate the ghetto.

But none of these actions effected meaningful changes in the fundamental economic and social proscriptions that continued to endure and that prevented full Negro equality in the city. The point may be illustrated by a look at the schools. What value was an education, segregated or integrated, to a youngster whose economic vistas were limited to jobs for "beggarly paid menials?"[36] There was no doubt of the mental capacities of Negro students in the Jacksonian period. Those who attended African Free School No. 2, for example, were taught map drawing, astronomy, logarithms and navigation in addition to the standard subjects. Examinations were public, and given by specialists in the various fields. Some Negro students demonstrated their abilities by scoring impressively on these tests.[37]

Yet many were too poor to come to school at all. Some lacked proper clothing and were apparently ashamed to register.[38] Others, forced to work at very young ages, remained in school only long enough to "attain a knowledge of mere monosyllable spelling and reading. . . ."[39] Negro parents sometimes removed youngsters and put them to work "It is a common complaint of colored teachers," a Negro New Yorker commented in 1859, "that their pupils are taken from school at the very time when their studies became most useful and attractive."[40] About half the black youngsters in New York City and in Philadelphia in the pre-Civil War era had no formal education.[41] A well-known nineteenth century Negro educator, Charles B. Ray, also complained that the city's black school facilities were "painfully neglected," "old and dilapidated." "Caste Schools," they were called.[42]

And those who managed to complete a public school education regularly entered a hostile world which refused to recognize and employ their talents. "After a boy has spent five or six years in the school," a teacher observed in 1830, "and . . . is spoken of in terms of high approbation by respectable visitors . . . he leaves school, with every avenue closed against him, which is open to the white boy for honorable and respectable rank in society, doomed to encounter as much prejudice and contempt, as if he were not only destitute of that education . . . but as if he were *incapable* of receiving it."[43] The black Reverend Theodore S. Wright made the same point a few years later. The most gifted children, he said, could find no place willing to use their skills: "He can't work. Let him be ever so skilled as a mechanic, up starts prejudice, and says 'I won't work in the ship if you do.' Here he is scourged by prejudice and has to go back, and sink down to some of the employments which white men leave for the most degraded."[44]

What followed then, as now, was the debasing cycle of low economic status, low self-esteem, limited aspiration, self-destructive or publicly destructive behavior. Parents employed as menials could offer their children little hope for a brighter future. "Instead of seeing their parents in honor and office with power to command and be obeyed," a sensitive observer recorded in the 1850's, the Negro child "sees them at the command of others. Instead of the deferential greeting, and the respected salutation, he hears his father nicknamed 'Dick,' 'Jake,' or 'Ole uncle,' or perhaps 'Cuffy,' or 'Old nigger'; his mother he hears addressed as 'Moll Dinah,' 'Suke,' or 'Black Bets.' Thus in early childhood the circumstances that surround his parents, and the treatment they receive from the community all tend to diminish his respect and reverence for them, hence to depreciate his respect for himself." It was not surprising to overhear a five or six year old girl in 1859 saying to herself: "O dear, I do wish I was white."[45]

Similar problems are encountered in the late nineteenth and twentieth centuries. Black educator, William Lewis Bulkley, who entered the city school system in the 1890's and made a distinguished career for himself, said his students left school "to open doors, run bells or hustle hash" for the rest of their lives. "On every hand avenues of employment are shut tight, discouragement begins and Negro children leave school to work at any menial employment that offers itself," Bulkley wrote.[46] Social worker Frances Blascoer made a comprehensive study of Negro school children in 1915 and found the same to be true then. "There was a general belief among school principals, social workers and colored clergymen that the restriction of industrial opportunities because of their race was sapping the ambition of the colored boys and girls," Blascoer wrote.[47] School administrators throughout the twentieth century hesitated to raise the aspirations of black youngsters in fear, they said, that it would only lead to frustrations after graduation. In 1937 an educator bluntly told an investigating commission of the state legislature: "Let's not mince words; let's be practical about this matter—the Negro is not employed in certain trades, so why permit him to waste his time taking such courses."[48] Malcolm X, one of the smartest students in his Lansing school, once told his English teacher he'd like to become a lawyer. He was immediately advised to be more "realistic" in his aspirations and since his woodworking was admired by all he was told to take up carpentry.[49]

The continuing crisis of ghetto education has received unprecedented attention in the last decade. Studies of the 1950's and 1960's demonstrate that about half of Harlem youngsters who go to high school drop out before completing their degrees. Most who graduate receive "general" diplomas—little more than a recognition of attendance—and their economic status differs not at all from the others who dropped out.[50] James B. Conant, shocked by what he discovered, maintained that such conditions threatened the future of America: "Potentialities for trouble —indeed possibilities of disaster—are surely there," he says.[51] What is new in this situation is not that it exists, but in the willingness of Conant and others to see it for the first time. "Our Children Have Been Dying" for generations.[52]

Other comparative examples may be studied and it is the primary intention of this essay to spur such interests—those relating to health, family structure and social disorganization, to cite a few—but my guess is that the thesis would remain unchanged. Despite occasional periods of racial reform, little has ever been done that permanently improved the fundamental conditions of life of most Negroes in Northern cities, nor if New York City is a representative model has any ideology or program radically improved the tone of race relations in the North. What has in our time been called the social pathology of the ghetto,[53] is evident throughout history; the wounds of centuries have not healed because they've rarely been treated. By all standard measurements of human troubles in the city, the ghetto has always been with us—it has tragically endured.

## NOTES

1. As there is relatively little published data on antebellum Negro life in New York City I have included some comparative material from Philadelphia in these years.

2. Florence M. Cromien, *Negroes in the City of New York: Their Number and Proportion in Relation to the Total Population, 1790–1960* (New York, nd); *Census of the State of New York for 1875* (Albany, 1877), p. 29.

3. Gilbert Osofsky, *Harlem: The Making of a Ghetto* (New York, 1966), *passim*.

4. *A Statistical Inquiry into the Condition of the People of Colour of the City and Districts of Philadelphia* (Philadelphia, 1849), p. 37. Early nineteenth century writers assumed that all-Negro neighborhoods were the dominant pattern in the North. Such folk designations as "Stagg Town," "Little Africa," and "Nigger Hill" referred respectively to New York's, Boston's, and Cincinnati's black sections in the Jacksonian period. Leon F. Litwack, *North of Slavery: The Negro in the Free States, 1790–1860* (Chicago, 1961), pp. 168–170.

5. *A Statistical Inquiry*, pp. 5–8; Pennsylvania Society for Promoting the Abolition of Slavery, *The Present State and Condition of the Free People of Color of the City of Philadelphia* (Philadelphia, 1838), pp. 3–6.

6. Rhoda G. Freeman, "The Free Negro in New York City in the Era Before the Civil War" (Ph.D. dissertation, Columbia University, 1966), p. 440; *Census of the State of New York for 1875* (Albany, 1877), pp.

116–119; *Eleventh Census, 1890; Population* (Washington, D. C., 1894), I, 564.

7. Robert C. Weaver, *The Negro Ghetto* (New York, 1948), pp. 4–6.

8. *Report of the Committee of Merchants for the Relief of the Colored People, Suffering from the Late Riots in the City of New York* (New York, 1863), *passim*; Osofsky, *Harlem*, pp. 46–52.

9. Charles Dickens, *American Notes for General Circulation* (London, 1850), pp. 61–63.

10. James Ford, *et al.*, *Slums and Housing: With Special Reference to New York City* (Cambridge, Mass., 1936), II, 673; *New York Daily Tribune*, June 5, 1850; Robert Ernst, *Immigrant Life in New York City, 1825–1863* (New York, 1949), p. 39.

11. *Report of the Committee of Merchants for the Relief of The Colored People*, pp. 7, 22.

12. *A Statistical Inquiry*, pp. 37–38.

13. The Federation of Churches and Christian Workers in New York City, *Second Sociological Canvass* (New York, 1897), p. 85; *The New York Freeman*, March 7, 1885.

14. Reid, "Twenty-four Hundred Negro Families in Harlem: An Interpretation of the Living Conditions of Small Wage-Earners" (Typescript, Scholburg Collection, 1927); Frazier, "The Negro in Harlem: A Report on Social and Economic Conditions Responsible for the Outbreak of March 19, 1935" (Typescript, La Guardia Papers).

15. Joan Gordon, *The Poor of Harlem: Social Functioning of the Underclass* (New York, 1965), p. 142. On the harmful psychological implications of inadequate housing for present ghetto residents see *ibid.*, pp. 33–48, and the unpublished study, "A Report of Attitudes of Negroes in Various Cities" (Summer 1966), prepared for the Senate Subcommittee on Executive Reorganization.

16. Michael Harrington popularized the findings of the United States Civil Rights Commission. The Commission concluded that the entire American population could fit into three New York City boroughs if its density were equal to some of Harlem's worst blocks. Harrington, *The Other America: Poverty in the United States* (New York, 1962), p. 62.

17. James Freeman Clarke, "Condition of the Free Colored People of the United States," *The Christian Examiner*, LXI (March 1859), 258.

18. See, for example, William Wells Brown, *The Black Man: His Antecendents, His Genius, and His Achievements* (Boston, 1863); and Martin Robison Delany, *The Condition, Elevation and Destiny of the Colored People of the United States* (Philadelphia, 1852).

19. Charles H. Wesley, *Negro Labor in the United States, 1850–1925* (New York, 1927), pp. 29–68, 142.

20. *Census of the State of New York for 1855* (Albany, 1857), pp. 8 and *passim*; Ernst, *Immigrant Life*, pp. 214–217; Franklin B. Hough, *Statics of the Population of the City and County of New York . . .*, (New York, 1866), p. 240; Leon F. Litwack, *North of Slavery: The Negro in the Free States, 1790–1860* (Chicago, 1961), pp. 153–186.

21. *Report of the Committee of Merchants for the Relief of the Colored People*, p. 7; Pennsylvania Society, *The Present State and Condition*, p. 21.

22. Samuel Ringgold Ward, *Autobiography of A Fugitive Negro: His Anti-Slavery Labours in the United States, Canada, and England* (London, 1855), pp. 29–30. "Less than two-thirds of those Negroes who have trades follow them. A few of the remainder pursue other avocations from choice, but the greater number are compelled to abandon their trades on account of the unrelenting prejudice against their color." Benjamin C. Bacon, *Statistics of the Colored Population of Philadelphia* (Philadelphia, 1859), p. 15. When a register of Negro craftsmen was compiled in 1838 it was considered necessary to mark the names of those *presently* following their trades with asterisks. *Register of Trades of the Colored People in the City of Philadelphia* (Philadelphia, 1838).

23. Nathan Glazer and Daniel Patrick Moynihan, *Beyond the Melting Pot* (Cambridge, Mass., 1963), p. 230; Arthur M. Ross and Herbert Hill, eds., *Employment, Race and Poverty* (New York, 1967), pp. 40–47.

24. Osofsky, *Harlem*, *passim.*; Kenneth Clark, *Dark Ghetto* (New York, 1965), pp. 34–41, 55–62; Harlem Youth Opportunities Unlimited, *Youth in the Ghetto* (New York, 1964), pp. 245–290; Glazer and Moynihan, *Beyond the Melting Pot*, pp. 29–44.

25. Charles C. Andrews, *The History of the New-York African Free-Schools from their Establishment in 1787 . . .* (New York, 1830), p. 56.

26. *The Liberator*, June 23, 1854.

27. Florence E. Gibson, *The Attitudes of the New York Irish Toward State and National Affairs, 1848–1892* (New York, 1951), p. 66; *The New York Age*, January 26, 1905; W.L. Bulkley, "Race Prejudice As Viewed from an Economic Standpoint," *Proceedings of the National Negro Conference*, 1909 (New York, 1909?), 94.

28. "Black-White," *Newsweek*, LXVIII (August 22, 1966); William Brink and Louis Harris, *Black and White: A Study of U. S. Racial Attitudes Today* (New York, 1967), p. 136.

29. Quoted in Charles M. Wiltse, ed., *David Walker's Appeal . . . To the Coloured Citizens of the World* (New York, 1965), p. 57.

30. James McCune Smith, "The German Invasion," *Anglo-African Magazine*, I (February 1859), 50.

31. *The Liberator*, November 10, 1854.

32. Quoted in Freeman, "The Free Negro in New York City," p. 131.

33. Quoted in Benjamin Quarles, *Frederick Douglass* (Washington, D. C., 1948), p. 217.

34. *Malcolm X Speaks* (New York, 1965), pp. 25-26.

35. See, for example, the changing responses to poll-taker samples since the 1930's presented in Mildred Schwartz, *Trends in White Attitudes Toward Negroes* (Chicago, 1967).

36. Frazier, "The Negro in Harlem," pp. 27–32.

37. Andrews, *New-York African Free-Schools*, pp. 85–103.

38. *Ibid.*, pp. 57–58; *A Statistical Inquiry*, p. 22. The American Moral Reform Society, the Black Garrisonian organization in Philadelphia, repeatedly spoke of the problem of black children who didn't attend school because of inadequate clothing, and also of their struggles to raise some money to outfit such youngsters, *Pennsylvania Freeman*.

39. Andrews, *New-York African Free-Schools*, p. 117.

40. "A Word to Our People," *Anglo-African Magazine*, I (September 1859), 293. "What Are We Doing?" *The Mirror of Liberty*, I (July 1838), 4.

41. "When we call to mind, that . . . there are at least 1200 children between the ages of 5 and 20, of whom no account is received, the greater part of whom are probably growing up in idle and viscious habits; it is clear that this is one of the most painful facts brought to light by this inquiry . . ." *A Statistical Inquiry*, p. 22. See also Andrews, *New-York African Free-Schools*, pp. 113–127; Bacon, *Statistics of the Colored Population*, pp. 8–12; Pennsylvania Society, *The Present State and Condition*, p. 19.

42. Charles B. Ray, "Communication from the New York Society for the Promotion of Education Among Colored Children," *Anglo-African Magazine*, I (July 1859), 222–224. "The managers of the different Anti-Slavery Societies in this city will permit us to suggest whether they might not employ a portion of their time and influence . . . in doing something for the cause of education among those of the despised caste." David Ruggles, "African Free Schools in the City of New York," *The Mirror of Liberty*, I (January 1839), 32–33.

43. Andrews, *New-York African Free-Schools*, pp. 117–118. The emphasis is Andrews'.

44. *Proceeding of the New England Anti-Slavery Convention: Held in Boston*, May 24, 25, 26, 1836 (Boston, 1836), pp. 48–49. "The colored people are almost altogether deprived of the opportunity of bringing up their children to mechanical employments, to commercial business, or other more lucrative occupations, whereby so many of our white laborers are unable to rise above the drudgery in which they commence their . . . life . . ." Pennsylvania Society, *The Present State and Condition*, p. 12.

45. M.H. Freeman, "The Educational Wants of the Free Colored Population," *Anglo-African Magazine*, I (April 1859), 116.
46. Bulkley, "The School as a Social Center," *Charities*, IV (October 7, 1905), 76.
47. Frances Blascoer, *Colored School Children in New York* (New York, 1915), p. 18.
48. New York State, *Second Report of the New York State Temporary Commission on the Condition of the Colored Urban Population* (Albany, 1939), p. 108.
49. *The Autobiography of Malcolm X* (New York, 1966), p. 36.
50. *Youth in the Ghetto*, pp. 161–244.
51. James Bryant Conant, *Slums and Suburbs: A Commentary on Schools in Metropolitan Areas* (New York, 1961), p. 18.
52. The phrase is Elliott Shapiro's, a former Harlem educator. See Nat Hentoff, *Our Children Are Dying* (New York, 1966).
53. Clark, *Dark Ghetto, passim*.

## 2 | Black Powerlessness in Chicago

*Harold M. Baron*

*With Harriet Stulman, Richard Rothstein, and Rennard Davis*

Until recently, the three principal targets of the civil-rights movement in the North were discrimination and inferior conditions in (1)
housing for Negroes, (2) jobs for Negroes, and (3) the education of
Negroes. But after failing to bring about major changes, many Negroes
realized that one reason the status quo in housing, jobs, and education
continues is that *the black community lacks control over decision-
making.* Negroes remain second-class citizens partly because of the
discrimination of individual whites, but mainly because of the way
whites control the major institutions of our society. And therefore the
fourth major goal of Negro organizations and the civil-rights movement
has become the acquisition of power.

It was because of this concern with power for black people that, more
than two years ago, the Chicago Urban League—a social-welfare
organization dedicated to changing institutions so as to achieve full
racial equality—started to study the decision-making apparatus in
Cook County, Ill., and particularly how it affects or ignores Negro
citizens. (Cook County takes in the city of Chicago, and two-thirds of
the population of the surrounding suburban ring included in the
Chicago Standard Metropolitan Statistical area.) Among the questions
we posed were:

• What is the extent of Negro exclusion from policy-making positions
in Chicago?

• Where Negroes *are* in policy-making positions, what type of positions
are these, and where are Negroes in greatest number and authority?

• Do Negroes in policy-making positions represent the interests of the
Negro community? and

Reprinted from *TRANS-action* VI, no. 1 (November 1968): 27–33. Copyright
© 1968 by *TRANS-action* Magazine, New Brunswick, New Jersey.

• How might an increase in the percentage of Negro policy-makers affect socio-economic conditions for Negroes in general?

What we found was that in 1965 some 20 percent of the people in Cook County were Negro, and 28 percent of the people in Chicago were Negro. Yet the representation of Negroes in policy-making positions was minimal. Of the top 10,997 policy-making positions in the major Cook County institutions included in our study, Negroes occupied only 285—or 2.6 percent.

In government (see Table 1), out of a total of 1088 policy-making

TABLE 1   *The Exclusion of Negroes from Government*

| Policy Making Positions in the Cook County Public Sector (1965) | Policy-Making Positions | Positions Held by Negroes | Percent |
|---|---|---|---|
| 1. Elected Officials | | | |
| U.S. House of Representatives | 13 | 1 | 8 |
| State Legislature | 120 | 10 | 8 |
| Cook County—nonjudicial | 34 | 3 | 9 |
| Chicago—nonjudicial | 59 | 7 | 12 |
| Cook County—judicial | 138 | 8 | 6 |
| Total: | 364 | 29 | 8 |
| 2. Appointive Supervisory Boards | | | |
| Total: | 77 | 10 | 13 |
| 3. Local Administrative Positions | | | |
| City of Chicago | 156 | 2 | 1 |
| Chicago Board of Education | 72 | 7 | 9 |
| Metropolitan Sanitary District | 7 | 0 | 0 |
| Cook County Government | 13 | 1 | 8 |
| Total: | 248 | 10 | 4 |
| 4. Federal Government | | | |
| Civil Service | 368 | 8 | 2 |
| Presidential Appointments | 31 | 1 | 3 |
| Total: | 399 | 9 | 2 |
| Grand Total: | 1088 | 58 | 5 |

positions Negroes held just 58. This 5 percent is about one-fourth of the percentage of Negroes in the total county population. Of the 364 elective posts in the survey, however, Negroes occupied 29, or 8 percent, indicating that the franchise has helped give Negroes representation. Yet Negroes had the most positions, percentagewise, on appointed supervisory boards, such as the Board of Education and the Chicago

Housing Authority. There they occupied 10 of the 77 policy-making positions, or about 13 percent.

Negroes were better represented on appointed supervisory boards and in elected (nonjudicial) offices than they were in local administrative positions, or in important federal jobs based in Chicago. Thus, Negroes held 12 percent of the nonjudicial elected posts in Chicago's government, but only a little over 1 percent of the appointive policy-making positions in the city administration. The same anomaly appears at the federal level. There is one Negro out of the 13 U.S. Congressmen from Cook County (8 percent), but Negroes held only one out of 31 Presidential appointments (3 percent), and eight of the 368 top federal civil-service posts (2 percent).

Nonetheless, Negroes have—proportionately—two-and-a-half-times as many important posts in the public sector as they have in the private sector. As Table 2 indicates, Negroes are virtually barred from policy-

TABLE 2   *The Exclusion of Negroes from Private Institutions*

| Policy Making Positions in the Cook County Private Sector (1965) | Policy-Making Positions | Positions Held by Negroes | Percent |
|---|---|---|---|
| 1. Business Corporations | | | |
| Banks | 2258 | 7 | 0 |
| Insurance | 533 | 35 | 6 |
| Nonfinancial Corporations | 4047 | 0 | 0 |
| Total: | 6838 | 42 | * |
| 2. Legal Profession | | | |
| Total: | 757 | 0 | 0 |
| 3. Universities** | | | |
| Total: | 380 | 5 | 1 |
| 4. Voluntary Organizations | | | |
| Business & Professional | 324 | 3 | 1 |
| Welfare & Religious | 791 | 69 | 9 |
| Total: | 1115 | 72 | 6 |
| 5. Labor Unions | | | |
| Internationals | 94 | 15 | 16 |
| District Councils | 211 | 20 | 9 |
| Locals | 514 | 73 | 14 |
| Total: | 819 | 108 | 13 |
| Grand Total: | 9909 | 227 | 2 |
| Grand Total for Public & Private Sectors: | 10997 | 285 | 2 |

* Below 1 percent.
** Includes the University of Illinois, which is a public body.

making positions in the large organizations that dominate the private institutions in the Chicago area. Out of a total of 9909 positions, Negroes fill a mere 227. This 2 percent representation is only one-tenth of the proportionate Negro population.

The whitest form of policy-making in Chicago is in the control of economic enterprises. Out of 6838 positions identified in business corporations, Negroes held only 42 (six-tenths of 1 percent). Thirty-five of these were in insurance, where Negroes occupy 6 percent of the 533 posts. But all 35 were in two all-Negro insurance firms. The other seven positions were in four smaller banks. In banks in general, Negroes occupied three-tenths of 1 percent of the policy posts. There were no Negro policy-makers at all in manufacturing, communications, transportation, utilities, and trade corporations.

Out of the 372 companies we studied, the Negro-owned insurance companies were the only ones dominated by blacks (see Table 3). And

TABLE 3   The Exclusion of Negroes from Private Establishments

| Percentage of Negro Policy-Makers in the Cook County Private Sector by Establishment (1965) | Total Establishments | Percentage of Negro Policy-Makers | | | | |
|---|---|---|---|---|---|---|
| | | None | 1-5% | 6-15% | 16-50% | 51%+ |
| 1. Business Corporations | | | | | | |
|     Banks | 102 | 98 | 0 | 4 | 0 | 0 |
|     Insurance | 30 | 28 | 0 | 0 | 0 | 2 |
|     Nonfinancial Corporations | 240 | 240 | 0 | 0 | 0 | 0 |
| 2. Legal Professions | 54 | 54 | 0 | 0 | 0 | 0 |
| 3. Universities* | 7 | 5 | 0 | 2 | 0 | 0 |
| 4. Voluntary Organizations | | | | | | |
|     Business & Professional | 5 | 3 | 2 | 0 | 0 | 0 |
|     Welfare & Religious | 14 | 2 | 4 | 7 | 1 | 0 |
| 5. Labor Unions | | | | | | |
|     Internationals | 4 | 0 | 1 | 1 | 2 | 0 |
|     District Councils | 23 | 13 | 0 | 5 | 5 | 0 |
|     Locals | 33 | 14 | 2 | 8 | 7 | 2 |
|     Total: | 512 | 457 | 9 | 27 | 15 | 4 |

* Includes the University of Illinois, which is a public body.

if we had used the same stringent criteria for banks and insurance companies that we used for nonfinancial institutions, there would have been no black policy-makers in the business sector at all.

Now, amazingly enough, Chicago has proportionately more Negro-controlled business, larger than neighborhood operations, than any other major city in the North. Therefore, similar surveys in other Northern metropolitan areas would turn up an even smaller percentage of Negro policy-makers in the business world.

The legal profession, represented by corporate law firms, had no Negroes at high policy levels. We are convinced that the same situation would be found in other professions, such as advertising and engineering.

The very prestigious universities—the University of Chicago, Northwestern University, Loyola University, DePaul University, Roosevelt University, the Illinois Institute of Technology, and the University of Illinois (the only public university of the seven)—had a negligible 1 percent Negro representation. Most of these universities had few Negro students, faculty members, or administrators. Five of the seven had no Negro policy-makers. The University of Illinois had one. Roosevelt University, the sole institution that had a number of Negroes at the top, was the newest, and the one with the *least* public support. When this university was founded, its leaders had made a forthright stand on racial questions and a firm commitment to liberal principles.

We included these major universities in our survey because other institutions—public and private—have been placing increasingly greater value on them. Every year hundreds of millions of dollars in endowment and operating funds are given to the Chicago-area schools. After all, their research activities, and their training of skilled personnel, are considered a key to the region's economic growth. One indication of the tremendous influence these universities have is that they have determined the nature of urban renewal more than any other institutional group in Chicago (aside from the city government). Without a doubt, the universities have real—not nominal—power. And perhaps it is a reflection of this real power that only five out of 380 policy-making positions in these universities are held by Negroes.

The exclusion of Negroes from the private sector carries over to its voluntary organizations: Negroes are found in only 1 percent of the posts there. It is in the voluntary associations that it is easiest to make symbolic concessions to the black community by giving token representation, yet even here Negroes were underrepresented—which highlights the fundamental norms of the entire sector.

The sector and individual groups in the Chicago area with the highest Negro representation were those with a Negro constituency—elective offices, supervisory boards, labor unions, and religious and welfare organizations. These four groups accounted for 216 of the posts held by Negroes, or 75 percent, although these four groups have only

19 percent of all the policy-making positions we studied. Labor unions had a larger percentage—13 percent—than any other institution in the private sector. In welfare and religious organizations, whose constituents were often largely Negro, Negroes occupied 8 percent of the positions, the same percentage of the elected public offices they held.

Now, either the black constituency elected the Negroes directly (in the case of elective offices and trade unions); or the Negroes were appointed to posts in an operation whose clients were largely Negro (principal of a Negro school, for example); or Negroes were given token representation on bodies that had a broad public purpose (like religious organizations). By "token representation," we mean—following James Q. Wilson—that "he is a man chosen because a Negro is 'needed' in order to legitimate [but not direct] whatever decisions are made by the agency."

Of the three ways a black constituency had of getting itself represented, the most important was the first. The statistics clearly show the importance of the Negro vote. The elected political offices and the elected trade-union offices account for only 11 percent of all the policy-making positions in Cook County. Yet almost half of all the Negro policy-makers were found in these two areas—137 out of 285.

Nonetheless, even in the major areas where Negro representation was the greatest—labor unions, elective offices, supervisory boards, and religious and welfare organizations—many institutions still excluded Negroes from positions of authority.

There are, of course, few Negroes in the building-trade unions, most of which bar Negroes from membership. Only two out of the 12 building-trade-union organizations we studied had even one Negro in a decisive slot. These two Negroes made up a mere one and a half percent of the policy-making positions in the building-trade unions.

The greatest degree of black representation was found in the former C.I.O. industrial unions. Only one-fourth of these units in the survey totally excluded Negroes from leadership. In almost half, the percentage of Negro policy-makers was over 15 percent—which is above token levels.

The former A.F. of L. unions (not including those in the building trades) had a higher rate of exclusion than those of the C.I.O. Two-fifths of these A.F. of L. unions had no Negroes at all in policy-making posts. But one-third of this group had leaderships that were 15 percent or more Negro. And the only two black-controlled locals large enough to be included in this study were in A.F. of L. unions.

In elective offices, the Negro vote certainly does give Negroes some representation—though far below their proportionate number. In public administration, however, where advancement to policy-making offices comes through appointment and influence, Negroes are all but excluded from decisive posts, at both the federal and local levels. Although a very high percentage of all Negro professionals are in public service, they do not reach the top.

The only major governmental operation that had a goodly number of Negroes at the upper level of the bureaucratic hierarchy was the public-school system. Nine percent of the top positions were occupied by Negroes. This unique situation is the result of some fairly recent appointments, made as concessions after an intense civil-rights campaign directed at the Chicago Board of Education. In this instance, one can consider these civil-rights actions as a proxy for Negro votes. Still, this high-level representation in the Chicago school hierarchy did not seem to reflect any uniform policy of including Negroes in management. At the level of principalship that was not included as a policy-making position in this study, only 3 percent of the positions were occupied by blacks.

The voluntary welfare and religious associations that were sufficiently important to be included in the study usually had at least a few Negro policy-makers. Only two out of 14 bodies had no Negroes in policy positions (see Table 3), while four organizations had token representation—below 5 percent. None had a Negro majority in the key posts. Only the Chicago Urban League (with 43 percent) had Negroes in more than 15 percent of its policy slots. If individual religious denominations had been among the organizations counted in the survey, there would have been some black-dominated groups. As it was, Negro representation in the United Protestant Federation, which *was* included, came largely from the traditionally Negro denominations. It is of interest to note that, in recent years, Protestant groups have provided some of the few instances in which Negroes have been elected to important offices by a constituency that was overwhelmingly white.

Not only were Negroes grossly underrepresented in Chicago's policy-making posts, but even where represented they had less power than white policy-makers. The fact is that *the number of posts held by Negroes tended to be inversely related to the power vested in these positions—the more powerful the post, the fewer the black policy-makers.*

As we have seen, Negroes were virtually excluded from policy-making in the single most powerful institutional sector—the business world. In *all* sectors, they were generally placed in positions in which the authority was delegated from a higher administrator, or divided among a board. Rarely were Negroes in positions of ultimate authority, either as chief executive or as top board officer.

When Negroes ran for a board or for a judicial office on a slate, their number had been limited by the political parties apportioning out the nominations. The percentage of Negroes on such boards or (especially) in judicial offices tended to run lower than the number of Negroes in legislative posts, for which Negroes run individually.

It is also true that no Negro has *ever* been elected to one of the key city-wide or county-wide executive positions, such as Mayor, City Clerk, or President of the Cook County Board. These are the positions with the greatest power and patronage.

In welfare agencies, where Negroes have token representation, they are virtually excluded from the key posts of executive director. Only five of the 135 directors of medium and of large welfare agencies were Negro.

Now, it was in the trade-union sector that the highest percentage of Negroes had policy posts—13 percent. We asked several experts on the Chicago trade-union movement to list the number of Negroes among the 100 most powerful trade unionists in the area. Among the 100 people they named, the number of Negroes ranged from two to five. This did not surprise us, for it was compatible with our general knowledge of the number of Negroes with truly powerful posts in other sectors.

## A RULE OF THUMB ON NEGRO POWER

All in all, then, we would suggest the following rule of thumb: *The actual power vested in Negro policy-makers is about one-third as great as the percentage of the posts they hold.*

Thus when Negroes elected other Negroes to office, these officers tended to represent small constituencies. For example, the greatest number of Negroes in legislative posts came from relatively small districts that happen to have black majorities. Indeed, according to Cook County tradition, Negroes simply do not hold legislative posts in city, state, or federal government *unless* they represent a district that is mostly black. No district with Negroes in the minority had a Negro representative, even when Negroes constituted the single largest ethnic group. And some districts with a Negro majority had a *white* representative.

Then too, the smaller the district, the more likely it would be homogeneous, and the greater the chances of its having a black majority that could return a Negro to office. In the Chicago area, consequently, Negroes were best represented on the City Council, which is based on 50 relatively small wards, each representing about 70,000 people; Negroes were represented most poorly in the U.S. House of Representatives, for which there are only nine rather large districts in Chicago, each representing about 500,000 people.

Most of the government policy-making posts that Negroes had been appointed to were in operations that had a large Negro clientele, if not a majority—as in the case of the Chicago public schools; or in operations that had largely Negro personnel, as in the case of the post office. On the appointed supervisory boards, in fact, those with as many as two Negro members were the Chicago Board of Education and the Board of Health, both of which served very large numbers of Negroes.

This limiting of Negro policy-makers to Negro constituencies was quite as evident in the private sector. Three of the four banks with Negroes in policy-making posts were in Negro neighborhoods; and two were the smallest of the 102 banks we studied, and the other two were not much larger. The two insurance firms had mainly Negro clients, and were among the smallest of the 30 studied. In the voluntary organizations, the more they served Negroes, the higher the percentage of Negroes on their boards (although representation was by no means proportionate). Thus, the five Negro executive directors of welfare organizations we studied headed all-Negro constituencies: Three directed moderate-sized neighborhood settlements in the ghetto; one directed a virtually all-Negro hospital; and one directed an interracial agency that has traditionally had a Negro executive.

Still another way of limiting the power of Negro policy-makers, we discovered, was by "processing" them. Public and private institutions, as indicated, tend to have a token representation of Negroes. And many Negroes in these positions have totally identified with the traditional values and goals of the institution, regardless of what they mean to the mass of Negroes. Some of these Negro policy-makers, because of their small numbers and lack of an independent source of power, are neutralized. Others, if they are firm in representing the needs and outlook of the black community, are isolated. The two Negro members of the Chicago Board of Education represented these extremes. Mrs. Wendell Green, a longtime Board member and the elderly widow of a former judge, had been the most diehard supporter of Benjamin Willis, the former Schools Superintendent, through all of his fights against the civil-rights movement. The other Negro—Warren Bacon, a business executive—sympathized with the campaign against inferior, segregated housing and, as a result, has been largely isolated on the Board. He was rarely consulted on critical questions. His vote was usually cast with a small minority, and sometimes alone.

The fact is that the norms and traditions of *any* organization or enterprise limit the amount of power held by black policy-makers. It is no longer bold to assert that the major institutions and organizations of our society have an operational bias that is racist, even though their *official* policies may be the opposite. The Negro policy-maker in one of these institutions ( or in a small black-controlled organization dependent upon these institutions, such as the head of a trade-union local) has a certain degree of conflict. If he goes along with the institution, from which he gains power and prestige, he ends up by implementing operations that restrict his minority group. Edward Banfield and James Q. Wilson have neatly pinpointed this dilemma in the political sphere:

> Not only are few Negroes elected to office, but those who are elected generally find it necessary to be politicians first and Negroes second. If they are to stay in office, they must soft-pedal the racial issues that are of the most concern to Negroes as Negroes.

This pattern is seen in the failure of William Dawson, Cook County's one Negro Congressman, to obtain many Presidential appointments or top federal civil-service posts for Negroes. Theoretically he is in a more strategic position to influence government operations than any other Chicago-based Congressman, since he has 23 years' seniority and holds the important chairmanship of the Government Operations Committee. Yet in 1965 Negroes held only 2 percent of the top federal jobs in Chicago.

Any examination of the real power of Negroes in Chicago requires an examination of the strongest single organization in the Negro community—the Democratic Party. Wilson's study, *Negro Politics*, points out that the strength and cohesiveness of the Negro Democratic organization is largely dependent upon the strength of the total Cook County Democratic organization. The Negro organization is a "sub-machine" within the larger machine that dominates the city. The Negro sub-machine, however, has basically settled for lesser patronage positions and political favors, rather than using its considerable strength to try to make or change policy. Therefore, this Negro organization avoids controversial questions and seeks to avoid differences with the central organization on such vital issues as urban renewal and the schools.

In short, then, not only are Negroes underrepresented in the major policy-making positions in Cook County, but even where represented their actual power is restricted, or their representatives fail to work for the long-term interests of their constituency. It is therefore safe to estimate that Negroes really hold less than 1 percent of the effective power in the Chicago metropolitan area. Realistically, the power structure of Chicago is hardly less white than that of Mississippi.

From these figures it is clear that, at this time, Negroes in the Chicago area lack the power to make changes in the areas of housing, jobs, and education. The basic subjugation of the black community, however, would not end if there were simply more Negroes in policy-making posts. We have seen the prevalence of tokenism, of whites' choosing Negro leaders who are conservative, of their boxing in Negro leaders who are proved to be liberal, of their giving these leaders less actual power than they give themselves.

Our analysis suggests that the best way to increase both the number *and* the power of Negro policy-makers is through unifying the black constituency. Access to policy-making positions could come through both the development of large, black-controlled organizations, and through getting Negroes into white-dominated organizations. If the constituency lacks its own clear set of goals and policies, however, things will surely remain the same. For success depends not just upon formal unity, but upon the nature of the goals set by the black community. In this situation, the overcoming of black powerlessness seems to require the development of a self-conscious community that has the means to determine its own interests, and the cohesiveness to command the loyalty of its representatives. We can safely predict that more and more Negroes will be moved into policy-making positions. The fundamental conflict, therefore, will take place between their cooptation into the established institutions and their accountability to a black constituency.

## APPENDIX: THE METHODOLOGY OF THE STUDY

In studying the exclusion of Negroes from the decision-making structure in Chicago, our working assumption was that the men who hold power are those who have been elevated to policy-making positions in powerful institutions, like banks, law firms, and unions. This approach differed from the more popular methodologies of studying community power—thus, we did not try to identify the top decision-makers, and we did not assume that a power élite was at work.

To identify policy-making posts, we relied on these assumptions:

• In each major area of metropolitan life, certain enterprises have a disproportionate amount of power—because of their control over human and material resources, or because of their responsibility for making public policy.

• Individuals who occupy policy-making posts in these key enterprises have a disproportionate amount of power *within* these institutions.

• Policy decisions are made at every level of a bureaucracy. But certain posts within a bureaucracy will structure the range of decision-making for all other posts. Posts that have this responsibility we call "policy-making," and these are the posts we studied.

Under stable conditions, policy-making is the most important way in which power is exercised. In any firm or government department, policy-makers are relatively few. They are the ones who set the major goals and orientation, while the more numerous *management* is responsible for their implementation.

Just as our definition of "policy-making position" was restrictive, so was our definition of "power." In our study, power means the ability to make and enforce decisions for an institution, for a community, or for society at large—and the ability to determine in whose interest these decisions are made.

Our study began with a census of those Negroes occupying public or private policy-making positions. First we identified Cook County's major institutional areas—that is, related types of formally organized activities, such as local government, religious organizations, and business firms. In those areas where we could *not* be exhaustive in our research, we selected one or more representative groups. Corporate law firms, for example, were chosen to represent business-oriented professions and services.

Within each institutional area, we developed criteria to determine how large an individual enterprise or organization had to be before it has significant potential influence and power over other organizations. Next, we determined which positions within these powerful enterprises or organizations had policy-making authority. Finally, we conducted interviews with knowledgeable informants to learn which of the policy-making positions were held by Negroes.

In our study, the chairman of the board of the largest industrial firm was given the same statistical weight as the vice-president of the smallest bank included in the survey. While differentiating between them would have been useful for a study of the total process of decision-making in the Chicago area, our aim was to document only the inclusion or exclusion of Negroes. If there is any methodological bias in our study, then, it operates in favor of employing less strict criteria in determining important positions in order to include at least a few Negroes.

Our census was based on information for the year 1965. Since then, although there have been some shifts in the number and percentage of Negroes in particular organizations, the pattern of power traced remains fundamentally the same.

# III | The Forging of a Black Nation in America

The history of blacks in America is radically different
from that of other Americans. This fact is of perhaps equal
importance to the institutionalized structure of racism
which they confront. Many black intellectuals, and some
white intellectuals, have concluded that these experiences
of black Americans have been so distinctive that black
Americans comprise a separate nationality with a unique
culture and consciousness: a black nation.

At first it seems anomalous to assert that a new
nationality has arisen within the geographical and political
boundaries of the United States. All the common-sense
wisdom of our culture argues against such an interpretation.
But multi-national states have existed throughout the
world (e.g., India, U.S.S.R., Great Britain, etc.); and it
is not unusual for national consciousness to develop among
a people who did not previously possess it, as for instance
among French-Canadians today, or among Italians
during the nineteenth century.

Upon further consideration, the rise of black national
consciousness is not so surprising. The twentieth century
has seen a remarkable rise of nationalism throughout
the world, in particular among oppressed colored groups
throughout the world. This consciousness is closely linked
to resistance to foreign domination. Indeed, the *national
liberation movements* of Asia, Africa, and Latin America
are one of the most vital aspects of contemporary history.
That the same historical forces and psychological attitudes
which engender these movements should also affect
black America is not remarkable; nor is it at all strange

that large numbers of black Americans increasingly view their plight as part of the international struggle of colonial and neo-colonial nations for self-determination.

The selections which follow attempt to indicate that this growing black national consciousness is neither a fad nor a rhetorical metaphor. Rather, as a result of the distinctive historical experiences of black Americans, a deeply rooted nationalist movement is arising; so far it lacks organizational coherence, but undoubtedly it corresponds to an irrevocable change in the self-image of black Americans.

Blacks came to America as slaves, and for over two centuries were held as legal chattels. This situation endured until the middle of the nineteenth century, and it was decisive for the formation of the black nation which is today becoming conscious of itself. Professor Eugene D. Genovese and Herbert Aptheker of the American Communist Party, the two most notable white American Marxist historians of slavery, clash over its historical import for today. "The Legacy of Slavery and the Roots of Black Nationalism," was originally delivered as a paper at the Socialist Scholars Conference in 1966; and Dr. Aptheker's "Comment" as a reply on the same panel. Their debate explores many of the implications of the experience of slavery for today's black movement.

It is worth noting for further exploration that the debate between Aptheker and Genovese has been sharply continued through the debate between white and black intellectuals over William Styron's historical novel, *The Confessions of Nat Turner*. In particular, see John H. Clarke (ed.), *William Styron's Nat Turner: Ten Black Writers Respond* (Boston: Beacon Press, 1968), and Genovese's highly critical review in *The New York Review of Books* (September 12, 1968), pp. 34–37. A contrasting posture on the question of the development of black cultural identity has been articulated by the black intellectual Harold Cruse in *The Crisis of the Negro Intellectual* (New York: William Morrow, 1967), a profoundly provocative work essential to an understanding of the question. Moreover, in "American Slaves and Their History," *The New York Review of Books* (December

3, 1970), pp. 34–43, Genovese has confessed that his earlier position was "dangerously distorted" and has sharply revised it.

The churches which black Americans have established have played a key role as institutions and sources of ideology in the elaboration of the political culture of black America. For a general background on black religious institutions, students are referred to the work of black sociologist E. Franklin Frazier, *The Negro Church in America* (New York: Schocken Books, 1963).*

This *Reader* includes two articles on black religion in its relation to black politics. "Black Muslims in America: A Reinterpretation," was written by W. Haywood Burns, now a practicing black attorney, while he was still a student. It addresses itself to the religious sect from which Malcolm X emerged as a major black figure. "Religion: Opiate or Inspiration of Civil Rights Militancy Among Negroes," is by a white sociology professor, Gary T. Marx, who attempts to utilize the tools of empirical sociology to discover the effects of black religion on civil rights activity.

The next three articles form a natural group. They discuss the efforts by black political activists of the thirties and early forties (with some help by radical whites), to overcome segregation by protest politics on the margin of respectable political life in America. By going back to the stage of radical protest which preceeded even the civil rights movement of the fifties and early sixties, these selections deal with some of the directly political roots of the contemporary black power movement.

Of course, these selections should not be seen as a substitute for learning about the history of black politics in America—a history which includes such giants as Frederick Douglass, Booker T. Washington, W. E. B. DuBois, Marcus Garvey, and Paul Robeson. Readers are referred to Herbert Aptheker (ed.), *A Documentary*

* For a comparative study of the effects of religious culture in shaping the consciousness of exploited people, and fostering a tradition of resistance to their oppression, see E. P. Thompson's brilliant *The Making of the English Working Class* (New York: Vintage Books, 1966).

*History of the Negro People in the United States,* 2 vols.
(New York: Citadel Press, 1952); Lerone Bennett, Jr.,
*Before the Mayflower: A History of the Negro in America,*
*1619–1962* (Chicago: Johnson, 1962); and August Meier
and Elliott Rudwick (eds.), *The Making of Black America:*
*Essays in Negro Life and History,* 2 vols. (New York:
Atheneum, 1969), for a general historical introduction to
the subject.

Nor should these selections be seen as precluding the
necessary evaluation of the nationalist period of the
twenties, and the role played by black organizations such
as the NAACP throughout modern times. They are
merely intended to illuminate the firm stance of a James
Foreman, Malcolm X, or Huey P. Newton within a
tradition of black radicalism—a tradition which played
a major, though much misrepresented part, in the life
of black America, especially during the Depression and
its aftermath.

## 3 | An Encounter on the Origins of Black Nationalism

## a | The Legacy of Slavery and the Roots of Black Nationalism

*Eugene D. Genovese*

American radicals have long been imprisoned by the pernicious notion that the masses are necessarily both good and revolutionary, and by the even more pernicious notion that, if they are not, they should be. The principal task of radical historians therefore has too often been to provide the masses with historical heroes, to make them aware of their glorious tradition of resistance to oppression, and to portray them as having been implacably hostile to the social order in which they have been held. This viewpoint now dominates the black liberation movement, which has been fed for decades by white radical historians who in this one respect have set the ideological pace for their liberal colleagues. It has become virtually sacrilege—or at least white chauvinism—to suggest that slavery was a social system within which whites and blacks lived in harmony as well as antagonism, that there is little evidence of massive, organized opposition to the regime, that the blacks did not establish a revolutionary tradition of much significance, and that our main problem is to discover the reasons for the widespread accommodation and, perhaps more important, the long-term effects both of the accommodation and of that resistance which did occur.

In 1831 Nat Turner led a slave revolt on which has hung most of the legend of armed black resistance to slavery. Of the 250 or so revolts chronicled and analyzed in Herbert Aptheker's *American Negro Slave Revolts*,[1] Turner's has pride of place and was described by Aptheker as

Reprinted from *Studies on the Left* VI, no. 6 (November–December, 1966): 3–26. By permission of *Studies on the Left*, Inc.

a "cataclysm." Yet, when we look closely, this revolt, like the total history of such revolts, recedes in importance and magnitude. As many of Aptheker's critics have pointed out, most of the 250 revolts probably never happened, being the imagination of hysterical or self-serving whites, insignificant plots that never matured, or mere local disturbances of a questionable nature. Of the three major revolts, one, Denmark Vesey's, was crushed before it came to fruition; only Gabriel Prosser's in 1800 and Turner's reached impressive proportions. Even so painstaking and thorough a scholar as Aptheker has been unable to discover  firm evidence of a major revolt between 1831 and 1865. As for Turner's, less than one hundred slaves joined. A revolt of this size would rate little more than a page or two in a comprehensive work on slave revolts in Brazil. To cite only two outstanding examples, runaway slaves in the Brazilian Northeast organized their own colony, Palmares, and waged a 65-year struggle for autonomy with as many as 20,000 people.[2] During the first four decades of the nineteenth century there were a series of violent and extensive risings in Bahia, culminating in the great Muslim-led holy war of 1835.[3] We need not dwell on Haiti,[4] as the record of Jamaica, Cuba and other countries is also impressive. Even if, as Aptheker suggests, news of many smaller risings was suppressed, the effect would have been to prevent the accumulation of a tradition to encourage and sustain revolt-prone slaves. On balance, we find the absence or extreme weakness of such a tradition.

There were many reasons for this extreme weakness. First, we need to consider the kind of Africans brought here. It has long been falsely assumed that, since slave traders mixed their cargoes, all parts of the hemisphere received similarly mixed bags. But Brazil, for example, received large numbers of Angolans and Congolese, whose military, religious and cultural traditions made them especially difficult to control.[5] Brazil also received a large number of Muslim slaves from Upper Guinea who proved intractable everywhere in the hemisphere. The United States, on the other hand, largely drew its slaves from those portions of Lower Guinea which had a population previously disciplined to servitude and domination. Ironically, these Africans were, in some respects, among the most advanced in technical culture.

Second, the slave trade to the United States came to an end in 1808, although illegal importations continued to trickle in; in contrast, the trade to Cuba and Brazil continued well into the nineteenth century. The presence of large numbers of newly imported Africans can generally be correlated with incidence of revolt. In the United States the great majority of slaves during the antebellum period had been born

and raised on Southern plantations. Their ranks received little rein-
forcement from newly enslaved and aggressive Africans.

Third, a review of the history of Brazil and the Caribbean suggests
that an important ingredient in the development of revolts out of local
disturbances was the division of the whites into warring factions and
the general weakness of the state apparatus. Together with these conditions went the general influence of geography in relation to state power.
Where suitable terrain was combined with a weak state, runaway slaves
could and did found maroon colonies, which directly fomented revolts
and kept alive a tradition of armed resistance. With minor qualifications, these conditions did not exist in the United States.

Fourth, a substantial revolt presupposed the formation of ideology
and leadership. In Brazil and the Caribbean two circumstances combined to encourage both: the cultivation of sugar led to the establishment of plantations averaging perhaps 200 slaves or more, and the size
of the white population was small. As a result the blacks could keep
alive much of their African culture or could develop a syncretized
Afro-Brazilian or Afro-Cuba culture, which militated against the loss
of identity and which could, under proper conditions, nurture resistance
movements. Apart from Islam, non-Christian religious cults, generally
of a syncretized type, played a great role in hemispheric slave revolts.
In the United States an imposed Protestantism, when effective, generally kept the slaves docile.

Half the slaves in the United States lived on units of twenty or less;
most of the others lived on plantations of fifty or less. Although blacks
heavily outnumbered whites in large areas of the South, they were, in
general, floating in a white sea. The white planters were residents, not
absentees; the non-slaveholders were loyal, armed and disciplined; the
country immediately beyond the plantation areas was inhabited by
armed whites completely hostile to the blacks. Death, not refuge, lay
beyond the plantation. For this reason, among others, blacks often
looked to their masters to protect them against the depredations and
viciousness of the poorer whites. We may therefore understand how,
during race riots like that in Atlanta in 1906, blacks reportedly ran to
whites—or at least to some whites—for protection.

The residency of the planters and their hegemony across the South
gave American slavery its particular quality and especially set it off
from Caribbean slavery. Between the Revolutionary War and the War
for Southern Independence the treatment of slaves, defined as day-to-
day conditions of life (housing, food, rigor of work routine, leisure time,
incidence and character of corporal punishment) improved steadily

and perceptibly. Although manumission was made increasingly difficult and escape from the system was sealed off, the harsh slave codes were steadily tempered by community sentiment and the interpretations of the state supreme courts. During the late antebellum period steady pressure built up to reform the slave codes in order to protect slave family life and to check glaring abuses of the slave's person. The purpose and effect of this amelioration in practice and at law was not to pave the way to freedom, but to consolidate the system from within and without. Like all liberal reformism it aimed to strengthen the social system.

For the planters these trends formed part of a developing world view within which paternalism became the specific manifestation of class consciousness. Paternalism did not mean kindness or generosity or love, although it embraced some of each; essentially it meant a special notion of duty and responsibility toward one's charges. Arbitrary power, harshness toward disobedience, even sadism, constituted its other side. For our immediate purposes, paternalism and the trend of treatment are especially noteworthy in confronting the slave with a world in which resistance could be quickly, severely and legitimately punished, whereas obedience placed him in a position to benefit from the favor of a master who more often than not had a genuine interest in his welfare. The picture of the docile and infantilized Sambo, drawn and analyzed so brilliantly by Stanley M. Elkins, is one-sided, but he is not far from the mark when he argues that the Southern regime greatly encouraged acceptance of and dependence upon despotic authority.[6] Elkins errs in thinking that the Sambo personality arose only in the United States, for it arose wherever slavery existed. He does not err in thinking that it was especially marked and extensive in the United States, where recourse to armed resistance was minimal and the tradition of paternalism took such firm root.

To say that slaves generally accommodated is not to say that they were so dehumanized as to be incapable of all forms of protest. Historians are quick to claim rebelliousness every time a slave broke a plow or stole a hog, but at least some room might be left for lack of initiative, thoughtlessness, stupidity and venality. Yet, we do know of enough instances of deliberate acts of day-to-day resistance to permit us to speak of a strong undercurrent of dissatisfaction and hostility, the manifestations of which require analysis.

One of the more prominent and irritating habits of recalcitrant slaves was stealing. Plundering the hog pen and the smokehouse was an especially happy pastime. Radical and liberal historians have taken particular delight in insisting that slaves might "steal" from each other but only "took" from their masters. After all, their labor being unpaid, they only took that which was rightfully theirs. I can understand this viewpoint from liberals because I can understand almost anything from liberals; I cannot understand it from Marxists. Since Marxists regard all surplus value as deriving from unpaid labor time, we ought, by the same logic, to be delighted every time a worker commits robbery at his plant. I do not wish to discuss the general problem of ethics in relation to class oppression, but I do insist that the encouragement given by the slave system to thefts had dangerous effects on the slaves themselves. The slaves understood the link between conventional morality and the civilized behavior of the whites; by rejecting that morality they registered a protest, but they simultaneously underscored their own isolation from that standard of civilization. Few masters got upset over slave thefts. They expected their slaves to steal, and by doing so, the slaves accepted their master's image of themselves.

Southern folklore abounds with charming stories of slaves outwitting masters by behaving like black versions of the Good Soldier Schweik. The trouble is that too often the masters enjoyed being outwitted in the same way that a tyrannical father sometimes enjoys being outwitted by a child. Every contortion necessary to the job implied inferiority. It proved the slave a clever fellow; it hardly proved him a man. It gained a few privileges or crumbs but undermined self-respect and confirmed the master's sense of superiority. The postslavery tradition of obsequiousness, indirection and the wearing of a mask before white men has played a similar role in the South ever since.

Arson and the mishandling of tools stand out as more positively rebelliousness acts. As expressions of frustration and resentment they are understandable, and might, in a general context of rebellion, have had considerable social value. As it was, they amounted to individual and essentially nihilistic thrashing about. With luck a few slaves might do enough damage to ruin a planter, in which case he would be forced to sell out and perhaps have to break up slave families and friendships. Advocates of the philosophy of "burn-baby-burn," whether on a Mississippi plantation in the 1850's or in a Northern ghetto in the 1960's, would do well to bear in mind that of necessity it is primarily the blacks who get burned. On occasion a slave took direct action against a particularly unpleasant master or overseer and killed him. For that manly act he would, if lucky, be hanged.

As we review these actions, which by no means exhaust the range, we find the formation of a tradition of recalcitrance but not revolution,

action but not politics, dim awareness of oppression but not cumulative, ideological growth. Thus, whereas most slaves came out of slavery
with a psychology of dependence conditioned by paternalism, the most
active spirits came out having learned little more than that they could
get away with individual acts of undirected, misdirected or naively
directed violence. What was missing was that sense of group consciousness, collective responsibility and joint political effort which is the
essence of a revolutionary tradition.

The formation of class leadership presents another side of this
development. Legend has it that house slaves and drivers, by virtue of
their special positions, arrayed themselves on the side of the master
against the field hands, who as the most oppressed were of course the
most revolutionary and pure. Examination of plantation documents
casts grave doubts on this legend. Few plantations were big enough to
carry a staff of servants large enough to constitute a separate caste.
Even then the social life of the plantation proved too enticing for them
to maintain total separation. With much of their everyday world conditioned by contacts with field slaves, they could ill-afford to be wholly
on the side of the whites. The range of behavior was wide, but there
were many instances of identification and sympathy.

The drivers, or slave foremen, present an even clearer case. These
men often dominated the everyday life of the plantation. On the whole
masters trusted them more than they trusted their white overseers;
overseers came and went after a year or two, but drivers usually stayed
on in positions of authority for many years. Masters relied on their
drivers to tell them if an overseer was too lax or too harsh and if the
hands respected him. Rarely did a planter take his overseer's word
against that of a trusted driver. Some drivers undoubtedly were themselves severe taskmasters who lorded it over their fellow slaves, but
drivers, too, had no social life apart from that of the slave quarters
and had to live with the others. In general, they compromised as best
they could between the master to whom they had pledged loyalty and
to whom they were indebted for special favors, and the slaves who
constituted their everyday fellows. Often the driver stood as a protector
or interpreter between slave and master or overseer. Drivers and house
slaves often, although certainly not always, comprised a leading
stratum in the eyes of the blacks as well as in the eyes of the whites.

In the Caribbean these privileged slaves led revolts; in the United
States they served as agents of accommodation. Toussaint L'Ouverture
was only the most prominent of insurrectionary leaders who had been
trained to leadership within the system. The problem in the United

States was not that the system did not create such privileged strata, nor that these strata were more docile or less courageous than those in the Caribbean. The problem was that the total environment reduced the possibilities for successful insurrection virtually to zero, and therefore made accommodationists out of the most high-spirited slave leaders. When the mass exodus from the plantations took place during the War for Southern Independence, drivers and house slaves often led their people to the Union lines. Not docility but lack of a tradition of armed resistance conditioned their leadership.

Potential recruitment of insurrectionary leaders was hampered by many other circumstances, of which three are especially noteworthy. For reasons already indicated little anti-Christian religious sentiment could develop. Religion (Islam, voodoo, or Afro-Catholic syncretisms) proved to be an essential ingredient in slave cohesion and organized resistance throughout the hemisphere, but in the United States the enforced prevalence of Protestant Christianity played an opposite role. The second group of potential leaders recruited from all strata were those who had sufficient strength, daring and resourcefulness to flee. The runaways are black folk heroes, with good reason, but they also drained the best elements out of the slave class. In much of Brazil and the Caribbean runaways had nowhere to go except into the back country to form maroon colonies, the existence of which encouraged slave disorder and resistance. Finally, the free blacks and mulattoes in the United States had little opportunity for self-development and rarely could or would provide leadership to slaves. Elsewhere in the hemisphere, where whites were relatively few, these free blacks and mulattoes were needed to fill a wide variety of social and economic functions. Often they prospered as a middle class. In some cases, feelings of racial solidarity or, as in Haiti, the racist stupidity of the whites, led them into partial identification with the cause of black freedom. Thus, with the exception of a rare Nat Turner, black leadership fell to those whose position within the plantation itself encouraged accommodation and negated the possibilities of effective political organization.

The War for Southern Independence brought these tendencies to a head. The staggering truth is that not one full-scale slave revolt broke out during a war in which local white police power had been drastically reduced. In only a few isolated cases did slaves drive off their masters and divide the land among themselves. Many, perhaps most, struck for freedom by fleeing to Union lines at the first opportunity. The attitude of the slaves toward the federals varied, but the great majority welcomed them with an adulation, trust and dependence that suggests the full force of the old paternalism.[7] Many blacks, free and slaves, Northern and Southern, entered the Union Army, where despite humiliating discrimination they gave a creditable account of themselves in action.

For all that, the record of the slaves and ex-slaves during the war constituted a disaster. Having relied previously on the protection and guidance of their masters, they now threw themselves on the mercies of the Union Army. As might be expected, untold thousands died in and out of virtual concentration camps, countless women were raped by Union troops, black soldiers generally found themselves used as menials or cannon fodder. Many decent and selfless white and black abolitionists accompanied the Union Army South and earnestly worked to educate and organize the freedmen; they deserve all the praise and attention historians are now heaping on them. The fact remains that no black movement and only a weak black leadership emerged from the war.

As the war years passed into the period of Reconstruction, these patterns were reinforced. The blacks could and did fight for their rights, but rarely under their own leadership. When they offered armed resistance under competent leadership they did well enough, but mostly they relied on the leadership of white politicians, or on the protection of federal troops, or on the advice of their own inexperienced leaders who in turn relied on whites. As Vernon Lane Wharton has observed, "The lesson learned was that the Negroes, largely unarmed, economically dependent, and timid and unresourceful after generations of servitude, would offer no effective resistance to violence."[8] When Whitelaw Reid asked black school children what they would do if someone tried to reenslave them, most responded that the troops would not permit it. No wonder Northern public opinion asked contemptuously in 1875 why a black majority in Mississippi constantly had to call for outside help.

The blacks sealed their own fate by relying on the protection of others. The Republican Party, the Union Army and the Freedman's Bureau all took on the role of protectors, but, if anything, the new paternalism proved much more flimsy and more insincere than the old. the best illustration may be found in the history of the Republican-sponsored, largely black militias. Ex-slaves, urged on and even threatened by their women, who were generally more militant than the men, responded to the calls of Republican governors and filled the ranks of state militias, which were put to effective use in guaranteeing Republican electoral victories. In several instances, especially toward the end of Reconstruction, militia units opposed each other on behalf of rival Republican factions. In the most appalling of these instances, the so-called Brooks-Baxter War in Arkansas in 1874, the Republican machine so discredited itself that the Democrats soon rode back to power. As Otis A. Singletary has sardonically observed, "The Negroes had been called to arms to fight in behalf of two white claimants for the governorship, as a consequence of which the Negro was eliminated as a political factor in Arkansas."[9] In Mississippi the radical governor, Adelbert Ames, called the blacks to arms in 1875 to counter Democratic violence, and then lost his nerve and disarmed them in return for a worthless pledge from the opposition. Significantly the black politicians in his party almost unanimously opposed using the black troops in a showdown. The militia movement failed because it faced greater force, but no less because its leaders were never willing to see it steeled in battle, especially in defense of specifically black interests.

In other respects the Reconstruction experience followed parallel lines. In the famous Sea Island experiment the blacks placed their trust in white generals, some of whom meant well and tried hard but could not prevail in the face of Washington's duplicity. When the old plantation owners returned with federal support, the blacks protested but ultimately accepted defeat without recourse to arms. Here, as with the militias, the masses seem to have been well ahead of their leaders. Demands for resistance were heard, anti-white feeling was manifest and the desire for land grew apace, but the leadership proved timid or mortgaged, and action independent of whites was deemed impractical. Black Congressmen and state legislators rarely fought for basic black interests and even opposed disfranchisement of ex-Confederate whites. With no powerful separate organizations and paramilitary units, without experience in leading their masses, they temporized and collapsed. Their fault did not lie in having coalesced with Northern whites, but in having coalesced from a position of weakness, without independent demands, organization and force. The masses moved sharply to the left and expressed an intense desire for land, but the old pattern persisted; they could not cut loose from accommodating leaders and from dependence on the ultimate authority of the whites. They did not so much demand, much less fight for, land, as they hoped it would be given them as a Christmas present.

The black leaders saw the duplicity of their white Republican allies, but had nowhere to go. Most had been Northerners or privileged Southern mulattoes; their links with the masses had never been firm. When election time arrived they swallowed their doubts and frustrations and, with the best of intentions, lied to their people. Without adequate traditions and without confidence in their masses they made the best deals they could. This lying carried on an old habit. Every slave, at some time or other, would outwit the white folks by pretending to be stupid or docile; unfortunately too often he simultaneously outwitted himself. When carried into slave leadership, it was generally impossible to outwit the whites without also outwitting the blacks. During the war, for example, the respected black pastor of a Baptist Church in Virginia offered a prayer for the victory of Confederate arms. Subsequently he was berated by his deacons for betraying the cause of the slaves, but he pacified them by saying, "Don't worry children; the Lord knew what I was talking about."[10] Undoubtedly, the Lord did, but the good pastor apparently never wondered whether or not his flock did also.

Some of the Reconstruction leaders simply sold out. As a distinguished South Carolina planter noted, they promised their people land and mules at every election but delivered only offices and jobs for themselves and their friends.[11] (Any resemblance to the War on Poverty is not of my making.)

Slavery and its aftermath left the blacks in a state of acute economic and cultural backwardness, with weak family ties and the much-discussed matriarchal preponderance. They also left a tradition of accommodation to paternalistic authority on the one hand, and a tradition of nihilistic violence on the other. Not docility or infantilization, but innocence of organized effort and political consciousness plagued the black masses and kept plaguing them well into the twentieth century. As a direct result of these effects and of the virtually unchallenged hegemony of the slaveholders, the blacks had little opportunity to develop a sense of their own worth and had every opportunity to learn to despise themselves. The inability of the men during and after slavery to support their families adequately, and especially to protect their women from rape or abuse without forfeiting their own lives, has merely served as the logical end of an emasculating process.

The remarkable ascendancy of Booker T. Washington after the post-Reconstruction reaction must be understood against this background. We need especially to account for his enormous influence over the black nationalists who came after him. Washington tried to meet the legacy of slavery on its own terms. He knew that slavery had ill-prepared his people for political leadership; he therefore retreated from political demands. He knew that slavery had rendered manual labor degrading; he therefore preached the gospel of hard work. He knew that slavery had undermined the family and elementary moral standards; he therefore preached the whole gamut of middle-class virtues and manners. He knew his people had never stood on their own feet and faced the whites as equals; he therefore preached self-reliance and self-help. Unhappily, apart from other ideological sins, he saw no way to establish self-reliance and self-respect except under the financial and social hegemony of the white upper classes. Somehow he meant to destroy the effects of paternalism in the long run by strengthening paternalism in the short run. It would be easy to say that he failed because of this tactic, but there is no way to be sure that the tactic was wrong in principle. He failed for other reasons, one of which was his reliance on the paternalistic, conservative classes at a time when they were rapidly losing power in the South to racist agrarian demagogues.

Washington's rivals did not, in this respect, do much better. The leaders of the NAACP repeatedly returned to a fundamental reliance on white leadership and money. Even Du Bois, in his classic critique of Washington, argued:

> While it is a great truth to say that the Negro must strive and strive mightily to help himself, it is equally true that unless his striving be not simply seconded, but rather aroused and encouraged by the initiative of the richer and wiser environing group, he cannot hope for great success.[12]

The differences between these militants and Washington's conservatives concerned emphases, tactics and public stance much more than ideological fundamentals. The differences were important, but their modest extent was no less so. The juxtaposition of the two tendencies reveals how little could be done even by the most militant without white encouragement and support. The wonder is that black Americans survived the ghastly years between 1890 and 1920 at all. Survival and more impressive, growing resistance to oppression—came at the price of continuing many phases of a paternalistic tradition that had already sapped the strength of the masses.

The conflict between Washington and Du Bois recalled many earlier battles between two tendencies that are still with us. The first has accepted segregation at least temporarily, has stressed the economic development of the black community and has advocated self-help. This tendency generally prevailed during periods of retrogression in race relations until the upsurge of nationalism in our own day. Washington was its prophet; black nationalism has been its outcome. The second has demanded integration, has stressed political action and has demanded that whites recognize their primary responsibility. Frederick Douglass was its prophet; the civil rights movement has been its outcome. Yet, the lines have generally been blurred. Du Bois often sounded like a nationalist, and Washington probably would have thought Malcolm X a madman.[13] This blurring reflects the dilemma of the black community as a whole and of its bourgeoisie in particular: How do you integrate into a nation that does not want you? How do you separate from a nation that finds you too profitable to release?

To probe the relationship between this past and the recent upsurge of the black masses requires more speculation and tentative judgment than one would like, but they cannot be avoided. Let us, at the risk of being schematic and one-sided, select several features of the developments of the last few decades and especially of the recent crisis for such analysis. In doing so let us bear in mind that the majority of blacks today live outside the South; that they are primarily urban, not rural, in all parts of the country; that whole cities are on the way to becoming black enclaves; that the problem increasingly centers on the urban North and West.[14] Let us bear in mind also that the only large-scale, organized black mass movements until recently have been nationalist. Garvey commanded an organization of hundreds of thousands; the Muslims have tens of thousands and influence many more. No integrationist organization has ever acquired such numerical strength; none has ever struck such deep roots in the black ghettoes.

Garvey's movement emphasized blackness as a thing of beauty, and struggled to convince the black masses to repudiate white leadership and paternalism. The pompous titles, offices, uniforms and parades did and do evoke ridicule, but their importance lay, as Edmund David Cronon says, "in restoring the all but shattered Negro self-confidence." There was enormous ideological significance in Garvey's delightful description of a light-skinned mulatto opponent as "a white man passing for Negro."[15]

A decisive break with the white man's church, if not wholly with his religion, has formed a major part of black nationalist thinking. In view of the central role of anti-Christian ideology in the slave risings of Brazil and the Caribbean and the generally accommodationist character of American Christianity, this has been a rational response to a difficult problem. Garvey tried to organize his own African Orthodox Church. The Islamic tendency, including Elijah Muhammed's Nation of Islam, has followed the maxim of Noble Drew Ali's Moorish Science Movement, "Before you can have a God, you must have a nationality." Garvey's Black Jesus and Muhammed's Allah have had many attributes of a tribal deity. Of special importance in Muhammed's teaching is his decidedly un-Islamic denial of an afterlife. In this way Black Muslim eschatology embodies a sharp reaction against accommodationist ideology. The tendency to turn away from the white man's religion has taken many forms, including conversion to Catholicism ostensibly because of its lack of a color line. In Catholic Brazil, on the other hand, an equivalent reason is given by blacks who embrace Protestantism.[16]

Black Protestants in the United States have largely attended self-segregated churches since Reconstruction. With the collapse of Reconstruction these churches, especially in the South, played an increasingly accommodationist role, but they also served as community centers, protective agencies, marriage counseling committees and leadership training schools. As objective conditions changed, so did many ministers, especially the younger ones. One of the great ironies of the current struggle for integration has been the leading role played by ministers whose training and following have been made possible by segregated organizations. The experience of the Protestant churches and their anti-Christian rivals brings us back to slavery's legacy of accommodationist but by no means necessarily treasonable leadership, of an absence of collective effort, of paternalistically-induced dependence and of emasculation. Theoretically, a militant mass leadership could have arisen from sources other than enforced segregation; historically there seems to have been no other way.[17]

The first difficulty with the integrationist movement arises not from its ultimate commitment, which may or may not be desirable, but from the determined opposition of the whites, whose hostility to close association with blacks recedes slowly if at all. Integration may only mean desegregation, and outstanding black intellectuals like Killens and Baldwin insist that that is all they want it to mean; it need not mean assimilation. In fact, the line is difficult to hold, and segregationists probably do not err in regarding one as the prelude to the other. In any case, de facto segregation in education and housing is growing worse, and many of the professed goals of the civil rights movement look further away than ever. Communities like Harlem face substantially the same social problems today as they did forty years ago.[18] I need not dwell on the worsening problem of black unemployment and its implications.

Even where progress, however defined, occurs, the frustration of the black masses deepens. The prosperity of recent decades has widened the gap between blacks and whites even of the same class. The rise of the African peoples has inspired blacks here but has also threatened to open a gap in political power and dignity between Africans and Afro-Americans.[19]

The resistance of whites and the inflexibility of the social system constitute only half the problem. A. James Gregor, in an article published in *Science & Society* in 1963, analyzes an impressive body of sociological and psychological literature to demonstrate that integration under the disorderly conditions of American capitalist life more often than not undermines the development and dignity of the participating blacks. He shows that the problems of the black masses, in contradistinction to those of the bourgeoisie, become intensified by an integration which, in the nature of things, must pass them by. As Gregor demonstrates, black nationalism has been the political reply of these masses and especially of the working class.[20] Similarly, in his honest and thoughtful book, *Crisis in Black and White*, Charles E. Silberman analyzes cases such as that in New Rochelle, in which poor black and rich children had the wonderful experience of integrating in school. Why should anyone be surprised that the experiment proved a catastrophe for the black children, who promptly lost whatever ambition they might have had.[21]

When liberals and academics speak of a "crisis of identity," they may sometimes merely wish to divert attention from the prior fact of oppression, but, by whatever name, that crisis exists. Slavery and its aftermath emasculated the black masses; they are today profoundly sick and shaking with convulsions. It does us no good to observe, with Kardiner and Ovesey, that a psychology of oppression can only disappear when the oppression has disappeared.[22] It does us no good to admit that the sickness of white racism is more dangerous than the sickness it has engendered. We face an aroused, militant black community that has no intention of waiting for others to heal themselves. Those who believe that emasculation is the figment of the liberal imagination ought to read the words of any militant leader from David Walker to W. E. B. Du Bois, from Frederick Douglass to Martin Luther King, from Robert F. Williams to Malcolm X. The cry has been to assert manhood and renounce servility. Every outstanding black intellectual today—Killens, Baldwin, Ellison—makes the point in one way or another. Let me quote only one, Ossie Davis on the death of Malcolm X:

[Negroes knew] that Malcolm—whatever else he was or was not— *Malcolm was a man!*

White folks do not need anybody to remind them that they are men. We do! This was his one incontrovertible benefit to his people. Protocol and common sense require that Negroes stand back and let the white man speak up for us, defend us, and lead us from behind the scene in our fight. This is the essence of Negro politics. But Malcolm said to hell with that! Get up off your knees and fight your own battles. That's the way to win back your self-respect. That's the way to make the white man respect you. And if he won't let you live like a man, he certainly can't keep you from dying like one.[23]

Is it any wonder, then, that Dr. King could write, almost as a matter of course, that the blacks of Birmingham during the summer of 1963 shook off 300 years of psychological slavery and found out their own worth?[24] It is no less instructive that his aide, the Reverend Wyatt T. Walker, denounced as "hoodlums" and "winos" those who responded to the attempt on King's life by attacking the white racists. King himself put it bluntly when he pleaded that the black militant be allowed to march and sit-in, "If his repressed emotions do not come out in these nonviolent ways, they will come out in ominous expressions of violence."[25]

King and his followers apparently believe that concerted action for integration can cure the ills engendered by slavery and subsequent oppression and break down discrimination at the same time. In one sense they are right. Their greatest achievement has been to bring order and collective effort to a people who had learned little of the necessity for either. But King must deliver victory or face grave consequences. As we have seen, not all slaves and freedmen yielded meekly to the oppressor. Many fought, sometimes with great ferocity, but they generally fought by lashing out rather than by organized revolutionary effort. It would be the crowning irony if the civil rights movement has taught just enough of the lesson of collective effort to guarantee greater and more widespread nihilism in the wake of its inability to realize its program.

More and more young black radicals are currently poring over Frantz Fanon's psychopathic panegyric to violence. Fanon argues that violence frees the oppressed from his inferiority complex and restores his self-respect.[26] Perhaps, but it is also the worst way to do either. Black Americans, like colonials, have always resorted to violence without accomplishing those goals. A slave who killed his overseer did not establish his manhood thereby—any wild animal can kill—he merely denied his docility. Violence can serve Fanon's purpose only when it is collective and disciplined—that is, political—but then it is precisely the collective effort, not the violence, that does the healing.[27]

The legend of black docility threatens to betray those who perpetuate it. They are ill-prepared for the yielding of one side of the slave tradition—accommodation and servility—to the other side—antisocial and nihilistic action. The failure of integration and the lawlessness to which the blacks have for so long been subjected and subject combine to produce that result. James Baldwin and Malcolm X, especially in his remarks on the prestige of the ghetto hustler, have each warned of this danger.[28] Bayard Rustin has made a similar point with gentle irony:

> From the point of view of motivation, some of the healthiest Negro youngsters I know are juvenile delinquents: vigorously pursuing the American Dream of material acquisition and status, yet finding the conventional means of attaining it blocked off, they do not yield to defeatism but resort to illegal (and sometimes ingenious) methods. They are not alien to American culture.[29]

Those historians who so uncritically admire the stealing of hogs and smashing of plows by slaves might consider its modern equivalent. In the words of Silberman:

> There are other means of protest, of course: misbehaving in school, or dropping out of school altogether; not showing up for work on time, or not showing up at all (and lying about the reason); breaking school windows or ripping telephone receivers out of outdoor phone booths; or the oldest form of protest of all, apathy—a flat refusal to cooperate with the oppressor or to accept his moral code.[30]

Black nationalism, in its various manifestations, constitutes a necessary response on the part of the black masses. The Muslims, for example, have understood the inner needs of the working-class blacks who have filled their ranks and have understood the futility—for these people at least—of integrationist hopes. Their insistence on the forcible assertion of a dignified, disciplined, collectively responsible black community represents a rational response to a harsh reality.[31] We need not dwell on what is unrealistic, romantic or even reactionary in the Nation of Islam or other nationalist groups; they are easy to see. Ralph Bunche, in his radical days, Gunnar Myrdal and many others have for years pointed out that the idea of a separate black economy is a will-o-the-wisp and that the idea of a separate territory is less than that. Yet I am not sure how to answer Marc Schleifer who in 1963 asked whether these goals were less realistic than those of equality under capitalism or a social revolution in the forseeable future.[32] I am not sure, either, that Malcolm X, Harold W. Cruse and Stokely Carmichael have not been wiser than their Marxist critics in demanding black ownership of everything in Harlem.[33] Such ownership will do little toward the creation of a black economy, but many of its advocates are easily bright enough to know as much. The point is that it may, as Malcolm X suggested, play a decisive role in the establishment of community stability and self-respect.

The black struggle for equality in America has always had two tendencies—integrationist and separatist—and it is likely to retain both. Since a separate economy and national territory are not serious possibilities, the struggle for economic integration will undoubtedly be pressed forward. For this reason alone some degree of unity between the civil rights and nationalist tendencies may be expected. The black bourgeoisie and its allied stratum of skilled and government clerical workers will certainly continue its fight for integration, but the interest of the black workers in this fight is, at bottom, even greater. At the same time there will clearly be serious defeats, as well as some victories, and the slogan "Freedom Now!" may soon turn to ashes.

The cumulative problems of past and present nonetheless demand urgent action. The assertion of black hegemony in specific cities and districts—nationalism if you will—offers the only politically realistic hope of transcending the slave heritage. First, it seems the only way for black communities to police themselves, to curb antisocial elements and to enforce adequate health and housing standards, and yet break with paternalism and instill pride and a sense of worth. Second, it seems the best way to build a position of strength from which to fight for a proper share of jobs and federal funds as a matter of right not privilege. Black nationalism may yet prove to be the only force capable of restraining the impulse to violence, of disciplining black rebelliousness and of absorbing the nihilistic tradition into a socially constructive movement. If this seems like a conservative rendering of an ostensibly revolutionary movement, I can only answer that there are no ingredients for a successful, independent black revolution, and that black nationalism can ultimately go only a few steps further to the left than the white masses. The rise of specifically black cities, counties and districts with high quality black schools, well paid teachers, as well as political leaders, churches and community centers, could and should uproot the slave tradition once and for all, could and should act as a powerful lever for structural reform of the American economy and society.

I do not offer these remarks as a program for a black movement, for the time is past when white men can offer programs to black militants. They are, happily, no longer listening. But I do submit that they are relevant to the formation of a program for ourselves—for the American left. If this analysis has merit, the demands of the black community will increasingly swing away from the traditional appeal to federal power and toward the assertion of local and regional autonomy. Even now Bayard Rustin and others warn that federal troops can only preserve the status quo. I should observe, further, that the appeals to Washington reflect the convergence of two powerful and debilitating traditions: slave-engendered paternalistic dependence and the growing state paternalism of white America. Let us admit that the naive fascination of leftists for centralized power has, since the 1930's, greatly strengthened this tendency. With such labels as "progressive" and even "socialist," corporate liberalism has been building what William Appleman Williams has aptly called a nonterroristic totalitarian society. Yet American socialism has never even posed a theoretical aternative. When Professor Williams called for a program of regional and local reassertion and opposition to centralization, he was dismissed by most radicals as a Utopian of doubtful mental competence. We may now rephrase his question: How do we propose to support an increasingly nationalistic black radicalism, with its demands for local hegemony, unless we have an ideology and program of opposition to the centralization of state power?

The possible courses for the black liberation movement include a total defeat in an orgy of violence (we ought to remember that there is nothing inevitable in its or our victory), a compromise with imperialism in return for some degree of local rule or the integration of its bourgeois strata, and the establishment of black power on the basis of a developing opposition to American capitalism. Since its future depends to a great extent on the progress of its integrationist struggle for a place in the economy, the black community must for a while remain well to the left of the current liberal consensus by its demands for public works and structural reform. But reform could occur under the auspices of an expansion rather than a contraction of state centralization, and the most militant of the black leaders may have to settle for jobs and local political control in return for allegiance to a consolidating national and international empire. The final result will be decided by the struggle within white America, with the blacks playing the role of an increasingly independent ally for one or another tendency. Notwithstanding some offensive and pretentious rhetoric, the advocates of black power have judged their position correctly. They are determined to win control of the ghettoes, and we would be foolish not to bet on them. The use to which they put that power, however, depends not on our good wishes or on their good intentions, but on what they are offered as a *quid pro quo*. For American socialism the black revolt opens an opportunity for relevance that has been missing for decades. What we do with that opportunity, as the leaders of SNCC have rather rudely reminded us, is our problem, not theirs.

## NOTES

1. Aptheker, Herbert, *American Negro Slave Revolts* (New York, 1943, 1963).

2. Carneiro, Edison, *O Quilombo dos Palmares, 1630–1695* (Sao Paulo, 1947).

3. Cf., Abbé Ignace Etienne, "La Secte musulmane des Malès du Brésil et leur révolte en 1835," *Anthropos*, IV (1909), 99–105; 405–415.

4. Cf., esp. C.L.R. James, *The Black Jacobins: Toussaint L'Ouverture and the San Domingo Revolution* (2nd ed., rev.; New York, 1963), which deserves to rank as a classic of Marxian historiography but has been largely ignored, perhaps because of the author's Trotskyist politics.

5. For example, Palmares was established by Angolans. See "Carta do Governador Fernao de Souza Coutinho . . ." in Ernesto Ennes, *As Guerras nos Palmares* (Sao Paulo, 1938), pp. 133–138, Nina Rodrigues, *Os Africanos no Brasil* (3rd ed., Sao Paulo, 1945), Ch. III.

6. Elkins, Stanley M., *Slavery: A Problem in American Institutional and Intellectual Life* (Chicago, 1959), esp. Ch. III.

7. Wiley, Bell Irvin, *Southern Negroes, 1861–1865* (New Haven, 1965; first pub., 1938), esp. pp. 14–15.

8. Wharton, Vernon Lane, *The Negro in Mississippi, 1865–1900* (New York, 1965; first pub. 1947), p. 190.

9. Singletary, Otis A., *Negro Militia and Reconstruction* (Austin, 1952), p. 65.

10. Wiley, *Southern Negroes*, p. 107.

11. Manigault, Charles, "Souvenirs of Our Ancestors & of My Immediate Family," ca. 1873. Ms. in the Manigault Papers, University of North Carolina.

12. Du Bois, W. E. Burghardt, *The Soul of Black Folk* (New York, 1964; first pub. 1903), p. 53.

13. For the period 1890–1915 see August Meier's careful and illuminating *Negro Thought in America: Racial Ideologies in the Age of Booker T. Washington* (New York, 1964).

14. For a perceptive discussion of these trends see Charles E. Silberman, *Crisis in Black and White* (New York, 1964), esp. pp. 7, 29–31.

15. Cronon, Edmund David, *Black Moses: The Story of Marcus Garvey and the Universal Negro Improvement Association* (Madison, 1955, 1964), p. 174. It was never Garvey's intention to send all blacks back to Africa; he wanted a strong African nation to serve as a protector to blacks everywhere. See esp. the interview with Garvey in James Weinstein, ed., "Black Nationalism: The Early Debate," *Studies on the Left*, IV, no. 3 (1964), pp. 50–58.

The idea of black nationality in America stretches back to the beginnings of the nineteenth century, if not earlier. See esp. Herbert Aptheker, "Consciousness of Negro Nationality to 1900," *Toward Negro Freedom* (New York, 1956), pp. 104–111; also, Benjamin Quarles, *The Negro in the Making of America* (New York, 1964), p. 157.

16. Bastide, Roger, and Fernandes, Florestan, *Brancos e negros em Sao Paulo* (2nd ed.; Sao Paulo, 1959), p. 254.

17. This recent experience, especially of SCLC, reveals the legacy of the past in other ways as well. Louis E. Lomax has criticized Dr. King for organizational laxness and has related the problems of the SCLC to the structure of the Baptist Church, "The Negro Baptist Church is a nonorganization. Not only is each congregation a sovereign body, dictated to by no one, but it would appear that the members who come together and form a Baptist Church are held together only by their mutual disdain for detailed organization and discipline." *The Negro Revolt* (New York, 1962), p. 86. As a result, according to Lomax, the SCLC is a loose, scattered organization that mobilizes itself only with great difficulty. Lomax makes good points but fails to note the extent to which this weakness flows from the entire history of black America and especially the black South. With justice, one could argue that the remarkable strength of SCLC in the face of this amorphousness is a singular tribute to Dr. King's political genius. He has mobilized masses who are ill-prepared for the kind of puritanical discipline preached by Elijah Muhammed.

18. Osofsky, Gilbert, *Harlem: The Making of a Ghetto* (New York, 1966), p. 179.

19. See the perceptive remarks on these two kinds of gaps in Oscar Handlin, *Fire-Bell in the Night: The Crisis in Civil Rights* (Boston, 1964), pp. 21–22, 53; C. Eric Lincoln, *The Black Muslims in America*

(Boston, 1961), p. 45; and James Baldwin, *The Fire Next Time* (New York, 1964), pp. 105–106.

20. Gregor, A. James, "Black Nationalism: A Preliminary Analysis of Negro Radicalism," *Science & Society*, XXVII (Fall 1963), 415–432.

21. Silberman, *Crisis in Black and White*, p. 298. Even under more favorable conditions, as John Oliver Killens has noted, black children in the South often have a feeling of belonging that is undermined when they move north. *Black Man's Burden* (New York, 1965), pp. 84–85.

22. Kardiner, Abram, and Ovesey, Lionel, *The Mark of Oppression: Explorations in the Personality of the American Negro* (New York, 1951, 1962), p. 387.

23. Davis, Ossie, "On Malcolm X," in *The Autobiography of Malcolm X* (New York, 1965), p. 453.

24. King, Martin Luther, Jr., *Why We Can't Wait* (New York, 1964), p. 111.

25. Silberman, *Crisis in Black and White*, pp. 122, 199.

26. Fanon, Frantz, *The Wretched of the Earth* (New York, 1965). But see also two good critiques in *Studies on the Left*, VI, no. 3 (May-June, 1966): Samuel Rohdie, "Liberation and Violence in Algeria," pp. 83–89, and esp. A. Norman Klein, "On Revolutionary Violence," pp. 62–82.

27. The warning of so humane and sensitive a man as Killens on this matter is worth quoting:
    The advocates of absolute non-violence have reckoned without the psychological needs of Black America. Let me state it plainly: There is in many Negroes a deep need to practice violence against their white tormentors. *Black Man's Burden*, p. 113.
    The Muslims understand this very well, as does Dr. King; they try to substitute internal discipline and collective effort for the violence itself.

28. Baldwin, *The Fire Next Time*, pp. 35–37; *The Autobiography of Malcolm X*, pp. 315–316.

29. Rustin, Bayard, "From Protest to Politics: The Future of the Civil Rights Movement," in F. L. Broderick and A. Meier, eds., *Negro Protest Thought in the Twentieth Century* (Indianapolis, 1965), p. 410.

30. Silberman, *Crisis in Black and White*, pp. 47–48.

31. The best study of the Muslims is E. U. Essien-Uudom, *Black Nationalism: A Search for Identity in America* (New York, 1964). Elijah Muhammed has demonstrated remarkable awareness of the persistence of the slave tradition, even in its most elusive forms. His denunciation of black conspicuous consumption, for example, correctly views it as essentially a reflection of the mores of the slaveholders and counter-

poses to it standards that recall those of revolutionary petty-bourgeois puritanism.

32. Schleifer, Marc, "Socialism and the Negro Movement," *Monthly Review*, XV (Sept. 1963), pp. 225–228.

33. For a suggestive theoretical defense of such a demand see Harold W. Cruse, "Revolutionary Nationalism and the Afro-American," *Studies on the Left*, II, no. 3 (1962), 12–25; and his subsequent communication in III, no. 1 (1962), esp. p. 70. See also *The Autobiography of Malcolm X*, p. 318.

# b | Comment

## Herbert Aptheker

American radicals have not been imprisoned by the notion that the masses are necessarily both good and revolutionary. This is a travesty and a caricature. American radicals have insisted that radicalism is not alien to the United States, that radicalism has been present among the Negro people of the United States, that there existed valid reasons for such radicalism, and that insofar as this radicalism sought an end to exploitative and oppressive relationships, it was "good."

American radicals have not been imprisoned by the "pernicious" notion that if the masses have not been or are not "good and revolutionary," they should be. There is nothing pernicious in the idea that it is the masses rather than the elite who represent a superior morality and a revolutionizing potential. American radicals have believed that with good reason. The history of the United States and of the Negro people in the United States, and the realities of life in this country today, offer convincing substantiation of such views.

That these views do dominate the Negro liberation movement today is one of the happiest and most significant realities, and is the result of many decades of effort. That effort was not simply or mainly the work of "white radical historians" who allegedly have in this one respect set the ideological pace for their liberal colleagues. First, the views of these white radical historians have not yet triumphed among their liberal colleagues—nor, from the evidence of the paper just presented—among some radical colleagues. Second, some note should be taken of the fact that many of the historians and professors are neither radical nor liberal, as the gubernatorial candidate recently selected by the New York Conservative Party makes clear. Third, the

Reprinted from *Studies on the Left* VI, no. 6 (November–December, 1966): 27–35. By permission of *Studies on the Left*, Inc.

white radical historians followed and learned from Negro historians; this is of great importance for the record and is directly pertinent here since in the paper just presented and in the book *The Political Economy of Slavery* there is no reference to the work of Du Bois or Woodson, Wesley or Johnston, Franklin or Jackson or Greene. . . .

The point is not that in slavery, "whites and blacks lived in harmony as well as in antagonism." Any social system, as a system, functions and hence contains within it "harmony"—i.e., is viable. But the point is, is its existence based upon invidious features, is it parasitic in character, antagonistic, filled with contradictions? Do these features reflect themselves in who benefits and who suffers under the system, who rebels and/or endures; where lie the dynamics of the order, the seeds of change and of challenge? The historian—certainly the radical historian—should interest himself particularly in these seeds and challenges; not only in what is, but what is coming about—without which, of course, one cannot understand what is.

There is massive evidence of significant organized resistance to the slave regime. This has been offered in the work of those mentioned above and of many others, including this commentator. As for the latter, this appears not only in his *American Negro Slave Revolts*— more often alluded to than studied—but in many other books and papers and in other contemporaneous scholars, such as Stampp.

The main problem is not to discover the reasons for the widespread accommodation—that is the business of historians of the status quo— such as U. B. Phillips. Furthermore, it was not accommodation; it was domination, enforced subordination. The domination was planned, deliberate and required constant attention. There was not so much accommodation as there was an elaborate "machinery of control," as it is called in one of the longest chapters in *American Negro Slave Revolts*. An examination of the long-time effects of that machinery of control would have the greatest relevance to an understanding of "The Legacy of Slavery and the Roots of Black Nationalism," but, alas, this is nowhere considered.

There is no "legend of armed black resistance to slavery." It is not a legend—though the use of the word "armed" is disarming. There is the fact of Negro resistance to enslavement—armed and unarmed; that is the great fact and it is not legendary at all.

Describing the Turner revolt as a "cataclysm" is correct; when examined closely it does not "recede in importance or magnitude." On the contrary, it appears as one of the seminal events in the history of Negro slavery and antislavery in the United States.

It is not true that "most of the 250 revolts probably never occurred" that are described in *American Negro Slave Revolts*. The latter book very carefully affirms that it is considering not only actual uprisings, but also plots and conspiracies. It makes very clear that it considers only those referred to by two or more contemporary witnesses, that they must have described the events as slave plots or uprisings, that at least ten slaves were involved, and that at least two plantations were involved. Dozens of events that were mere rumors or (probably) the result of panic are carefully described that way in the book; further, the point is made that censorship existed and that it is entirely likely that genuine plots and perhaps even uprisings never were recorded.

That there were three major insurrectionary efforts in the first sixty years of the 19th century—Genovese omits reference to the preceding century which was filled with unrest—argues against the Phillipsian view; the more so when it is understood—and Genovese misses this crucial point altogether—that each of these major outbreaks was the climax of several years of heightened unrest. Indeed, that is characteristic of the history of American Negro slavery, i.e., *periods* of intensified unrest, namely, 1720–1740, 1790–1802, 1820–1831, 1850–1860.

It is not true that Aptheker was able to find no evidence of significant slave unrest and uprisings from 1831 through the Civil War; the evidence is contained on pages 325 through 367 of *American Negro Slave Revolts*, and in several other publications. Indeed, perhaps the highest point—qualitatively as well as quantitatively—of slave unrest came in the decade immediately preceding the Civil War, and without understanding that one can neither understand the meaning of John Brown, the movement of Abolitionism towards greater militancy, nor all the sources of the slaveholders' counterrevolution, quaintly called —twice—by Genovese, the War for Southern Independence!

There was—and to a large degree, there still is—an absence of a tradition of rebellion; but the reasons therefore are not those offered by Genovese. I find remarkable his failure to mention racism itself as the source of such an absence, but I think that is decisive. Ruling classes guard their past only somewhat less fervently than their present, and a racist society will have, of course, a racist historiography. Denial of a history on the part of racism's victim is a central element in racist ideology. This fundamentally explains, I think, the absence of a tradition of rebellion among the Negro people in the United States.

There is no good evidence that from 1785 to 1860 the conditions of the slaves improved. There was a "liberal" movement among some slaveowners, especially in the Border States and especially just after the intense slave unrest of the 1820's and the rise of a national anti-slavery movement, but this was weak at best and all its proposals were defeated. Genovese confines the phenomenon of maroons to the Caribbean and South America; in this he is wrong, for maroon settlements existed throughout the slave states and throughout the period of slavery.

Genovese fears that historians are too prone to read militancy into acts of the slaves—such as breaking tools, etc.—which might as easily be explained as acts of carelessness or stupidity or venality. I do not live in Genovese's world and do not find the state of historiography in the United States such as to require correction from the right, or that a significant problem is exaggeration of the militancy of Negro men and women. The same consideration applies to Genovese's quite remarkable discussion of the distinction *which the slaves themselves made* between stealing and taking, a distinction that seems to me to have much force and much illumination. Of course, there is a world of difference—or an era of difference—between a slave and a wage-worker; even in the latter case, however, surely there is a moral distinction between the stealing of a worker and the wholesale and institutionalized plundering of a General Motors or General Electric. Striking, too, in the rather elaborate discussion of this matter of taking and stealing by slaves, was the ignoring of the fact that slavery itself was a system of wholesale theft; the slaves, however, did not ignore this fact and so, I think, their moral acumen was sharper than Genovese's.

In noting impact upon personality, it would be well if Genovese had paid more attention—or some attention—to the devastating impact of racism, of holding others in subjugation, upon those who dominate. Genovese's paper not only omits this crucial point, but generally *assumes* that the practices and rules and codes of the dominant class were equivalent to civilized behavior.

There is, incidentally, a contradiction in Genovese's estimate of the impact of the slaves' "stealing." At one point he finds it to have been one of the "more irritating" habits of the slaves, while at another he finds that "few masters got upset" over the thievery. I am afraid he will have to pick between these two, and I suggest that the first is the more accurate.

Obsequiousness may have the debilitating effects noted by Genovese, and by many other writers. But there is much more present, and not so many have noticed this. There is the fact of outwitting the white boss, of surviving, of just being around so that one can continue bothering Charlie, and there is the fact of hating white yielding. Richard Wright, when operating an elevator, did bend down so that a particular white man might kick him in the buttocks; Wright did this because he needed the 25¢ the gentleman paid for his hilarious entertainment. But this was not simply obsequiousness. First of all, it was getting an extra quarter, and second, every kick was a hot iron to the rebelling genius within Wright. Need we comment upon the morality of the monster who paid the quarter?

The whole weight of Genovese's paper is in the direction of denying militancy on the part of American Negro slaves. This is not saved by his statement, at one point, that he sees in the slave period "the formation of a tradition of recalcitrance but not revolution." I think I understand the point—as developed in his ideas of a lack of politics—"a dim awareness of oppression" or the alleged absence of group consciousness.

First, if as Genovese says, most high-spirited slaves became accommodationists, how could a tradition of recalcitrance develop? And, second, there was not a dim awareness of oppression. On the contrary, everything about the history of the slaves (songs, folktales, religious heroes and deeds) cries out that the awareness was vivid.

Of course in slavery there was not politics in any traditional sense; rather, Genovese says, there was action. But in slavery and for a slave, action against slavery *was* politics, was political behavior and of a very high order.

The separation of domestics from field hands is reality and not myth. The enforced prevalence of Protestantism had a moderating influence, but even there nothing is said of the particular kind of religion developed by the slave, and this was far from a religion of repose or accommodation.

It is not true that local police power in the South was reduced during the Civil War; the contrary is true. And somehow Genovese gives the impression that the mass flight of slaves during the Civil War reflected accommodationism. On the contrary, it demonstrated discontent, and such flight was quite difficult for most of the years of the War and most of the areas of the Confederacy. Du Bois' characterization of this mass flight of scores of thousands as a kind of mobile general strike is very much nearer the mark than Genovese's treatment.

Of course the former slaves assumed the support of Lincoln's government. They constituted about 12% of its Army and 25% of its navy. Their condition had been decisive to the war. The transformation of that condition had been decisive to winning the war and preserving the government. That betrayal followed is another matter, and certainly the onus therefore in no way may be placed upon the former slaves. They pursued the only course open to them.

It is not true to say that no black movement and no black leadership emerged from the Civil War. On the contrary, there emerged a militant movement for enfranchisement, civil rights, land; all this was the heart of radical Reconstruction. It succeeded to significant degrees in several states for several years, and was crushed only after years of terror, chauvinism and after the complete betrayal by the federal government under the domination of the Republican Party. Even so, the crushing was partial and in twenty years the whole effort at full emancipation was renewed with fierceness.

The hegemony of the slaveowners not only was not "virtually unchallenged"; a central feature of the history of the pre-Civil War south is exactly that challenge, from the slaves and from the nonslaveholding whites. I do not find "innocence of organized effort and political consciousness" as plaguing black people in the United States until well into the twentieth century. On the contrary, organized effort was massive and political ingenuity was extraordinary.

Certainly the Negro masses were told incessantly to despise themselves, but I am much less certain that Genovese appears to be that this message succeeded. Surely the literature is self-critical, but the literature also shows that it is the white—especially the white boss— who is despised; and there is a decisive thread in the literature and thinking of the Negro people which holds (correctly) to the moral and ethical superiority of themselves as compared with a racist-infected white population.

I do not find an "enormous influence" exerted by Booker T. Washington upon black nationalists. And Genovese's acceptance of Mr. Washington's own public rationalizations for his program of acquiescence is extraordinary. Thus, Washington justified his insistence that Negroes avoid political activity on the grounds that they were not experienced in such activity; but this was not why he put forth the program of acquiescence. He put forth that program because of the insistence of Baldwin of the Southern Railroad, and Carnegie and Rockefeller who subsidized the Tuskegee machine. And they insisted on that program for obvious reasons.

The differences between Du Bois and Washington were basic and not simply tactical, and no single quotation from a 1903 essay will change that. Du Bois rejected subordination; Washington accepted it. Du Bois rejected colonialism; Washington assumed its continuance.

Du Bois was intensely critical of capitalism, long before World War I; Washington worshipped it.

Genovese asks: How do you integrate into a nation that does not want you? This is not and has not been the point. The point is that through integration one transforms. The effort is not simply to integrate *into* the nation; the demand is to transform a racist nation into an egalitarian one. Hence to battle for integration is to battle for basic transformation.

Further, integration is necessary to this nation exactly because the Negro is integral to it; the nation depends upon him and consists of him as surely as it depends upon and consists of those who are not Negro. Decisive here, too, is the class character of the nation and the class character of the Negro, considerations that are basic for a radical analysis but which are notably missing from the Genovese paper.

The realities of black nationalism are exaggerated by Genovese; the power and force of Negro-white efforts are minimized by him.

I join in Genovese's appeal for enhanced power in localities. I do not see this in any way, however, as contrary to enhancing power nationally, or of enhanced Negro-white unity and common action, or the development of an increasingly radical and independent *national* politics in the United States.

I reject the "state's rights" plea of Genovese. I deny a naive dependence upon central power by the left. And federal troops need not be merely guardians of the status quo, if the status quo is jim crow and if the law is anti-jim crow and if the executive office is sworn to carry out that law and uses—as it is supposed to do—all its force, including federal troops, to enforce the law, i.e., to extirpate jim crow.

No problem is a problem of the whites and not of the blacks. Whoever says this is in error. *Central* to this nation is the so-called Negro question. The fates of white people and of black people in this country are inextricably bound together.

If this nation is to be spared fascism, it will be by the efforts of blacks and whites together. If this nation is to reverse its present foul foreign policy it will be because of black and white struggle together. Genuine democratic, progressive and radical advance in this country has depended in the past, and most particularly depends in the present, upon popular mass power, united, and that means Negro-white mass power, together.

Without that, slavery would not have been destroyed in the United States. Without that, jim crow will not be destroyed in the United States. Absolutely fundamental to read radicalism in the United States is the building of that mass, popular, Negro-white political power.

| 4 | **The Black Muslims in America: A Reinterpretation** |

W. Haywood Burns

Much of the comment upon and analysis of the Black Muslims in America in both academic and popular accounts has tended to emphasise the racist aspects of the movement. The Muslims are generally depicted as a violent extremist group desiring separation from white America. While the racist aspects of the Muslim programme must be neither denied nor minimised, those who choose to interpret the group solely in terms of these ideas will fail to reach a true understanding of the movement, the problem to which it has addressed itself and the solutions at which it has arrived.

The growth and proliferation of the Black Muslims in America has been a peculiarly urban phenomenon. There are close to eighty temples and missions located throughout the United States—almost all in metropolitan areas. The Muslims find their greatest strength in the ghetto areas of large Northern cities—in New York's Harlem, in Boston's Roxbury and on Chicago's South Side. It is to the disillusioned and disaffected black man that the teachings of the Muslim leader, the Honourable Elijah Muhammad, have their greatest appeal.

Fifty years ago the ghettos in which the Muslims now thrive did not even exist. In 1919, 81 per cent of the nation's Negroes lived in the states of the old Confederacy. Over the years there has been a continual stream of Negroes out of the cotton fields, rice swamps and cane brakes into the Northern industrialised cities such as New York, Chicago and Detroit. This steady migration has continued to the point that the last census showed that only 52 per cent of America's Negro population are now living in the South. In addition to this South to North flow of Negro population, there has been a great deal of rural to

Reprinted from *RACE* V, no. 1 (July 1963): 26–37. Published for the Institute of Race Relations, London, by the Oxford University Press, © Institute of Race Relations.

urban movement within the South itself, so much so that today most Negroes live in metropolitan areas. There are fourteen metropolitan areas in America with Negro populations numbering from 200,000 to 1,500,000.

As the number of Negroes coming to the North increased, there was not a concomitant development in the amount of living area that was available to them. "Negro areas" in large cities were circumscribed and the new Negro immigrant often had little choice as to where he would live on coming to the big city or what he would pay for his living quarters. The rising number of people compressed into an area which was never meant to contain so many brought with it all the attendant problems of overcrowding and social disorientation. The Negro ghettos and slums were born.

The Negro ghetto problems of education, housing and employment were not unique; similar problems were faced by large numbers of other migrant groups who came to the city and had for a while to play a marginal role in the economy—entering on the bottom rung of the ladder, as it were. However, with the Negro there was one significant and perhaps all-important difference—the factor of colour prejudice. Other newcomers at earlier times had been able to escape the ghetto and move in the larger society, relatively free of their "Irish-ness", for example. This type of mobility and the possibility of recognition of individual merit helped to break down many of the strictly ethnic slums and provide for a dispersal throughout the society. But the black man's stigma—his blackness—is visible and in American society works to keep him at one end of the social spectrum.

Since the days of slavery "going up North" has been looked upon as a panacea by millions of Negroes. Even in times of greatest economic stress throughout the country, the Negro has exhibited a faith that things in the North would be better and that he had only to follow the North Star to a fuller life.

The reality of the situation has often been otherwise. All too frequently, the Negro has found that by coming North he has substituted one pattern of discrimination and deprivation for another; and often he is not able to cope with the new as well as with the old. The problems of urbanisation and industrialisation are modern problems faced not only by Negroes but by millions of men throughout the world, but the difficulty is so much the greater if the man happens to be a Negro in an American setting.

The recent Southern immigrant of the kind most likely to be attracted to Mr. Muhammad's brand of Islam is very often greatly affected by the insidious nature of Northern discrimination. He is already unsure of himself and of his effectualness and it takes only an "incident" or two to make him totally estranged in his new environment. In the South at least the lines were clear-cut and the accepted patterns of behaviour well-learned. The "Colored" sign in the waiting room, the white sheriff and his gun, the rope, the faggot were all "real". They could be touched and seen, and deprivation could be assessed, but in the alien environment of an impersonal metropolis the black man is quite often only able to *sense* his oppression. He knows that life in the ghetto is stifling, but the oppressor is not immediately identifiable. Should he wish to strike out at his foe, he might not be able to find him. It seems that "forces" are at work against him—"forces" much too large for him to control. Indeed, the horror comes from the sense that they are controlling him. These feelings of personal ineffectualness in alien surroundings give rise to a good deal of the restiveness among Negro communities in the large cities, and persons harbouring these feelings are fertile soil for the seeds of the Messenger, the Honourable Elijah Muhammad.

Mr. Muhammad teaches that the white man has robbed the American Negro of his "language, culture, religion and God". Leaving aside for the moment the fallacious belief that there ever was a Negro language, culture or religion, we see that Muhammad is striking at a profound truth concerning the Negro's cultural, or more properly sub-cultural, situation in America. The unique institution of American chattel slavery destroyed almost all vestiges of indigenous culture among the African slaves who made up the bulk of the ancestry of today's American Negroes. In many ways the American Negro is more American in his thinking and values than any other ethnic group in the United States. It has to be this way since he no longer has any other background from which to draw directly. The difficulty comes not from the Negro's having to accept an identity so very American, but from America's unwillingness to accept the Negro.

The Negro, calling himself "American", must wrestle to see what this really means. Can he identify with a nation that so often refuses even to recognise his presence? The American Negro looks in vain to find himself in the nation's magazine or billboard advertisements, television commercials or history books; America refuses to integrate the Negro into its consciousness. In so many cases, separation is a mental fact, a social reality. Elijah Muhammad has made it a virtue.

The Muslims are often tossed off lightly as appealing only to "lower-class urban Negroes". Those making this comment do not seem to realise that this category takes in most of the country's 20 million

Negroes, since the majority of them live in metropolitan areas and are from the lower socio-economic bracket of the country as a whole. In 1960 the average Negro family income was only 56 per cent that of the average white family income—a fact made all the more significant when it is considered that Negro families are, on an average, slightly larger than white families and have a greater average number of persons employed in each family. The average Negro can expect to receive three years less education and to die seven years sooner than his white counterpart.[1] In tangible terms, on an absolute scale, it is true that much progress has been made in the Negro community, particularly in the last two decades; but on a relative scale, where the true test of equality must be made, there is still a tremendous gap between the white and Negro economic situations.

Recent years have seen advances in laws and attitudes pertaining to the racial situation in America. The tangible results of these intangible gains in many cases, however, have not been felt in the real-life situation of individuals. Thus a fair housing law or desegregation order is often meaningless in terms of a person's daily existence because of the cultural lag between a legislated change and a realisation of that change and because people who pay lip service to recently acquired "liberal" attitudes often do not hold those attitudes honestly enough for their behaviour to be influenced by them. People living in an increasingly "liberal" social milieu, but whose real-life situation remains unchanged, often look upon the statements of white liberals as hypocritical and legislation for integration as schemes of deceit.

The identity problems of the Negro masses in America have been further complicated in recent years by the growth of the Negro middle class. The absolute progress in the economic situation of the Negro has increased the Negro middle class from 5 per cent of the Negro population in 1940 to 25 per cent in 1960 (as opposed to 55 per cent for whites).[2] The masses of Negroes in the lower socio-economic bracket have come to resent Negro middle-class leadership, saying that it is at variance with their interests. Of Negro leaders Muslim minister Malcolm X.* has said:

> . . . they don't speak for the black masses. They speak for the "BLACK BOURGEOISIE," the "brainwashed" (white minded) middle class minority . . . who, because they are ashamed of black and don't want to be identi-

---

* It is the practice for converts to the Black Muslim movement to drop their former surname and replace it with "X". "X" represents the lack of knowledge of the "true" (i.e. African) surname and the rejection of the one that has come down from the "Christian slave-masters" of their ancestors.

fied with black or as being black, are seeking to lose this "identity" by mingling, mixing, intermarrying, and integrating with the white man.[3]

The growing Negro middle class naturally has class attitudes, and these are not always commensurate with those of the masses. The middle-class American Negro is better able to rationalise his position in America than those Negroes of the less privileged majority, because with middle-class status his alienation is diminished; in other words this status carries with it a degree of acceptance in white society. The increasing bifurcation of the Negro community along class lines has made the question "Exactly who and what am I?" all the more salient for the masses.

Mr. Elijah Muhammad has recognised the economic as well as the psychological plight of the Negro masses and it is to these problems that he addresses himself and his programme.

### THE RESPONSE: MR. MUHAMMAD AND HIS PROGRAMME

Mr. Muhammad has set forth a twelve-point programme for the deliverance of the "lost-found nation of Islam in the wilderness of North America":[4]

1. Separate yourselves from the slave master.
2. Pool your resources, education and qualifications for independence.
3. Stop forcing yourself into places where you are not wanted.
4. Make your own neighbourhood a decent place to live.
5. Rid yourselves of the lust of wine and drink and learn to love self and kind before loving others.
6. Unite to create a future for yourself.
7. Build your own homes, schools, hospitals, and factories.
8. Do not seek to mix your blood through racial integration.
9. Stop buying expensive cars, fine clothes, and shoes before being able to live in a fine home.
10. Spend your money among yourselves.
11. Build an economic system among yourselves.
12. Protect your women.

The Muslims express the view that the Negro can never expect "freedom, justice and equality" from the white man in America. They maintain that if the white man wanted the Negro in America to be free, he would have been so a long time ago. Giving up all hopes for an honest democracy, Mr. Muhammad and his followers then state that *separation* is the only answer, and ask for land in order to set up a black nation. Mr. Muhammad has said:

> We must become as a people producers and not remain consumers and employees. We must be able to extract raw materials from the earth: manufacture them into something useful for ourselves. We must remember that without land there is no production.[5]

To the Muslims the white man is anathema and representative of the total forces of evil. In temple meetings and in general parlance he is referred to as "the devil". Mr. Muhammad teaches that in the last days the forces of good will do battle with the forces of evil in the war of Armageddon. Good, of course, will triumph. Since in Mr. Muhammad's teachings the forces of good are represented by Islam and those of evil by Christianity, and since further Muhammad maintains that no white man can be a true Muslim, the battle becomes a battle between the coloured peoples of the world and the white race—in which the white race will be destroyed. The day of this great reckoning was first set for some time in 1970. However, at the last report Allah has given the white man a fourteen-year extension, which takes him to the ominous date of 1984.

The attacks upon the white race in temple meetings are of the most strident and scurrilous nature. One Muslim minister has summed up Muslim goals as:

> To get the white man's foot off my neck, his hand out of my pocket and his carcass off my back. To sleep in my own bed without fear, and to look straight into his cold blue eyes and call him a liar every time he parts his lips.[6]

Another Muslim minister, on explaining the prohibition of pork in the Muslim diet, said:

> The hog is dirty, brutal, quarrelsome, greedy, ugly, foul, a scavenger which thrives on filth. It is a parasite to all other animals. It will even kill and eat its own young. Do you agree? In short the hog has all the characteristics of a white man![7]

It is statements like these and other even more intemperate renderings of the teachings of Mr. Muhammad that have attracted widespread attention and provided adequate fodder for the sensationalised popular accounts of the Muslims which usually depict them as a hate group bent on retribution. The latent guilt feelings of many an American white are already so close to the surface that it does not take much to convince them that a veritable "black Ku Klux Klan" is in their midst. However, anyone who took the trouble to investigate further would be quick to notice the difference between the Muslims and many other extreme racist groups. There is nothing of the terrorist approach in this movement. Muslims are taught never to be the aggressor, and to be non-violent unless attacked. This is not inconsistent with the Muslim promise of a settling of accounts between black and white at Armageddon, as this is divine retribution, the details of which are not specified in the ideology.

The Muslims' vitriolic attacks upon white America should not be ignored, but neither should the wrong construction be put upon them or their role in the movement. They are ends in themselves. Functionally they are most significant for their cathartic value, in that they permit followers to gather three times a week (usually on Wednesday, Friday and Sunday) and excoriate the white man. The hate and the bitterness are real (as are most of the grievances from which they arise) but in terms of a programme of action based upon these sentiments the aggressive verbal attacks have little direct relevance, because there is at present no such programme.

The Muslims have organised for power and now refuse to use it. They are far from revolutionaries in their ideas of how change should come about. Use of sheer power to bring about change *within* the society goes against the American ethos, and the Muslims have not chosen to breach that ethos. They not only shun the use of force, but eschew the more accepted ways of bringing about change, having thus far declined to take part in elections or have anything to do with the American political process.* Their real concern seems to be the unity and uplift of the American black man.

It is difficult to believe that the Muslims actually expect the United States Government to give them any number of states any time in the near future. However, for the time being, the *idea* of a nation is a very useful concept in a programme bent on withdrawal, unification and the creation of a certain spiritual bouyancy. "If Muhammad actually

---

* There is some indication that this may be changing as increasingly in recent months Muslim ministers have taken an interest in the Negro voting potential and emphasized the role the Negro vote will play in deciding the 1964 elections. There has been no major change, however, in the Muslim policy of non-involvement in American politics.

expects to set up a nation somewhere in the United States", the question is often asked, "Why then is he spending so much money developing the Nation of Islam throughout America?" At present, for example, there are plans for a £20 million Islamic centre in Chicago. Certainly Muhammad does not expect that Illinois would be one of the states the Government would consider giving away.

Although the Muslims inveigh against "other worldly-ness" in religion, theirs is far from an activist faith. Instead of the Christian idea that Christ will make things aright in the end, which they denounce so sharply, the Muslims believe that Allah will settle all accounts in the War of Armageddon, here on earth. Not long ago at a temple meeting in Boston a Muslim minister preached against ever taking matters into one's own hands. He said that Allah had his army to take care of the white man. "Cancer is Allah's weapon! Influenza! Hepatitis! Poliomyelitis! Spinal myelitis!" The same minister repeatedly emphasised that "Islam" means "peace" and is a religion of peace. "We don't teach you to turn the other cheek", he said, but admonished all good Muslims to avoid trouble at almost any cost.

At times this Minister sounded like the conventional "Uncle Tom". His message was "Don't get the white man excited; his day is coming. Treat him like a ravenous dog. Speak softly and don't get him excited. Nice doggie. Nice doggie."[8] Muslims make assertions as to how angry and militant they are, but in practical terms they realise the necessity of staying as law abiding and respectable as possible. They are under the constant surveillance of the F.B.I. It has been remarked wisely that Mr. Muhammad is fairly successful in "treading the thin line between religious license and political sedition".

In creating a sense of dignity and racial pride among the masses of American Negroes, much of what Mr. Muhammad teaches is black supremacist in doctrine and distorted in historical fact. However, Muhammad seems to realise that the Negro's current sense of inferiority stems from racial myths and historical distortions, and only hopes to counter with his own myths and so to rectify the balance. From his teachings about "the devil", black supremacy and racial history, it is clear that Mr. Muhammad has no compunction about making the means suit the end. Minister Malcolm X. has said that if it is "necessary" for Mr. Muhammad to tell his followers that the white man is the devil, Mr. Muhammad will tell them that the white man is the devil. "It's like stones spaced out across a river. Elijah sees that you can't get over the way the stones are now, so he is bringing them closer together". It is the getting across that is important (i.e. deliverance from current degradation) even if it means moving a few stones a little bit.

When questioned recently on the matter of black supremacy a Muslim adherent replied, "Well, you shoot for the stars and maybe you'll get the moon. Tell the black man that he is better than the white man and maybe you'll get him to believe that he is equal." The Muslims want no part of a self-conscious equality. Elijah Muhammad feels the need for an intense pride among the Negro masses as a prerequisite to full dignity and self-awareness. In their present depressed psychological state he sees no better way of instilling this feeling than by telling the black masses that "black is best".

Aside from all other considerations about the lack of any real threat from the Black Muslim community, there is the very practical consideration of numbers. The Muslims are not nearly as strong numerically as most popular accounts have supposed. Estimates vary from 100,000 to half a million, and the Muslims themselves are only too glad to encourage the most generous of these estimates. It is impossible to say exactly how many Black Muslims there are in America, since statistics are one of the things about which they are most secretive. Malcolm X. has said on this subject, "Those who say don't know, those who know don't say." Although this is quite correct, there are certain indicators as to the precise size of the movement. The number of Muslim converts is high but, as is often true of evangelical sects with high conversion rates, the rate of turn-over is also quite high. This is due to the number of on-the-spot converts who do not go any further, and those who are unable to accept the discipline of the movement for any great length of time. A visit to the New York, Boston and Chicago temples of the Black Muslims gives an indication of how small a number of practising members there are. Though these three cities have some of the largest Negro populations in the country and are supposedly areas of great strength for the Muslims, the *total* seating capacity for the three temples probably does not exceed 2,000 persons. One of the closest students of the movement estimates that there are about 15,000 "registered" (i.e. fully active) Muslims, 50,000 professed believers, and an unknown number of sympathisers.[9] The Muslims draw their greatest significance not from their numbers but from their importance as social barometers. They reflect a mood that in some form is pervasive in the American Negro community—a certain anger and frustration arising out of the Negro's position in American society and the rate at which it is being changed. The Muslim indictment of the white power structure is one to which millions of American Negroes would subscribe.

It is in Muhammad's economic programme that the greatest amount of change is taking place and the white middle-class *mores* most visible. Here, rather than a rejection of the white man or any fight against him, we see what is often a conscious effort to emulate him. At one point Mr. Elijah Muhammad has even said:

> Observe the operations of the white man. He is successful. He makes no excuse for his failures. He works hard in a collective manner. You do the same.[10]

Muslims place a very high value on education, and there is a strong middle-class belief in it as a panacea. Though the movement has definite anti-intellectual strains, this feeling is against the "white man's education" that brainwashes. Knowledge of self is held at a premium and is seen as the only path to full dignity. In Muslim schools most subjects, with the exception of history, are taught in the same way as in other schools. Children at the state-accredited Muslim schools in Detroit and Chicago go to school fifty weeks in the year and start learning Arabic ("the language of their fathers") in the third grade (about eight years old). Other Muslim communities have schools of their own which have not received state accreditation, but which the Muslim children attend in addition to the state school.

It is the attraction of an opportunity for personal improvement and social mobility that brings many to Mr. Muhammad's Islam. Much has been made of the fact that many of his converts are former convicts or represent the "dregs" of society. This is true, but critics do not often go beyond this point to see the amazing transformation that becoming a Muslim often works in a person's life. The Muslims do not mind receiving the "marginal" types and social rejects for, to a great extent, they themselves have rejected society. Muslim emphasis upon courtesy, cleanliness and morality challenges the early Puritans in its austerity and unrelenting enforcement. The way up and the way out, as far as the Muslims are concerned, seems to be in being more middle-class than the middle class. John Dollard's description of the middle class in the towns he studied in the American South as reported in his classic work, *Caste and Class in a Southern Town*, could well be a description of the drive of the Muslims—a drive which differentiates them so much from the other "unredeemed" Negroes of the lower socio-economic class:

> One feels the spirit to be energetic and acquisitive. In the main they intend to make their way by their exertions and personal contributions

to the welfare of the community. Their personal standards of behaviour, on questions of drinking, divorce, and profanity seem to be more rigorous than those of the classes above or below them. They seem to be religious. . . .[11]

For women, Mr. Muhammad's programme is often a way to a better existence, because of the tremendous amount of emphasis it lays upon respecting and protecting black womanhood. Through Mr. Muhammad's economic policy of "buying black" and "hiring your own", it is often easier for the man of the family to assume the traditional role of bread-winner and the woman of homemaker. She is taught to be a better mother and homemaker in one of the main subgroups of the temple, the "Muslim Girls' Training and General Civilization Class".

Elijah Muhammad's followers strive for economic independence in so far as it is possible. There are Muslim-operated restaurants, farms, grocery stores, barber and beauty shops, cleaning plants, clothing stores, used car lots, real estate offices and various other business establishments.

The newspaper *Mr. Muhammad Speaks*, the official organ of the Black Muslims in America, illustrates how very middle-class in orientation this supposedly "radical" group can be. In one issue there is an article entitled "University of Islam Parent-Teachers Association Sponsors Brilliant Musical Program at School". In the same issue the advertisements for clothes from the Temple No. 2 Clothing Store look quite familiar—almost like clothing store advertisements in any other newspaper. The people depicted in the advertisement are handsome or attractive in conformity with what is regarded as "handsome" or "attractive" in typical middle-class white American society, in fact, they might very well be taken as white. On the advertisement appear the words:

> SEE the *smartest styles* at Temple No. 2 Clothing Store. . . Shop in comfort among friends. . . CASH LAY-A-WAY-BUDGET.[12]

There is also a similar looking advertisement for the Temple Cleaners, which advises:

> To be successful—LOOK SUCCESSFUL. By keeping Your Clothes Neat and *Cleaned* by Temple No. 2 Cleaners.[13]

Muslim men set great store by having a neat appearance. They usually wear Ivy-League suits and have closely cropped hair—a very middle-class approach to "respectability". In this same newspaper there is also an article headed "Trenton Marriage of Brother Edward Beautiful Affair", which might have come from the society page of any other newspaper—had not Black Muslims been involved. The "Melvin X. Barber Shop" in the same issue advises "It pays to look Smart!" and includes in the advertisement of its services "Men-Women Manicuring".

A latter issue of *Mr. Muhammad Speaks* carries an article on "The Family—most powerful Unit in Islam"; a section on Household Hints; Muslim Cookbook (the month's recipe is for "smothered chicken"), and an article on gardening which discusses the various tints and shades of delphiniums. On the back of the paper is a full-page advertisement headed: "BOYS! GIRLS! (MEN & WOMEN TOO!) WIN A SCHOLARSHIP TO COLLEGE!" The advertisement goes on to say:

Now Your Dream of A College Education CAN Come True
Because MUHAMMAD SPEAKS will give scholarship(s)
No need to "drop out" from lack of money
Get off the Relief Rolls!
An Education makes you independent! . . .
Win scholarships to the college of your choice,
from the Elijah Muhammed Scholarship Fund. . .
Let's beat the Drop out and Relief by advancing ourselves education-
ally and economically by participating in this program. . . Why?—
Remember, he who wishes to be free and independent, must work and
prepare himself to become a leader or resign himself to follow the
dictates of others. . . . Get started Today![14]

At present the Black Muslim movement draws its strength from the black masses in the lower socio-economic bracket; there are as yet very few professional or university-trained adherents, although there is one university professor who has been converted.

But the Muslims are trying to broaden the base of their appeal in the hope of making their movement more palatable to intellectuals and to the Negro population at large. This is a further restraint on their being too radical or openly offensive to some of the sentiments of other Negroes. A good example of their restraint can be seen in some of the changes that have been made in the Muslims' stage musical production "Orgena" ("a Negro" spelled backwards). As originally presented, the show sharply attacked the Christian religion and the white man. The last time that the show was presented, however, it was in a much softened form. It was the "colonialist" or "exploiter" who was under indictment, not "the white man". A long section ridiculing the Virgin

Birth was completely deleted, and the star, Minister Louis X., used his "Christian slavemaster" name, Gene Walcott, on the programme and advertisements. In general, there has recently been less emphasis in the teachings on the differences between Islam and Christianity and more of an appeal on the basis of black solidarity.

## CONCLUSION

In spite of the radical and racist form of its indictment of the white power structure in the United States, the Black Muslim movement, in its current state at least, poses no real threat. There is nothing in its present programme or course of action that is violently aggressive. And while on the surface the Muslims appear to be rejecting America, this is only partially true since there is much in America which they have not been able to reject and which leaves them very much inside the American social framework. Indeed what the Muslims are expressing is a fundamental disillusionment with the fulfillment of the American promise and a desire for many of its values which have been denied them. In many instances they have not found or invented new values, but simply reinterpreted or placed new constructions upon familiar American middle-class values. The Black Muslim movement under the leadership of Mr. Elijah Muhammad has provided many black men and women with a new identity where before there had been only the emptiness of the ghetto. It has provided them with a means of giving vent to their frustrations and anger and at the same time brought them to a new pride in self and an opportunity for self-improvement and upward mobility toward a higher socio-economic bracket. Through its creation of a community within a community it has been a vehicle to *respectability* and *acceptance* for thousands of American Negroes who had been denied both of these by the larger society.

## NOTES

1. Statistics supplied to the author by Whitney Young, Executive Director of the National Urban League.
2. *Ibid.*
3. Minister Malcolm X., Muhammad's Temple No. 7, New York City.
4. Quoted in William Worthy, "The Angriest Negroes", *Esquire*, February 1961, p. 103.

5. "Mr. Muhammad Speaks", *Los Angeles Herald-Dispatch*, 26 November 1960.

6. Quoted in C. Eric Lincoln, *The Black Muslims in America*, Boston, Beacon Press, 1961, p. 27. For the only other comprehensive study of the Muslims see E. U. Essien-Udom, *Black Nationalism*, London, Oxford University Press, 1962.

7. Lincoln, *op. cit.* p. 81.

8. Minister James X. of Muhammad's Temple No. 7, New York City, in a sermon at Muhammad's Temple No. 11, Boston, April 1962.

9. Interview with Dr. E. U. Essien-Udom, author of *Black Nationalism*, *op. cit.*, and formerly of the Center for International Affairs, Harvard University.

10. *Los Angeles-Herald Dispatch*, 6 January 1960.

11. John Dollard, *Caste and Class in a Southern Town*, New York, Anchor Books, 1957, p. 76. Quoted in Essien-Udom, *op. cit.*

12. *Mr. Muhammad Speaks*, April 1962.

13. *Ibid.*

14. *Mr. Muhammad Speaks*, May 1962.

# 5 | Religion: Opiate or Inspiration of Civil Rights Militancy Among Negroes?*

## Gary T. Marx

The implications of religion for protest are somewhat contradictory. With their stake in the status quo, established religious institutions have generally fostered conservatism, although as the source of humanistic values they have occasionally inspired movements of protest. For a nationwide sample of Negroes, analysis of the effect of religiosity on protest attitudes indicates that the greater the religious involvement, the less the militancy. However, among the religious, religion does not seem to inhibit, and may even inspire, protest among those with a temporal as distinct from an otherworldly orientation. Still, until such time as religion loosens its hold, or comes to embody more of a temporal orientation, it may be seen as an important factor inhibiting black militancy.

Let justice roll down like waters, and righteousness like a mighty stream.

*Amos* 5:24

But God . . . is white. And if his love was so great, and if he loved all his children, why were we the blacks, cast down so far?

James Baldwin

The relationship between religion and political radicalism is a confusing one. On the one hand, established religious institutions have generally had a stake in the status quo and hence have supported conservatism. Furthermore, with the masses having an otherworldly orientation, religious zeal, particularly as expressed in the more funda-

Reprinted from *American Sociological Review* XXXII, no. 1 (1967): 64–72. By permission of the American Sociological Association and the author.

* Revision of paper read at the annual meeting of the American Sociological Association, August, 1966. This paper may be identified as publication A-72 of the Survey Research Center, University of California, Berkeley. I am grateful to Gertrude J. Selznick and Stephen Steinberg for their work on the early phase of this project, and to the Anti-Defamation League for support.

mentalist branches of Christianity, has been seen as an alternative to the development of political radicalism. On the other hand, as the source of universal humanistic values and the strength that can come from believing one is carrying out God's will in political matters, religion has occasionally played a strong positive role in movements for radical social change.

This dual role of religion is clearly indicated in the case of the American Negro and race protest. Slaves are said to have been first brought to this country on the "good ship Jesus Christ."[1] While there was occasional controversy over the effect that religion had on them it appears that most slave-owners eventually came to view supervised religion as an effective means of social control. Stampp, in commenting on the effect of religion notes:

> . . . through religious instruction the bondsmen learned that slavery had divine sanction, that insolence was as much an offense against God as against the temporal master. They received the Biblical command that servants should obey their masters, and they heard of the punishments awaiting the disobedient slave in the hereafter. They heard, too, that eternal salvation would be their reward for faithful service . . .[2]

In discussing the period after the Civil War, Myrdal states that ". . . under the pressure of political reaction, the Negro church in the South came to have much the same role as it did before the Civil War. Negro frustration was sublimated into emotionalism, and Negro hopes were fixed on the after world."[3] Many other analysts, in considering the consequences of Negro religion from the end of slavery until the early 1950's reached similar conclusions about the conservatizing effect of religion on race protest.[4]

However, the effect of religion on race protest throughout American history has by no means been exclusively in one direction. While many Negroes were no doubt seriously singing about chariots in the sky, Negro preachers such as Denmark Vesey and Nat Turner and the religiously inspired abolitionists were actively fighting slavery in their own way. All Negro churches first came into being as protest organizations and later some served as meeting places where protest strategy was planned, or as stations on the underground railroad. The richness of protest symbolism in Negro spirituals and sermons has often been noted. Beyond this symbolic role, as a totally Negro institution, the church brought together in privacy people with a shared problem. It was from the church experience that many leaders were exposed to a broad range of ideas legitimizing protest and obtained the savoir faire, self-confidence, and organizational experience needed to challenge an oppressive system. A recent commentator states that the slave churches were "the nucleus of the Negro protest" and another that "in religion Negro leaders had begun to find sanction and support for their movements of protest more than 150 years ago."[5]

Differing perceptions of the varied consequences religion may have on protest have continued to the present time. While there has been very little in the way of empirical research on the effect of the Negro church on protest,[6] the literature of race relations is rich with impressionistic statements which generally contradict each other about how the church either encourages and is the source of race protest or inhibits and retards its development. For example, two observers note, "as primitive evangelism gave way to a more sophisticated social consciousness, the church became the spearhead of Negro protest in the deep South,"[7] while another indicates "the Negro church is a sleeping giant. In civil rights participation its feet are hardly wet."[8] A civil rights activist, himself a clergyman states: ". . . the church today is central to the movement . . . if there had been no Negro church, there would have been no civil rights movement today."[9] On the other hand, a sociologist, commenting on the more involved higher status ministers, notes: ". . . middle class Negro clergymen in the cities of the South generally advocated cautious gradualism in race activities until the mid-1950's when there was an upsurge of protest sentiment among urban Negroes . . . but most of them [ministers] did not embrace the more vigorous techniques of protest until other leaders took the initiative and gained widespread support."[10] Another sociologist states, "Whatever their previous conservative stance has been, the churches have now become 'spearheads of reform.' "[11] Still another indicates: ". . . the Negro church is particularly culpable for its general lack of concern for the moral and social problems of the community . . . it has been accommodating. Fostering indulgence in religious sentimentality, and riveting the attention of the masses on the bounties of a hereafter, the Negro church remains a refuge, and escape from the cruel realities of the here and now."[12]

Thus one faces opposing views, or at best ambiguity, in contemplating the current effect of religion. The opiating consequences of religion are all too well known as is the fact that the segregated church is durable and offers some advantages to clergy and members that might be denied them in a more integrated society. On the other hand, the prominent role of the Negro church in supplying much of the

ideology of the movement, many of its foremost leaders, and an institution around which struggle might be organized—particularly in the
South—can hardly be denied. It would appear from the bombings of
churches and the writings of Martin Luther King and other religiously
inspired activists that for many, religion and protest are closely linked.

Part of this dilemma may lie in the distinction between the church
as an institution in its totality and particular individual churches within
it, and the further distinctions among different types of individual
religious concern. This paper is concerned with the latter subject; it is
an inquiry into the relationship between religiosity and response to the
civil rights struggle. It first considers how religious denomination
affects militancy, and then how various measures of religiosity, taken
separately and together, are related to civil rights concern. The question is then asked of those classified as "very religious" and "quite religious," how an "otherworldly orientation"—as opposed to a "temporal"
one—affects militancy.

In a nationwide study of Negroes living in metropolitan areas of the
United States, a number of questions were asked about religious behavior and beliefs as well as about the civil rights struggle.[13] Seven of
the questions dealing with civil rights protest have been combined into
an index of conventional militancy.[14] Built into this index are a number
of dimensions of racial protest such as impatience over the speed of
integration, opposition to discrimination in public facilities and the sale
of property, percepton of barriers to Negro advancement, support of
civil rights demonstrations, and expressed willingness to take part in a
demonstration. Those giving the militant response to five or more of
the questions are considered militant, those giving such a response to
three or four of the questions, moderate, and fewer than three, conservative.[15]

## DENOMINATION

It has long been known that the more fundamentalist sects such as
the Holiness groups and the Jehovah's Witnesses are relatively unin-
terested in movements for secular political change.[16] Such transvalua-
tional movements with their otherworldly orientation and their promise
that the last shall be first in the great beyond, are said to solace the
individual for his lowly status in this world and to divert concern away
from efforts at collective social change which might be brought about
by man. While only a minority of Negroes actually belong to such

groups, the proportion is higher than among whites. Negro literature is rich in descriptions of these churches and their position on race protest.

In Table 1 it can be seen that those belonging to sects are the least likely to be militant; they are followed by those in predominantly Negro denominations. Ironically those individuals in largely white denominations (Episcopalian, Presbyterian, United Church of Christ, and Roman Catholic) are those most likely to be militant, in spite of the perhaps greater civil rights activism of the Negro denominations. This pattern emerged even when social class was held constant.

TABLE 1    *Proportion Militant (%) by Denomination**

| Denomination | % Militant |
|---|---|
| Episcopalian | 46  (24) |
| United Church of Christ | 42  (12) |
| Presbyterian | 40  (25) |
| Catholic | 40 (109) |
| Methodist | 34 (142) |
| Baptist | 32 (658) |
| Sects and Cults | 20 (106) |

\* 25 respondents are not shown in this table because they did not specify a denomination, or belonged to a non-Christian religious group, or other small Christian group.

In their comments members of the less conventional religious groups clearly expressed the classical attitude of their sects toward participation in the politics of the secular world. For example, an Evangelist in the Midwest said, "I don't believe in participating in politics. My church don't vote—they just depend on the plans of God." And an automobile serviceman in Philadelphia stated, "I, as a Jehovah's Witness, cannot express things involving the race issue." A housewife in the Far West ventured, "In my religion we do not approve of anything except living like it says in the Bible; demonstrations mean calling attention to you and it's sinful."

The finding that persons who belong to sects are less likely to be militant than the non-sect members is to be expected; clearly this type of religious involvement seems an alternative for most people to the development of radicalism. But what of the religious style of those in the more conventional churches which may put relatively less stress on the after-life and encourage various forms of secular participation? Are the more religiously inclined within these groups also less likely to be militant?

## RELIGIOSITY

The present study measured several dimensions of religious involvement. Those interviewed were asked how important religion was to them, several questions about orthodoxy of belief, and how frequently they attended worship service.[17] Even with the sects excluded, irrespective of the dimension of religiosity considered, the greater the religiosity the lower the percentage militant. (See Tables 2, 3 and 4.) For example, militancy increases consistently from a low of only 29 percent among those who said religion was "extremely important" to a high of 62 percent for those who indicated that religion was "not at

TABLE 2   *Militancy by Subjective Importance Assigned to Religion**

| Importance | % Militant |
|---|---|
| Extremely important | 29 (668) |
| Somewhat important | 39 (195) |
| Fairly important | 48 (96) |
| Not too important | 56 (18) |
| Not at all important | 62 (13) |

* Sects are excluded here and in all subsequent tables.

TABLE 3   *Militancy by Orthodoxy*

| Orthodoxy | % Militant |
|---|---|
| Very high | 27 (414) |
| High | 34 (333) |
| Medium | 39 (144) |
| Low | 47 (68) |
| Very low | 54 (35) |

TABLE 4   *Militancy by Frequency of Attendance at Worship Services*

| Frequency | % Militant |
|---|---|
| More than once a week | 27 (81) |
| Once a week | 32 (311) |
| Once a month or more but less than once a week | 34 (354) |
| Less than once a month | 38 (240) |

all important" to them. For those very high in orthodoxy (having no doubt about the existence of God or the devil) 27 percent were militant while for those totally rejecting these ideas 54 percent indicated great concern over civil rights. Militancy also varies inversely with frequency of attendance at worship service.[18]

Each of these items was strongly related to every other; when taken together they help us to better characterize religiosity. Accordingly they have been combined into an overall measure of religiosity. Those scored as "very religious" in terms of this index attended church at least once a week, felt that religion was extremely important to them, and had no doubts about the existence of God and the devil. For progressively lower values of the index, frequency of church attendance, the importance of religion, and acceptance of the belief items decline consistently until, for those scored "not at all religious," church is rarely if ever attended, religion is not considered personally important and the belief items are rejected.

Using this measure for non-sect members, civil rights militancy increases from a low of 26 percent for those labeled "very religious" to 30 percent for the "somewhat religious" to 45 percent for those "not very religious" and up to a high of 70 percent for those "not at all religious."[19] (Table 5.)

TABLE 5   *Militancy by Religiosity*

| Religiosity | Very Religious | Somewhat Religious | Not Very Religious | Not at All Religious |
|---|---|---|---|---|
| % Militant | 26 | 30 | 45 | 70 |
| N | (230) | (523) | (195) | (36) |

Religiosity and militancy are also related to age, sex, education, religious denomination and region of the country. The older, the less educated, women, Southerners and those in Negro denominations are more likely to be religious and to have lower percentages scoring as militant. Thus it is possible that the relationship observed is simply a consequence of the fact that both religiosity and militancy are related to some third factor. In Table 6 it can be seen however, that, even when these variables are controlled the relationship is maintained. That is, even among those in the North, the younger, male, more educated and those affiliated with predominantly white denominations, the greater the religiosity the less the militancy.

TABLE 6    *Proportion Militant (%) by Religiosity, for Education,
Age, Region, Sex, and Denomination*

|  | Very Religious | Somewhat Religious | Not Very Religious | Not at All Religious |
|---|---|---|---|---|
| **Education** | | | | |
| Grammar school | 17 (108) | 22 (201) | 31 (42) | 50 (2) |
| High school | 34 (96) | 32 (270) | 45 (119) | 58 (19) |
| College | 38 (26) | 48 (61) | 59 (34) | 87 (15) |
| **Age** | | | | |
| 18–29 | 33 (30) | 37 (126) | 44 (62) | 62 (13) |
| 30–44 | 30 (53) | 34 (180) | 48 (83) | 74 (19) |
| 45–59 | 25 (71) | 27 (131) | 45 (33) | 50 (2) |
| 60+ | 22 (76) | 18 (95) | 33 (15) | 100 (2) |
| **Region** | | | | |
| Non-South | 30 (123) | 34 (331) | 47 (159) | 70 (33) |
| South | 22 (107) | 23 (202) | 33 (36) | 66 (3) |
| **Sex** | | | | |
| Men | 28 (83) | 33 (220) | 44 (123) | 72 (29) |
| Women | 26 (147) | 28 (313) | 46 (72) | 57 (7) |
| **Denomination** | | | | |
| Episcopalian, Presbyterian, United Church of Christ | 20 (15) | 27 (26) | 33 (15) | 60 (5) |
| Catholic | 13 (15) | 39 (56) | 36 (25) | 77 (13) |
| Methodist | 46 (24) | 22 (83) | 50 (32) | 100 (2) |
| Baptist | 25 (172) | 29 (354) | 45 (117) | 53 (15) |

The incompatibility between piety and protest shown in these data becomes even more evident when considered in light of comments offered by the respondents. Many religious people hold beliefs which clearly inhibit race protest. For a few there was the notion that segregation and a lowly status for Negroes was somehow God's will and not for man to question. Thus a housewife in South Bend, Indiana, in saying that civil rights demonstrations had hurt Negroes, added: "God is the Creator of everything. We don't know why we all dark-skinned. We should try to put forth the effort to do what God wants and not question."[20]

A Negro spiritual contains the lines "I'm gonna wait upon the Lord till my change comes." For our respondents a more frequently stated belief stressed that God as the absolute controller of the universe would bring about change in his own way and at his own time, rather than expressing segregation as God's will. In indicating her unwillingness to take part in a civil rights demonstration, a Detroit housewife said, "I don't go for demonstrations. I believe that God created all men equal and at His appointed time He will give every man his portion, no one can hinder it." And in response to a question about whether or not the government in Washington was pushing integration too slowly, a retired clerk in Atlanta said: "You can't hurry God. He has a certain time for this to take place. I don't know about Washington."

Others who desired integration more strongly and wanted immediate social change felt that (as Bob Dylan sings) God was on their side. Hence man need do nothing to help bring about change. Thus a worker in Cleveland, who was against having more civil rights demonstrations, said: "With God helping to fight our battle, I believe we can do with fewer demonstrations." And in response to a question about whether Negroes should spend more time praying and less time demonstrating, an Atlanta clergyman, who said "more time praying," added "praying is demonstrating."[21]

## RELIGION AMONG THE MILITANTS

Although the net effect of religion is clearly to inhibit attitudes of protest it is interesting to consider this relationship in the opposite direction, i.e., observe religiosity among those characterized as militant, moderate, and conservative with respect to the civil rights struggle. As civil rights concern increases, religiosity decreases. (Table 7). Mili-

TABLE 7   Religiosity by Civil Rights Militancy

|  | Militants | Moderates | Conservatives |
|---|---|---|---|
| Very religious | 18% | 24% | 28% |
| Somewhat religious | 48 | 57 | 55 |
| Not very religious | 26 | 17 | 16 |
| Not at all religious | 8 | 2 | 1 |
| Total | 100 | 100 | 100 |
| N | 332 | 419 | 242 |

tants were twice as likely to be scored "not very religious" or "not at all religious" as were conservatives. This table is also of interest because it shows that, even for the militants, a majority were scored either "very religious" or "somewhat religious." Clearly, for many, a religious orientation and a concern with racial protest are not mutually exclusive.

Given the active involvement of some churches, the singing of protest spirituals, and the ideology of the movement as it relates to Christian principles of love, equality, passive suffering,[22] and the appeal to a higher moral law, it would be surprising if there were only a few religious people among the militants.

A relevant question accordingly is: Among the religious, what are the intervening links which determine whether religion is related to an active concern with racial matters or has an opiating effect?[23] From the comments reported above it seemed that, for some, belief in a highly deterministic God inhibited race protest. Unfortunately the study did not measure beliefs about the role of God as against the role of men in the structuring of human affairs. However, a related variable was measured which would seem to have much relevance—the extent to which these religious people were concerned with the here and now as opposed to the after-life.

The classical indictment of religion from the Marxist perspective is that by focusing concern on a glorious after-life the evils of this life are ignored. Of course there are important differences among religious institutions and among individuals with respect to the importance given to other worldly concerns. Christianity, as with most ideologies, contains within it, if not out-and-out contradictory themes, then certainly themes which are likely to be in tension with one another. In this fact, no doubt, lies part of the explanation of religion's varied consequences for protest. One important strand of Christianity stresses acceptance of one's lot and glorifies the after-life;[24] another is more concerned with the realization of Judeo-Christian values in the current life. King and his followers clearly represent this latter "social gospel" tradition.[25] Those with the type of temporal concern that King represents would be expected to be higher in militancy. A measure of temporal vs. otherworldly concern has been constructed. On the basis of two questions, those interviewed have been classified as having either an otherworldly or a temporal orientation.[26] The evidence is that religiosity and otherworldly concern increase together. For example, almost 100 percent of the "not at all religious" group were considered to have a temporal orientation, but only 42 percent of the "very religious." (Table 8). Those in predominantly white denominations were more likely to have a temporal orientation than those in all-black denominations.

Among the religious groups, if concern with the here and now is a relevant factor in overcoming the opiating effect of religion then it is to be anticipated that those considered to have a temporal religious orientation would be much higher in militancy than those scored as

TABLE 8    Proportion (%) with Temporal (as Against Otherworldly)
           Concern, by Religiosity

|  Religiosity | % with Temporal Concern |
|--------------|-------------------------|
| Very religious | 42 (225) |
| Somewhat religious | 61 (531) |
| Not very religious | 82 (193) |
| Not at all religious | 98 (34) |

otherworldly. This is in fact the case. Among the otherworldly religious,
only 16 percent were militant; this proportion increases to almost 40
percent among those considered "very religious" and "somewhat religious" who have a temporal religious outlook. (Table 9). Thus it
would seem that an important factor in determining the effect of reli-

TABLE 9    Proportion Militant (%) by Religiosity and Temporal or
           Otherworldly Concern

| Concern | Very Religious | Somewhat Religious |
|---------|----------------|---------------------|
| Temporal | 39 (95) | 38 (325) |
| Otherworldly | 15 (130) | 17 (206) |

gion on protest attitudes is the nature of an individual's religious
commitment. It is quite possible, for those with a temporal religious
orientation, that—rather than the effect of religion being somehow
neutralized (as in the case of militancy among the "not religious"
groups)—their religious concern serves to inspire and sustain race
protest. This religious inspiration can, of course, be clearly noted
among some active civil rights participants.

## CONCLUSION

The effect of religiosity on race protest depends on the type of religiosity involved. Past literature is rich in suggestions that the religiosity of the fundamentalist sects is an alternative to the development
of political radicalism. This seems true in the case of race protest as

well. However, in an overall sense even for those who belong to the more conventional churches, the greater the religious involvement, whether measured in terms of ritual activity, orthodoxy of religious belief, subjective importance of religion, or the three taken together, the lower the degree of militancy.

Among sect members and religious people with an otherworldly orientation, religion and race protest appear to be, if not mutually exclusive, then certainly what one observer has referred to as "mutually corrosive kinds of commitments."[27] Until such time as religion loosens its hold over these people or comes to embody to a greater extent the belief that man as well as God can bring about secular change, and focuses more on the here and now, religious involvement may be seen as an important factor working against the widespread radicalization of the Negro public.

However, it has also been noted that many militant people are nevertheless religious. When a distinction is made among the religious between the "otherworldly" and the "temporal," for many of the latter group, religion seems to facilitate or at least not to inhibit protest. For these people religion and race protest may be mutually supportive.

Thirty years ago Donald Young wrote "One function which a minority religion may serve is that of reconciliation with inferior status and its discriminatory consequences . . . on the other hand, religious institutions may also develop in such a way as to be an incitement and support of revolt against inferior status."[28] The current civil rights struggle and the data observed here certainly suggest that this is the case. These contradictory consequences of religion are somewhat reconciled when one distinguishes among different segments of the Negro church and types of religious concern among individuals.


## NOTES

1. Louis Lomax, *When the Word is Given*, New York: New American Library, 1964, p. 34. It has often been noted that when the missionaries came to Africa they had the Bible and the people had the land. When the missionaries left, they had the land and the Africans had the Bible.

2. Kenneth Stampp, *The Peculiar Institution*, New York: Alfred A. Knopf, 1956, p. 158.

3. Gunnar Myrdal *et al.*, *An American Dilemma*, New York: Harper, 1944, pp. 851–853. About the North he notes that the church remained far more independent "but on the whole even the Northern Negro

church has remained a conservative institution with its interests directly upon other-worldly matters and has largely ignored the practical problems of the Negro's fate in this world."

4. For example, Dollard reports that "religion can be seen as a mechanism for the social control of Negroes" and that planters have always welcomed the building of a Negro church on the plantation but looked with less favor upon the building of a school. John Dollard, *Caste and Class in a Southern Town*, Garden City: Doubleday Anchor, 1957, p. 248. A few of the many others reaching similar conclusions are, Benjamin E. Mays and J. W. Nicholson, *The Negro's Church*, New York: Institute of Social and Religious Research, 1933; Hortense Powdermaker, *After Freedom*, New York: Viking Press, 1939, p. 285; Charles Johnson, *Growing Up in the Black Belt*, Washington, D.C.: American Council of Education, 1941, pp. 135–136; Horace Drake and St. Clair Cayton, *Black Metropolis*, New York: Harper and Row, 1962, pp. 424–429; George Simpson and Milton Yinger, *Racial and Cultural Minorities*, New York: Harper, rev. ed., 1958, pp. 582–587. In a more general context this social control consequence of religion has of course been noted throughout history from Plato to Montesquieu to Marx to Nietzsche to Freud to contemporary social theorists.

5. Daniel Thompson, "The Rise of Negro Protest," *Annals of the American Academy of Political and Social Science*, 357 (January, 1965).

6. The empirical evidence is quite limited. The few studies that have been done have focused on the Negro minister. Thompson notes that in New Orleans Negro ministers constitute the largest segment of the Negro leadership class (a grouping which is not necessarily the same as "protest leaders") but that "The vast majority of ministers are primarily interested in their pastoral role . . . their sermons are essentially biblical, dealing only tangentially with social issues." Daniel Thompson, *The Negro Leadership Class*, Englewood Cliffs, New Jersey: Prentice-Hall, 1963, pp. 34–35. Studies of the Negro minister in Detroit and Richmond, California also stress that only a small fraction of Negro clergymen show any active concern with the civil rights struggle. R. L. Johnstone, *Militant and Conservative Community Leadership Among Negro Clergymen*, Ph.D. dissertation, University of Michigan, Ann Arbor, 1963, and J. Bloom, *The Negro Church and the Movement for Equality*, M.A. thesis, University of California, Berkeley, Department of Sociology, 1966.

It is worthy of mention that, although the number of cases was small, the Negro ministers in our sample had the lowest percentage militant of any occupational group. With respect to the sons of clergymen, the situation seems somewhat different. While the myth of the preacher's son gone bad is almost a part of American folklore, one would think that a comparable myth might develop within the Negro community—that of the preacher's son gone radical. Malcolm X, James Baldwin, A. Philip Randolph, Martin Luther King, James Farmer, Adam Clayton Powell, Elijah Muhammad, and a number of others had clergymen as fathers. To be taken into consideration is that clergymen make up a relatively larger segment of the Negro middle than of the white middle class.

7. Jane Record and Wilson Record, "Ideological Forces and the Negro Protest," *Annals, op. cit.*, p. 92.

8. G. Booker, *Black Man's America*, Englewood Cliffs, N.J.: Prentice-Hall, 1964, p. 111.

9. Rev. W. T. Walker, as quoted in William Brink and Louis Harris, *The Negro Revolution in America*, New York: Simon and Schuster, 1964, p. 103.

10. N. Glenn, "Negro Religion in the U.S." in L. Schneider, *Religion, Culture and Society*, New York: John Wiley, 1964.

11. Joseph Fichter, "American Religion and the Negro," *Daedalus* (Fall, 1965), p. 1087.

12. E. U. Essien-Udom, *Black Nationalism*, New York: Dell Publishing Co., 1962, p. 358.
    Many other examples of contradictory statements could be offered, sometimes even in the same volume. For example, Carleton Lee stresses the importance of religion for protest while Rayford Logan sees the Negro pastor as an instrument of the white power structure (in a book published to commemorate 100 years of emancipation). Carleton Lee, "Religious Roots of Negro Protest," and Rayford Logan, "Educational Changes Affecting American Negroes," both in Arnold Rose, *Assuring Freedom to the Free*, Detroit: Wayne University Press, 1964.

13. This survey was carried out in 1964 by the Survey Research Center, University of California, Berkeley. A non-Southern metropolitan area probability sample was drawn as well as special area samples of Negroes living in New York City, Chicago, Atlanta and Birmingham. Since the results reported here are essentially the same for each of these areas, they are treated together. More than 90% of the interviews were done with Negro interviewers. Additional methodological details may be found in Gary Marx, *Protest and Prejudice: A Study of Belief in the Black Community*, New York: Harper & Row, forthcoming.

14. Attention is directed to conventional militancy rather than to that of the Black Nationalist variety because a very small percentage of the sample offered strong and consistent support for Black Nationalism. As in studying support for the KKK, the Birch Society or the Communist Party, a representative sample of normal size is inadequate.

15. Each of the items in the index was positively related to every other and the index showed a high degree of internal validity. The index also

received external validation from a number of additional questions. For example, the percentage belonging to a civil rights organization went from zero among those lowest in militancy to 38 percent for those who were highest, and the percentage thinking that civil rights demonstrations had helped a great deal increased from 23 percent to 58 percent. Those thinking that the police treated Negroes very well decreased from 35 percent to only 2 percent among those highest in militancy.

16. Liston Pope, *Millhands and Preachers*, New Haven: Yale University Press, 1942, p. 137. J. Milton Yinger, *Religion, Society, and the Individual*, New York: The Macmillan Company, 1957, pp. 170–173.

17. These dimensions and several others are suggested by Charles Y. Glock in "On the Study of Religious Commitment," *Religious Education Research Supplement*, 57 (July–August, 1962), pp. 98–100. For another measure of religious involvement, the number of church organizations belonged to, the same inverse relationship was noted.

18. There is a popular stereotype that Negroes are a "religious people." Social science research has shown that they are "over-churched" relative to whites, i.e., the ratio of Negro churches to the size of the Negro population is greater than the same ratio for whites. Using data from a nationwide survey of whites, by Gertrude Selznick and Stephen Steinberg, some comparison of the religiosity of Negroes and whites was possible. When these various dimensions of religiosity were examined, with the effect of education and region held constant, Negroes appeared as significantly more religious *only* with respect to the subjective importance assigned to religion. In the North, whites were more likely to attend church at least once a week than were Negroes; while in the South rates of attendance were the same. About the same percentage of both groups had no doubts about the existence of God. While Negroes were more likely to be sure about the existence of a devil, whites, surprisingly, were more likely to be sure about a life beyond death. Clearly, then, any assertions about the greater religiosity of Negroes relative to whites are unwarranted unless one specifies the dimension of religiosity.

19. When the sects are included in these tables the results are the same. The sects have been excluded because they offer almost no variation to be analyzed with respect to the independent variable. Since virtually all of the sect members scored as either "very religious" or "somewhat religious," it is hardly possible to measure the effect of their religious involvement on protest attitudes. In addition the import of the relationships shown in these tables is considerably strengthened when it is demonstrated that religious involvement inhibits militancy even when the most religious and least militant group, the sects, are excluded.

20. Albert Cardinal Meyer notes that the Catholic Bishops of the U.S. said in their statement of 1958: "The heart of the race question is moral and

religious." "Interracial Justice and Love," in M. Ahmann, ed., *Race Challenge to Religion*, Chicago: H. Regnery, 1963, p. 126. These data, viewed from the perspective of the activist seeking to motivate Negroes on behalf of the civil rights struggle, suggest that this statement has a meaning which Their Excellencies no doubt did not intend.

21. A study of ministers in Richmond, California notes that, although almost all questioned were opposed to discrimination, very few had taken concrete action, in part because of their belief that God would take care of them. One minister noted, "I believe that if we all was as pure . . . as we ought to be, there would be no struggle. God will answer my prayer. If we just stay with God and have faith. *When Peter was up, did the people march to free him? No. He prayed, and God did something about it.*" (Bloom, *op. cit.*, italics added.)

22. Non-violent resistance as it relates to Christianity's emphasis on suffering, sacrifice, and privation, is discussed by James W. Vander Zanden, "The Non-Violent Resistance Movement Against Segregation." *American Journal of Sociology*, 68 (March, 1963), pp. 544–550.

23. Of course, a most relevant factor here is the position of the particular church that an individual is involved in. Unfortunately, it was difficult to obtain such information in a nationwide survey.

24. The Muslims have also made much of this theme within Christianity, and their militancy is certainly tied to a rejection of otherworldly religiosity. The Bible is referred to as a "poison book" and the leader of the Muslims states, "No one after death has ever gone any place but where they were carried. There is no heaven or hell other than on earth for you and me, and Jesus was no exception. His body is still . . . in Palestine and will remain there." (As quoted in C. Eric Lincoln, *The Black Muslims in America*, Boston: Beacon Press, 1961, p. 123).

However, while they reject the otherworldly theme, they nevertheless rely heavily on a deterministic Allah; according to E. U. Essien-Udom, this fact leads to political inactivity. He notes, "The attainment of black power is relegated to the intervention of 'Almighty Allah' sometime in the future . . . Not unlike other religionists, the Muslims too may wait for all eternity for the coming of the Messiah, the predicted apocalypse in 1970 notwithstanding." E. U. Essien-Udom, *Black Nationalism, op. cit.*, pp. 313–314.

25. He states: "Any religion that professes to be concerned with the souls of men and is not concerned with the slums that damn them, the economic conditions that strangle them, and the social conditions that cripple them is a dry-as-dust religion." He further adds, perhaps in a concession, that "such a religion is the kind the Marxists like to see— an opiate of the people." Martin Luther King, *Stride Toward Freedom*, New York: Ballantine Books, 1958, pp. 28–29.

John Lewis, a former SNCC leader and once a Baptist Divinity student, is said to have peered through the bars of a Southern jail and said, "Think not that I am come to send peace on earth. I came not to send peace, but a sword." (Matthew 10:34.)

26. The two items used in this index were: "How sure are you that there is a life beyond death?"; and "Negroes should spend more time praying and less time demonstrating." The latter item may seem somewhat circular when observed in relation to civil rights concern. However, this is precisely what militancy is all about. Still it would have been better to measure otherworldly vs. temporal concern in a less direct fashion; unfortunately, no other items were available. Because of this the data shown here must be interpreted with caution. However it does seem almost self-evident that civil rights protest which is religiously inspired is related to a temporal religious outlook.

27. Rodney Stark, "Class, Radicalism, and Religious Involvement," *American Sociological Review*, 29 (October, 1964), p. 703.

28. Donald Young, *American Minority Peoples*, New York: Harper, 1937, p. 204.

These data are also consistent with Merton's statement that it is premature to conclude that "all religion everywhere has only the one consequence of making for mass apathy" and his insistence on recognizing the "multiple consequences" and "net balance of aggregate consequences" of a given institution such as religion. Robert Merton, *Social Theory and Social Structure*, Glencoe: Free Press, 1957, revised edition, p. 44.

# 6 The "Forgotten Years" of the Negro Revolution

*Richard M. Dalfiume*

A recent president of the American Sociological Society addressed himself to a puzzling question about what we know as the Civil Rights Revolution: "Why did social scientists—and sociologists in particular —not foresee the explosion of collective action of Negro Americans toward full integration into American society?" He pointed out that "it is the vigor and urgency of the Negro demand that is new, not its direction or supporting ideas."[1] Without arguing the point further, the lack of knowledge can be attributed to two groups—the ahistorical social scientists, and the historians who, until recently, have neglected modern Negro history.

The search for a "watershed" in recent Negro history ends at the years that comprised World War II, 1939–1945. James Baldwin has written of this period: "The treatment accorded the Negro during the Second World War marks, for me, a turning point in the Negro's relation to America. To put it briefly, and somewhat too simply, a certain hope died, a certain respect for white Americans faded."[2] Writing during World War II, Gunnar Myrdal predicted that the war would act as a "stimulant" to Negro protest, and he felt that "There is bound to be a redefinition of the Negro's status in America as a result of this war."[3] The Negro sociologist E. Franklin Frazier states that World War II marked the point where "The Negro was no longer willing to accept discrimination in employment and in housing without protest."[4] Charles E. Silberman writes that the war was a "turning point" in American race relations, in which "the seeds of the protest movements of the 1950s and 1960s were sown."[5] While a few writers have indicated the importance of these years in the recent Negro pro-

Reprinted from *Journal of American History* LV (June 1968): 90–106. By permission of the Organization of American Historians.

test movement, the majority have failed to do so. Overlooking what went before, most recent books on the subject claim that a Negro "revolution" or "revolt" occurred in 1954, 1955, 1960, or 1963.[6] Because of the neglect of the war period, these years of transition in American race relations comprise the "forgotten years" of the Negro revolution.

To understand how the American Negro reacted to World War II, it is necessary to have some idea of the discrimination he faced. The defense build-up begun by the United States in 1940 was welcomed by Negroes who were disproportionately represented among the unemployed. Employment discrimination in the revived industries, however, was rampant. When Negroes sought jobs at aircraft factories where employers begged for workers, they were informed that "the Negro will be considered only as janitors and in other similar capacities. . . ."[7] Government financed training programs to overcome the shortages of skilled workers discriminated against Negro trainees. When government agencies issued orders against such discrimination, they were ignored.[8]

Increasing defense preparations also meant an expansion of the armed forces. Here, as in industry, however, Negroes faced restrictions. Black Americans were assigned a minimal role and rigidly segregated. In the navy, Negroes could enlist only in the all-Negro messman's branch. The marine and the air corps excluded Negroes entirely. In the army, black Americans were prevented from enlisting, except for a few vacancies in the four regular army Negro units that had been created shortly after the Civil War; and the strength of these had been reduced drastically in the 1920s and 1930s.[9]

Although the most important bread-and-butter issue for Negroes in this period was employment discrimination, their position in the armed forces was an important symbol. If one could not participate fully in the defense of his country, he could not lay claim to the rights of a full-fledged citizen. The NAACP organ, the *Crisis*, expressed this idea in its demand for unrestricted participation in the armed forces: "this is no fight merely to wear a uniform. This is a struggle for status, a struggle to take democracy off of parchment and give it life."[10] Herbert Garfinkel, a student of Negro protest during this period, points out that "in many respects, the discriminatory practices against Negroes which characterized the military programs . . . cut deeper into Negro feelings than did employment discrimination."[11]

Added to the rebuffs from industry and the armed services were a hundred others. Negroes, anxious to contribute to the Red Cross blood program, were turned away. Despite the fact that white and Negro blood is the same biologically, it was deemed inadvisable "to collect and mix caucasian and Negro blood indiscriminately."[12] When Negro citizens called upon the governor of Tennessee to appoint some black members to the state's draft boards, he told them: "This is a white man's country. . . . The Negro had nothing to do with the settling of America."[13] At a time when the United States claimed to be the last bulwark of democracy in a war-torn world, the legislature of Mississippi passed a law requiring different textbooks for Negro schools: all references to voting, elections, and democracy were to be excluded from the black student's books.[14]

The Negro's morale at the beginning of World War II is also partly explained by his experience in World War I. Black America had gone into that war with high morale, generated by the belief that the democratic slogans literally meant what they said. Most Negroes succumbed to the "close ranks" strategy announced by the crusading NAACP editor, W. E. B. Du Bois, who advocated subduing racial grievances in order to give full support to winning the war. But the image of a new democratic order was smashed by the race riots, lynchings, and continued rigid discrimination. The result was a mass trauma and a series of movements among Negroes in the 1920s which were characterized by a desire to withdraw from a white society which wanted little to do with them. When the war crisis of the 1940s came along, the bitter memories of World War I were recalled with the result that there was a built-in cynicism among Negroes toward the democratic slogans of the new war.[15]

Nevertheless, Negroes were part of the general population being stimulated to come to the defense of democracy in the world. When they responded and attempted to do their share, they were turned away. The result was a widespread feeling of frustration and a general decline of the Negro's morale toward the war effort, as compared with the rest of American society. But paradoxically, the Negro's general morale was both low and high.

While the morale of the Negro, as an American, was low in regard to the war effort, the Negro, as a member of a minority group, had high morale in his heightened race consciousness and determination to fight for a better position in American society. The same slogans which caused the Negro to react cynically also served to emphasize the disparity between the creed and practice of democracy as far as the Negro in America was concerned. Because of his position in society, the Negro reacted to the war both as an American and as a Negro. Discrimination against him had given rise to "a sickly, negative attitude toward national goals, but at the same time a vibrantly positive attitude toward racial aims and aspirations."[16]

When war broke out in Europe in 1939, many black Americans tended to adopt an isolationist attitude. Those taking this position viewed the war as a "white man's war." George Schuyler, the iconoclastic columnist, was a typical spokesman for this view: "So far as the colored peoples of the earth are concerned," Schuyler wrote, "it is a toss-up between the 'democracies' and the dictatorships. . . . [W]hat is there to choose between the rule of the British in Africa and the rule of the Germans in Austria?"[17] Another Negro columnist claimed that it was a blessing to have war so that whites could "mow one another down" rather than "have them quietly murder hundreds of thousands of Africans, East Indians and Chinese. . . ."[18] This kind of isolationism took the form of anti-colonialism, particularly against the British. There was some sympathy for France, however, because of its more liberal treatment of black citizens.[19]

Another spur to isolationist sentiment was the obvious hypocrisy of calling for the defense of democracy abroad while it was not a reality at home. The NAACP bitterly expressed this point:

> THE CRISIS is sorry for brutality, blood, and death among the peoples of Europe, just as we were sorry for China and Ethiopia. But the hysterical cries of the preachers of democracy for Europe leave us cold. We want democracy in Alabama and Arkansas, in Mississippi and Michigan, in the District of Columbia—*in the Senate of the United States*.[20]

The editor of the Pittsburgh *Courier* proclaimed that Negroes had their "own war" at home "against oppression and exploitation from without and against disorganization and lack of confidence within"; and the Chicago *Defender* thought that "peace at home" should be the main concern of black Americans.[21]

Many Negroes agreed with columnist Schuyler that "Our war is not against Hitler in Europe, but against the Hitlers in America."[22] The isolationist view of the war in Europe and the antagonism toward Great Britain led to an attitude that was rather neutral toward the Nazis and the Japanese, or, in some extreme cases, pro-Axis. Appealing to this latent feeling, isolationist periodicals tried to gain Negro support in their struggle against American entrance into the war.[23] By 1940 there were also Negro cults such as the Ethiopian Pacific Movement, the World Wide Friends of Africa, the Brotherhood of Liberty for the Black People of America, and many others, which preached

unity among the world's darker people, including Japanese. Many of
these groups exploited the latent anti-semitism common among Negroes
in the urban ghettos by claiming that the racial policies of Germany
were correct.[24]

Reports reached the public that some black Americans were expressing a vicarious pleasure over successes by the "yellow" Japanese and
by Germany. In a quarrel with her employer in North Carolina, a
Negro woman retorted: "I hope Hitler does come, because if he does
he will get you first!" A Negro truck driver in Philadelphia was held
on charges of treason after he was accused of telling a Negro soldier
that he should not be in uniform and that "This is a white man's government and war and it's no damned good." After Pearl Harbor, a
Negro share cropper told his landlord: "By the way, Captain, I hear
the Japs done declared war on you white folks." Another Negro declared that he was going to get his eyes slanted so that the next time a
white man shoved him around he could fight back.[25]

It is impossible to determine the extent of this kind of pro-Axis
sentiment among Negroes, but it was widespread enough for the Negro
press to make rather frequent mention of it.[26] In 1942 and 1943 the
federal government did arrest the members of several pro-Japanese
Negro cults in Chicago, New York, Newark, New Jersey, and East St.
Louis, Illinois. Although the numbers involved were small, the evidence
indicated that Japanese agents had been at work among these groups
and had capitalized on Negro grievances.[27]

By the time of the Pearl Harbor attack, certain fundamental changes
were taking place among American Negroes. Nowhere is this more
evident than in a comparison of Negroes' reactions to World Wars I
and II. The dominant opinion among them toward World War I was
expressed by Du Bois. In World War II, most Negroes looked upon the
earlier stand as a great mistake. The dominant attitude during World
War II was that the Negro must fight for democracy on two fronts—
at home as well as abroad. This opinion had first appeared in reaction
to the discriminatory treatment of Negro soldiers;[28] but with the attack
on Pearl Harbor, this idea, stated in many different ways, became the
slogan of black America.[29]

American Negroes took advantage of the war to tie their racial
demands to the ideology for which the war was being fought. Before
Pearl Harbor, the Negro press frequently pointed out the similarity of
American treatment of Negroes and Nazi Germany's treatment of
minorities. In 1940, the Chicago *Defender* featured a mock invasion of
the United States by Germany in which the Nazis were victorious

because a fifth column of southern senators and other racists aided them.[30] Later the *Crisis* printed an editorial which compared the white supremacy doctrine in America to the Nazi plan for Negroes, a comparison which indicated a marked similarity.[31] Even the periodical of the conservative Urban League made such comparisons.[32]

Many Negroes adopted a paradoxical stand on the meaning of the war. At the same time that it was labeled a "white man's war," Negroes often stated that they were bound to benefit from it. For example, Schuyler could argue that the war was not for democracy, but "Peace means . . . a continuation of the status quo . . . which must be ended if the Negro is to get free." And accordingly, the longer the war the better: "Perhaps in the shuffle we who have been on the bottom of the deck for so long will find ourselves at the top."[33]

Cynicism and hope existed side by side in the Negro mind. Cynicism was often the attitude expressed after some outrageous example of discrimination. After Pearl Harbor, however, a mixture of hope and certainty—great changes favorable to the Negro would result from the war and things would never be the same again—became the dominant attitude. Hope was evident in the growing realization that the war provided the Negro with an excellent opportunity to prick the conscience of white America. "What an opportunity the crisis has been . . . for one to persuade, embarrass, compel and shame our government and our nation . . . into a more enlightened attitude toward a tenth of its people!" the Pittsburgh *Courier* proclaimed.[34] Certainly that a better life would result from the war was based on the belief that revolutionary forces had been released throughout the world. It was no longer a "white man's world," and the "myth of white invincibility" had been shattered for good.[35]

There was a growing protest against the racial status quo by black Americans; this was evidenced by the reevaluation of segregation in all sections of the country. In the North there was self-criticism of past acceptance of certain forms of segregation.[36] Southern Negroes became bolder in openly questioning the sacredness of segregation. In October 1942, a group of southern Negro leaders met in Durham, North Carolina, and issued a statement on race relations. In addition to endorsing the idea that the Negro should fight for democracy at home as well as abroad, these leaders called for complete equality for the Negro in American life. While recognizing the "strength and age" of the South's racial customs, the Durham meeting was "fundamentally opposed to the principle and practice of compulsory segregation in our American society." In addition, there were reports of deep discontent among southern Negro college students and evidence that political activity among the blacks of the South, particularly on the local level, was increasing.[37]

The American Negro, stimulated by the democratic ideology of the war, was reexamining his position in American society. "It cannot be doubted that the spirit of American Negroes in all classes is different today from what it was a generation ago," Myrdal observed.[38] Part of this new spirit was an increased militancy, a readiness to protest loud and strong against grievances. The crisis gave Negroes more reason and opportunity to protest. Representative of all of the trends of black thought and action—the cynicism, the hope, the heightened race consciousness, the militancy—was the March on Washington Movement (MOWM).

The general idea of exerting mass pressure upon the government to end defense discrimination did not originate with A. Philip Randolph's call for a march on Washington, D.C., in early 1941.[39] Agitation for mass pressure had grown since the failure of a group of Negro leaders to gain any major concessions from President Franklin D. Roosevelt in September 1940.[40] Various organizations, such as the NAACP, the Committee for Participation of Negroes in the National Defense, and the Allied Committees on National Defense, held mass protest meetings around the country in late 1940 and early 1941.[41] The weeks passed and these efforts did not seem to have any appreciable impact on the government; Walter White, Randolph, and other Negro leaders could not even secure an appointment to see the President. "Bitterness grew at an alarming pace throughout the country," White recalled.[42]

It remained, however, for Randolph to consolidate this protest. In January 1941, he wrote an article for the Negro press which pointed out the failure of committees and individuals to achieve action against defense discrimination. "Only power can effect the enforcement and adoption of a given policy," Randolph noted; and "Power is the active principle of only the organized masses, the masses united for a definite purpose." To focus the weight of the black masses, he suggested that 10,000 Negroes march on Washington, D.C., with the slogan: "We loyal Negro-American citizens demand the right to work and fight for our country."[43]

This march appeal led to the formation of one of the most significant —though today almost forgotten—Negro protest movements. The MOWM pioneered what has become the common denominator of today's Negro revolt—"the spontaneous involvement of large masses of Negroes in a political protest."[44] Furthermore, as August Meier and

Elliott Rudwick have recently pointed out, the MOWM clearly fore-shadowed "the goals, tactics, and strategy of the mid-twentieth-century civil rights movement." Whites were excluded purposely to make it an all-Negro movement; its main weapon was direct action on the part of the black masses. Furthermore, the MOWM took as its major concern the economic problems of urban slumdwellers.[45]

Randolph's tactic of mass pressure through a demonstration of black power struck a response among the Negro masses. The number to march on Washington on July 1, 1941, was increased to 50,000, and only Roosevelt's agreement to issue an executive order establishing a President's Committee on Fair Employment Practices led to a cancella-tion of the march. Negroes then, and scholars later, generally inter-preted this as a great victory. But the magnitude of the victory is diminished when one examines the original MOWM demands: an executive order forbidding government contracts to be awarded to a firm which practiced discrimination in hiring, an executive order abolishing discrimination in government defense training courses, an executive order requiring the United States Employment Service to supply workers without regard to race, an executive order abolishing segregation in the armed forces, an executive order abolishing dis-crimination and segregation on account of race in all departments of the federal government, and a request from the President to Congress to pass a law forbidding benefits of the National Labor Relations Act to unions denying Negroes membership. Regardless of the extent of the success of the MOWM, however, it represented something different in black protest. Unlike the older Negro movements, the MOWM had captured the imagination of the masses.[46]

Although overlooked by most recent writers on civil rights, a mass militancy became characteristic of the American Negro in World War II. This was symbolized by the MOWM and was the reason for its wide appeal. Furthermore, older Negro organizations found them-selves pushed into militant stands. For example, the NAACP underwent a tremendous growth in its membership and became representative of the Negro masses for the first time in its history. From 355 branches and a membership of 50,556 in 1940, the NAACP grew to 1,073 branches with a membership of slightly less than 450,000 in 1946.[47] The editors of the Pittsburgh Courier recognized that a new spirit was present in black America. In the past, Negroes

made the mistake of relying entirely upon the gratitude and sense of fair play of the American people. Now we are disillusioned. We have neither faith in promises, nor a high opinion of the integrity of the American people, where race is involved. Experience has taught us that we must rely primarily upon our own efforts. . . . That is why we protest, agitate, and demand that all forms of color prejudice be blotted out. . . .[48]

By the time of the Japanese attack on Pearl Harbor, many in America, both inside and outside of the government, were worried over the state of Negro morale. There was fear that the Negro would be disloyal.[49] The depth of white ignorance about the causes for the Negro's cynicism and low morale is obvious from the fact that the black press was blamed for the widespread discontent. The double victory attitude constantly displayed in Negro newspapers throughout the war, and supported by most black Americans, was considered as verging on disloyalty by most whites. White America, ignorant of the American Negroes' reaction to World War I, thought that black citizens should subdue their grievances for the duration.

During World War II, there was pressure upon the White House and the justice department from within the federal government to indict some Negro editors for sedition and interference with the war effort. President Roosevelt refused to sanction this, however. There was also an attempt to deny newsprint to the more militant Negro newspapers, but the President put an end to this when the matter was brought to his attention.[50] The restriction of Negro newspapers from military installations became so widespread that the war department had to call a halt to this practice in 1943.[51] These critics failed to realize that, although serving to unify black opinion, the Negro press simply reflected the Negro mind.

One of the most widely publicized attacks on the Negro press was made by the southern white liberal, Virginius Dabney, editor of the Richmond *Times Dispatch*. He charged that "extremist" Negro newspapers and Negro leaders were "demanding an overnight revolution in race relations," and as a consequence they were "stirring up interracial hate." Dabney concluded his indictment by warning that "it is a foregone conclusion that if an attempt is made forcibly to abolish segregation throughout the South, violence and bloodshed will result."[52] The Negro press reacted vigorously to such charges. Admitting that there were "all-or-nothing" Negro leaders, the Norfolk *Journal and Guide* claimed they were created by the "nothing-at-all" attitude of whites.[53] The Chicago *Defender* and Baltimore *Afro-American* took the position that they were only pointing out the shortcomings of American democracy, and this was certainly not disloyal.[54] The NAACP and the

Urban League claimed that it was patriotic for Negroes to protest against undemocratic practices, and those who sought to stifle this protest were the unpatriotic ones.[55]

The Negro masses simply did not support a strategy of moderating their grievances for the duration of the war. After attending an Office of Facts and Figures conference for Negro leaders in March 1942, Roy Wilkins of the NAACP wrote:

> . . . it is a plain fact that no Negro leader with a constituency can face his members today and ask full support for the war in the light of the atmosphere the government has created. Some Negro educators who are responsible only to their boards or trustees might do so, but the heads of no organized groups would dare do so.[56]

By 1942, the federal government began investigating Negro morale in order to find out what could be done to improve it. This project was undertaken by the Office of Facts and Figures and its successor, the Office of War Information.[57] Surveys by these agencies indicated that the great amount of national publicity given the defense program only served to increase the Negro's awareness that he was not participating fully in that program. Black Americans found it increasingly difficult to reconcile their treatment with the announced war aims. Urban Negroes were the most resentful over defense discrimination, particularly against the treatment accorded black members of the armed forces. Never before had Negroes been so united behind a cause: the war had served to focus their attention on their unequal status in American society. Black Americans were almost unanimous in wanting a show of good intention from the federal government that changes would be made in the racial status quo.[58]

The government's inclination to take steps to improve Negro morale, and the Negro's desire for change, were frustrated by the general attitude of white Americans. In 1942, after two years of militant agitation by Negroes, six out of ten white Americans felt that black Americans were satisfied with things the way they were and that Negroes were receiving all of the opportunities they deserved. More than half of all whites interviewed in the Northeast and West believed that there should be separate schools, separate restaurants, and separate neighborhoods for the races. A majority of whites in all parts of the country believed that the Negro would not be treated any better after the war than in 1942 and that the Negro's lesser role in society was due to his own shortcomings rather than anything the whites had done.[59] The white opposition to racial change may have provided the rationale for governmental inactivity. Furthermore, the white obstinance must have added to the bitterness of black Americans.

Although few people recognized it, the war was working a revolution in American race relations. Sociologist Robert E. Park felt that the racial structure of society was "cracking," and the equilibrium reached after the Civil War seemed "to be under attack at a time and under conditions when it is particularly difficult to defend it."[60] Sociologist Howard W. Odum wrote from the South that there was "an unmeasurable and unbridgeable distance between the white South and the reasonable expectation of the Negro."[61] White southerners opposed to change in the racial mores sensed changes occurring among "their" Negroes. "Outsiders" from the North, Mrs. Franklin Roosevelt, and the Roosevelt Administration were all accused of attempting to undermine segregation under the pretense of wartime necessity.[62]

Racial tensions were common in all sections of the country during the war.[63] There were riots in 1943. Tensions were high because Negro Americans were challenging the status quo. When fourteen prominent Negroes, conservatives and liberals, southerners and northerners, were asked in 1944 what they thought the black American wanted, their responses were almost unanimous. Twelve of the fourteen said they thought that Negroes wanted full political equality, economic equality, equality of opportunity, and full social equality with the abolition of legal segregation.[64] The war had stimulated the race consciousness and the desire for change among Negroes.

Most American Negroes and their leaders wanted the government to institute a revolutionary change in its race policy. Whereas the policy had been acquiescence in segregation since the end of Reconstruction, the government was now asked to set the example for the rest of the nation by supporting integration. This was the demand voiced by the great majority of the Negro leaders called together in March 1942 by the Office of Facts and Figures.[65] *Crisis* magazine summarized the feelings of many black Americans: Negroes have "waited thus far in vain for some sharp and dramatic notice that this war is not to maintain the status quo here."[66]

The White House, and it was not alone, failed to respond to the revolutionary changes occurring among the nation's largest minority. When the Fraternal Council of Negro Churches called upon President Roosevelt to end discrimination in the defense industries and armed forces, the position taken was that "it would be very bad to give encouragement beyond the  point where actual results can be accomplished."[67] Roosevelt did bestir himself over particularly outrageous incidents. When Roland Hayes, a noted Negro singer, was beaten and jailed in a Georgia town, the President dashed off a note to his attorney general: "Will you have someone go down and check up . . . and see if any law was violated. I suggest you send a northerner."[68]

Roosevelt was not enthusiastic about major steps in the race relations field proposed by interested individuals within and without the government.[69] In February 1942 Edwin R. Embree of the Julius Rosenwald Fund, acutely aware of the growing crisis in American race relations, urged Roosevelt to create a commission of experts on race relations to advise him on what steps the government should take to improve matters. FDR's answer to this proposal indicates that he felt race relations was one of the reform areas that had to be sacrificed for the present in order to prosecute the war. He thought such a commission was "premature" and that "we must start winning the war . . . before we do much general planning for the future." The President believed that "there is a danger of such long-range planning becoming projects of wide influence in escape from the realities of war. I am not convinced that we can be realists about the war and planners for the future at this critical time."[70]

After the race riots of 1943, numerous proposals for a national committee on race relations were put forward; but FDR refused to change his position. Instead, the President simply appointed Jonathan Daniels to gather information from all government departments on current race tensions and what they were doing to combat them.[71] This suggestion for what would eventually become a President's Committee on Civil Rights would have to wait until a President recognized that a revolution in race relations was occurring and that action by the government could no longer be put off. In the interim, many would share the shallow reasoning of Secretary of War Stimson that the cause of racial tension was "the deliberate effort . . . on the part of certain radical leaders of the colored race to use the war for obtaining . . . race equality and interracial marriages. . . ."[72]

The hypocrisy and paradox involved in fighting a world war for the four freedoms and against aggression by an enemy preaching a master race ideology, while at the same time upholding racial segregation and white supremacy, were too obvious. The war crisis provided American Negroes with a unique opportunity to point out, for all to see, the difference between the American creed and practice. The democratic ideology and rhetoric with which the war was fought stimulated a sense of hope and certainty in black Americans that the old race structure was destroyed forever. In part, this confidence was also the result of the mass militancy and race consciousness that developed in these years. When the expected white acquiescence in a new racial order did not occur, the ground was prepared for the civil rights revolution of the 1950s and 1960s; the seeds were indeed sown in the World War II years.

## NOTES

1. Everett C. Hughes, "Race Relations and the Sociological Imagination," *American Sociological Review*, XXVIII (Dec. 1963), 879.

2. Quoted in T. Milton Yinger, *A Minority Group in American Society* (New York, 1965), 52. Many Negroes agreed with James Baldwin in recalling the bitterness they experienced. William Brink and Louis Harris, *The Negro Revolution in America* (New York, 1964), 50.

3. Gunnar Myrdal, *An American Dilemma: The Negro Problem and Modern Democracy* (New York, 1944), 756, 997.

4. E. Franklin Frazier, *The Negro in the United States* (rev. ed., New York, 1957), 682.

5. Charles E. Silberman, *Crisis in Black and White* (New York, 1964), 60, 65.

6. See, for example, Lewis M. Killian and Charles Grigg, *Racial Crisis in America* (Englewood Cliffs, 1964); Louis E. Lomax, *The Negro Revolt* (New York, 1962); Leonard Broom and Norval D. Glenn, *Transformation of the Negro American* (New York, 1965); Brink and Harris, *Negro Revolution in America*.

7. Quoted in Louis Coleridge Kesselman, *The Social Politics of FEPC: A Study in Reform Pressure Movements* (Chapel Hill, 1948), 7.

8. Charles H. Thompson, "The American Negro and the National Defense," *Journal of Negro Education*, IX (Oct. 1940), 547–552; Frazier, *Negro in the United States*, 599–606; Robert C. Weaver, "Racial Employment Trends in National Defense," *Phylon*, II (4th Quarter, 1941), 337–358.

9. See Richard M. Dalfiume, "Desegregation of the United States Armed Forces, 1939–1953" (doctoral dissertation, University of Missouri, 1966), 30–57; Ulysses Lee, *United States Army in World War II: Special Studies: The Employment of Negro Troops* (Washington, 1966), 32–87.

10. "For Manhood in National Defense," *Crisis*, 47 (Dec. 1940), 375.

11. Herbert Garfinkel, *When Negroes March: The March on Washington Movement in the Organizational Politics for FEPC* (Glencoe, Ill., 1959), 20.

12. General James C. Magee, Surgeon General, to Assistant Secretary of War John J. McCloy, Sept. 3, 1941, ASW 291.2, Record Group 335 (National Archives); Pittsburgh *Courier*, Jan. 3, 1942.

13. Pittsburgh *Courier*, Nov. 2, 1940.

14. "Text Books in Mississippi," *Opportunity*, XVIII (April 1940), 99.

15. Kenneth B. Clark, "Morale of the Negro on the Home Front: World Wars I and II," *Journal of Negro Education*, XII (Summer 1943), 417–428; Walter White, " 'It's Our Country, Too': The Negro Demands the Right to be Allowed to Fight for It," *Saturday Evening Post*, 213 (Dec. 14, 1940), 27, 61, 63, 66, 68; Metz T. P. Lochard, "Negroes and Defense," *Nation*, 152 (Jan. 4, 1941), 14–16.

16. Cornelius L. Golightly, "Negro Higher Education and Democratic Negro Morale," *Journal of Negro Education*, XI (July 1942), 324. See also Horace R. Cayton, "Negro Morale," *Opportunity*, XIX (Dec. 1941), 371–375; Louis Wirth, "Morale and Minority Groups," *American Journal of Sociology*, XLVII (Nov. 1941), 415–433; Kenneth B. Clark, "Morale Among Negroes," Goodwin Watson, ed., *Civilian Morale* (Boston, 1942), 228–248; Arnold M. Rose, *The Negro's Morale: Group Identification and Protest* (Minneapolis, 1949), 5–7, 54–55, 122–124, 141–144.

17. Pittsburgh *Courier*, Sept. 9, 1939.

18. P. L. Prattis in *ibid.*, Sept. 2, 1939. Similar sentiments were expressed by Chicago *Defender* editorials, May 25, June 15, 1940.

19. Pittsburgh *Courier*, Sept. 9, 16, 1939.

20. "Lynching and Liberty," *Crisis*, 47 (July 1940), 209.

21. Pittsburgh *Courier*, Sept. 9, 1939; Chicago *Defender*, May 25, 1940.

22. Pittsburgh *Courier*, Dec. 21, 1940.

23. Lee, *The Employment of Negro Troops*, 65–67; Horace Mann Bond, "Should the Negro Care Who Wins the War?" *Annals*, CCXXIII (Sept. 1942), 81–84; Adam Clayton Powell, Jr., "Is This a 'White Man's War'?" *Common Sense*, XI (April 1942), 111–113.

24. Roi Ottley, "A White Folk's War?" *Common Ground*, II (Spring, 1942), 28–31, and *'New World A-Coming'* (Boston, 1943), 322–342; Lunnabelle Wedlock, *The Reaction of Negro Publications and Organizations to German Anti-Semitism* (Washington, 1942), 116–193; Alfred M. Lee, "Subversive Individuals of Minority Status," *Annals*, CCXXIII (Sept. 1942), 167–168.

25. St. Clair Drake and Horace R. Cayton, *Black Metropolis* (New York, 1945), 744–745; Ottley, *'New World A-Coming'*, 306–310; Horace R. Cayton, "Fighting for White Folks?" *Nation*, 155 (Sept. 26, 1942), 267–270.

26. "The Negro and Nazism," *Opportunity*, XVIII (July 1940), 194–195; Horace R. Cayton in Pittsburgh *Courier*, Dec. 20, 1941; J. A. Rodgers in *ibid.*, Dec. 27, 1941; Chandler Owen in Norfolk *Journal and Guide*, Dec. 13, 1941; report in Baltimore *Afro-American*, Nov. 21, 1942.

27. New York *Times*, Sept. 15, 22, 1942, Jan. 14, 28, 1943.

28. "Conference Resolutions," *Crisis*, 47 (Sept. 1940), 296; "Where the Negro Stands," *Opportunity*, XIX (April 1941), 98; Lester M. Jones, "The Editorial Policy of Negro Newspapers of 1917–1918 as Compared with that of 1941–1942," *Journal of Negro History*, XXIX (Jan. 1944), 24–31.

29. Baltimore *Afro-American*, Dec. 20, 1941, Feb. 7, 1942; Norfolk *Journal and Guide*, March 21, 1942; "Now Is the Time Not to Be Silent," *Crisis*, 49 (Jan. 1942), 7; "The Fate of Democracy," *Opportunity*, XX (Jan. 1942), 2. Two Negro newspapers adopted this theme for their war slogans. The Pittsburgh *Courier*, Feb. 14, 1942, initiated a "Double V" campaign—"victory over our enemies at home and victory over our enemies on the battlefields abroad." When a Negro was brutally lynched in Sikeston, Missouri, a few weeks after Pearl Harbor, the Chicago *Defender*, March 14, 1942, adopted as its war slogan: "Remember Pearl Harbor and Sikeston too." See also Ralph N. Davis, "The Negro Newspapers and the War," *Sociology and Social Research*, XXVII (May–June 1943), 373–380.

30. Chicago *Defender*, Sept. 25, 1940.

31. "Nazi Plan for Negroes Copies Southern U. S. A.," *Crisis*, 48 (March 1941), 71.

32. "American Nazism," *Opportunity*, XIX (Feb. 1941), 35. See also editorials in Pittsburgh *Courier*, March 15, April 19, 26, 1941, May 30, 1942; Chicago *Defender*, Sept. 7, 1940; Norfolk *Journal and Guide*, April 19, 1941; Baltimore *Afro-American*, Feb. 17, 1940, Sept. 6, 1941.

33. Pittsburgh *Courier*, Oct. 5, 1940; George S. Schuyler, "A Long War Will Aid the Negro," *Crisis*, 50 (Nov. 1943), 328–329, 344. See also J. A. Rodgers in Pittsburgh *Courier*, June 28, 1941; Horace R. Cayton in *ibid.*, March 22, 1941; Baltimore *Afro-American*, Sept. 12, 16, 1939; Guion Griffis Johnson, "The Impact of War Upon the Negro," *Journal of Negro Education*, X (July 1941), 596–611.

34. Pittsburgh *Courier*, Jan. 10, Aug. 8, 1942. Charles S. Johnson, "The Negro and the Present Crisis," *Journal of Negro Education*, X (July 1941), 585–595. Opinion surveys indicated that most Negro soldiers expressed support for this kind of opportunism. Samuel A. Stouffer and others, *The American Soldier* (2 vols., Princeton, 1949), I, 516–517.

35. Baltimore *Afro-American*, June 12, Oct. 31, 1942; Walter White in Pittsburgh *Courier*, May 23, 1942. The impact of world affairs on the

American Negro is detailed in Harold R. Isaacs, *The New World of Negro Americans* (New York, 1963).

36. See editorials in Pittsburgh *Courier*, Dec. 28, 1940; Feb. 1, June 28, 1941; May 30, 1942; Baltimore *Afro-American*, May 23, 1942.

37. Charles S. Johnson, *To Stem This Tide* (Boston, 1943), 131–139; Malcolm S. MacLean, president of Hampton Institute, to Marvin H. McIntyre, Nov. 20, 1942, OF 93, Roosevelt Papers (Franklin D. Roosevelt Library, Hyde Park); George B. Tindall, "The Significance of Howard W. Odum to Southern History: A Preliminary Estimate," *Journal of Southern History*, XXIV (Aug. 1958), 302. Anthropologist Hortense Powdermaker, *After Freedom: A Cultural Study of the Deep South* (New York, 1939), 331–333, 353, supports the observations of a tendency to rebel among the younger Negroes of the South. See also Ralph J. Bunche, "The Negro in the Political Life of the United States," *Journal of Negro Education*, X (July 1941), 567–584; Myrdal, *American Dilemma*, 499; Henry Lee Moon, *Balance of Power: The Negro Vote* (Garden City, 1948), 178–179.

38. Myrdal, *American Dilemma*, 744.

39. Garfinkel, *When Negroes March*, fails to emphasize this point.

40. Walter White, *A Man Called White* (New York, 1948), 186–187; "White House Blesses Jim Crow," *Crisis*, 47 (Nov. 1940), 350–351, 357; Dalfiume, "Desegregation of the United States Armed Forces, 1939–1953," 46–51.

41. Pittsburgh *Courier*, Dec. 7, 14, 21, 1940; Jan. 4, 25, Feb. 8, 1941.

42. White, *A Man Called White*, 189–190.

43. Pittsburgh *Courier*, Jan. 25, 1941.

44. Garfinkel, *When Negroes March*, 8.

45. August Meier and Elliott M. Rudwick, *From Plantation to Ghetto: An Interpretive History of American Negroes* (New York, 1966), 222.

46. "Proposals of the Negro March-on-Washington Committee to President Roosevelt for Urgent Consideration," June 21, 1941, OF 391, Roosevelt Papers. The standard versions of a Negro "victory" are Garfinkel, *When Negroes March*; Kesselman, *The Social Politics of FEPC*; and Louis Ruchames, *Race, Jobs, & Politics: The Story of FEPC* (New York, 1953). For a different interpretation, see Dalfiume, "Desegregation of the United States Armed Forces, 1939–1953," 172–177. The Negro press generally recognized that the MOWM represented something new. The Pittsburgh *Courier*, July 5, 1941, claimed: "We begin to feel at last that the day when we shall gain full rights . . . of American citizenship is now not far distant." The Chicago *Defender*, June 28, July 12, 1941, felt that the white man will be convinced that "the American black man has decided henceforth and forever to abandon

the timid role of Uncle-Tomism in his struggle. . . ." The tactics of the MOWM had "demonstrated to the doubting Thomases among us that only mass action can pry open the iron doors that have been erected against America's black minority."

47. Frazier, *The Negro in the United States*, 537; Charles Radford Lawrence, "Negro Organizations in Crisis: Depression, New Deal, World War II" (doctoral dissertation, Columbia University, 1953), 103; Myrdal, *American Dilemma*, 851–852. Such close observers of American race relations as Will Alexander, Edwin Embree, and Charles S. Johnson recognized the changing character of Negro protest. They believed that "the characteristic movements among Negroes are now for the first time becoming proletarian, as contrasted to upper class or intellectual influence that was typical of previous movements. The present proletarian direction grows out of the increasing general feelings of protest against discrimination, especially in the armed forces and in our war activities generally. The present movements are led in part by such established leaders as A. Philip Randolph, Walter White, etc. There is likelihood (and danger) that the movement may be seized upon by some much more picturesque figure who may be less responsible and less interested in actual improvement of conditions. One of the most likely of the potential leaders is A. Clayton Powell, Jr." Memorandum of Conferences of Alexander, Johnson, and Embree on the Rosenwald Fund's Program in Race Relations, June 27, 1942, Race Relations folder, Rosenwald Fund Papers (Fisk University).

48. Pittsburgh *Courier*, Sept. 12, 1942. See also Roscoe E. Lewis, "The Role of Pressure Groups in Maintaining Morale Among Negroes," *Journal of Negro Education*, XII (Summer 1943), 464–473; Earl Brown, "American Negroes and the War," *Harper's Magazine*, 184 (April 1942), 545–552; Roi Ottley, "Negro Morale," *New Republic*, 105 (Nov. 10, 1941), 613–615; Thomas Sancton, "Something's Happened to the Negro," *New Republic*, 108 (Feb. 8, 1943), 175–179; Stanley High, "How the Negro Fights for Freedom." *Reader's Digest*, 41 (July 1942), 113–118; H. C. Brearley, "The Negro's New Belligerency," *Phylon*, V (4th Quarter 1944), 339–345.

49. Memorandum to Assistant Secretary of War McCloy from G-2, June 27, 1942, ASW 291.2, Record Group 335.

50. White, *A Man Called White*, 207–208; R. Keith Kane to Ulric Bell, May 14, 1942, OFF 992.11, Record Group 208; Memorandum to Robert A. Lovett from McCloy, March 6, 1942, ASW 291.2, Record Group 335.

51. Baltimore *Afro-American*, Sept. 30, 1941; Pittsburgh *Courier*, March 8, 1941, Nov. 13, 1943. Assistant Secretary of War McCloy, who was also head of the war department's Advisory Committee on Negro Troop

Policies, held a critical view of the Negro press that was common in the army. McCloy to Herbert Elliston, editor of the Washington *Post*, Aug. 5, 1943, ASW 292.2, Record Group 335.

52. Virginius Dabney, "Nearer and Nearer the Precipice," *Atlantic Monthly*, 171 (Jan. 1943), 94–100; Virginius Dabney, "Press and Morale," *Saturday Review of Literature*, XXV (July 4, 1942), 5–6, 24–25.

53. Norfolk *Journal and Guide*, Aug. 15, 1942. See also *Journal and Guide* editorials of Oct. 17, April 25, 1942; and March 6, 1943, for a defense of Negro militancy.

54. Chicago *Defender*, Dec. 20, 1941; Baltimore *Afro-American*, Jan. 9, 1943.

55. Pittsburgh *Courier*, May 8, June 19, 1943. A few conservative Negroes joined whites in criticizing the growing militancy. James E. Shepard, Negro president of North Carolina College for Negroes, asked the administration to do something to undercut the growing support of the militants among young Negroes: "Those who seek to stir them up about rights and not duties are their enemies." Shepard to Secretary of the Navy Frank Knox, Sept. 28, 1940, OF 93, Roosevelt Papers. Frederick D. Patterson, president of Tuskegee Institute, made it clear in his newspaper column and in talks with administration officials that he believed in all-out support for the war effort by Negroes regardless of segregation and discrimination. "Stimson Diary," Jan. 29, 1943 (Yale University Library), and columns by Patterson in the Pittsburgh *Courier*, Jan. 16, July 3, 1943. Such conservatives were bitterly attacked in the Negro press. The black leader who urged his people to relax their determination to win full participation in American life was a "misleader and a false prophet," the Norfolk *Journal and Guide*, May 2, 1942, proclaimed. Such people "endangered" the interests of Negroes by "compromising with the forces that promote and uphold segregation and discrimination," wrote the editor of the Chicago *Defender*, April 5, 1941. The *Crisis* charged that those Negroes who succumbed to segregation as "realism" provided a rationale for those whites who sought to perpetuate segregation. "Government Blesses Separatism," *Crisis*, 50 (April 1943), 105.

56. Memorandum to White from Roy Wilkins, March 24, 1942, Stephen J. Spingarn Papers (Harry S. Truman Library, Independence).

57. Memorandum to Archibald MacLeish from Kane, Feb. 14, 1942; Bell to Embree, Feb. 23, 1942, OFF 002.11, Record Group 208. Some government agencies displayed timidity when it came to a subject as controversial as the race question. Jonathan Daniels, Assistant Director in Charge of Civilian Mobilization, Office of Civilian Defense, urged the creation of a Division of American Unity within the OCD, but his superiors decided Negro morale was "too hot a potato." Memoranda to

James Landis, April 1, 7, 1942; Daniels to Howard W. Odum, Aug. 24, 1942, Jonathan Daniels Papers (University of North Carolina).

58. "Reports from the Special Services Division Submitted April 23, 1942: Negro Organizations and the War Effort"; Cornelius Golightly, "Negro Morale in Boston," Special Services Division Report No. 7, May 19, 1942; Special Services Division Report No. 5, May 15, 1942: "Negro Conference at Lincoln University"; Special Services Division Memorandum, "Report on Recent Factors Increasing Negro-White Tension," Nov. 2, 1942. All are in OFF and OWI files in Record Group 44.

59. "Intelligence Report: White Attitudes Toward Negroes," OWI, Bureau of Intelligence, Aug. 5, 1942; same title dated July 28, 1942, Record Group 44. Hazel Gaudet Erskine, "The Polls: Race Relations," *Public Opinion Quarterly*, XXVI (Spring 1962), 137–148.

60. Robert E. Park, "Racial Ideologies," William Fielding Ogburn, ed., *American Society In Wartime* (Chicago, 1943), 174.

61. Howard W. Odum, *Race and Rumors of Race: Challenge to American Crisis* (*Chapel Hill*, 1943), 7; for a similar view, see Johnson, *To Stem This Tide*, 67–68, 73, 89–107, 113, 117.

62. John Temple Graves, "The Southern Negro and the War Crisis," *Virginia Quarterly Review*, 18 (Autumn 1942), 500–517; Clark Foreman, "Race Tension in the South," *New Republic*, 107 (Sept. 21, 1942), 340–342.

63. Alfred McClung Lee and Norman Daymond Humphrey, *Race Riot* (New York, 1943); Carey McWilliams, "Race Tensions: Second Phase," *Common Ground*, IV (Autumn 1943), 7–12.

64. Rayford W. Logan, ed., *What the Negro Wants* (Chapel Hill, 1944).

65. Memorandum to White from Wilkins, March 23, 1942, Spingarn Papers; Pittsburgh *Courier*, March 28, 1942; Norfolk *Journal and Guide*, March 28, 1942.

66. "U. S. A. Needs Sharp Break With the Past," *Crisis*, 49 (May 1942), 151.

67. "A Statement to the President of the United States Concerning the Present World Crisis by Negro Church Leaders Called by the Executive Committee of the Fraternal Council of Negro Churches of America," Feb. 17, 1942; McIntyre to MacLean, Chairman of the President's Committee on Fair Employment Practice, Feb. 19, 1942, OF 93, Roosevelt Papers.

68. Memorandum to the Attorney General from the President, Aug. 26, 1942, OF 93, *ibid.*

69. Franklin Roosevelt's conservative and "leave well enough alone" attitude toward Negro rights is discussed in Arthur M. Schlesinger, Jr., *The Age of Roosevelt: The Politics of Upheaval* (Boston, 1960), 431; Frank Freidel, *F. D. R. and the South* (Baton Rouge, 1965), 73, 81,

97; Mary McLeod Bethune, "My Secret Talks with F. D. R.," *Ebony*, IV (April 1949), 42–51. Perhaps Roosevelt's conservative attitude is responsible for his privately expressed dislike of the NAACP. In 1943 Arthur B. Spingarn, president of the NAACP, asked him to write a letter praising the twenty-five years of service by White to that organization. On one version of the proposed letter there is an attached note which reads: "Miss Tully brought this in. Says the President doesn't think too much of this organization—not to be to[o] fullsome—tone it down a bit." Roosevelt to Spingarn, Oct. 1, 1943, PPF 1226, Roosevelt Papers.

70. Roosevelt to Embree, March 16, 1942, in answer to Embree to Roosevelt, Feb. 3, 1942, OF 93, Roosevelt Papers. In his covering letter to the President's secretary, Embree emphasized that his proposed commission should address itself to the problem of race around the world as well as at home: "A serious weakness both in America and among the united nations is the low morale of the 'colored peoples' to whom this war is being pictured as simply another struggle of the white man for domination of the world. This condition is becoming acute among the Negro group at home and among important allies abroad, especially the Chinese and the residents of Malaya, the East Indies, and the Philippines." Embree to McIntyre, Feb. 3, 1942, Commission on Race and Color folder, Rosenwald Fund Papers.

71. In June 1943, Embree and John Collier, Commissioner of Indian Affairs, developed an idea for a committee established by the President "to assume special responsibility in implementing the Bill of Rights of the Constitution, particularly in defending racial minorities at a time of crisis." Memorandum to Johnson and Alexander from Embree, June 16, 1943, Race Relations folder, Rosenwald Fund Papers. See also John Collier and Saul K. Padover, "An Institute for Ethnic Democracy," *Common Ground*, IV (Autumn 1943), 3–7, for a more elaborate proposal.

Embree probably passed along his idea to Odum of the University of North Carolina so that he could discuss it with a fellow North Carolinian in the White House, Daniels, administrative assistant to the President. Odum and Daniels had a conference in August 1943 from which emerged a recommendation for a "President's Committee on Race and Minority Groups." Odum to Daniels, Aug. 23, 1943; Memorandum to Daniels from Odum, Aug. 30, 1943, Howard W. Odum Papers (University of North Carolina).

Although Daniels apparently gave Odum the impression that he was interested in a national committee, this was not the case. "It has been suggested that a committee of prominent men be named to study this situation," he wrote the President. "I am sure the naming of such a committee would not now halt the procession of angry outbreaks which are occurring. I doubt that any report could be made which would be so effective as a statement now from you would be. I am very much afraid, indeed, that any committee report would only serve as a new ground for controversy." Memorandum to the President from Daniels, Aug. 2, 1943, Daniels Papers. Roosevelt apparently agreed with Daniels, and Odum was informed that "My boss does not think well of the idea that we discussed." Daniels to Odum, Sept. 1, 1943, Odum Papers.

Daniels' appointment as White House coordinator of information on race relations was actually suggested by him to the President in June 1943. Memorandum to the President from Daniels, June 29, 1943, Daniels Papers. By July 1943, Roosevelt had approved of the new role for his administrative assistant, and Daniels was hard at work gathering information. Daniels to Secretary of War Stimson, July 28, 1943, ASW 291.2, Record Group 335.

72. "Stimson Diary," June 24, 1943.

# 7 | The "Impossible" Candidate

*Benjamin Davis*

When, in 1943, my candidacy for the New York City Council on the Communist ticket was announced, the press was unanimous in declaring my election impossible. For entirely different reasons, some of my friends joined them. The difficulties were considered insurmountable.

Shortly after I was designated as a candidate by the Manhattan County Committee of the Communist Party, I telephoned my father in Atlanta to inform him of my nomination. I had run for office before on the Communist ticket; consequently my father was not inclined to attach any special importance to this particular instance. But I assured him that this was different—this time I was going to win. An old hand in politics, too worldly-wise to be moved by youthful enthusiasm, he replied:

"Son, this election is going to be like all the rest. Remember the time you ran for District Attorney or something on the Communist ticket? Well, you didn't get elected then; and you won't be elected this time. You Communists are always running for offices, but you never catch them. The day of your party hasn't come yet."

But the impossible happened. I was elected. The opposition and its two-party machine were shocked and dismayed. They had already had to swallow the bitter pill of the election of Peter V. Cocchione, Brooklyn Communist leader, in 1941, and they had hoped to get rid of him in 1943. Instead, they were now faced with two Communists in the city council.

My friends and supporters were jubilant. My election was another high-water mark in the achievement of the labor-Negro people's progressive coalition. Independent political action had scored a signal victory. And the Negro people of Harlem, demonstrating tremendous political maturity, had fired a shot that was heard not only in the share-cropper's cabin in Mississippi, but in the trenches in Europe and the Far East. It was, above all, a victory for unity behind our country's patriotic, national war to defeat the Rome-Berlin-Tokyo axis.

The combination of circumstances and relationships which had led to this triumph had thrust upon me the honor of being the first Negro Communist elected to office in the history of the United States. While I regarded it as a great distinction and an unprecedented opportunity, uppermost in my mind was the feeling of responsibility. My task was not only to advance the movement which alone could improve the jim-crow conditions imposed upon my community in Harlem, but also to make the whole of New York City a better place for the people. There was no contradiction, but rather a dynamic unity, between the two.

A part of the campaign against me was that I would never get elected because I had two strikes against me. I was a Negro and a Communist. An amusing incident as to this "deadly" combination occurred when I called my father the night I was elected. He thought it was a gag and wouldn't believe me. I finally gave up—I knew how stubborn father could be, especially when he had predicted another outcome.

The next morning I got a call from him. Excited and happy, he exclaimed: "Son, I guess you were right. I see there's a headline in the paper here which says 'Black Red elected in New York. White Yankees vote for him.'"

My father represented a link between the period of the struggle for Negro rights in which he had lived and fought and another stage of this struggle in which I was living and fighting. He still was inclined to think his period would last forever, and still believed pretty much, as did Frederick Douglass, that "the Republican Party was the ship, and all else was the sea." He found it difficult to acknowledge the beginning of another era. Before he died, however, he had become somewhat reconciled to the inevitable; he even went so far as to completely forgive my abandonment 28 years earlier of the comfortable and lucrative bourgeois career he had arranged for me.

The reaction of the Atlanta paper was a small measure of the shock sustained by the bourgeoisie. The New York *Herald Tribune* sought to explain my election on the basis of my "personal following." Other papers and bourgeois experts on elections said it was a political accident.

Often in my campaign I would share with the audience the episodes involving my father. They never failed to get a big laugh, especially when there were many Southern-born Negroes among the listeners. For they were intimately acquainted with the utterly absurd—as well as murderous—forms that white supremacy could take in the deep South. Sometimes I would use the description of me as a "Black Red" to answer the favorite argument of A. Philip Randolph, the Social-Democratic Negro labor leader: "Why should the Negro add to the handicap of being Black, the handicap of being Red?"

Far from considering it a handicap to be a Negro and a Communist simultaneously, I considered it a double weapon against the ruling class. An American Negro has a background of 300 years of oppression in this country, and great indeed is the Negro's anger. When that same Negro is a Communist, he is equipped with a science—Marxism-Leninism—which alone can help realize his 300-year aspiration for freedom and equality.

In 1943, the only Negro member of the city council was Adam Clayton Powell, Jr., who had been elected as the first Negro member in 1941. He had been elected pretty much as an independent, securing designations from the City Fusion Party, the American Labor Party and the Democratic Party. He was the symbol of the progressive people's coalition in the city. This was the dramatic start of Powell's political power as an independent, when he first proclaimed his motto: "I will wear no man's collar." He was swept into office in 1941 on the crest of a wave of demands by the Negro people and their supporters for representation in the city legislature. His election was made possible technically by Proportional Representation, which had become the law of the city under the new Charter adopted in 1936.

Powell was a powerful orator, dramatic and colorful, and capable of manipulating the emotions of his audience. A shrewd politician, he had the gift of sensing the popular yearnings and trends of the masses, which he voiced as their leader. His church, the Abyssinian Baptist, built by his father, was famous as the largest in the United States, numbering 15,000 members. A wealthy institution, its members were very politically and nationally alert, and constituted a formidable election machine.

As the chief executive functionary of the Harlem Communist Party, I had a deep concern in having the community retain the seat held in trust, as it were, by Councilman Powell. I had heard that he did not intend to run for re-election but, putting no stock in rumors, I decided to have a personal talk with him. We had a long discussion, a friendly one, but not successful, on the question of the city council. He said, in effect, that he had already announced his candidacy for congress in

1942. The new congressional district which made it possible to elect a Negro representative from Harlem had been carved out in 1941, and Powell was determined to be the first Negro congressman from that district.

I placed the issues squarely before him, giving the point of view of my party, namely, that it was incumbent upon the progressive forces of the community to do everything possible to guarantee the retention by a Negro of the seat he now held and, if at all possible, to elect an additional Negro. I emphasized that we were faced with the prospect of losing the one place in the council, and that would amount to a set-back of such proportions as to damage the united struggles of the Negro people. I asked him to reconsider his decision not to run and, failing that, to assist in establishing unity around a progressive Negro candidate of independence and integrity who would be worthy of support.

Powell declined on both scores. He stated that to run for re-election to the city council in 1943 and then to make the race for congress in 1944 was more than he could bear either physically or financially, and that he considered it best to relinquish his position in the council in order to prepare for the congressional race in 1944. On the second point, he preferred a hands-off policy.

This was late spring of 1943 and time was passing rapidly. It would be no easy or simple matter to achieve Harlem unity around a candidate who could win and there was not much time left. I had heard that Dr. Channing Tobias was considering the race and made an appointment with him at his offices in the YMCA headquarters on Madison Avenue. He was, of course, neither as militant nor as close to the man on the street as Powell, although he was pro-labor and had associated himself on various occasions with the progressive coalition. He would have made a good candidate at that time; he was part of the Roosevelt coalition among the Negro people in a vague sort of way. He was a typical liberal, but I was not looking for a Communist candidate but one around whom the broadest unity of the Negro people and labor could be achieved in this specific situation.

When I placed the question before him, he respectfully declined, on the ground that he wanted to remain independent politically and had no desire for public office.

I finally went to Dr. George Cannon, who later became the chairman of the non-partisan committee for my election. Although he declined to run, he helped in every way, calling conferences, having personal chats with friends, trying to convince representative Negroes to run.

George Cannon was an able physician and surgeon who had not lost any of his youthful passion against jim-crow. He would not sacrifice his militant views to further his medical career, and although he was a Roosevelt Democrat, he did not quail at my Communist convictions, but rather believed that if a cause was worthy, people should not permit political or other differences to prevent them from supporting it.

Nevertheless, the problem had not been solved. The nominations for the city council by all parties had been made, but no representative Negro from Harlem had been nominated. The Democrats had not nominated a Negro. Even the Negro Tammany leaders in the community were up in arms. They felt they had been put in a very bad position before the Negro people, upon whom they depended in the election district for the Democratic vote. Many of them protested and showed their disapproval but without going so far as breaking with the Tammany machine.

Our Harlem Communist Party surveyed the situation, consulted with Negro and labor leaders. My own conversations with various Negro spokesmen demonstrated that all felt that the place in the council must not be lost. They felt that the failure of the two major parties to designate a candidate of the community's choice should be exposed during the campaign. Our party had nominated a candidate, Carl Brodsky, well known in labor and progressive circles. He offered to withdraw in my favor and to permit the party to substitute my name for his as candidate on the Communist ticket. After due consideration, the county committee made the switch and my name was substituted for Brodsky's within the time permitted by the law. This decision was based upon the record of our Harlem party among the Negro people, their response to its program, and on the basis of our contact with the community. At least, I was an integral part of the people's coalition in Harlem, had shared in their struggles and activities, and had been accepted as one of their recognized spokesmen. Moreover, as my election proved, our party had correctly judged the desires and sentiment of the Negro people and their white supporters as well.

The honor of my designation as the Communist candidate belonged rightfully not to me but to the people from whom I sprang. Whatever spark of determination I possessed in the struggle was instilled in me by the hardihood of my people in resisting oppression in America, Africa, the West Indies and wherever black men fight to live. I had seen that same flame burn in my father; a little of it burns in every

Negro, if he does not permit it to be extinguished by violence or intimidation, or if he does not deny it for a mess of pottage.

Carl Brodsky was truly a representative of the Jewish people. In withdrawing in my favor, under circumstances in which the Jewish people needed a representative in the City Council, he demonstrated the close bonds of cooperation that could exist between the Jewish and Negro people. His action was a warm, human and generous symbol of recognition on the part of progressive Jewish workers of their own profound stake in the cause of Negro liberation.

It was not only I who was deeply impressed; this dramatic and genuine demonstration of solidarity was not lost among the people of Harlem. Although Brodsky spent most of his time during the campaign trying to win the lower East Side Jewish workers to my support, he would occasionally come to Harlem, often speaking on the same platform with me. He would receive a rousing ovation from the people.

The tremendous vote I received from the Jewish community was one of the highlights of my election. I was told by experienced election campaigners that my name had become as familiar as one of their own, and that never before had a Negro candidate received such a high percentage of votes in a white neighborhood.

The metropolitan newspapers merely noted the fact that I had been substituted for Carl Brodsky. I was listed along with the candidates of the other parties. After this, there ensued a conspiracy of silence in these papers; the bourgeois election experts and commentators paid me no mind. I didn't have a chance, according to them, so why waste printer's ink? Tammany paid no serious attention to my candidacy; nor did the Republicans. This attitude even affected the people in my own ranks. Many friends said, "Yes, you'll make a good campaign, a very fine one indeed; but you won't be elected—too many odds against you. Besides, the two party machines are too strong; if you look as though you might become a serious threat, they'll pour in thousands of dollars to defeat you," and so on, ad infinitum.

These friends and supporters were not the only ones with serious doubts. Some of my own comrades were skeptical. They were only a small minority among the party membership, still their views deserved serious consideration. They doubted that the estimate of a possible victory was correct, although during the campaign they worked with great skill and energy; I would have liked to have had more "skeptics" like them. Such differences illustrate a cardinal distinction of our party—a working class organization operating on the principle of democratic centralism. Once a decision was made it was binding and carried out by all members alike. Some of these skeptics pointed out that a Communist councilmanic candidate in Manhattan had never received more than 13,000 votes, and in Harlem no more than 5,000 votes. They estimated that I would have to receive almost twice the number of votes in the trade union and progressive white areas that a Communist candidate had ever received in the whole of Manhattan under the best circumstances. Furthermore, the campaign was late and I had only a bare six weeks. Other arguments were that any attempt to shoot for victory would tax our organization too heavily and run the danger of not securing the re-election of Councilman Cacchione in Brooklyn. Still others held that I should aim to secure enough second-choice votes to elect the ALP candidate, which would be a big advance since Manhattan had never had a labor councilman.

These arguments could not be brushed aside willy-nilly. They proved to be very valuable in pitching and focusing the campaign and in touching up weak points. Besides, these exchanges of opinion were part of the thorough way in which our party considered all angles of a problem and then charted its course. It was this same Marxist consideration of many-sided factors that led to the election victory and rallied and strengthened our ranks.

All the doubts expressed by the skeptics failed to dent my enthusiasm. My campaign staff and I prepared to involve all these friends, not in a "very fine" campaign, but in a winning one. I was buoyed up by the fact of Pete Cacchione's election in 1941. What was basically new in the situation was the tremendous upsurge among the Negro masses and the unprecedented support they were receiving from white workers—particularly from the CIO, but also from the AFL—as well as from white intellectuals, artists, progressives, liberals. The Negro people, wholeheartedly supporting the war against fascist-racism abroad, were demanding more and more earnest of eventual victory at home. Their democratic aspirations were released under the impetus of the anti-fascist war. The war, under Roosevelt's leadership, brought forward the most democratic and progressive traditions of our country. What was apparent here was the possibility of a qualitative leap forward for the Negro people and for independent political action. It had to be grasped then or it would be lost.

The circumstances that had dictated my nomination also shaped my campaign, which was pitched upon the theme of winning the war and demonstrating against Hitler racism by advancing the cause of

Negro representation at home. In the local and city program were: the banning of jim-crow in Stuyvesant Town, the appointment of a Negro on the Board of Education, a public market for Harlem, the end of police brutality, rent and price controls, slum clearance, the enforcement and expansion of the multiple dwelling laws, and the outlawing of all forms of racial discrimination, anti-Semitism, jim-crow and segregation.

But I was also running on the Communist ticket. It was my duty and responsibility, as well as my privilege, to explain to the voters why I was running on that ticket, what the Communist Party stood for and why I was a member. If I couldn't trust the people, why should they trust me? I did not believe in hiding "the light of Marxism-Leninism" under a bushel. It was necessary to point out that though I had backers of other parties in my corner, I nevertheless was a Communist whose program went much farther than the present election campaign; that I believe in socialism and would ever strive for its triumph at home.

My campaign spread like wildfire. Overnight the nonpartisan committee for my election leaped from about 50 to approximately 2,000 —a real cross-section of ministers, doctors, lawyers, businessmen, trade unionists, social leaders, women, youth, foreign-born, native-born, workers, artists—indeed, people from every conceivable stratum of life. The committee became so large and unwieldy that it had to divide up into smaller committees. The major power in these committees and among the campaign workers were the Negro masses and the trade unionists. The accomplishments of our party, which numbered less than 2,000, were nothing short of miraculous. Only hard work, devotion and skill—climbing six and seven flights of stairs, tramping the streets in the roughest weather, seeing ministers, arranging conferences, holding street meetings, distributing literature, and so on— could achieve such "miracles."

Resolutions of endorsement and support soon began to pour in from unions, churches, groups of almost every description. Friends in the deep South, especially from Atlanta, sent long public statements of good wishes, accompanied by donations. Soldiers in the trenches sent best wishes. The campaign took on an international aspect. The two Harlem Negro weeklies reflected in as much space as they dared to give the snowballing character of the campaign.

A group of artists and layout experts produced excellent campaign literature. An enterprising chap even got hold of an old Amherst year-

book of my class (1925)—from an unsuspecting Wall Street classmate
—and reproduced my entire college career in pictures. My campaign
literature was of "printer's excellence"; even experienced Democrats
and Republicans wanted to know whether they could borrow my layout staff—"for a price," of course. They were amazed to find that not
everyone was for sale. Many of the people of Harlem wanted certain
campaign pieces as ornaments for their walls.

We held street rallies at the liveliest corners in Harlem, in the garment workers' district, before union and people's organizations in the
course of their regular meetings. It was impressive to see the revolutionary tradition of the Negro church assert itself during the campaign.
They became bulwarks of support to my campaign. Ministers invited
me to speak "for a few minutes" at their 11 o'clock Sunday morning
religious services.

The campaign was becoming irresistible; the smell of victory was in
the air. Councilman Powell was now ready to take his stand. He issued
a statement declaring that I was the "worthy successor" to his seat
in the city council, and called upon his supporters and friends to vote
for me. Accurately gauging the enthusiasm of the campaign, the Non-
Partisan Committee decided on a rally in Golden Gate Ballroom—a
mammoth auditorium in the center of Harlem, holding about 5,000
people.

A top price of $2.75 was placed on reserved seats and 50¢ on general
admission. "Who ever heard of charging for admission to an election
rally?" the doubting Thomases said. "Most candidates are only too
glad to get a full house, with free admission." But the committee
wouldn't be daunted.

There was scarcely a name brand or a popular entertainer who did
not volunteer their services. The Golden Gate was sold out ten days
before the rally. On the day of the event, the fire department closed
the hall two hours before the performance. When I appeared on the
scene, it was all I could do to get in. One of the more prominent artists
had to intercede with the police and fire department in my behalf.

Finally another 5,000 people had gathered outside the Golden Gate.
We decided to rent an additional hall about six blocks away. We then
routed the artists to this hall after their Golden Gate performance.

There were no speeches. Paul Robeson introduced me at both halls.
I told the audience that I was but a part in a cause much bigger than
any one of us and that we would struggle jointly until our country
and the world were rid of Hitler racism and all humankind could
live in dignity and walk in freedom.

This type of campaign rally was new, and we continued with it. At our street corner rallies we featured outstanding Negro and white artists. They performed with dignity, and they gave their talent because of their convictions.

In Harlem, support came from all sorts of quarters and for all sorts of reasons. A score or more old-timers who were Georgia-born supported me because they knew and admired my father. Some of them would slap me on the back and say: "Davis, your father was a Lincoln Republican. You must be a Lincoln Communist. I'm going to vote for you."

The large vote I received from the Porto Rican community was indispensable to my victory. During the campaign two things struck me with great force: First, that the Porto Rican community in lower Harlem, victimized by discrimination, had no representation whatever at any level of government*; second, that I could not speak Spanish. I resolved to do something to help correct both these conditions.

In the course of the five-week whirlwind campaign, the Communist Party had built a smooth and powerful people's election machine that cut across all party lines. It was based on the crusading spirit of the advanced trade unionists—the leaders of the working class. They had ties with thousands of families, churches and people's organization in Harlem and throughout the city. When they moved in their full strength, the whole community moved. Naturally, our heaviest concentration was in Harlem, for without a large base vote in Harlem, it was not possible to win.

When election day came, the trade unionists took over all our poll-watching assignments—most outstanding were the organized seamen, the furriers (CIO) and the food workers (AFL). Church women prepared hot coffee and sandwiches at various assembly spots on election day. Many elderly Negroes voted for the first time in their lives. As a candidate, I had the right to visit the polls—and I did. Whenever I walked in, there were cheers and assurances of victory.

The heaviest voting in New York City is done in the last two hours —between 5 and 7 P.M., the period when the workers are returning from their jobs. At about 4:30 P.M. the worst downpour of the season started. It lasted until about 8 P.M., an hour beyond the closing of the

---

* The so-called racial pattern of the United States must appear quite bewildering to the Porto Rican people. In New York they are jim-crowed and treated like Negroes. But here in Terre Haute federal penitentiary they are integrated with the white inmates, while the Negro is segregated. It shows the utter insanity of racism and discrimination.

polls. All we could do was hope. I continued to visit the polls even during the downpour and was surprised to see that the polling places were crowded. We took heart from this.

When the polls closed, our task had just begun. The count began next morning and was to last about eight days. These days seemed like years. To watch the count is a bewildering, nerve-wracking experience. One had to be on his toes against vote stealing, chicanery, every conceivable brand of trickery—as well as some honest errors. The Democrats and Republicans held all the official positions as counters, tellers, etc., and they did not want me to win. And it later appeared that they planned to count me out.

From the first day of the count, I was leading the field. Radio commentators blasted out that this was the upset of the election. Actually, they were counting those districts which included Harlem. But after the first two or three days, my vote began to level off as the count reached other parts of the city. I remained among the first three, however, and five were to be elected. It seemed that my election was assured. But then the stealing began in earnest. The votes for me began to disappear from my table, and the closest Tammany candidates began to congregate around my table, seeking to create an incident. We appealed to Mayor La Guardia, to the Honest Ballot Association, to every clean-government group. Statements were issued informing the public of the conspiracy to count me out.

On the fourth day Pete Cacchione, his own election in Brooklyn now assured, brought his entire staff over to the Manhattan court to assist me. Soon after he arrived, I discovered that some of my Harlem districts were missing and hadn't been counted. One of the ablest of our party election workers demanded a halt to the count, and demanded the right to search for the missing votes. He dug through the huge pile, district by district, and found not only the missing votes we knew of but also some unknown ones. In all, 1,500 votes had been stacked away, stolen right before our eyes. How perilous this was could be seen in the fact that I won by a little over 2,000 votes. It was a dramatic moment.

When, at the end of the long, gruelling count, my election was announced, every Negro in the Armory jumped up and yelled. They were to maintain their representation in the city council and white supremacy had taken a licking. The machine had been beaten. The wrath of an aroused electorate outweighed the fraud, deceit, corruption and vote-stealing of the party bosses. The unity of Negro and white had done the "impossible." History had been made.

Major party lines had been badly shattered. In the whole of Manhattan in 1943, there were not more than 6,000 Communists. My vote was more than 43,000. My election represented a qualitative leap forward for the Negro people, for the Negro-labor alliance and for our party. It was the result of years of conscientious and consistent work of the party in Harlem in the battles of the Negro people. And it went far beyond the state lines of New York, reflecting the leading role that Harlem plays in the political thinking of the Negro, nationally. From all over the country came messages of congratulations, greetings, best wishes. And I felt a sense of responsibility to the Negro people, nationally, and to fighters for Negro and colonial liberation all over the globe.

In this campaign for the City Council, as well as in my subsequent campaigns in 1945 and 1947, the dominant note was its people's character. By this I mean that my platform which was based upon the major issues facing the electorate was shaped in such a manner as to facilitate the coming together of the largest sector of the people in defense and extension of their all-around welfare. Republican and Democratic voters rallied to my support no less than independents. It was the difference between a narrow partisan campaign designed to reach primarily those who agreed with my Marxist socialist views, and a people's nonpartisan campaign designed to reach those who could unite on immediate issues such as housing, equality, police violence and civil liberties, irrespective of their party affiliation or long-range political perspective. The latter was especially adapted to Harlem, characterized by the all-people's character of the movement against the jim-crow ghetto system.

However, there was no contradiction between my being a Communist candidate and at the same time a people's candidate. The two supplemented each other. Moreover, only such an approach could guarantee Negro representation on the city council. Besides, living Marxism is itself the broadest approach to the mass of people, encompassing all who work by hand and brain. Since my party was part of the people's movement in its electoral coalition form, I could pledge support of the Communists to this broad people's platform. Some of my well-meaning supporters who were either Democrats or Republicans hoped I would stop there and go no further, fearing that an espousal of my views would frighten away voters. I rejected this view. Some agreed, others tried to reconcile themselves with my position; but none bolted. My campaigns were an excellent example of the united or people's front in which many forces work together on a common platform, even though they disagree on many other important questions.

At the same time, the foundation of my victorious campaign was the alliance of the Negro people and important sections of the labor movement. Upon this foundation was erected the structure of mass support among all sections of the population. The solid vote of Harlem was not enough to elect me; I needed the trade union and white progressive vote. That was shown clearly after the ALP candidate was counted out, when I received enough second-choice votes from him to assure my election by a comfortable margin.

It was significantly shown in the elections that among the Negro people there was a tremendous trend toward independent political action, toward breaking with the two-party system. They also showed great solidarity and a high degree of political maturity. Cacchione's vote was scattered widely over the Borough of Brooklyn, while my base vote was largely in a single community, which rebuffed solidly any red-baiting during the campaign.

Although our party received such a fine reception in Harlem it failed to become a mass party in that community. The basic requisites were present, except for one: the will to do so. As the leader of the party in Harlem, I was making one of the biggest mistakes in my political life. For I had become, no less than many other party leaders, deeply influenced by the revisionism of Browder, which led to the liquidation of the party as an independent working class force. Our party began to merge with the masses of militants and progressives, losing its own identity. True, the party had played a significant role by drawing together and leading the combination of forces that achieved my election and made possible continued Negro representation on the city council at a crucial moment when all other parties failed to meet the test. All the more pity that we failed to build a strong, mass party in Harlem.

Our campaign did make clear certain important characteristics of our party. My candidacy did not result from a careerist desire to run for office, as is generally the case with other parties. It was a response to the needs of the given situation—to guarantee that the Negro people should not lose their place on the city council. My nomination came only after the party had offered its full support to other candidates, none of whom were Communists but who merited the support of the Negro people and had a good chance of winning. In fact, it had not occurred to me that I might be the candidate.

The campaign also showed that only a progressive Negro candidate could serve as the symbol of unity. A conservative Negro spokesman identified with either of the major parties could not have united the Negro people. Such a candidate would have led to disunity, to certain defeat and to the loss of the council seat. The ruling class can unite only on a reactionary program, the working class only on a progressive one.

Thus, now the so-called unity of the CIO and AFL behind the pro-imperialist policies of the top labor leadership is a false facade. Badly confused and temporarily hogtied by the collaborationist policies of the officialdom, predominant sections of the labor movement are following the line of least resistance behind their treacherous leadership, although a significant section opposes these policies. On the other hand, a positive policy, clearly put before the rank and file and courageously fought for, together with further experiences in struggle, can eventually turn the tide. So much the better for America. Let us hope that this will happen in time—in time to avert the third world war and the catastrophe into which the ruling class, abetted by the top labor officialdom, is pushing the nation.

My electoral victory rested upon years of conscientious and consistent work of the Communist Party in Harlem in the struggles of the Negro people. Many gave their lives or served in prison, victims of police brutality, frame-ups or what have you. Progress seems slow and then, all at once, when conditions are ready, it takes a big leap forward. Communist open-air speakers were pelted with cabbages and tomatoes by Garveyites back in 1929, but a dozen years later even the neo-Garveyites joined in my campaign. It is always toward the qualitative leap forward that the Communist works, for it is only in this way that socialism can be established. There is no such thing as capitalism gradually growing into socialism. But the Communist also works, even at the risk of his life, to prevent a qualitative step backward. For this can mean only one thing—fascism, which in our country might well be worse than Hitlerism.

## 8 | How CORE Began

*August Meier*
*Elliott Rudwick*

The Congress of Racial Equality (CORE) first achieved national prominence as a result of the Freedom Ride to Alabama and Mississippi in 1961; but what is not so widely known is the fact that CORE—until 1965 the most interracial of all the nonviolent, direct action, civil rights organizations—is also the oldest of them. In this paper we will describe how CORE, with its ideology and program of nonviolence and interracialism, was founded a quarter of a century ago.

### ORIGINS AND IDEOLOGY

CORE was initiated in Chicago in the spring of 1942 by a small band of pacifists who were active members of the Fellowship of Reconciliation (FOR), a Christian pacifist organization established during World War I. They belonged to a wing within the fellowship which was intensely interested in social action and wished to apply Gandhian techniques of nonviolent direct action to the resolution of racial and industrial conflict in the United States. FOR was chiefly white, but it numbered several Negroes among its officials, even in the South, and had clearly exhibited a concern about race relations. It was not, however, until the activist A. J. Muste became co-secretary of FOR in 1940, that the fellowship encouraged experimentation with nonviolent, direct action projects.[1]

FOR members were organized, into units called "peace teams" or "cells"; and at the University of Chicago a cell devoted to race relations was formed in October, 1941. The cell had 10 or 12 members, at least three of whom were Negroes. Four of the six individuals who were

Reprinted from *Social Science Quarterly* 49 (March 1969): 789–799. By permission of *Social Science Quarterly* and August Meier.

largely responsible for the creation of CORE belonged to this race relations cell. The other two were staff members of FOR who worked out of the fellowship's Chicago office, maintained close relationships with the cell's members, and participated in its projects. It was from the activities of this race relations cell that the first CORE group, the Chicago Committee of Racial Equality, was born.[2]

Of the six figures whom we can appropriately call the founders of CORE, all but one had come to Chicago in the fall of 1941. Two, James Farmer and George Houser, had taken up their work with the Chicago FOR office in October. During the 1930's both had been prominent figures in Methodist student circles. Farmer, son of a professor at Methodist Wiley College in Texas, had received his B.D. from Howard University. There, as a student of the noted Negro Methodist pacifist and FOR Vice-Chairman Howard W. Thurman, he had become "deeply versed in Christian pacifist thinking." He had been working part-time as a FOR youth secretary when, in the summer of 1941, he accepted an appointment as the fellowship's race relations secretary.[3]

Houser, son of a Methodist minister, had attended Union Theological Seminary. In his third year there he was sentenced to prison for refusing to register under the Selective Service Act. After serving a year in Danbury Penitentiary he came to Chicago to complete his studies at the Chicago Theological Seminary and to work part-time as a field secretary for FOR.

Two other founders—Bernice Fisher and Homer Jack—were also divinity students at the University of Chicago. Both had been social activists in their student days in Rochester. Jack was studying for the Unitarian ministry. Miss Fisher, an active member of the Baptist Young People's Union, had long been interested in labor and race questions.

The remaining two founders were liberal arts students at the University of Chicago. Joe Guinn, a Chicago Negro, was head of the local NAACP Youth Council, and would later be imprisoned as a conscientious objector. James R. Robinson, a graduate student in English, was the only non-Protestant in the group. A Catholic from upstate New York, his interest in pacifism had been stimulated by reading the *Catholic Worker*, and he had been active in peace circles while an undergraduate at Columbia University. Later, as a conscientious objector, he served time in a CPS camp.[4]

Thus, not only were the six persons most responsible for founding CORE all pacifists, but three of them served terms in jail or CPS camp as conscientious objectors. Four were white, two were Negro. All were religiously oriented products of the Christian student movement of the

1930's, which had an ideological commitment to interracialism, pacifism, and industrial unionism. In a recent interview, one of the founders of CORE recalled that "the 1930's was the pacifist era," and that "the trend in pacifist-Christian circles was on nonviolence as an alternative to violence. It was natural that this was combined with Gandhi-ism." Thus it is noteworthy that the young people who, in their twenties, founded CORE had belonged to a respected, reformist segment of campus leaders in their college years. Unlike the majority of their Christian-pacist fellow students, however, they retained their earlier ideology even after the onset of World War II.

As heirs of the Christian radicalism of the 1930's, the founders of CORE were not only conscientious objectors to war, but exhibited their social idealism in other ways. Half were Socialists, and all of them favored industrial unions. They admired the direct action techniques of the sit-down strikers, and as Farmer expressed it, "similar instrumentalities for racial brotherhood in America must be developed." Indeed, when the sit-in technique was first invented, it was called a "sit-down."

The race relations cell met as a Saturday afternoon discussion group. Its two dominant personalities were James Robinson and Bernice Fisher. "All of us," Bernice Fisher recalled later, "were afire with the ideas of Gandhian nonviolence." The cell's members studied and debated, chapter by chapter, Shridharani's *War without Violence*, a description of Gandhi's philosophy and methods, and they discussed ways of adapting them to end American racism. Skeptical of the programs of the NAACP and Urban League and believing that, in Houser's words, discrimination "must be challenged directly, without violence or hatred, yet without compromise," the cell members regarded the Saturday afternoon meetings as preparation for real action.[5]

The first action emerged directly from their experiences as students. Negroes studying at the University of Chicago faced serious problems in finding housing in the neighborhood. Dr. Arthur Falls, a Negro physician and civic leader who became a valued adviser to Chicago CORE, was the first to describe to the youthful members the operation of the restrictive covenant system. The University itself was a party to the system that excluded Negroes from Woodlawn and Hyde Park. Disturbed by the housing situation, and inspired by the example of Gandhian cooperative communities, or "ashrams," of India, the race relations cell decided to establish an interracial men's cooperative, or Fellowship House, as a means of challenging the restrictive covenants in the university area. White members of the cell secured a six-month lease on an apartment, and in January, 1942 an interracial group of about a dozen men, including three or four Negroes, moved in. They regarded this action, uncontested by the owners (evidently because of the short term of the lease) as a successful example of nonviolent direct action against residential segregation.[6]

## LOOKING TOWARD A NATIONAL MOVEMENT

Farmer, although not a member of the cell, had been active in arranging the strategy for securing the Fellowship House and was one of its residents.[7] In the course of his speaking tours of midwestern colleges and southern Negro campuses, Farmer wrestled with the problem of developing a nonviolent, direct action approach to race relations. In February and March, in two memoranda addressed to A. J. Muste and the FOR National Council, he outlined his proposal for a "brotherhood mobilization." Farmer called for a nationwide organization to be started, using FOR cells as nuclei, but to be autonomous and to include non-pacifists. He anticipated that in 5 or 10 years it might become a mass movement. It would be based upon Gandhian principles of love, nonviolence, and non-cooperation. Farmer's proposal reflected a distrust of the capitalist system, urged the formation of consumers and producers cooperatives to finance the mobilization, and even exhibited a Gandhian predilection for handicraft industries. Finally the proposal combined elitist assumptions with plans for a mass movement. Realizing that all persons would not be equally dedicated, Farmer recommended three classes of membership, ranging from a broad base of those who would lend general support to the aims of the movement to the few who would engage, at the appropriate time, in the most extreme forms of civil disobedience.[8]

The FOR National Council approved Farmer's memoranda, and the race relations cell discussed them at length.[9] Nevertheless Farmer's memoranda and the cell's activities were parallel and converging, rather than causally related, developments.[10] Farmer's proposal was part of the general ferment in FOR regarding race relations, and was the first suggestion for a *national* nonviolent, direct action organization to fight race discrimination. Moreover there were some notable parallels between Farmer's proposal and CORE as it actually emerged. These involved using FOR members as a nucleus for an organization including non-pacifists, and CORE's elitist distinction between active members and the less dedicated associate members.

In March, 1942 the cell created an informal preliminary organizing committee.[11] After several meetings the committee decided first to establish a "concrete action project" and then to create an organization. The project utilized was an attack upon discrimination at the White City Roller Rink. Located in a changing neighborhood, the rink excluded Negroes in violation of the state civil rights law on the fictitious grounds that it was a private club. One evening early in April, a group of 24 cell members and friends, including Farmer, sought admission to the rink and disproved the private-club claim, for while Negro and mixed contingents were excluded, all-white ones were admitted. On the basis of this experience a committe was appointed to visit the rink manager.[12]

By today's standards this action seems inconsequential, yet it produced considerable excitement among the participants and their friends. Stimulated by this enthusiasm, 50 people met in late April to form "a permanent interracial group committed to the use of non-violent direct action opposing discrimination." Bernice Fisher became the first chairman.[13]

## CHARTER MEMBERS

Of these charter members, consisting of 22 women and 28 men, we have been able to secure data on 39. They were primarily unmarried people in their early twenties. Of the 39, 12 were Negroes, 26 were white, and 1 was of mixed Japanese and white ancestry. Most of the whites were university students, mainly at the Federated Theological Seminary at the University of Chicago. Most of the Negroes were college graduates, engaged in white-collar jobs. The overwhelming majority of members were Christian. Ironically, in view of the important role Jews have had in the twentieth century civil rights movement, and particularly in CORE, only three or four of the charter members were Jews. The Christian-pacifist orientation of FOR, and the exodus of Jews from the pacifist movement because of the war against Nazi Germany, served to limit Jewish participation. Of the 39, about half were definitely pacifist—3 of the 12 Negroes and 15 or 16 of the 26 whites. Thus, as Bernice Fisher later emphasized, "There was never a time when CORE was composed only of philosophical pacifists." Nevertheless, the role of the pacifist nucleus was critical. In addition to founding the group, pacifists held most of the offices during the Chicago CORE's early years, and decisively influenced its philosophy and style.[14]

While the whites of early CORE were more likely than the Negroes to be pacifists, the Negroes were more likely to be active in the traditional civil rights organizations. Of the three charter members identified as being active with either the NAACP or Urban League, all were Negroes. Thus, even at this early date, CORE showed something of a tendency to attract different types of persons from each race, foreshadowing later trends and cleavages within the organization. The whites tended to be wide-ranging social idealists, often as much interested in the nonviolent means as in the racial egalitarian goals to which they were also passionately dedicated. The Negroes, on the other hand, tended more often to be concerned solely with destroying discrimination, and to be interested in nonviolent direct action not on ideological grounds but as a practical technique to achieve their goal.

Thus began this small, interracial, nonviolent, direct action group, led by a nucleus of FOR members. In one sense, early CORE was an elitist organization. From the start, members were required to be well versed in the principles of nonviolent philosophy, to be active in some phase of the organization's work, and to accept the "CORE Action Discipline," which set forth (in leaflet form) the modified Gandhian methods by which CORE worked. All this was in direct contrast to the NAACP, where a dollar contribution made one a full-fledged member for a year, without requiring active participation.

Internally, CORE functioned as a small, highly democratic, tightly knit group that absorbed much of the time and energies of its members. The "Statement of Purpose" and the "CORE Action Discipline," which were adopted at an early date, directed members to "commit themselves to work as an integrated, disciplined group," and provided that "all decisions on general policy shall be arrived at only through democratic group discussion." As Bernice Fisher later recalled, "Democracy became almost an obsession. Hours of debate consumed every meeting." Democratic functioning was facilitated both by frequent meetings and by holding elections every two or three months. Gradually, over a period of half a year or so, an organizational structure evolved. Each active member was expected to serve on at least one of the group's committees or one of the action units. These units, the real heart of the organization, were three in number, devoted to investigating and planning action against discrimination (1) in schools and hospitals, (2) in housing, and (3) in places of public accommodation. Ordinarily a member would attend a meeting each week—either of the group as a whole or of his committee or his action unit. There was constant discussion of philosophy and program and, except in emergency, any

action taken had to be approved by the membership as a whole.[15] Thus
there developed a decentralized, yet cohesive, group of about 20 to
25 active members. For such people, as was often said of the more
dynamic CORE chapters in later years, CORE had become a way
of life.

## RATIONALE, PURPOSES, AND PROCEDURES

Gandhian nonviolence and interracial action were the twin ideological beliefs underpinning CORE's organizational structure. As the
"CORE Action Discipline" declared, the nonviolent method "confronts
injustice without fear, without compromise, and without hate." CORE
literature expressed the belief that direct action should always be accompanied by a spirit of good will toward the discriminator, a frame
of mind calculated to change not only his action, but his attitudes as
well. As Bernice Fisher put it, "Reading 'War without Violence' was a
prerequisite in the early days. We adhered seriously to the steps of
Satyagraha."

The leaders also articulated the religious foundations of their belief
in nonviolence. Bernice Fisher once wrote, "As a young Christian I had
been caught up with the idea that we should live life now as if the
Kingdom of God were at hand. . . . To many of us [nonviolence] was
a philosophy of life." Farmer asserted that "At the very foundation of
the pacifist philosophy is the Jewish-Christian faith in the universal
community," a faith which "urges that putting an end to racial discrimination become one of our major emphases."

Beyond the philosophical argument there was a practical justification for interracial, nonviolent direct action. As the "CORE Action
Discipline" put it, nonviolent direct action "assumes that it is suicidal
for a minority group to use violence, since to use it would simply result
in complete control and subjugation by the majority group." To Farmer
and other CORE leaders, nonviolent direct action was the only
alternative to the ineffectiveness of the traditional organizations.

If nonviolence was one cornerstone of the early CORE ideology,
interracialism was the other. As the CORE "Statement of Purpose"
succinctly put it, "CORE has one method—interracial, non-violent
direct action." CORE members were exceedingly ambivalent in their
attitudes toward what was, at the time, a more celebrated example of
a nonviolent direct action movement—the deliberately all-Negro March
on Washington movement of A. Philip Randolph. Farmer believed that
the religious pacifist faith in the universal community required the

eschewing of anything that "smacks of racial chauvinism." He maintained that "no great and oppressive evil can ever be truly wiped out
until those oppressed by that evil, in collaboration with men of conscience everywhere, refuse cooperation with its oppression." Among
the whites, no one expressed the ideology of interracialism more pun-
gently than Bernice Fisher. As she recollected, "One of our motivations
had been the determination that there should be a thoroughly interracial organization . . . not another Negro group with a token membership of whites." Fisher took her interracialism so seriously that it
became a central part of her life. She joined the church of the minister-
politician Archibald Carey, Jr., pastor of Woodlawn AME Church,
who became one of CORE's most prominent backers in Chicago. She
recalled that "Negro block voting to us was anathema . . . the building
up of the myth of differences." Once, when a noted Negro cleric spoke
of his pride in the historic heroes of the race, she "indignantly claimed
the equal right to be proud of them as a part of the human race. Negro
History Week seemed mere chauvinism. . . . My avowed intention was
to fight for the time that race would be a term of importance only to
anthropologists."[16]

Chicago CORE developed a procedure that was an adaptation of
Gandhian techniques to the American scene. Gandhi's method was to
start with an attempt to convert the opponent through negotiations,
and then successively move on to more militant actions. Thus, if negotiations failed, agitation was employed to arouse public opinion as a
means of putting pressure on the evildoer. Next, if this did not succeed,
came parades and other forms of colorful demonstrations, and eventually an ultimatum threatening more radical actions. Before undertaking
these radical steps the Satyagrahis would undergo rites of prayer and
fasting to purify themselves of the share of the guilt for the existence
of evil practices, arising from their previous failure to resist them.
Then came picketing, strikes, boycotts, and sit-downs. Finally, if all
else failed, out-right civil disobedience was employed. Throughout,
the Satyagrahis would seek to love their opponents and refrain from
committing violence, no matter what the provocation, even if this
meant accepting death. The Chicago Committee of Racial Equality
(CORE), in adapting this procedure, omitted certain items in the
series. Because of the organization's small membership, parades survived only as occasional "poster walks." Rites of self-purification were
discarded as inapplicable to the American scene. Civil disobedience
was a subject of discussion, but it is nowhere mentioned in the CORE
literature. Possibly this was because CORE was fighting business firms,

not the government. On other points CORE followed Gandhi rather faithfully, and the "Action Discipline" stressed the importance of acting without malice and in a "spirit of good will and creative reconciliation," submitting to assault without retaliating in kind.[17]

## EARLY EFFORTS IN CHICAGO

The Chicago Committee of Racial Equality in its first year attacked discrimination on several fronts. "Good will" failed the members in the White City case. After considerable discussion, they took the matter to court, only to find their skepticism about legal action justified by the judge's unfavorable decision.[18] "Good will" proved more successful when the men living in the second Fellowship House, established in the fall of 1942, were haled into court. Because of the friendly attitude which the co-op's members displayed toward their neighbors, the real estate agent found it impossible to obtain witnesses to testify that Negroes lived in the apartment.[19] Other activities included a successful effort to end discrimination at the University of Chicago barbershop,[20] and the beginning of a campaign against discrimination at the university's hospital and medical school.[21] Restaurant discrimination, however, was the area that proved "the most important and time-consuming."[22]

The majority of Chicago restaurants observed the state civil rights law, but CORE found some that did not, most notably the Jack Spratt Restaurant at 47th Street, near the Fellowship House, and Stoner's, downtown in the Loop. In both cases CORE strove to negotiate and change the minds of the management in a spirit of Gandhian good will. Both proprietors proved adamant, however. Interracial groups visiting the restaurant received a hostile reception. Sometimes they were served at Jack Spratt's, but in an uncivil manner, and once the dishes Negroes had used were smashed by the manager. Stoner adopted a policy of seating the test groups after a long wait, and then serving them, as George Houser reported, "meat with egg shells scattered on it, or a plate of food salted so heavily that it could not be eaten, or a sandwich composed of tomato and lettuce cores picked out of the garbage can. . . ."[23]

Negotiations having failed, CORE, following Shridharani's outline, undertook to mobilize public opinion against Stoner's through agitation. For one entire week in December, 1942, CORE members passed out leaflets to Stoner patrons, asking them to protest the discrimination as they paid their bills. Accused of "picking on" Stoner's, CORE investigated the policies of other downtown restaurants, and circulated its findings in a leaflet entitled "50 Loop Restaurants which do not Discriminate."[24] In January, four months after the start of the Stoner campaign, CORE justified its lengthy procedure and suggested that it was about to pass on to the next stage of the Gandhian method. It announced that "we are an action group, and within the month the investigation will grow into the demanding of justice from any restaurant with such undemocratic policies yet unremedied. Remember technique! . . . Gather facts, Negotiate. Rouse public opinion, and then, if absolutely necessary, and only as a last resort, Take Direct Action. . . ."[25]

Finally, two months later in March, 1943, CORE decided to try a sit-down at Stoner's, but it quickly became evident that CORE was too small to successfully adapt this technique of the industrial unions to a restaurant seating over 200 persons. Thus it was decided to delay the attack until the June planning conference for a national federation on nonviolent, direct action groups would bring enough participants into the city. Accordingly the first sit-in took place at Jack Spratt's, which accommodated only 40 people. Twenty-one CORE members entered on a Saturday in May just at the dinner hour; together with the regular patrons they filled the premises. When white CORE members "politely but firmly" refused to eat until the Negroes were served, the manager called the police, who announced that they could do nothing. Some of the other white patrons followed the example of the white CORE members and declined to eat until the Negroes were served. Finally, two hours after the sit-in began, the manager took the orders from the mixed groups, and the first CORE sit-in ended successfully.[26] The demonstration at Stoner's in early June, in which the out-of-town delegates participated, followed a similar pattern.[27]

The contrast between CORE's method in these first sit-ins and the character of the direct action of the 1960's is obvious and profound. Farmer has written:

> When I look back at that first sit-in, I am amazed at our patience and good faith. No action group today would prolong the attempts at negotiation for more than a month before finally deciding to demonstrate. No militant Negro today would dream of trying to persuade a manager to serve him on the grounds that Negro patronage would not be bad for business. We have grown too proud for that. But in those days we were childishly literal-minded. . . . We regarded the sit-in as the successful culmination of a long campaign to reach the heart of the restaurant owner with the truth. What we took to be his conversion was as important as the fact that the restaurant had indeed been desegregated.[28]

While Chicago CORE was thus engaged, similarly minded groups had appeared in several other cities. In the main these groups were initiated by the FOR Race Relations Department, which had been established in October, 1943 with Farmer and Bayard Rustin as secretaries. In their travels for FOR the two men encouraged the formation of nonviolent, direct action groups. FOR members were usually the leaders.[29] Although some in FOR wanted the fellowship to maintain control over the projected national federation which Farmer and Fisher had planned, Farmer was able to win A. J. Muste over to the view that the direct action groups initiated by the Race Relations Department should be independent of FOR.[30]

While Farmer and Rustin were establishing these groups, Bernice Fisher shouldered the responsibility of organizing the conference called to create a national organization.[31] Meeting in Chicago during the first weekend in June, 1943, the delegates created a loose federation, the Committees of Racial Equality, elected Farmer as chairman and Fisher as secretary, and adopted as their official doctrines Chicago CORE's "Statement of Purpose" and "Action Discipline."[32]

## CONCLUSION

Thus the small band of pacifists, mainly students, who started the Chicago Committee of Racial Equality in the spring of 1942, not only pioneered in applying nonviolent direct action to the elimination of racial discrimination, but, along with FOR's Race Relations Department, did a critical service in setting the stage for the national federation, subsequently known as the Congress of Racial Equality. The new federation bore the stamp of their vision in its democratic organization, in its specific adaptations of Gandhian philosophy and techniques, and in its explicitly interracial approach; and for over 20 years CORE's style of operation was characterized by the ethos which the founders of the Chicago Committee of Racial Equality developed. Only in the 1960's, under the impact of rapid changes in the nature of its membership and disillusionment arising from the frustration of vastly heightened expectations, did this early ethos erode and ultimately disappear.

## NOTES

1. For a general overview of FOR concerns with race relations, industrial conflict, and the use of nonviolent direct action techniques, see its official publication, *Fellowship*, 1 (1935).

See especially "Statements of the FOR National Council on Sit-Down Strikes," *Fellowship*, 3 (Jan., 1937), p. 14, and 3 (May, 1937), p. 6; A. J. Muste, "Sit Downs and Lie Downs," 3 (March, 1937), pp. 5–6; Claud D. Nelson (FOR's Southern Secretary, 1934–1938), column entitled "Interracial News and Views," *passim*; James R. Robinson, "The Yogi and the Commisar," 12 (Feb., 1946), pp. 25–26; John Dillingham, "Our Racial Caste System," 2 (Dec., 1936), pp. 6, 13–14.

In the FOR Minutes Books (FOR Archives, Nyack, New York) see especially "Reports of the Southern Secretaries," 1939–1940; J. Holmes Smith, "Report of Secretary of Committee on Non-Violent Techniques," March 28–May 25, 1941; A. J. Muste, "Report to Annual Conference," Sept. 5–7, 1941; James Farmer, Letter read at FOR National Council Meeting, Nov. 29, 1941.

Very helpful in preparing this article were confidential interviews which the authors had with three of CORE's principal founders.

2.  To avoid an identification with pacifism, CORE literature spoke of an informal discussion group rather than a FOR peace team. Confidential interviews and materials in the FOR Archives revealed the crucial role of this FOR group in organizing CORE.

    See George M. Houser, Report of Youth Field Worker, Sept. 30–Nov. 28, 1941, FOR Archives; and Report of Youth Secretary, Sept. 12, 1942, FOR Archives.

    Identification of the six prime movers was based on a combination of data obtained through interviewing and from the following written sources: Houser, "CORE: A Brief History," mimeographed pamphlet [1949], CORE Archives, State Historical Society of Wisconsin, Madison, Wisc.; Bernice Fisher, "Confessions of an Ex-Liberal" [ca. 1960], MS in James Farmer Papers, New York City; and Houser to Juanita Morrow, July 7, 1948, CORE Archives.

3.  *Fellowship*, 6 (Feb., 1940), p. 30; 6 (April, 1940), p. 65; 7 (Oct., 1941), p. 173; Donovan E. Smucker, "Reports of Youth Secretary to FOR Council and Executive Committee," Jan. 12 and July 9, 1940; Farmer, "Reports of Middle-Atlantic Student Secretary," Sept. 1939–Sept. 1940, and Sept.–Dec. 1940; Farmer, "Report of Youth Field Worker," Sept. 30–Nov. 28, 1941; "FOR National Council Minutes," Sept. 7, 1941 (all in FOR Minutes Books, FOR Archives).

4.  Information on Houser, Robinson, Jack, and Guinn was obtained chiefly from confidential interviews; on Bernice Fisher, from her "Confessions of an Ex-Liberal." On Houser see also *Fellowship*, 7 (Oct., 1941), p. 173; 7 (Nov., 1941), p. 190; and "FOR National Council Minutes," Sept. 9, 1941.

5.  Houser, "CORE: A Brief History," p. 1; Houser to Juanita Morrow, July 7, 1948, CORE Archives; Confidential interviews; Fisher, "Confessions of an Ex-Liberal"; *What Is CORE?* Leaflet [1943], CORE Archives; Krishnalal Shridharani, *War without Violence* (New York,

1939); Houser, "We Say No to Jim Crow," *Fellowship*, 11 (April, 1945), p. 62.

6. Fisher, "Confessions of an Ex-Liberal"; Houser, "CORE: A Brief History," pp. 1–2. On "ashrams," see Farmer, *Freedom—When?* (New York, 1965), p. 58.

7. Houser, "CORE: A Brief History," p. 2.

8. Farmer, "Memorandum to A. J. Muste on Provisional Plans for Brotherhood Mobilization," Feb. 19, 1942; and "Additional Memorandum from James Farmer," March 9, 1942, FOR Archives (reprinted in Francis Broderick and August Meier, eds., *Negro Protest Thought in the Twentieth Century* [Indianapolis, 1966], pp. 211–219).

9. "Minutes of FOR National Council Meeting," April 11, 1942 (reprinted in *ibid.*, pp. 219–221).

10. Houser, "CORE: A Brief History," p. 3; and Farmer, *Freedom—When?*, p. 55, both suggest this, an interpretation also supported by interview data.

11. Houser, "CORE: A Brief History," p. 3; Fisher, "Confessions of an Ex-Liberal."

12. Houser, "CORE: A Brief History," p. 4; Houser, *Erasing the Color Line*, 3d ed., (New York, 1951), pp. 37–38; Farmer, *Freedom—When?*, pp. 58–59.

13. Houser, "CORE: A Brief History," p. 5.

14. H. A. J. [Homer A. Jack], "Charter Members of CORE," 1942, Farmer Papers; Fisher, "Confessions of an Ex-Liberal." Names of officers were obtained from the Chicago Committee of Racial Equality's mimeographed newsletter, *CORE Comments*, 1942–1943, *passim*, CORE Archives. Data on individual charter members and officers were obtained chiefly from confidential interviews.

15. See, for example, Houser, "Report of Chicago Youth Secretary," Sept. 12, 1942, FOR Minutes Books, FOR Archives; "CORE Statement of Purpose," Leaflet [1942], Farmer Papers; "CORE Action Discipline," Leaflet, 1946, Farmer Papers. On development of internal structure and method of operations, see *CORE Comments*, 1942–1943, *passim*.

16. Fisher, "Confessions of an Ex-Liberal"; Farmer, "The Race Logic of Pacifism," *Fellowship*, 8 (Feb., 1942), pp. 24–25; "Action Discipline" and "Statement of Purpose." See also Bayard Rustin, "The Negro and Non-Violence," *Fellowship*, 8 (Oct., 1942), pp. 166–167.

17. Krishnalal Shridharani, *War without Violence*, pp. 3–47; Confidential interviews; "Action Discipline."

18. Houser, *Erasing the Color Line*, p. 38; *CORE Comments* [Jan., 1943]; Houser, "CORE: A Brief History," pp. 4–5; Farmer, *Freedom—When?*, p. 59.

19. Houser, "CORE: A Brief History," p. 6; *CORE Comments*, Sept. 16 [1942]; Aug. 25 [1942]; Oct. [1942]; Dec. 10 [1942]; Farmer to Fisher, Oct. 14, 1942, Farmer Papers; Houser, *Erasing the Color Line*, p. 46; Houser, "We Say No to Jim Crow," p. 63; Farmer, *Freedom—When?*, p. 58.

20. Houser, *Erasing the Color Line*, pp. 26–27; *CORE Comments*, Dec. 10 [1942]; "Discrimination at the University of Chicago: Background for Action, Pamphlet no. 2" [1943], p. 4, CORE Archives.

21. "Discrimination at the University of Chicago," p. 4; *CORE Comments*, Oct. [1942].

22. Houser, "CORE: A Brief History," p. 6.

23. Houser, "We Say No to Jim Crow," pp. 61–62; Farmer, *Freedom—When?*, pp. 60–61; Houser, *Erasing the Color Line*, pp. 22–23.

24. Houser, *Erasing the Color Line*, p. 23; *CORE Comments*, Dec. [1942]; Feb. 12, 1943.

25. *CORE Comments* [Jan., 1943].

26. Houser, *Erasing the Color Line*, p. 23; Fisher, "Confessions of an Ex-Liberal"; Houser, "We Say No to Jim Crow," p. 62; Farmer, *Freedom—When?*, pp. 61–62; *CORE Comments* [May, 1943]; *Chicago Bee*, May 16, 1943, confidential interviews.

27. "Minutes of the First National Planning Conference of the Congress of Racial Equality, June 4, 5 and 6, 1943," Farmer Papers; also Houser, *Erasing the Color Line*, pp. 23–25.

28. Farmer, *Freedom—When?*, p. 62.

29. "Minutes of FOR Executive Committee," Sept. 22, 1942 and April 27, 1943; James Farmer, "Report of Field Secretary," Sept. 12, 1942; Bayard Rustin, "Report of Youth Secretary," Sept. 12, 1942; "Minutes of Non-Violent Action Committee," Oct. 26, 1942 (all in FOR Archives). Farmer to Fisher, Oct. 14, 16, Nov. 2, 24, 1942, and Jan. 18, 1943, Farmer Papers; *Fellowship*, 8 (Dec., 1942), p. 214; 9 (Feb., 1943), p. 35; "Minutes of First National Planning Conference"; Margaret Rohrer, "Memorandum to Fellowship of Reconciliation," Dec. 9, 1942; "Syracuse CORE, Brief History," Feb. 19, 1943 (both in CORE Archives).

30. Farmer to Fisher, Oct. 16, Nov. 2, 5, 24, 1942, and Jan. 18, 1943, Farmer Papers; Fisher, "Confessions of an Ex-Liberal."

31. Farmer to Fisher, Nov. 2, 24, 1942; Feb. 27, March 5, 17, 23, 1943, Farmer Papers; *CORE Comments*, Dec. 10 [1942] and [May, 1943].

32. "Minutes of the First National Planning Conference."

# IV | A Case Study of Gary, Indiana

Gary, Indiana, is probably the most important current
example of black political power in the United States, since
blacks control the city's key executive position—the
mayoralty. There are other cities with black mayors, such as
Washington, D.C. and Cleveland. But in Washington the
powers of the mayor are distinctly subordinate to the U.S.
Congress. And although Cleveland is a much larger
and more important city than Gary, its large white
majority implies that black executive control rest on
the support of a significant bloc of white voters.

Gary, however, has an absolute black majority in its
population of 200,000. It is thus the pure case—the instance
of black power which can rest exclusively on black votes
and support, regardless of the posture of the local white
population. (For an impressionistic view of the city, see
Marshall Frady, "Gary, Indiana," *Harper's*, August 1969,
pp. 35–45). Although few cities seem likely to achieve black
majorities in this century—and thus situations similar to
Cleveland are more likely to occur—the fact remains that
the Gary case defines most clearly the possibilities
open to black power through the political system.

The four articles in this section attempt to create a basis
for a judgment about Gary. The article by the historian
Emma Lou Thornbrough, "Segregation in Indiana During
the Klan Era of the 1920's," sets the stage by placing the
city in a precise historical context. Political sociologist
Michael Rogin, in "Politics, Emotion, and the Wallace Vote,"
illustrates how such regional developments manifest
themselves in the present day through racist attitudes and

voting patterns among white Gary residents. Rogin's article
uses empirical political science tools to illuminate part
of Gary's reality; and it provides information
useful to an evaluation of the situation.

The excerpt from Chuck Stone's *Black Political Power
in America* provides some background material on the
Hatcher election campaign, written by a black politician
who is deeply immersed in the realities of electoral
politics. The editor's contribution, "The First Year of Black
Power in Gary, Indiana," represents an effort to interpret
his experiences one year earlier as a member of
Mayor Richard Gordon Hatcher's personal staff. The
selection should be viewed as an initial attempt, by a
white socialist, to describe the effects of black control and
to place them in a theoretical framework as a guide
to further practical efforts.

## Segregation in Indiana during the Klan Era of the 1920's

*Emma Lou Thornbrough*

During the First World War there began a mass migration of Negroes from the rural South to the cities of the North which was to have marked effects upon the character and institutions of these cities. The number of Negroes moving into Indiana was not as great as the number moving into the neighboring states of Ohio, Michigan, and Illinois, but in the years from 1910 to 1930 the colored population of Indiana doubled.[1] Hopes for economic betterment were probably the most important reason for the migration, but the desire for greater personal freedom, for political and civil rights, and for opportunities to educate their children also brought Negroes northward. In Indiana the newcomers found little of the legalized Jim Crowism which they had known in the South, but they encountered much prejudice and discrimination. Although there were no racial disorders comparable to the riots in East St. Louis, Chicago, and Detroit, the influx of Negroes led to a movement for segregation on a scale previously unknown. In these same years the Ku Klux Klan, an organization which was habitually a strong advocate of white supremacy, was also rising to a position of unprecedented power in Indiana. It is not unusual for present-day commentators to see a close link between these two developments and to conclude that the increase in segregation measures was due primarily to Klan influence. This is a relationship, however, which has never been closely analyzed, and before the nature of the Klan's role can be understood it is necessary to look first at the segregation measures as they were originated in the state in the years following World War I.

These measures were confined for the most part to urban areas, because it was there that the Negro population was concentrated. In an earlier period, Negroes entering the state had settled in Evansville and

Reprinted from *Mississippi Valley Historical Review* XLVII (March 1961): 594–618. By permission of the Organization of American Historians.

the other Ohio River communities; but by the time of World War I new arrivals moved farther north, to Indianapolis, in the central part of the state, or to the cities in the Calumet region, especially Gary. The largest number went to Indianapolis, where the colored population increased from 21,816 in 1910 to 43,967 in 1930 (when it comprised about 12 per cent of the total population of the city). A more spectacular increase occurred in the extreme north, where a steel empire was arising on the shores of Lake Michigan. The population of Gary, which was little more than a small town in 1910, had grown to just over 100,000 in 1930. In this same twenty-year period the city's Negroes had increased from 383 to almost 18,000—approximately 18 per cent of the total population. In the neighboring city of East Chicago, where there were only 28 Negroes in 1910, the number had grown to more than 5,000 by 1930. By the latter date nearly 60 per cent of the Negro population of the state was found in Indianapolis and the Gary-East Chicago area. Most of the remainder was in other cities and towns, census figures showing that over 92 per cent of the Negro population lived in urban areas.

Although the new arrivals settled in cities, most of them came from rural areas in the South, and an increasingly large number came from the Lower South. Before 1900 most Negroes migrating to Indiana had come from the Upper South, especially Kentucky, while a very few had come from the Lower South. By 1930, when the census showed that 67 per cent of the total Negro population had been born outside of Indiana, persons from Kentucky still outnumbered by a large margin those from any other single state. In Indianapolis the number of Kentucky-born Negroes was only slightly smaller than the number native to Indiana. But in the Calumet area most Negroes came from the Lower South. In Gary in 1930 the largest single group came from Mississippi, and the second largest from Alabama. Each of these groups was substantially larger than the number born in Indiana. In 1930 more than 86 per cent of the Negroes in the steel city had been born outside of Indiana, and of these an overwhelming majority came from the South.[2]

The problems of assimilation created by the abrupt transition from a simple, rural way of life to the more complex patterns of city life were complicated by Indiana's long tradition of racism. In the pre-Civil War period the Black Code of Indiana had scarcely been equaled in its harshness by the law of any other northern state. In the years following the Civil War the adoption of the Fourteenth and Fifteenth Amendments removed most of the legal disabilities against Negroes in the state,[3] and by the time of the migration of the First World War era only a few remnants of earlier racial distinctions remained in the law code. One of these was a severe prohibition against marriages between white persons and persons with as little as one-eighth Negro blood. Another was the school law, which gave local school authorities the option of maintaining segregated schools or of allowing members of both races to attend the same school.[4]

In spite of the fact that there was little legal segregation, in practice there was little mingling of the races. In the larger cities Negroes were unable to find housing outside of well-defined areas, which were largely slums. Since 1885 there had been a civil rights law prohibiting discrimination in the use of public accommodations, but it was largely a dead letter. Negroes almost never ventured into a "white" hotel or restaurant, and signs announcing that the proprietor "catered to white trade only" were not uncommon. When Negroes went into a theater or concert hall they sat in the gallery. In the rural parts of the state there were many small communities in which a Negro was not allowed to settle or even spend the night.[5]

In Indianapolis, where the bulk of the Negro population lived, race relations were normally peaceful. At least there were few overt signs of antagonisms. The leading Negro newspaper, the *Freeman*, which was far from militant in its editorial policy, frequently asserted that racial harmony prevailed, but some of its content seems to indicate that friction was avoided in part by the failure of Negroes to take advantage of all the rights which were legally theirs. One editorial admitted: "We have learned to forego some rights that are common, and because we know the price. We would gain but little in a way if certain places were thrown open to us. We have not insisted that hotels should entertain our race, or the theaters, rights that are clearly ours." But even the conservative *Freeman* insisted that Negroes could not give up the right to live where they chose.[6]

The rapid increase in Negro population created new tensions, especially in housing. The parts of the city which had been the Negro districts simply could not house both the older residents and the newcomers. As immigrants from the South took over these districts, older residents sought to buy homes in hitherto all-white neighborhoods. The largest concentration of Negroes in Indianapolis had always been just northwest of the downtown business area. After the war this area began to expand northward—toward upper middle class white neighborhoods. Property owners, faced with the prospect of Negro neighbors and fearful of a decline in real estate values, organized themselves into local civic leagues, which had as their chief purpose the barring of Negro residents. One novel device to which one group, the Capitol Avenue Protective Association, resorted was to try to isolate and humiliate Negroes who bought property by building spite fences on either side of the property. But a young Negro dentist, faced with this form of retaliation, obtained an injunction which prohibited the practice.[7]

Sometimes opposition to Negro neighbors took a more sinister form. When, despite warnings, a Negro family moved into a white neighborhood in 1924, a hand grenade was thrown through a window of their house. Following this episode handbills were circulated in an adjacent neighborhood, asking "DO YOU WANT A NIGGER FOR A NEIGHBOR?" The handbills appear to have been the work of a group which unabashedly called itself the White Supremacy League and which had as its objective not only barring Negroes from white neighborhoods but excluding them from most forms of employment as well. Members were bound by oath not to employ Negroes in their homes or trade at stores which employed Negroes.[8] This group represented an extremist element, but its president was also active in the Mapleton Civic Association, an organization which included in its membership eminently respectable businessmen. A printed statement of the aims of the Mapleton group frankly stated: "One of our chief concerns is to prevent members of the colored race from moving into our midst, thereby depreciating property values fifty per cent, or more." Members of the association pledged themselves not to sell or lease property to anyone except a white person. The agreement was reported to have worked so well that for three years no more Negroes had moved into the Mapleton area, and some who were already residents had moved away.[9]

Although private efforts of this sort met with some success in stemming the Negro tide, stronger measures were sought. In response to pressure from civic groups, including particularly the White Citizens Protective League, the Indianapolis city council enacted a residential zoning ordinance in March, 1926. Declaring that "in the interest of public peace, good order and the general welfare, it is advisable to foster the separation of white and negro residential communities," the measure made it unlawful for white persons to establish residence in a "portion of the municipality inhabited principally by negroes," or for Negroes to establish residence in a "white community," except with the written consent of a majority of persons of the opposite race inhabiting the neighborhood.[10]

The measure was sponsored by a Republican member of the council who said he had received petitions containing more than five thousand names asking for the enactment of the ordinance. The only member to oppose it was a Democrat, who insisted that it was unconstitutional and violated "the spirit of American institutions." More than eight hundred cheering, hand-clapping, stamping spectators crowded into the council chambers while the ordinance was under consideration. After the favorable vote the president of the White Citizens Protective League declared with satisfaction: "Passage of this ordinance will stabilize real estate values . . . and give the honest citizens and voters renewed faith in city officials."[11]

The mayor, asserting that it was not the duty of the executive to pass upon the validity of an act of the legislative branch, signed the ordinance, even though he admitted that the entire legal staff of the city was of the opinion that it was unconstitutional. In a lengthy message justifying his action the mayor expressed the opinion that there was no intention to discriminate against either whites or Negroes in adopting the ordinance and that its "tenor" precluded either race from obtaining any advantage over the other. He went so far as to say that if critics would study the law with "open minds" they would "hail with delight this step toward the solution of a problem that has long caused deep thought and serious study by members of both races."[12]

Doubts as to the constitutionality of the ordinance arose because of its similarity to a Louisville ordinance which had been declared unconstitutional by the United States Supreme Court in 1917. Backers of the Indianapolis ordinance, who declared themselves ready to take a test case to the Supreme Court, were not unaware of this precedent, but were hopeful that in the years which had elapsed since the Louisville case the highest tribunal might have changed its mind. The principal reason for their optimism was the fact that the Supreme Court of Louisiana had recently upheld the constitutionality of a New Orleans racial zoning ordinance which had served as a model for the Indianapolis enactment. The court had held that the Louisville precedent did not apply because the New Orleans ordinance (like the Indianapolis ordinance) did not prohibit outright the buying or selling of property but merely restricted the right of purchasers to *occupy* property. They ruled that the ordinance was not discriminatory because it applied equally to whites and blacks and dealt with "social relations" rather than civil or political rights.[13]

The optimism of members of the Protective League proved to be unwarranted. By 1926 there was a vigorous chapter of the National Association for the Advancement of Colored People in Indianapolis, which was eager to take every possible step to invalidate the ordinance. The national office of the NAACP, which had won one of its first vic-

tories in the United States Supreme Court in connection with the
Louisville case, was also interested in the situation in Indianapolis.
Funds amounting to about five thousand dollars were quickly raised
to carry on the fight, and a case which bears the signs of having been
arranged with the deliberate purpose of testing the ordinance was soon
on the docket of a local court. The case arose from the refusal of a
Negro physician to fulfill a contract for the purchase of real estate in a
predominantly white neighborhood. He based his refusal on the
grounds that the zoning ordinance would prevent him from occupying
the property. The judge who heard the case ruled in favor of the
Negro, declaring the zoning ordinance unconstitutional in the light of
the precedent established by the Louisville case. He held that the
ordinance deprived a citizen of his constitutional rights by making his
right to live in his own property depend upon the consent of other
citizens.[14] Hopes of supporters of the ordinance for an appeal to the
Supreme Court of the United States were dashed when that tribunal
reversed the Louisiana Supreme Court decision as to the New Orleans
ordinance.[15]

The successful attack on the zoning ordinance was the only significant legal victory in the fight in Indiana against segregation during the
1920's. On other fronts, and especially in connection with segregation
in the schools, there were some serious defeats. In Indianapolis the
movement for residential restrictions went hand in hand with a movement to remove Negroes from hitherto mixed schools. From the time
that colored children were first admitted to the city elementary schools
in 1869, the general policy had been to require that they attend separate schools, but there had always been a few schools with mixed en-
rollments. Inasmuch as most Negroes lived in all-Negro neighborhoods
children had usually attended the school nearest them, but sometimes
there were complaints that children were required to travel long distances to attend Negro schools rather than schools nearer to their
homes. Indianapolis high schools had never been segregated. As early as
1872 a Negro student had been admitted to Indianapolis High School,
which was later renamed Shortridge High School. Thereafter, although
their numbers were not large, there were always Negroes enrolled in
the school, which had the reputation of being one of the best public
academic institutions in the country. In later years as two new high
schools were built, Negroes attended them also. It was always the
policy to employ Negro teachers in the all-Negro elementary schools,
but Negro teachers were never assigned to the mixed elementary
schools or the high schools.[16]

The growth of the Negro population after World War I and the consequent movement of Negroes into new neighborhoods led to demands for a more restrictive policy. Two principal arguments were used by those favoring segregation. First, they insisted that the presence of Negroes in the same schools as the whites menaced the health of the latter and that Negroes should be segregated to protect the white children. Second, they argued that Negroes would benefit from segregation—that in their own schools they would take more pride in their work, their scholarship would improve and that they would develop more initiative. The latter argument more than the first, dealt with intangibles, and proponents never made clear how segregation would bring about the desired results. Their conclusions, too, now appear to be completely at variance with the views of the Supreme Court in the segregation cases of 1954 and with a large body of sociological studies.

A resolution presented to the Indianapolis Board of School Commissioners in 1922 on behalf of the Federation of Civic Clubs was a forceful statement of the health argument and a revealing commentary on Negro housing. It pointed out that, while Negroes constituted only about one tenth of the total population of Indianapolis, about one fourth of the deaths in the city were among Negroes. "For years," it asserted, "the Marion County Tuberculosis Society has emphasized the care of incurable consumption among the colored people as the greatest social need in this city." Because crowded housing conditions made it impossible for a tubercular patient to be cared for at home without endangering other members of the family, a large number of cases of incipient tuberculosis were believed to exist among colored school children. For this reason the school board was asked to establish separate schools for all Negro children and to staff them with Negro teachers.[17]

At the same session a letter in support of segregation was presented to the school board on behalf of the Mapleton Civic Association and the White Supremacy League. The contents have not been preserved, but they were of such a nature as to cause the president of the board to remark that the letter "contained such statements as rendered it impossible to properly be received by the Board, without the reservation that its receipt was in no sense to be construed as endorsement on the part of the Board of the sentiments which it contained."[18]

In response to such pressures the Board of School Commissioners set up new boundaries for fourteen elementary schools for Negroes and required that Negroes attend them. Groups of Negro parents protested in vain. When the attorney for the school board ruled that under the law the children could be required to attend the Negro schools even though they had to travel long distances, two parents sought court orders to permit attendance at the schools nearest their homes. But in both cases the court upheld the right of the school board to carry out the transfer.[19] After these transfers, which occurred in 1923, elementary schools were predominantly all white or all Negro. The process of separation of the races was carried almost to completion in 1929 when Negroes were removed from three more schools.[20]

Before the latter date segregationists in Indianapolis had also been successful in removing Negroes from the mixed high schools and putting them in an all-Negro school. The demand for separate high schools was backed by many white groups. Among them was the Indianapolis Chamber of Commerce, which presented a petition to the Board of School Commissioners in September, 1922, setting forth the "necessity" for a "separate, modern, completely equipped and adequate high school building for colored students."[21]

This movement met with strong and bitter opposition in the Negro community. Various delegations representing Negro civic and ministerial groups appeared before the school board, while other groups sent written protests. A petition from the Better Indianapolis Civic League forcefully and eloquently presented the arguments against a separate school. Declaring that the public school system was the most powerful factor in American society for the "engendering and transmission of sound democratic ideals," it emphasized that "no one section of the population" could be "isolated and segregated without taking from it the advantages of the common culture." Since money for the public schools came from taxation of all the people it was "unjust, un-American, and against the spirit of democratic ideals that one section of the citizenship should subvert the funds of the common treasury to discriminate against another section solely on the basis of ancestry."[22]

The report which the board adopted on December 12, 1922, recommending a separate school, embodied a different point of view. It declared that the enrollment of over eight hundred Negroes in the city high schools showed a "laudable desire on their part and on the part of their parents" for an education, but that a "new, modern, well equipped high school" of their own would provide them with the "maximum educational opportunity" and the fullest opportunity for the development of initiative, self-reliance, and the other qualities needed for good citizenship.[23]

The movement for a Negro high school was closely linked with the movement to relocate Shortridge High School, which was regarded as the best college preparatory school in the city and which included in its enrollment a number of students from wealthy and influential white families. The school occupied ancient and inadequate buildings in an older part of the city, not far from a Negro slum area. That new quarters for the school were badly needed was undeniable, but the zeal of some of its patrons for a new building and a new location on the north side of the city was clearly motivated by a desire to get rid of Negro students, who constituted 10 to 15 per cent of the enrollment. In a report of a survey of the school, made by one of the leading women's clubs of the city, it was emphasized that one of the reasons for planning a new building was the fact that "there are numbers of colored students packed into crowded class rooms with the white children." The *Freeman* commented bitterly that it was "evidently thought that to call attention to the Negroes as mixed with white children would be the weightiest argument for action on the part of the School Commissioners."[24]

After the school board decided to build both a Negro high school and a new Shortridge at a new location, a delegation of whites appeared before it to request "in the interest of economy" that the old buildings at Shortridge be used for the Negro school, "thus releasing building funds for other construction projects."[25] But the school board, instead of acting on this suggestion, went ahead with the construction of a Negro school, which was substantially equal to new schools being built for white students so far as construction and equipment were concerned. The board no doubt hoped that the new school and the employment of Negro teachers to staff it would make segregation less offensive to the Negro community.[26]

But before the building was started, a group of Negroes, backed by the NAACP, brought suit to enjoin construction on the grounds that the proposed school could not meet the requirements of "equality" under the "separate but equal" doctrine. Lawyers for the Negroes argued that the new school could not be equal to the three Indianapolis high schools already in operation because no single school could offer the range of subjects—academic and technical—which were offered in these schools. To build a Negro school truly equal to the combined three schools would be so expensive as to be prohibitive. After the local court in Marion County refused to grant the injunction an appeal was taken to the Indiana Supreme Court. That court, sustaining the action of the lower court, held that the suit was premature—that the mere fear that the proposed school might not offer courses of equal caliber was no reason for not building it. If, after the school was in operation, a case arose in which a colored pupil was denied some "educational advantage accorded white children of equal advancement," then proceedings could be taken "to secure the constitutional rights of such a child." In the meantime, the court declared, an injunction would not be granted "merely to allay the fears and apprehension of individuals."[27]

As the new school, which was named Crispus Attucks after the Negro of Revolutionary War fame, was nearing completion in 1927 the Board of School Commissioners announced that it would be the policy of the board to require all colored high school students to attend that school.[28] The board, in fact, followed this policy until the state legislature adopted a law in 1949 which required the desegregation of all public schools in the state.

In Gary, where the Negro population was increasing at a faster rate than in Indianapolis, the school segregation provoked a more militant response. In that city there had been a policy since 1908 of maintaining separate elementary schools for Negroes, which were staffed by Negro teachers,[29] but until 1927 Negroes were not required to attend a separate high school. Nearly all of the burgeoning Negro population of Gary was concentrated in the central part of the city, known as "the Patch." In that area was located Froebel High School, a four-year institution, with a racially mixed student body. Some Negroes were also enrolled for the first two years of high school work in two Negro elementary school buildings. A few Negroes—not more than fifty—were scattered in schools in other parts of the city.[30]

Racial tension was occasionally evident at Froebel, but no serious racial disturbances occurred in the Gary schools until September, 1927. These disturbances broke out not at Froebel but at Emerson High School when twenty-four Negroes were transferred there from a Negro school, known as the Virginia Street school. A few days after the transfer white students at Emerson went on strike in protest. About six hundred of them paraded down the main street of the city, some of them carrying placards which said: "We won't go back to Emerson 'til it's white." In spite of the fact that the school principal threatened them with expulsion the number of strikers grew, until by the third day over thirteen hundred were absent from classes. At a mass meeting of students the superintendent of schools and the vice-president of the school board declared that the Negroes must remain at Emerson for the time being, but implied that they would be removed when a new Negro high school could be erected—in two or three years. In the meantime the superintendent indicated that it would not be necessary to include Negro students in the social and athletic activities of the school. The members of the board of education, after a conference with the mayor, also gave assurances that the transfer of the Negro students was intended to be temporary, that there was no intention of making Emerson permanently a mixed school, and gave promises that no more Negroes would be transferred there.[31]

At the end of four days the strike was settled by what the local newspaper referred to as a "peace treaty" between the students and the school and city authorities. The strikers were not to be penalized and the city council voted $15,000 for the purpose of erecting a temporary structure for a Negro school. The appropriation was carried in spite of negative votes of the three Negro members of the council and over the protests of a group of Negroes who crowded into the council chamber.[32]

Plans to remove the Negroes from Emerson to the temporary building ran into a snag when the local branch of the NAACP secured an injunction to prevent the expenditure of funds for that purpose.[33] The authorities then changed their tactics and decided to make some renovations in the school from which the Negroes had been transferred in the first place. At the end of the Christmas vacation, in January, 1928, less than four months after the strike, all Negroes except for three seniors were removed from Emerson and transferred either to the Virginia Street school or to Froebel.

Efforts by Negroes to block the transfer were unsuccessful. One parent, with the backing of the local and the national office of the NAACP sought a mandamus ordering the superintendent of schools to readmit his daughter to Emerson. The lawyers for the Negro student tried to prove that the Virginia Street school, which she was ordered to attend, did not meet the state requirements for a four-year high school, but both a local court and the Indiana Supreme Court rejected their plea.[34] The segregationists won a complete victory so far as Emerson High School was concerned. In addition to transferring the Negroes back to the Virginia Street school, the school board rearranged school districts in such a way as to provide that students who finished the tenth grade in that school would continue at Froebel instead of Emerson. As a final step, the city council appropriated $600,000 to build a high school for Negroes which would be equal in all respects to the other high schools. When completed this school was named

Roosevelt and made an all-Negro institution with a Negro faculty. Froebel High School, which was on the same side of the tracks, continued to have a mixed enrollment and to be the only unsegregated school in Gary. Emerson, on the other side of town, remained all white until 1945, when another student strike, this time at Froebel, led to the abandonment of segregation throughout the Gary school system.[35]

Thus in Gary and Indianapolis, two major centers of Negro concentration, the decade of the 1920's saw impressive gains by the advocates of segregation. In the southern part of the state, where Negroes had first settled, the schools had always been completely segregated. A few northern towns, where the number of Negroes was small, moved toward segregation for the first time in this decade. One of these was Elkhart, where the total Negro population was only about five hundred. Other northern cities, including South Bend and East Chicago, where the number of Negroes was larger, never adopted segregation.[36]

It is difficult to generalize on the course of racial discrimination in institutions of higher learning, since the number of Negroes enrolled in them was small. At least one private institution is known to have adopted a quota system in the 1920's limiting the number of Negroes admitted. In the state universities there were no racial restrictions in admission policies, but Negroes were not allowed to live in the residence halls maintained by the institutions and were barred from a number of university activities. At Indiana University a house for Negro women erected with private funds was opened in 1929.[37]

Some of the same discriminatory pattern that developed in the public schools during the 1920's may be discerned also in the city regulations governing places of public accommodation. Although discrimination in such places was prohibited by law, it continued to be customary in the decade for Negroes and whites to patronize different establishments. One place where the color line was drawn for the first time was in the public parks of Indianapolis and Gary. In Indianapolis, Douglass Park was acquired in 1921. It was not officially designated as a park for Negroes, but the swimming pool and playgrounds which were subsequently built there were marked with signs which said "Negroes only." After the opening of this park Negro groups found it impossible to get permission to hold functions in the other city parks. In Gary, one park was divided into two areas with "separate but equal" recreational facilities for members of each race. Negroes were excluded from the only park in the area which had a beach on Lake Michigan, and as a result a group of Negro businessmen leased private property on the lake-front for a beach in 1926.[38]

These illustrations of segregationist practices, whether in places of public accommodation or in the public schools, are evidence of the increasing sharpness of racial discrimination during the 1920's. It was a period, at least in the larger urban areas of Indiana, when the color line seemed marked more indelibly than before. The question which remains is that of the responsibility of the Klan—the extent to which the segregationist measures may be attributed to its influence.

Of the strength of the Klan there can be no doubt. The Klan moved into Indiana in the years following the First World War. By 1923 there were klaverns all over the state, with a membership estimated at between a quarter and half a million. The Klan infiltrated Protestant churches, social organizations, and politics. For a time it dominated the Republican party, which in turn controlled state government. But its heyday was short-lived. It collapsed in the midst of a series of disclosures which shook the complacency of Indianans, even though they were inclined to be fairly tolerant of wrongdoing in political circles. David C. Stephenson, former Grand Dragon and dominant figure in the Klan, was sentenced to life imprisonment for a particularly revolting sex crime. A few months later a whole series of public officials identified with the Klan had been accused of various kinds of malfeasance. Some of them escaped conviction but all were disgraced. Ever since that time politicians have frantically sought to dissociate themselves from any hint of Klan ties. Because the Klan was so thoroughly discredited there has been a tendency in recent years to make it a scapegoat and blame it for segregation measures which a later generation finds discreditable. The evidence in support of this belief, however, is tenuous.

In exploiting popular prejudices the Indiana Klan relied most heavily upon traditional fears of Roman Catholicism.[39] The theme which was harped on most consistently in the pages of the official Klan publication, the *Fiery Cross*, was the alleged desire of the Church of Rome to dominate the government and schools of the United States, a theme in which existing prejudice against foreigners was fully exploited. Appeal to race prejudice, in comparison to the appeal to anti-Catholicism, was relatively slight despite Indiana's long history of racial bigotry. In fact, efforts were sometimes made to convince Negroes that the Klan was their friend.

But white supremacy was one of the avowed tenets of the Klan, and part of the appeal to Hoosiers was the use of the well-worn argument of the necessity of maintaining racial purity. One Klansman explained that in "selling" the Klan to prospective members one approach was to bring up the subject of white supremacy "in this way—not anti-negro, but to keep the black man black and the white man white." A full-page advertisement in the *Fiery Cross* from the Wayne County Klan declared that it unalterably opposed "contamination of the pure blood of the Anglo-Saxon race with an inferior nationality." A Junior Klan had among its ideals, along with "shielding the chastity of the home and the purity of our womanhood" and "the practical value of the Scriptures," a pledge "to maintain forever white supremacy."[40]

At the same time the *Fiery Cross* and Klan spokesmen frequently asserted that they were not enemies of Negroes but were in reality their best friends. One editorial declared: "The fact that the Ku Klux Klan believes in white supremacy has furnished much propaganda for the enemy to use among the negro population, inciting hatred for the Klan in that quarter, although thousands of intelligent negroes realize the meaning of the sentiment expressed by 'white supremacy,' and are not excited by the slanderers of the Klan." It insisted that there were many cases "wherein worthy negroes have been materially aided in time of misfortune by the Klan." One form of aid cited was gifts made to "worthy" Negro churches. It was reported that a gift to the Edinburg Colored Baptist Church was "gratefully received by the secretary of the church, who knows that the Klan is not the enemy of the negro as alien propaganda would have his people believe."[41] The *Fiery Cross* insisted, also, that Klansmen were law-abiding and that they were opposed to lynching. In one instance, it was claimed, members of the Klan were responsible for preventing the lynching of a Negro accused of assaulting a white woman.[42] In spite of these protestations of good will, however, it was well known that processions of white-robed Klansmen sometimes paraded through Negro districts as warning to Negroes to be law-abiding and to "keep in their place."

Attitudes among Negroes toward the Klan were mixed. Because it was identified with Protestantism and was publicly opposed to sin, some Negro clergymen either praised it or refrained from criticism, but other Negro ministers were frankly opposed to it. Negro intellectuals generally were openly suspicious and hostile. Most disturbing to them was the power which the Klan displayed in the Republican Party.

The identification of the Klan with the party of Lincoln created a curious dilemma for Negro voters. As a legacy from the days of Reconstruction, Negroes had always retained an unquestioning loyalty to the Republican party. In the Democratic party, which in the South, at least, was the symbol of white supremacy, Negroes were a rarity. The injection of the Klan issue into the 1924 election campaign created the possibility of a change in the traditional political alignment. In the May primaries the Klan-backed candidates on the Republican ticket were victorious almost without exception. No Negro Republicans were nominated, but for the first time in history a Negro Democrat was nominated as a candidate for the Indiana house of representatives. One Negro newspaper, the Indianapolis *Ledger*, was undoubtedly subsidized by the Klan, and its editor was active in support of Ed Jackson, whom the Klan backed for the Republican nomination as governor. In an effort to hold the support of Negroes the Jackson group attempted to promote a kind of Klan for Negroes—an organization called "The Ritualistic Benevolent Society for American Born Citizens of African Blood and Protestant Faith." Members pledged themselves to support the American government, the Protestant faith, "protection of honor and chastity of womanhood," free public schools, laws punishing lynching, and immigration laws to check the influx of "undesirables who threatened the jobs of colored workers. The organization apparently met with little success, and on the day of the primary the Negro vote was light.[43]

From the beginning the *Freeman*, whose owner and publisher George L. Knox, had been active in Republican politics in an earlier period, was strongly anti-Klan. After the primary it declared "The Republican party as now constituted is the Ku Klux Klan of Indiana. The nominees for Governor, House, Senate, and Courts offices with one possible exception are all Klansmen, in fact there is no Republican party." The *Freeman* called upon Negroes to support the Democrats; otherwise they would show that they were not worthy to vote. "The ballot is the only weapon of a civilized people and it is up to the Negro to use that weapon as do other civilized groups."[44]

Throughout the campaign the Democratic leaders in Indiana adopted an anti-Klan position. The Democratic state platform condemned efforts to make political issues out of race and religion. While not calling the Klan by name, it declared that the Republican party had been "delivered into the hands of an organization which has no place in politics and which promulgates doctrines which tend to break down the safeguards which the constitution throws around every citizen." The Klan responded by circulating a bulletin during the campaign declaring that the Democratic candidate for governor, Dr. Carleton McCulloch, was "antagonistic" toward the Klan and had "openly and publicly denounced the Klan," and should therefore be defeated.[45]

The Klan issue in Indiana attracted nationwide attention and aroused apprehension among Negroes in other states. During the campaign the *Freeman* asserted that because of the Klan, nationally known Negro Republican leaders refused to come into the state to campaign. At the national convention of the National Association for the Advancement of Colored People, James Weldon Johnson, the executive secretary, declared that the most important issue before Negroes in the coming election was the Klan. In spite of protestations by Klan leaders that it was not anti-Negro, he insisted that if the Klan gained political power the rights of Negroes would be endangered. In Indiana, he declared, it was the plain duty of Negroes to vote against Republican candidates who were "touched with the tar brush of the Ku Klux Klan."[46]

Members of the NAACP in Indiana made strenuous efforts to defeat the Klan-backed candidates and organized an Independent Voters League for this purpose. In October the NAACP and the recently organized League called a meeting in Indianapolis of Negroes from all parts of the state for the purpose of alerting voters to the Klan issue. At a session which several thousand Negroes attended it was voted to endorse the entire Democratic ticket.[47]

Some Negro clergymen were outspoken in their opposition to the Klan. At the general conference of the African Methodist Episcopal Church, meeting in Louisville, Kentucky, a resolution was adopted condemning Senator James E. Watson of Indiana for endorsing Jackson for governor. In Indianapolis, the minister of the leading A.M.E. church was known to be a foe of the Klan. On the other hand, Negro ministers, who were traditionally active in Republican politics, in many instances continued to give their support to that party. Several A.M.E. ministers were listed as speakers by the Republican speakers' bureau. As might be expected, the Negroes most vocal in support of the Republican cause were those holding political jobs. Anti-Klan Negroes were bitter in their denunciation of those "Jim Crow" Negroes who continued to work in the Klan dominated Republican organization.[48]

Democrats tried to convince Negro voters that the real issue in the campaign was not between Democrats and Republicans but between Democrats and the Klan.[49] Republicans tried to hold the Negro vote by pointing up traditional political loyalties. Representative Leonidas C. Dyer, of Missouri, author of an anti-lynching bill in Congress, told Indiana Negroes that their real enemy was the Democratic party. "There is no such thing," he said in Indianapolis, "as a colored man being loyal to his race and at the same time voting the Democratic ticket."[50]

As the campaign wore on Republican leaders apparently began to feel concern over the possibility of a defection of the normally loyal

Negroes. The director of the Republican state campaign bureau for Negroes told party workers that the Klan question had frightened Negroes. "The heart of the colored man is with you," he said, "but his mind is confused." The Klan itself was also apprehensive about the Negro vote. One bulletin from Klan headquarters warned that "the amalgamated enemies of the organization [Klan] are influencing the negro and foreigner to such an extent that practically the entire negro and foreign vote will be cast for the anti-Klan candidates. We must overcome this loss by seeing to it that all Protestant people support those candidates whom we favor."[51] Headlines in the *Fiery Cross* proclaimed: "Rome Dictates to Indiana Voters: Attempt Is Made to Stampede the Negro Vote." The paper accused the Democrats of "waging a war of hate, misrepresentation, coercion and party destruction with the hope of driving the Negro out of the Republican party and into the Democratic camp." "Roman agents" were said to be busily trying to create trouble at every Negro political meeting. But the *Fiery Cross* expressed confidence that Negroes were too intelligent to be misled. The agents of Rome, it said, "may control the Roman Catholic vote, but their task of driving like a herd of sheep, the negro voter into the McCulloch fold is too big for the Roman corporation. It can't be done."[52]

In spite of these brave words there were marked defections among Negro Republicans on election day. In Indianapolis, Negro wards which normally were solidly Republican, now went Democratic.[53] But these Republican losses were more than offset by the large numbers of white Democrats and independents who voted the Klan-backed Republican ticket. The result was the election of a governor and other state officers who were known to have Klan ties. More than half of the members of the Indiana house of representatives as well as a large number of state senators were elected with Klan support, while innumerable local officials owed their victories partly to the Klan.

During the campaign Democrats had warned Negroes that if the Klan got control of the state government it would enact severe segregation measures, but no such measures materialized. In the 1925 session of the state legislature, in which Klan-supported members were in a majority, several measures were proposed against Roman Catholic influence in the public schools. But not a single segregation measure nor any other proposal to establish racial discrimination was introduced.[54]

By the autumn of 1925, when municipal elections were held in the larger cities in the state, the prestige and influence of the Klan were already badly shaken. The trial of D. C. Stephenson, former Grand

Dragon, got under way at the same time as the fall campaigns. But in spite of Stephenson's disgrace the Klan had not yet lost its power in Indianapolis and Gary. In Indianapolis the Republican candidates for mayor and the city council were openly supported by the Klan. In the election of members of the Board of School Commissioners, which was held at the same time as the municipal election, a slate of candidates known as "the United Protestant Clubs ticket" also had Klan backing. Although the election of the school board was supposed to be nonpartisan, Republican workers as well as Klan members were active in support of the Protestant ticket. In the closing days of the campaign a huge rally was held at which the Exalted Cyclops of Marion County Klan No. 3 presided. Prayers and speeches were made on behalf of the Republican candidates for mayor and city council and the Protestant school ticket, all of whom were present.[55]

All of the Klan-backed candidates were elected. Negroes do not appear to have been aroused over the Klan issue during the campaign as they had been in 1924. Except for a few party workers they showed little enthusiasm for the Republican candidates, but neither did they show much disposition to support the Democrats. On election day the Negro vote was light, but the Republicans carried the day. Negro wards which had been Democratic the year before were once again in the Republican column. In Gary, as in Indianapolis, the Klan scored a victory. Floyd E. Williams, who was reputed to be a member of the Klan, was elected mayor, and five members of the Gary city council were persons nominated and elected with Klan support.[56]

There is a widespread belief that the Indianapolis school board elected with Klan backing was responsible for the segregation measures which became so controversial a part of the city's school administration in the remaining years of the decade. A recent book on desegregation in the schools says that "the Klan secured the erection of Crispus Attucks High School in 1927 and established it as a segregated school. In the same year a Klan dominated school board initiated the policy of transporting Negroes away from the elementary school in their neighborhood to more distant schools for Negroes." In a newspaper statement in 1957 the superintendent of the Indianapolis schools also placed the blame for segregation in the schools on the Klan.[57]

The accuracy of these statements is questionable in view of what we know about the development of segregation measures after World War I. Certainly the Klan did not "initiate" the policy of requiring Negro children to travel long distances to Negro schools. Negro parents were complaining about this policy before the Klan made its appearance in Indiana.[58] In September, 1923, as noted above, the policy of requiring elementary school children to attend segregated schools was greatly extended. In December of that same year the building of a Negro high school was authorized. These developments, of course, all took place before 1925, when the Klan-backed school board was elected. In 1923 the board was made up of members nominated and elected with the support of the Citizens School Committee, a group which in 1925 ran candidates in opposition to the Klan-backed slate; in fact, members of the school board who had voted for the segregation measures in 1923 were defeated by Klan-backed candidates in 1925. In 1923, moreover, the Indianapolis school board had been under constant attack by the Klan because of alleged Roman Catholic influence, especially because the president of the board was a Catholic. The *Fiery Cross* regularly published articles and editorials on this subject, charging that Catholic influence was impeding the construction of needed public schools. But during 1923 there was not a single item in the columns of that paper on the subject of segregation in the Indianapolis schools.

The Klan-backed school board elected in 1925 instead of initiating segregation merely carried forward policies begun by its predecessor. In 1927, when the Negro high school, Attucks, was completed, the board adopted a policy which apparently had been intended all along, that all Negro high school students must attend this school. The action of the board in 1929 in removing Negro pupils from three mixed elementary schools was a continuation of an already established policy. By that year Negro leaders in Indianapolis, including the president of the NAACP, were active in a campaign to defeat the members of this board who were seeking re-election. Publicly, at least, they did not base their opposition on the board's segregationist policies but rather on discrimination against Indianapolis Negroes in the hiring of teachers.[59]

The fact that the Klan did not work openly for the segregation of the Indianapolis schools does not mean that Klan influence was nonexistent. Since Klan membership and Klan influence were pervasive in the early 1920's, undoubtedly Klan views were represented in the Indianapolis Chamber of Commerce and other civic groups which worked for the separation of the races in the schools. By 1926, Klan influence no doubt contributed to passage of the racial zoning ordinance in Indianapolis and the segregation movement in the Gary schools; at that time the influence of the Klan was indirect and covert rather than direct and open. But throughout these years the mayors of both Indianapolis and Gary were reputed to be members of the Klan, and a majority of the city councils of both cities had been elected with Klan support.

Klan influence may have played some part in the tightening of racial barriers in the 1920's, but it does not appear to have been the prime mover. Actually, the rapid influx of Negroes from the rural South into urban centers of a state where there had always been a tradition of racism seems to offer a sufficient explanation of the demand for segregation. The same attitudes among the people of Indiana which caused them to embrace the Klan caused them to favor separation of the races. Although Klan propaganda may have intensified race feeling, it is still conceivable that the segregation measures which were adopted in the 1920's might have been adopted if the Klan had not existed.

## NOTES

1. In Indiana the Negro population increased from 60,320 in 1910 to 111,982 in 1930, in Illinois, from 104,049 to 328,972; in Ohio, from 111,452 to 309,304; in Michigan, from 17,115 to 169,453. United States Bureau of the Census, *Negroes in the United States, 1920–1932* (Washington, 1935), 9, 12, 15.

2. *Ibid.*, 34–36, 44, 49, 53, 55; John Foster Potts, "A History of the Growth of the Negro Population in Gary, Indiana" (M. A. thesis, Cornell University, 1937), 6, 9, 18, 27; Powell A. Moore, *The Calumet Region: Indiana's Last Frontier* (Indianapolis, 1959), 252.

3. See Emma Lou Thornbrough, *The Negro in Indiana before 1900* (Indianapolis, 1957), *passim*, especially 68–70, 120–127, 162–166, 233, 249. The Indiana constitution of 1851 absolutely prohibited Negroes from coming into the state to reside. Before 1868 Negroes were not allowed to testify in court in a case in which a white man was a party. Until 1869 Negro children were not admitted to the public schools.

4. *Ibid.*, 266–270, 329.

5. For example, one county history published in 1916 contains the statement: "Washington County has for several decades boasted that no colored man or woman lived within her borders." Quoted, *ibid.*, 225.

6. *The Freeman* (Indianapolis), April 22, 1916. When there were signs of opposition to the use of the public parks by Negroes, the *Freeman* warned that it was wiser not to go to the parks in large numbers. It asserted: "What we wish is our right of enjoyment rather than to be in the parks at all times. If we are careful in not overdoing the matter . . . the right to go where we wish will not be opposed." *Ibid.*, August 12, 1916.

7. Indianapolis *World*, May 6, 1921.

8. The group was said to aim at securing the dismissal of Negroes from positions in the federal civil service and from employment by local government. *Freeman*, July 26, 1924. The president of the White Supremacy League wrote a long letter to the Ku Klux Klan publication, *The Fiery Cross*, justifying white supremacy. She insisted that she had no animosity toward Negroes but had a "marked respect for the negro who keeps his own kind, who does not display an anomalous desire for 'social equality' and who respects the white authority of the United States." *Fiery Cross* (Indianapolis), January 19, 1923.

9. *Freeman*, March 1, 1924.

10. *Journal of the Common Council of the City of Indianapolis, Indiana, from January 1, 1926, to December 1, 1926* (Indianapolis, 1927), 54. Persons who owned property before the adoption of the ordinance were permitted to reside in it and also to sell it, but if a Negro sold property to a white, or a white sold property to a Negro, the purchaser was not allowed to take up residence without obtaining the written consent of a majority of persons of the opposite race in the neighborhood. The term "community" as used in the ordinance was defined as every residence within 300 feet of the property involved.

11. The vote was five to one in favor of adoption. Three members of the council, two Republicans and one Democrat, where not present. *Ibid.*, 77–78; Indianapolis *News*, March 16, 1926; Indianapolis *Star*, March 16, 1926.

12. *Journal of the Common Council, 1926*, p. 82. The mayor was John L. Duvall, a Republican, who was elected with the backing of the Ku Klux Klan and subsequently sent to jail for violation of the Corrupt Practices Act.

13. *Tyler v. Harmon*, 158 La. 439 (1925). On a second hearing the Louisiana Supreme Court refused to reverse its decision. *Tyler v. Harmon*, 160 La. 943 (1926). In the Louisville case, *Buchanan v. Warley*, 245 U. S. 60 (1917), the Supreme Court ruled that the ordinance violated the Fourteenth Amendment because it interfered with property rights without due process of law. The decision did not rest on the equal protection clause.

14. National Association for the Advancement of Colored People, *Seventeenth Annual Report* (1927), 10. The case was Edward S. Gaillard versus Dr. Guy L. Grant, decided in the Marion County Superior Court, November 23, 1926. Indianapolis *News*, November 24, 1926.

15. *Harmon v. Tyler*, 273 U. S. 668 (1927). In a per curiam decision the Louisiana court was reversed on the authority of *Buchanan v. Warley*. After the invalidation of the racial zoning ordinance, white property owners turned increasingly to the use of racially restrictive covenants,

which continued to be enforceable in the courts until the decision of the United States Supreme Court in *Shelley v. Kraemer* (334 U. S. 1) in 1948.

16. Thornbrough, *Negro in Indiana*, 332–334, 341; Indianapolis *News*, May 13, 1919.

17. Indianapolis Board of School Commissioners (Office of the Board, Indianapolis), Minutes, Book W, 227.

18. *Ibid.*, 226–227.

19. *Ibid.*, Book Y, 22, 85, 159, 185, 304–305. See also Indianapolis *Times*, January 14, 1957, for a later survey of these problems.

20. Indianapolis Board of School Commissioners, Minutes, Book FF, 293.

21. *Ibid.*, Book W, 396. The Mapleton Civic Association also worked for a separate high school. A statement of its accomplishments said: "Through our efforts the School Board has promised to provide separate schools for the colored pupils of the city, especially a high school, this season, and we believe this will be of assistance in segregating these people." *Freeman*, March 1, 1924.

22. Indianapolis Board of School Commissioners, Minutes, Book X, 29, 50, 51.

23. *Ibid.*, 64.

24. Report of the Women's Department Club, *ibid.*, Book Y, 321; *Freeman*, March 21, 1924.

25. Indianapolis Board of School Commissioners, Minutes, Book Y, 319.

26. The *Freeman*, June 28, 1924, objected to the location chosen for the Negro school on the grounds that it was in a depressed residential area, near a glue factory and the city dump. Such a location, it declared, would have a depressing effect upon pupils "already humiliated by the fact that they are being forced from rooms of Shortridge, Manual and Arsenal Tech solely because of color."

27. *Greathouse v. Board of School Commissioners of City of Indianapolis*, 198 Ind. 95–107 (1926).

28. Indianapolis Board of School Commissioners, Minutes, Book CC, 166. Negro groups protested when the Board of School Commissioners announced that the new school would be known as Jefferson High School. As a result the name was changed to Crispus Attucks, a name suggested by some Negroes. *Ibid.*, Book BB, 113.

29. In 1910 the superintendent of schools, William A. Wirt, was quoted as saying: "We believe that it is only justice to the Negro children that they be segregated. There is naturally a feeling between the Negroes and the whites in the lower grades and we believe that the Negroes will be better cared for in their own schools. Besides they will take pride in

their work and will accomplish better results." Moore, *Calumet Region*, 392.

30. Gary *Post Tribune*, September 27, 1927.

31. *Ibid.*, September 26, 27, 28, 29, 1927.

32. *Ibid.*, October 4, 1927.

33. National Association for the Advancement of Colored People, *Nineteenth Annual Report* (1928), 17.

34. *State ex rel. Cheeks v. Wirt*, 203 Ind. 121 (1932). The court pointed out that the Virginia Street school was but one of six elementary school buildings in Gary in which courses equivalent to the first two years of high school work were offered and that pupils were transferred from these schools to the four-year high schools to finish their work. This was held to meet the requirements of the state law.

35. *Ibid.*, 134; Federal Writers Project, Works Progress Administration, *The Calumet Region Historical Guide* (Gary, 1939), 54; Indianapolis *Times*, April 4, 1947.

36. Robin M. Williams, Jr., and Margaret W. Ryan (eds.), *Schools in Transition: Community Experiences in Desegregation* (Chapel Hill, 1954), 68–69, 118. In the cities with segregated school systems there were opportunities for employment for Negro teachers. South Bend, on the other hand, did not employ a single Negro teacher until 1950.

37. Indianapolis *Star*, June 8, 1929. Residence halls at Indiana University were opened to Negro men in 1948 and to Negro women in 1950. Indianapolis *News*, April 23, 1959.

38. Indianapolis *World*, July 18, 1921; *Freeman*, August 9, 1924; Moore, *Calumet Region*, 391.

39. Norman F. Weaver, "The Knights of the Ku Klux Klan in Wisconsin, Indiana, Ohio, and Michigan" (Ph.D. dissertation, University of Wisconsin, 1954), *passim.*, especially 11–31.

40. Deposition of Hugh F. Emmons, p. 377, in Papers Relating to the Ku Klux Klan and D. C. Stephenson (Archives Division, Indiana State Library); *Fiery Cross*, February 16, September 28, 1923. In a typical piece of Klan oratory, defending the fact that the Klan was open to white members only, one speaker declared: "We are not anti anything. We are just white. We are not only white, but you just bet your life we are going to stay white. Whenever a man goes to mixing God's colors he gets into trouble, and he is not only doomed but he is damned and they [*sic*] ought to be." *Ibid.*, December 6, 1922.

41. *Fiery Cross*, July 6, August 31, 1923.

42. This incident occurred near Culver, Indiana. *Ibid.*, May 25, 1923. In another instance it was claimed that Klan members protected a Negro

minister in Hammond who was threatened by Catholics and foreigners when he sought to have a Negro church built near a Catholic church. *Ibid.*, December 5, 1924.

43. *Freeman*, March 29, May 17, 1924; Indianapolis *News*, May 6, 1924.
44. *Freeman*, May 17, 1924.
45. *Ibid.*, February 14, 1924; Weaver, "The Knights of the Ku Klux Klan," 206.
46. *Freeman*, July 12, September 27, 1924.
47. *Ibid.*, September 20, October 4, October 25, 1924.
48. *Ibid.*, May 17, September 20, October 25, 1924.
49. This theme was used repeatedly by the Democrats. See, for example, Indianapolis *News*, October 17, 1924.
50. *Ibid.*, October 16, 1924.
51. *Freeman*, September 20, 1924; Mimeographed bulletin, October 25, 1924, The Papers Relating to the Ku Klux Klan.
52. *Fiery Cross*, October 24, 1924.
53. Indianapolis *News*, November 5, 1924; Indianapolis *Star*, November 4, 1925.
54. A bulletin issued from the office of the Grand Dragon of the Realm of Indiana, October 20, 1924, said that enemies of the Klan were importing Negro speakers, who were advising Negro voters that a Klan victory would mean that Negroes would be segregated or forced to return to the South. See Papers Relating to the Ku Klux Klan. The only measure mentioning race introduced in the 1925 session was a senate bill sponsored by William E. English, Republican of Marion County, which would have provided a training school in domestic arts for Negro girls. The bill passed the senate but not the house. Indiana Senate, *Journal*, 74th Session (1925), 132, 792; Indiana House of Representatives, *Journal*, 74th Session (1925), 751.
55. Indianapolis *News*, October 21, October 26, November 2, 1925.
56. *Ibid.*, November 2, November 4, 1925; Indianapolis *Star*, November 4, 1925. Moore, *Calumet Region*, 556
57. Williams and Ryan (eds.), *Schools in Transition*, 50; statement of Dr. Herman Shibler, in Indianapolis *Times*, January 14, 1957.
58. See, for example, Indianapolis *News*, May 13, 1919.
59. Indianapolis *Times*, November 2, 1929.

# 10 | Politics, Emotion, and the Wallace Vote*

## Michael Rogin

### ONE

George Wallace's campaign for the Presidency of the United States began not in 1968 but in 1964. That spring Governor George Wallace, nationally prominent for his role defending school segregation in Alabama, ran in the presidential primaries of three northern states. Before the April Wisconsin primary few expected Wallace to get a significant vote;[1] yet he garnered 34 per cent of the Democratic primary total in Wisconsin, 31 per cent in Indiana, and 42.7 per cent in Maryland, including a majority of the white vote.

Wallace's strength in the industrial centres of the three states was even more impressive. Wisconsin, Maryland, and Indiana contain large metropolitan areas, heavily populated by Negroes and by workers of Southern- and East-European stock. The Negro ghettoes have grown substantially since the 1960 census, and no exact measure of their size is available. Estimates placed Negroes at 10–15 per cent of the Milwaukee population, and approximately 35 per cent of the Baltimore population; in Gary, Indiana, Negroes outnumbered non-Spanish-speaking whites. Wallace ran better in Milwaukee than in Wisconsin as a whole, carried virtually every white precinct in Gary—most by more than two-thirds of the Democratic vote—and carried most of the non-Jewish, white Baltimore precincts.

Much of the impact of the Wallace showings was shattered by the

Reprinted from *British Journal of Sociology* XX, no. 1 (March 1969): 27–49. By permission of Routledge and Kegan Paul Ltd., and the London School of Economics.

* My thanks to Sheila Stern and Michael Parker for help in the preparation of the quantitative sections of this article, and to the Chancellor's office, University of California at Berkeley, for a summer research fellowship which made the interviewing possible.

Johnson landslide a few months later. But Johnson's authoritative victories in the cities and states where Wallace had done so well simply added to the host of unanswered questions. Four of these questions provide the focus for the present discussion:

1. What were the *specific* sources of support and opposition to Wallace?
2. What was the relationship between the support for Wallace and the support for Goldwater in the subsequent presidential contest?
3. What do these campaigns indicate about the nature and extent of racism at the mass political level?
4. How did pragmatic, urban politicians respond to extremist racist appeals?

To determine the sources of support for Wallace and Goldwater, I analysed county, township, and precinct voting returns in Maryland, Wisconsin, and Indiana. In addition, I interviewed politicians, newspapermen, and union officials in Baltimore, Milwaukee, Gary, and East Chicago, and read the local newspaper reports of the Wallace campaigns. Here I will discuss the *vote* in Wisconsin and Indiana only, and then analyse the *campaigns* for and against Wallace in all three states.[2]

### Wisconsin: The Wallace Vote

What social groups most favoured Wallace? Many social scientists distinguished between the sources of support for economic and non-economic liberalism. These theorists will hold that economic liberalism (support for the welfare state) is strongest among working class and ethnic minority elements. They find support for civil rights, civil liberties, political tolerance, a moderate foreign policy, and the other elements of 'non-economic' liberalism greater among middle class and better educated people, who are more sophisticated in understanding democracy, more tolerant and less authoritarian in personal outlook.[3]

This view is not confined to social scientists. Explaining Wallace's strong showing inside Milwaukee, politically knowledgeable residents invariably reported the anti-Negro feeling on the heavily Polish, working class, south side of the city. A veteran newspaperman, a prominent union leader, and a Democratic politician all believed Wallace had run best on the south side. However, the working class, Polish precincts gave Wallace a smaller percentage of their votes than any other white precincts in the city. Of thirty-one neighbourhoods, the five more than 18 per cent Polish[4] gave Wallace an average of 31 per cent of the vote. The sixteen neighbourhoods less than 5 per cent Polish averaged 38 per cent for Wallace. Similarly, the eight neighbourhoods with more than 45 per cent of their employed population engaged in white collar occupations averaged 41 per cent for Wallace. The eight neighbourhoods less than 25 per cent white collar averaged 33 per cent for the Alabama governor. (For the over-all correlations, see Table 1.)

Republican neighbourhoods also voted consistently more for Wallace than Democratic ones. Because of reapportionment, we have only a September 1964 gubernatorial primary as a measure of the normal party vote, and there are difficulties with its use. Nevertheless, the Republican percentage of total turnout in that primary is probably a broadly valid indicator of regular Republican strength,[5] and its correlation with the Wallace vote is striking (see Table 1).

TABLE 1   *The Wallace Vote in Milwaukee*

|  | Wallace | *Wallace with:* | | |
|  | | 1964 Repub. primary constant | White collar constant | Polish constant |
|---|---|---|---|---|
| White collar | .68 | .08 | | .46 |
| Polish | −.74 | −.32 | −.57 | |
| 1964 Sept. Repub. primary | .79 | | .55 | .50 |
| Goldwater | .77 | | | |

In the Milwaukee suburbs the principal support for Wallace also came not from workers but from middle class Republicans; Wallace was stronger in middle class suburbs than anywhere else in Wisconsin.[6] In Gary, Indiana, however, the pattern was much different.

### Gary: Working Class Authoritarianism?

Whites in Gary and the other working class towns of Lake County voted overwhelmingly for Wallace. He received his strongest support in Gary from two groups: Southern, white, working class homeowners; and homeowners of Southern- and East-European stock. A relatively homogeneous census tract of Southern, white, working class homeowners voted 77 per cent for Wallace.[7] The large section of

Gary south of the Little Calumet River, heavily populated by South-
ern- and East-European homeowners, was 76 per cent for Wallace.[8]
This part of Gary is predominantly working class. However, the more
white collar precincts in south Gary supported Wallace just as strongly
as the most blue collar neighbourhoods.[9]

The area of Gary north of the Negro ghetto contains far fewer
homeowners, and fewer of the residents are of Southern- and East-
European stock. Both working and lower middle class north Gary
precincts voted less for Wallace than comparable precincts in south
Gary. Six north Gary lower middle class precincts averaged 69 per
cent for Wallace, as did ten adjoining working class precincts. The
wealthiest Gary neighbourhood gave least support to Wallace, 'only'
57 per cent. Perhaps class was a factor here, but a significant minority
of the residents are Jewish.[10] The Jewish precinct in downtown Gary
was also substantially less for Wallace than surrounding precincts,
and the Milwaukee suburbs with Jewish residents voted less for
Wallace than other middle class Milwaukee suburbs.

Thus ethnicity and home ownership seem more important than
class in revealing who would support the Alabama governor and who
oppose him. The fact remains that Gary is predominantly blue collar,
and workers voted overwhelmingly for Wallace. But given the contrasting behaviour of Milwaukee workers, abstract "working class
authoritarianism" explanations divorced from concrete political realities
hardly provide an adequate explanation of the Gary vote. The size and
visibility of the Gary Negro ghetto is more relevant.

### Indiana: The "Black Belt" Effect

In the south, racist voting has been strongest where the race issue
is most salient, i.e. in the counties with the heaviest Negro concentration.[11] Black belt patterns now entered northern politics as well. Half
the Gary population is Negro, more than three times the Milwaukee
proportions. And while one-third of Milwaukee's whites voted for
Wallace, more than two-thirds of Gary's did.

Black belt voting extended within Lake County itself. The Negro
ghetto fills the centre of Gary, and proximity to it did not affect
voting within the city. However, the closer suburban whites lived to
the ghetto, the more likely they were to vote for Wallace. Hobart,
Ross, and Calumet, which surround south Gary on three sides, gave
Wallace 69 per cent, 73 per cent, and 65 per cent of their vote,
respectively. (Calumet is 7 per cent Negro, so the white vote there

was more than 65 per cent.) Residents of these townships are probably more likely to work in and travel to Gary. In the other white
cities and villages of Lake County Wallace received 50–60 per cent
of the Democratic vote, his lowest total recorded at the south end of
Lake County, furthest from the Gary Negro ghetto.

Outside of Lake and suburban Porter counties, the Wallace vote
fell off precipitously, duplicating the pattern in outstate Wisconsin.[12]
Omitting Lake County, Wallace averaged only 28 per cent of the
Indiana vote. None of the twelve counties which gave Wallace the
smallest percentage of their vote was as much as 2 per cent non-white;
four of the twelve most pro-Wallace counties, in addition to the Lake–
Porter metropolitan area, had small but visible Negro ghettos.[13]

### Indiana: The Bible Belt

Wallace's strength in outstate Indiana was in part explained by
Negro proximity. But many counties with virtually no Negroes voted
30–45 per cent for Wallace. Much of southern Indiana was settled by
southerners, and Civil War traditions continue to influence party
patterns in the state. But perhaps these traditions have become
divorced, as so often happens, from the live issues which created them;
"southern" counties did not disproportionately support Wallace.[14]

Instead more recent Indiana political history may have been relevant. The Ku Klux Klan dominated Indiana politics in the 1920's,
and was stronger in that state than anywhere else in the country.
Wallace ran best in a wide belt of counties across central Indiana,
many with middle size Anglo-Saxon cities, and most dominated by
fundamentalist Protestant sects. He ran worst in rural counties
originally settled by German Catholics and Protestants, who had felt
the lash of nativist sentiment in the 1920's (see Table 2).[15] Thus

TABLE 2   *The Wallace Vote in Indiana*

| Counties | % Urban | % Rural-farm | % Non-white | % 'German' religions (1936) | % German (1930) |
|---|---|---|---|---|---|
| Ten non-metropolitan, pro-Wallace (37–45%) | 45.7 | 12.6 | 2.2 | 3.0 | 0.1 |
| Twelve anti-Wallace (7–17%) | 28.9 | 25.4 | 0.0 | 25.4 | 5.2 |

nativism augmented the black belt effect; the Wallace vote had "ideo-logical" as well as "pragmatic" roots. This was also true in Wisconsin, where Republicans in counties with few Negroes, who generally vote for conservative candidates, voted for the southern segregationist.[16]

### The Support for Wallace: Conclusion

In outlying Wisconsin and Indiana, general right-wing sentiments apparently contributed votes for Wallace. But he received most of his support from anti-Negro prejudice activated by proximity to Negroes. This explains why the ethnic working class supported Wallace in Gary and opposed him in Milwaukee.[17] Negroes are a majority of the English-speaking population in Gary, less than 15 per cent in Milwaukee. To add to the visibility of the Gary Negro ghetto, at the time of the Wallace campaign the president and two other members of the Gary city council were Negroes. Gary's large and active civil rights movement had staged a 10,000-man housing march and a successful school boycott in the months before the primary. No comparable events had yet occurred in Milwaukee. Moreover, the civil rights activity in neighbouring Chicago must have had some impact on Gary residents, many of whom read Chicago newspapers (particularly the *Chicago Tribune*).[18]

I have speculated elsewhere[19] that educated members of the middle class do not require immediate and concrete realities to unleash anti-democratic predispositions. Abstract fears and distant threats can be more salient to them. Workers, on the other hand, lead a more concrete and present-oriented existence. This can be a protection against the political expression of emotions like racism; caught up in their immediate daily concerns, workers—whatever their abstract attitudes —are less easily mobilized. Traditional party loyalty kept many in Milwaukee from voting for Wallace. But where a reality that seems unpleasant is immediate and visible, workers can react intensely. Active working class racism may depend more than middle class racism on a large and visible Negro ghetto.[20]

### TWO

If Wallace's strength was the first act of the 1964 racial drama, Gold-water's weakness was the second. Whatever other forces caused the Republican Party to depart from tradition and nominate an outspoken conservative, Wallace's showing among Democrats was surely a factor. Here was concrete evidence—and such evidence was scarce—of potential electoral support more likely to go to a conservative than to a moderate Republican. Many observers argued that Goldwater's nomination would realign American political parties. The racial issue would benefit Goldwater by shifting the Republican base of support toward ethnic minorities and lower class whites, allegedly more vulnerable to racial appeals. What in fact was the impact of the racism reflected in the Wallace vote on Goldwater's strength?

To determine whether racism reoriented Republican strength, we must first calculate the Goldwater deviations from the "normal" party vote. I chose the 1962 Wisconsin gubernatorial contest and the 1962 Indiana senatorial race, both won by Democrats, as measures of party normality.[21] Deviations were determined by plotting the Goldwater vote against the 1962 Republican vote. Those geographical units (countries, precincts, etc.) most distant from the regression line were the deviant units. The greater the number and size of the deviations, the lower the correlation between Goldwater and party normality. If the pro-Goldwater deviating units had supported Wallace, the anti-Goldwater ones opposed him, then racism would have influenced the Goldwater vote.

### Wisconsin: The Goldwater Vote

Goldwater ran consistently beneath normal Republican strength in Wisconsin, but he tended to be strong and weak in the same areas as previously Republican candidates. Within Milwaukee, among the suburbs, and among the counties, the relationship between Goldwater's support and previous Republican strength was extremely high. In the city Goldwater's vote correlated .97 with the Republican vote in the September primary. In the suburbs of the correlations between Goldwater's vote and other Republican elections were all .95+.[22] In the counties Goldwater's vote was as close to normal Republican elections as these were to each other (see Table 3).[23] The Goldwater election did not radically alter the sources of support for the Republican Party.

TABLE 3   *The Republican Vote in Wisconsin*

|  | 1960 Rep. Gov. | 1962 Rep. Gov. | 1964 Rep. Pres. |
|---|---|---|---|
| 1958 Rep. Sen. | .92 | .89 | .83 |
| 1960 Rep. Gov. |  | .92 | .89 |
| 1962 Rep. Gov. |  |  | .92 |

However, those shifts that did occur were strongly related to the Wallace vote. Three shifts stand out. First, Goldwater's strength fell off much less in the city of Milwaukee, the working class suburbs, and the middle class suburbs than in the counties of Wisconsin as a whole (see Table 4). Second, Goldwater's strength held up better in the

TABLE 4  *Percentage Drop in Republican Vote, 1962–1964*

| Milwaukee city | Working class suburbs | Middle class suburbs | Wisconsin counties |
|---|---|---|---|
| 17.8 | 18.4 | 17.1 | 29.1 |

lower middle class Milwaukee suburbs than in the upper middle class, Jewish suburbs (see Table 5).[24] Third, Goldwater ran behind the 1962 Republican gubernatorial candidate in every county in the state. But he was deserted more in the poorer, rural counties of Wisconsin which had opposed Wallace than in the wealthier urban ones which had supported him (see Table 6).[25]

In the folklore of American politics, Goldwater represented the nineteenth-century rural American, out of touch with modern prob-

TABLE 5  *Goldwater and the Wisconsin Suburban Middle Class*

|  | % Wallace | % Drop 1962 Rep. Gov. to 1964 Rep. Pres. | % Upper white collar* | Median family income (in dollars) |
|---|---|---|---|---|
| Three upper-middle class partly Jewish suburbs | 48 | 23 | 53 | 14,700 |
| Three lower-middle class suburbs | 51 | 16 | 30 | 8,300 |

* Percentage employed as professionals, managers, proprietors, and officials.

lems and cosmopolitan developments. But Goldwater's candidacy, tied to the backlash, hurt the Wisconsin Republican Party more in the countryside than in urban areas.

## Lake County: Race and Realignment

Unlike Milwaukee, the white backlash in Lake County had a pronounced effect on the presidential contest. In spite of the Johnson

TABLE 6   *Support and Opposition to Goldwater in Wisconsin*

| Counties | % For Wallace | % Urban | % Rural farm | Median income (dollars) |
|---|---|---|---|---|
| Seven pro-Goldwater, Republican | 39.7 | 46.6 | 14.4 | 5,564 |
| Six anti-Goldwater, Republican | 27.8 | 28.3 | 34.9 | 4,409 |
| Eight pro-Goldwater, Democratic | 31.3 | 41.6 | 23.1 | 5,348 |
| Nine anti-Goldwater, Democratic | 24.7 | 27.8 | 29.6 | 4,884 |

landslide elsewhere in Indiana, Goldwater actually improved on the normal Republican vote in south Gary, and ran as well as Republicans normally do in the suburbs. The effects of the white backlash on traditional party lines was greater in Lake County than anywhere else in Indiana or Wisconsin.

To discover the impact of the Wallace vote on Goldwater support, the Goldwater vote in every predominantly English-speaking, white precinct in Gary was plotted against the percentage garnered by the Republican senatorial candidate in 1962. The correlation between the two elections was .85, which seemed relatively low, indicating a greater Goldwater departure from the normal party pattern than was true in Milwaukee.[26] Two main groups of precincts deviated from the normal party pattern.

Several north Gary working class precincts disproportionately opposed Goldwater, but most of these probably had substantial Latin minorities. A cluster of precincts, all from south Gary, disproportionately supported Goldwater, actually voting more for him than for the Republican senatorial candidate in 1962. Indeed, of the twenty-six south Gary precincts, all but three were above the regression line, and all but four were more Republican than two years previous. In south Gary as a whole Republican strength rose from 41 per cent in 1962 to 46 per cent in 1964. This, of course, flies in the face of the Johnson landslide; only three other Gary precincts voted more Republican in 1964 than in 1962.

Goldwater's success was not restricted to south Gary alone. The total Republican vote in Lake County outside of Gary and East Chicago dropped less than 1 per cent between 1962 and 1964. As in

Wisconsin, the metropolitan centre, where Wallace had been strongest, failed to oppose Goldwater in the proportions found in the outlying areas.

### Indiana: Realignment and Religion

Outside of Lake County the Goldwater election did not noticeably disrupt party lines. But the religious split, important in the Wallace vote, was equally significant in November. This split cannot be explained by proximity to Negroes. It rather lends support to speculation about the fundamentalist Protestant underpinnings of the contemporary American right.[27]

As in Wisconsin, the Goldwater election was as close to recent Republican elections as these were to each other (see Table 7). However, a substantial number of counties deviated somewhat from party tradition. Almost invariably, those counties disproportionately for

TABLE 7    *The Party Vote in Indiana*

|                    | 1958 Rep. Sen. | 1960 Rep. Pres. | 1962 Rep. Sen. | 1964 Rep. Pres. |
|--------------------|----------------|-----------------|----------------|-----------------|
| 1956 Rep. Pres.    | .80            | .80             | .85            | .75             |
| 1958 Rep. Sen.     |                | .80             | .86            | .75             |
| 1960 Rep. Pres.    |                |                 | .90            | .84             |
| 1962 Rep. Sen.     |                |                 |                | .91             |

Goldwater had strongly supported Wallace, those disproportionately against Goldwater had strongly opposed the Alabama governor.[28] The anti-Goldwater counties averaged 18 per cent for Wallace; the pro-Goldwater counties averaged 37 per cent. The religious component of the Wallace vote also remained important. Those adhering to the 'German' religions were more than 15 per cent of the population in six of the eight anti-Goldwater counties, and in none of the ten non-metropolitan pro-Goldwater counties. Goldwater ran best in the Protestant bible belt; yet even here he could not match normal Republican strength. Race helped Goldwater more than religion in Indiana.

### Goldwater and Wallace: Conclusion

Goldwater clearly benefited from pro-Wallace sentiment. Lake County aside, shifts of normally Democratic voters into the Republican camp were too small either to realign substantially the sources of support for the parties, or to counteract the Democratic landslide. In 1964 racism was still less important than traditional party loyalty, economic issues, and foreign policy; these factors all hurt Goldwater. Nevertheless, the more salient race—in metropolitan as opposed to rural areas, in Lake County, in south Gary—the greater his support. The white backlash was a marginal factor in November 1964, but it had entered a northern, Presidential general election for the first time.

## THREE

Wallace's strength had ethnic and economic correlates. But even where these were clear-cut—class in Milwaukee, ethnicity in Gary— the differences they produced in voting behaviour were only a few percentage points.[29] Wallace sentiment was diffused throughout the urban population, falling off sharply only in rural counties far from Negro ghettoes. To account for Wallace's remarkable metropolitan showing, we must investigate features of urban life and politics shared across class and ethnic lines.

Wallace mobilized his remarkable support without the public backing of a single, established political leader or political faction in Gary, Milwaukee, or Baltimore. All the symbols of public authority—newspapers, church leaders, state and national politicians—issued strong public statements against the Alabama governor. Support for Wallace, moreover, violated obvious public norms about tolerance and equal rights. Wallace had few physical resources to overcome his failure to win any public legitimacy. He lacked a political organization, did not even campaign in Lake County, and virtually no precinct work was done in his behalf.

To vote for Wallace under these circumstances was to reject the ordinary bearers and standards of public authority. The Wallace campaign permitted the expression of feelings that had heretofore lacked a political outlet.[30] As a woman said after a rally in Madison, Wisconsin, "Wallace is saying things that many of us are thinking, but are afraid to say."[31] One local observer of the Gary campaign echoed the views of many others when he remarked, "People were not going to be told what to do by politicians." Wallace pitched his campaign to these same feelings of popular rebelliousness, presenting himself as an underdog fighting the politicians.

In their attempt to minimize the Wallace threat, politicians fed the underdog image. In part this was wishful thinking, as they sought to deny a reality that they must have felt they could not control. But there were also considerations of strategy involved. Minimizing Wallace's strength was part of a general effort to deny him legitimacy; he was consistently attacked as a southern "carpetbagger" and an extremist. Similar efforts to isolate and undermine Goldwater were to succeed; these simply backfired.

Why did popular rebelliousness work for Wallace but not for Goldwater—or against Eisenhower for that matter? Here one must point not only to grassroots racial resentments, but also to the conditions under which they could be safely expressed.

There is little doubt but that the Wallace vote was racially motivated. Wallace chose to run against state administrations which had enacted unpopular tax measures, and many politicians and union leaders sought to blame the size of his showing on the tax increases. As a negative factor taxes may have been important; Wallace wisely did not pit himself against any highly popular state administrations. But why should tax increases have made the governors so much more unpopular in the industrial centres of their states, with substantial Negro ghettoes, than in the outlying areas? When politicians and union leaders stressed the sales tax, they seemed mainly anxious to disguise (from themselves as well as from others) the depth of racial feeling among their constituents. They wanted to insist on the normality of the politics involved in the Wallace campaigns. A Gary newspaperman with strong local ties remarked, "Politicians will tell you it was the sales tax; but I didn't hear one person mention the sales tax during the entire campaign."

As the sales tax was credited with mobilizing working class votes for Wallace, so Republican desire to "embarrass the Democrats" allegedly explained middle class cross-overs in Wisconsin. Middle class prejudice may well require more rationalization than working class prejudice; perhaps for some Republicans "embarrassing the Democrats" was analogous to the more common "states rights" and "property rights" slogans. The history of cross-over in Wisconsin indicates that most voters cross over to vote for the candidate they favour. And the middle class Wallace support, like the working class support, came near areas of Negro concentration.

The Wallace vote was first and foremost an anti-Negro vote. A lifelong Gary resident with obvious sympathy for Wallace explained,

People voted for Wallace because they don't like open occupancy laws shoved down their throats . . . because Dick Gregory and Al

Raby (Chicago civil rights leaders) lead these marches and demonstrations, tie up traffic, lie down in the streets . . . because a nineteen year old stewardess gets raped on an el [rapid transit] platform . . . People are afraid of Negroes . . . This had been building up for years . . . Negro housing projects ten years old have to be condemned; white projects twice as old are in fine condition. . . .

Without discoursing on the reasons for prejudice, anti-Negro feelings are almost a reflex on the part of American urban whites. When race becomes salient in American politics, one need not wonder that a Wallace will run so well.

Public opinion polls, however, show that three-quarters of northern whites favour integrated schools and neighbourhoods. Two-thirds of the American people supported the Civil Rights Act up before Congress that Wallace attacked in his campaigns. How reconcile Wallace's vote with the 1964 California public opinion poll in which two-thirds of the sample believed civil rights to be the most important issue in the presidential campaign, and two-thirds of these thought Johnson better able to deal with it than Goldwater?[32]

Those who take the polls at face value must deny the racism in white America and blame the Wallace vote on *deus ex machina* like the sales tax or Negro "extremism". But it would be equally mistaken to ignore the commitment to civil rights. How, we must ask, did voters adjust these abstract norms to their concrete fears; what made it safe to express racist emotion? And here most observers had the same explanation. One could vote for Wallace without having to live with the consequences. The Wallace voter was free to express his anger; it cost him nothing. As a veteran Baltimore newspaperman put it, "People knew Wallace wasn't going anywhere. For the average voter this was an emotional thing; there wasn't a bit of politics in it."

Again we encounter the anti-political character of the Wallace vote, this time expressed not as a revolt against the politicians, but as a rejection of the need to be practical. Many of those who voted for Wallace would probably not have wanted him to be governor of their state, or president of the United States. This would violate their abstract commitment to civil rights, as well as their need for order; it would make them feel too guilty. But in voting for Wallace one could express pent up feelings without having to live with their consequences. In much the same way many whites opposed to civil rights demonstrations probably voted for Johnson rather than Goldwater, just because Goldwater was an "extremist" and would not keep things under control.[33] Wallace provided the opportunity, rare in politics, to express anger without needing to fear its disordering consequences, to violate social values without having to feel guilt.

The vote for Wallace was thus double-edged. It suggested on the one hand that racist emotion was strongest when it was politically least meaningful. But future years might bring ways of making prejudice safe that would move racism closer to the centre of American politics. The Wallace vote was a reminder that the possibility of a mass-based racist movement was not completely remote.

At the same time, the sources of support for Wallace make irrelevant theories which rely on urban middle class, "non-economic" liberalism as a counter-weight to "working class authoritarianism". The size of the non-Jewish middle class Wallace vote—even the upper middle class vote—is telling. Perhaps there are upper middle class, highly educated groups whose non-economic liberalism can be relied upon, but they make up a small percentage of the voting population.


FOUR

Instead the Wallace vote seems to lend credibility to a different theory of non-economic liberalism—one which locates the sources of support for racial and political tolerance among political and community leaders, and urges that political issues be kept within the "political stratum" and away from the population at large.[34] Does not the Wallace vote, a rebellion of the population against its political leadership, give sustenance to this theory? Let us look more closely at the behaviour of politicians during the Wallace campaigns.

"For the average voter," said the Baltimore reporter, "this was an emotional thing. There wasn't a bit of politics in it." For the average politician, he might have added, this was a political thing; there wasn't a bit of emotion in it. A young Baltimore ward heeler was more wrong than right about the uniqueness of his own city when he said, "In other cities people play politics at election time; here we play it all year round." For what he calls attention to was the impact of private political intrigue upon public issues. And the gulf between public stance and private performance in all three cities was as significant as the gulf between political leaders and private citizens discussed above.

Baltimore, Gary, and Milwaukee are all strongly Democratic cities with chaotic party organizations. There are at least two major factions in each city, with a host of minor cliques around particular candidates, ethnic bosses, and ward heelers. In Baltimore, with extremely well-developed, grassroots politics, many precincts contain competing precinct organizations. In Milwaukee the party organization hardly exists at all at the precinct level, but individual incumbents have their own workers, and the major city politicians are allied with different factions in the state Democratic party. The fight for political control of Gary in 1964 was between a faction led by John Krupa, head of the Lake County Democratic Central Committee, and a faction which included the ex-mayor of Gary, convicted of criminal charges arising from political corruption. A powerful faction in each of the cities was in conflict with the state Democratic administration.

For ordinary citizens the Wallace campaign was about race. For the professional politicians it was just another chapter in an unending competitive struggle for political power. For many the most important candidate in the primary was not Wallace but his opponent. The mayor of Milwaukee, for example, at political loggerheads with Governor Reynolds, did not officially endorse Reynolds, or take part in the primary fight. The mayor is officially non-partisan, and, a member of his staff explained, does not get involved in primaries. Mayor Maier had four years earlier been elected thanks to his strength on the Polish south side. Voters here had a reputation for being anti-Negro, and the political calculation was simple. Why mobilize votes for the head of an opposing political faction against a candidate of undetermined but probably powerful political appeal?

Voters and readers of the nation-wide press might have thought the most important contest in the 1964 Indiana primary was that between Wallace and Governor Welsh. For Gary politicians there were more pressing matters of practical significance. More than one hundred candidates were running for the ten Lake County seats in the state assembly, and each faction had its own slate. One precinct worker, asked what he would say when he knocked on the door, explained he would start with the "top of ticket", by which he meant the top of his state slate. Asked if he would eventually talk about Wallace, he replied, "Usually", but that if there was any resentment he would not push matters. To do so might jeopardize the chances of the candidates about whom he cared.

Moreover, neither the steel union in Gary nor the leaders of the political faction currently controlling the county had any fondness for Governor Welsh. Many did not want Welsh to look too good in the primary fight (although none expected that Wallace would run as well as he did). The situation in Baltimore—strife between city and state politicians, disassociation of candidates for other offices from the Wallace campaign—duplicated that in the other cities.[35]

Did Democratic Party politicians fail to mobilize against Wallace simply because of indifference and fear? Was no more involved than calculations of political costs and benefits? Certainly the pervasive instrumentalism of these politicians was important. A local Baltimore politico explained that no established precinct worker or organization could support Wallace, since they depended for patronage jobs and advancement on the political higher-ups who opposed him. But a few young precinct workers, he said, had campaigned for Wallace, just so they could say they had won their precincts with him. If he were twenty-one, said the politico nostalgically, he might have done the same thing. For such a man love of the political game and its stakes ("here we play politics all year round") pre-empts any ideological consideration. Others, particularly further advanced in the political hierarchy, were sincerely opposed to Wallace, but they were more concerned with their continuing political rivalries and constituency relationships than with political issues like race. These politicians were adaptable, fearful of risks, anxious not to back a loser, pre-occupied with their political battles. They fit, in short, the traditional picture of the pragmatic, non-ideological American politician. How they would have responded to a local racist who actually challenged their power, or to a candidate with a chance for a concrete victory, it is impossible to say. But a Wallace success could not hurt them; like the ordinary voters, they had nothing political at stake.

For other politicians and local activists, indifference to the Wallace campaign masked covert sympathy for the Alabama governor. Often those who insisted that the sales tax rather than race had caused the Wallace vote were disguising their own racial feelings. Not wanting to face their own prejudice, such community activists could not admit the existence of prejudice anywhere.[36] Many politicians and union leaders withdrew from the Wallace campaign because of their own conflicted feelings.

Finally, in all three cities there was widespread sympathy for Wallace among grassroots political activists, even many who went through the motions of campaigning against him. Many precinct workers would wait until the first anti-Negro, pro-Wallace remark by their neighbour permitted them to express their own real feelings. To an important extent Wallace mobilized a community underground, divorced from the official sentiments of city and national leaders. This underground consisted not simply of precinct workers, but of other people respected in their neighbourhoods. A Gary reporter, whose father has been on the police force for twenty-one years, and who spent much of his own time at the police station, reported that all the policemen he talked to had voted for Wallace.[37]

Would clear political opposition to Wallace have made a difference? Certainly it would have had some impact. In Baltimore's Polish second ward, a well-manned precinct split fifty-fifty for Wallace; another in the same ward where the machine lay down supported Wallace two to one.[38] In the Italian section of Baltimore, a precinct of elderly, immigrant, homeowners is run by a short, barrelchested Italian in his middle sixties. He has the (local) reputation of being the best precinct worker in the country. His is generally the most Democratic white precinct in the city, and he was given an award by the then Vice-President Johnson at a Baltimore Democratic dinner a few years ago. His precinct voted two to one for Wallace. Surely such a precinct leader could have produced more votes for Brewster had he so desired.

It would be perverse to blame the political organizations for a Wallace vote so clearly produced by grassroots sentiment. That perversity is not intended. But it seems equally perverse to argue that pragmatic, non-ideological politicians in America insulate our politics from the consequences of ideology and extremism. Pragmatism, cross-pressures, and the related virtues of political moderation increased the Wallace vote. Perhaps the American style of urban politics only works against weakly felt ideologies—precisely the sort not themselves dangerous.

To blame the attitudes of ordinary citizens when racism, McCarthyism, and similar 'ideologies' gain political importance, and thank political activists when they do not, hardly seems sufficient. The real forces keeping ideological extremism out of American politics have been, I would argue, pre-political. Pragmatic politics have not kept racism, jingoism, and anti-Communism out of the political arena when these "ideologies" have become salient. Whatever has made extremism politically relevant, ordinary politicians adapt to it, pretending that nothing out of the ordinary has happened. This politics of avoidance is not necessarily the best way either to solve the problems which produced the hysteria or to meet anti-democratic threats.[39]

There is a gulf between expressed public sentiments of political leaders and their willingness actively to engage the population on the basis of those sentiments. Political pragmatism replaces political education.[40] In this situation the gulf between the expressed public sentiments of political leaders and the actual feelings of ordinary citizens becomes truly enormous. Since political leaders lack the authority of communicated conviction, no one really believes them.

When citizens feel strongly enough about an issue to rebel against the politicians, there is only the authority of hollow men standing in their way. And since the politicians hide from the issues which promote the rebellion, and insist on politics as usual, the rebellion meets only a hollow response.

Ought our aim to be, then, to keep issues like race out of the political realm, or at least to restrict attention to such issues to the political stratum itself? The difficulty is that race was kept out of the political arena only at the expense of Negroes; once race enters politics, how, and at what price, does one restrict interest in it to a few groups and individuals? For example, would reducing the scope of Negro demands or mass demonstrations (if one had this power) placate white racism? It is equally plausible to argue that public Negro demands and demonstrations push further the frontiers of legitimacy for Negro aspirations—even if they also produce such defensive reactions as the Wallace vote.

There is no running away from racism in white America through political formulas and mechanics. Perhaps that racism will ultimately be less important than economic issues, real feelings of toleration, indifference to Negroes, etc. Then the Wallace vote will appear in retrospect as a kind of political therapy for white Americans in the process of resisting change and changing themselves. Alternatively, white racism may culminate in a mass anti-Negro political movement. Perhaps both these things will happen. But given the consciousness now in the Negro community, and given the economic and political obstacles that inhibit the realization of Negro demands, race will disappear neither from American politics nor from mass attention. And the race issues is not like traditional American ethnic and economic political controversies. Because Negro–white relations involve serious conflict and deep feelings, Madisonian politics has not been successful in dealing with race. It has succeeded neither in preventing violence nor in incorporating the Negroes into the Madisonian system. And it has failed because it is not a system which saves us from ideological extremism, but that works in its absence. The Wallace vote should serve as a reminder both of racist emotion in America and of the consequent failure of a pragmatic politics of race.

## NOTES

1. Governor Reynolds, Wallace's Wisconsin opponent, conceded him 100,000 votes two weeks before the primary (*Milwaukee Sentinel*, 4

April 1964), far more than he had been expected to receive when the campaign started, and far fewer than the 260,000 votes he actually obtained. Predicting that Wallace would be "slaughtered" in Maryland, Governor Tawes remarked, "Governor Wallace won't get a vote of any significance." (*Baltimore Sun*, 23 March 1964.)

2. Changes in precinct boundaries in Gary and Milwaukee, and difficulties in aligning ward and precinct lines with census tracts, place obstacles in the way of statistical analysis. The Milwaukee findings are based on a sample of 31 white neighbourhoods—groups of precincts whose boundaries coincided closely (although often not exactly) with census tract lines. In Gary the paucity of white census tracts compounds the boundary problem, and there were too few white units to permit correlations. Instead I have simply compared all the white neighbourhoods for which demographic data is available.

Baltimore precinct boundaries were constant for several years, and ward lines corresponded to census tract divisions. A statistical analysis of Baltimore and Maryland data will be reported on in a subsequent publication.

3. Cf. the more extended discussion in my "Wallace and the Middle Class: The White Backlash in Wisconsin", *Public Opinion Quart.*, vol. 30 (Spring 1966), pp. 98–99, and the references there cited.

4. i.e., those born in Poland, or with at least one parent born there. Cf. *Bureau of the Census, U.S. Census of Population and Housing: 1960*, Census Tracts PHC (1)–92, Washington, D.C., G.P.O., 1961, pp. 15–29.

5. Space precludes an extended discussion of the validity of this primary as a measure of party strength. Suffice it to say that where the primary results can be compared to the party vote in the previous general elections—in the eighteen Milwaukee suburbs—correlations are extremely high (.95+).

6. Rogin, pp. 100–105.

7. This neighbourhood is known in Gary as a southern white working class community. Only 19% of the residents are of foreign stock; only 5% come from southern or eastern Europe. 65% of the labour force is blue collar; 89% of the homes are owner-occupied.

8. 65% of the employed population of south Gary is blue collar, 77% of the homes are owner-occupied, and 19% of the residents are immigrants or the children of immigrants from southern and eastern Europe. Poles make up the largest single ethnic group, but there are significantly more Italians, Czechs, and Hungarians in south Gary than in south Milwaukee.

9. Within south Gary there is no exact correspondence of census tracts and precincts, and I have compared precincts lying wholly within the most white collar and the most blue collar tract.

Moreover, the Republican (presumably more white collar) precincts supported Wallace as much as the Democratic precincts; the correlation between Wallace and the 1962 Democratic senatorial vote was —.16. (On the relationship between ethnicity, class, and party affiliation in Gary, cf. Phillip Cutright and Peter H. Rossi, "Grass Roots Politicians and the Vote," *Amer. Sociol. Rev.*, vol. 23 (April 1958), pp. 172–173.)

10. Gary residents report the Jewish concentration here. It is also suggested by the fact that this census tract has the highest percentage of Russians (usually indicating Jewishness, although not all Jews will be Russian) in Gary. 43% of the employed population is in upper status white collar jobs; only 30% is blue collar.

11. Cf. V. O. Key, Jr., *Southern Politics in State and Nation*, New York, Knopf, 1949, pp. 5–12, 42–43, 215–216, 344, 531, 666–667.

12. Cf. Rogin, pp. 104–106.

13. These were all counties containing middle-size cities; approximately 8% of the population in each city was non-white.

14. Cf. V. O. Key, Jr., and Frank Munger, "Social Determinism and Electoral Decision: The Case of Indiana", in Eugene Burdick and Arthur J. Brodbeck (eds.), *American Voting Behavior*, Glencoe, Ill.: The Free Press, 1955. I compared the map of Wallace's strength with their map of party voting in 1868.

15. For the suggestion that the religious split between Germans and fundamentalist Anglo-Saxon Protestants played a part in the Wallace vote, I am indebted to the American Jewish Committee Jewish Information Service. "The Politics of Prejudice: Wallace in the Presidential Primaries in Wisconsin, Indiana, and Maryland" (July 1964), pp. 17–19. The major fundamentalist-leaning Protestant sects in Indiana are the Methodists, the Disciples, the United Brethren, and the Baptists. Two of these (mainly the first two) were the two leading religions in each of the outstate pro-Wallace counties, and in less than half of the anti-Wallace counties. The "German" religions are the Catholics, Lutherans, Evangelicals, and Mennonites.

Rural German-Americans often live in tight-knit, church-oriented communities. The A.J.C. reports that in at least one county voters were influenced against Wallace by a local priest. (The religious figures are from the 1936 religious census, the most recent. I have used the 1930 census for the percentage of Germans and their children, because Germans, as fourth and fifth generation Americans by 1960, would not show up in more recent censuses. There has been little movement into the rural Indiana counties in recent times.)

In spite of the urban character of the Wallace vote, the Wallace counties were no more working class than the anti-Wallace counties.

16. Rogin, pp. 105–107.

17. The contrast is particularly striking since the comparable neighbour-hoods are each on the south side, across a river from the Negro ghetto. The ghetto has been able to expand across the river in neither city.

18. On Gary, cf. Victor Hoffman and John Strietelmeimer, "Gary's Rank-and-file Reaction", *Reporter*, vol. 31 (9 September 1964), pp. 28–29. Whites in East Chicago, where the Negro ghetto is much smaller and the civil rights movement more quiescent, gave Wallace substantially less support than those in Gary.

19. Rogin, pp. 106–107.

20. Other factors may also have affected the Gary/Milwaukee contrast. First, more voters had probably heard of Wallace by the Indiana campaign. Second, Milwaukee Republicans voted for Wallace in the Democratic primary (cf. Rogin, pp. 102–104). Cross-over is not a general feature of Indiana politics, and potentially pro-Wallace Republicans were supporting Goldwater against Stassen in their own primary. Abundant survey evidence shows that middle-class Democrats are more liberal on non-economic issues than middle-class Republicans; had the latter crossed over, middle-class Gary areas might have been even more for Wallace than working-class areas.

Third, Gary is a city of working-class homeowners; Milwaukee is not. There was some evidence in Gary and in the Milwaukee suburbs that working-class homeowners felt more threatened by Negroes, who could, by entering their neighbourhoods, upset their aspirations for a middle-class life-style. Finally, Milwaukee had had a strong Socialist tradition, based partly on the fact, unusual in America, that its Polish immigrants had been skilled workers rather than peasants.

21. Since 1958 was a big Democratic year, 1960 was distorted by the religious issue, and 1962 was the most recent, it seemed the best choice. Correlations of the county vote in Indiana and Wisconsin (Tables 2 and 7) further support its use.

22. Goldwater's vote was correlated .98 with the 1960 gubernatorial vote, .99 with the 1962 senatorial vote, .99 with the 1962 gubernatorial vote, and .96 with the 1964 September primary vote.

23. In this table the 1960 gubernatorial vote is used instead of the 1960 presidential vote because religion clearly distorted normal party strength in the presidential election. Cf. Andrew R. Baggeley, "Religious Influence on Wisconsin Voting 1928–1960", *Amer. Polit. Sci. Rev.*, vol. 56 (March 1962), pp. 66–70.

24. It is impossible to determine, with confidence, whether the non-Jewish upper middle class also deserted Goldwater disproportionately.

25. The regression equation for the scattergram of Goldwater and the 1962 Republican vote is $y = 3.54 + .81x$. Those counties furthest above the regression line had deserted Goldwater least; those furthest below the

line had deserted him the most. These deviant counties make up Table 6. They were further subdivided into Republican and Democratic counties; all counties more than 55% Republican in 1962 were called Republican. This figure was chosen because it divided Wisconsin's seventy-one counties approximately in half.

26. The equation for the regression line in Figure 2 is $y = 9\cdot01 + \cdot77x$. A wholesale reapportionment in 1961 prevents us from correlating the party vote in two non-Goldwater years. However, there is indirect evidence that party stability in Gary is normally very high. Cf. Cutright and Rossi, *Amer. Sociol. Rev.* vol. 23, pp. 172–173.

27. Cf. David Danzig, "The Radical Right and the Rise of the Fundamentalist Minority", *Commentary*, vol. 33 (April 1962), pp. 291–298; Raymond E. Wolfinger *et al.*, "America's Radical Right; Politics and Ideology," in David E. Apter (ed.), *Ideology and Discontent*, New York, The Free Press, 1964, pp. 262–293.

28. Among Indiana's eight most strongly Democratic counties, this relationship was not consistent. The calculations that follow report only on the eighty-four counties more than 42% Republican in 1962. (The relevant scattergram has not been reproduced; its regression equation is $y = 3\cdot25 + \cdot93x$.)

29. Research on the backlash in Baltimore reveals the same pattern.

30. My interviews indicated that support for Wallace at the grass roots was open and enthusiastic. Thus a Gary civil rights leader, wife of a steel worker, reported widespread talk for Wallace in the steel mills, virtually no open opposition to him. Among community and political leaders support for Wallace was illegitimate; in the discourse of ordinary people, almost the reverse seemed true. Cf. also *Baltimore Sun*, 15 May 1964.

31. *Milwaukee Journal*, 3 April 1964.

32. Cf. Herbert Hyman and Paul B. Sheatsley, "Attitudes Toward Desegregation," *Scientific American*, vol. 111 (July 1964), pp. 18–21; *San Francisco Chronicle*, "California Poll: The Rights Issue," 15 September 1964, p. 1. There may be an analogy between abstract commitment to civil rights and abstract commitment to free speech, which also often fails to apply in concrete cases. Cf. Herbert McClosky, "Consensus and Ideology in American Politics," *Amer. Polit. Sci. Rev.*, vol. 58 (June 1964), pp. 364–366.

33. To anyone watching the 1964 Democratic convention, particularly the unofficial interviews with politicians, the lesson was clear: civil rights was a good thing, but civil rights demonstrations were equated with race riots, Ku Klux Klan activity, and right-wing extremism.

34. For one version of this currently popular notion, cf. Robert Dahl, *Who Governs*, New Haven, Yale Univ. Press, 1961, pp. 80–94, 318–325. Cf.

also Samuel Stouffer, *Communism, Conformity, and Civil Liberties*, Garden City, N.Y., Doubleday, 1955, pp. 26–57.

35. Evidence from interviews, and *Baltimore Sun*, 5 May 1964.

36. Steel union leaders in East Chicago, for example, stressed the importance of anti-Negro feeling in the Wallace vote, and were forthright in their own pro-civil rights sentiments. Gary union leaders, much more ambivalent on civil rights themselves, insisted that the sales tax alone explained the Wallace vote.

37. Negro Richard Hatcher, campaigning against municipal corruption, defeated the Democratic incumbent in the 1967 Gary mayorality primary. The entire Gary Democratic organization moved into the Republican Party in the general election. John Krupa, still chairman of the Lake County Democratic Central Committee, denounced Hatcher as a "subversive," and denied him all party financial support. The weak Republican candidate in this overwhelmingly Democratic city received more than 80% of the white vote, but Hatcher was narrowly elected. Krupa, assuming an unprecedented posture of moral outrage, announced widespread evidence of illegal voting.

38. Cf. Charles Whiteford, "Negroes Show Vote Power, The Key to Wallace Defeat," *Baltimore Sun*, 21 May 1964.

39. These ideas are more fully developed in my *The Intellectuals and McCarthy: The Radical Specter*, Cambridge, Mass., M.I.T. Press, 1967, chs, 8–9.

40. Cf. Norman Jacobson, "Political Science and Political Education," *Amer. Polit. Sci. Rev.*, vol. 57 (September 1963), pp. 561–569.

# The Charisma of Blackness

*Chuck Stone*

In the new revolutionary era of Black Power and black pride, black people have begun to develop an ethnic consciousness of their political capabilities that is rooted solely in blackness. No longer need a black man apologize for his black skin in a subconscious hope that white people, too, will be inclined to overlook its white-originated odium. And just as John "Honey Fitz" Fitzgerald as Boston's first Irish Catholic mayor could proudly refer in 1906 to "this Catholic city," black people over a half century later could finally discover a dignity and power in the color of the skin of a black mayor.

"Black," as applied to a race of people, covers any person who is not only black, but brown, light-skinned, fair-skinned, mulatto, *café au lait*, or even white. The last would require a public self-identification as a black man—as have done Adam Clayton Powell and the late Walter White, the blue-eyed and dove-skinned executive secretary of the NAACP, who looked more like a Scandinavian than a black man.

Thus, "black," as Powell has repeatedly said, is a way of thinking, not a skin color. Many are the fair-skinned, mulatto, or white negroes who are far more "black" in their thinking than many black men.

A one-company-dominated city of 175,000, Gary is the home of U.S. Steel, which employs over 16,000 workers. It is a depressingly typical American city with all the ethnic conflicts, race hate, and crises of air pollution, transportation, urban decay, and inferior education plaguing all cities. For years, it has been a balanced composite of Czechoslovakians, Poles, Hungarians, Irish, Greeks, Jews, Latin-Americans, and, more recently, blacks. A community where gambling and prostitution were carried on openly, Gary was known for its corruption, its stagnancy, and its hard-working population.

Reprinted from *Black Political Power in America*, pp. 213–218. Copyright © 1968 by C. Sumner Stone. By permission of the publishers, The Bobbs-Merrill Company, Inc.

As rapidly as whites left the city, blacks moved in, and by 1966, black people were a majority of the population. This fact was not lost on the Democratic Party, which controlled the city, and there were whispers of a black candidate for mayor in the 1967 election.

The incumbent mayor, A. Martin Katz, had probably done more for black people than any previous mayor. Under his administration, every city commission was integrated for the first time, and black men were appointed as corporation counsel (third-ranking city official), superintendent of sanitation, deputy controller, assistant director of general services, and two assistant fire chiefs. Katz also appointed thirty-two black men as firemen, as many as had been appointed in the entire fifty-seven-year history of Gary. But this was still not enough, as far as many black leaders were concerned. Richard Gordon Hatcher was one of them. Gary was now a black city. Black people should control it or have a majority share in its administration.

By Stone's Index of Proportional Equality, Gary was more advanced than any other city in America, yet it still fell short of fulfilling an ideal pattern. Of the twenty-six city departments, only two, or 7 per cent, were headed by black people. Of Gary's four state representatives, none was black. In the nine-man city council, three, or 33 per cent, were black (including Hatcher, who had been elected as one of three at-large councilmen). Both the judges serving Gary, the City Court judge and the Criminal Court judge, were white, the former Jewish and the latter Irish. According to an Indiana Civil Rights Commission report which Hatcher used extensively in his campaign, only 28 per cent of the 2000 City Hall jobs were held by black people.

In the fall of 1966, Hatcher began to think seriously about running for mayor. He knew he would never be acceptable to the Gary political machine because of what many of the more conservative leaders regarded as his extremist views on many subjects. In an interview in the Black Muslims' newspaper *Muhammad Speaks* in the September 16, 1966, issue, Hatcher covered everything from black power to the war in Vietnam:

> As far as I'm concerned, the white community's interpretation of black power is irrelevant. Before a white man can talk to me about this, he'll first have to talk about white power which has been exercised so ruthlessly against black people. When he explains that, I'll talk about black power.
>
> If a man bombs my home, from a plane or any other way, and he is caught, I would demand that he be tried. Why can't the North Vietnamese try men who are bombing their homes? In any event, the United States should certainly find a way to get out of Vietnam. It's getting

worse instead of better, and there is no way of winning against the huge forces of Asia.

The article, entitled "Struggle for Black Power in Gary," indicated that Hatcher had not decided to run for mayor then, but "modestly agrees that he would have an excellent chance of winning."

Hatcher's black militancy made him anathema to the essentially conservative political machine, and he knew that in 1971, when the Democratic Party was almost certain to slate a black man for mayor, he would not be that man. The favorite would more likely be Dr. Alexander Williams, a successful physician who had made history by becoming elected as the first black Lake County Coroner. Williams was as fair of skin as Hatcher was black. Had Williams had less integrity and a sense of honor, he would have been Gary's mayor today, instead of Hatcher. But Williams kept the faith, and it was a black man, not a white man, who broke it. What happened was a series of events that subsequently made Hatcher's election possible.

The behind-the-scenes political boss of Gary is George Chacharis, a well-read, friendly, burly Greek who had risen from a steel worker to become mayor of Gary. Convicted of income-tax evasion, Chacharis served time and then was released from the Federal penitentiary, returning to Gary to assume his former position as boss of the party. Chacharis had broken with Mayor Katz for political reasons and approached Williams in 1966 to run for election. With Chacharis' support, Williams would have won. But the coroner, who believed in fair play (an old-fashioned commodity in today's cauldron of corrupt politics), asked Chacharis for time to consider the request. He instead approached Katz, informed him of the offer and asked his reaction. Katz replied he knew Williams could defeat him with Chacharis' backing, but that he (Katz) strongly felt he deserved a second chance in adhering to the political tradition of Gary that "one good term deserves another." He also pointed out to Williams that the reason he (Katz) was in political trouble was because of his liberalism in racial appointments, which the white community deeply resented. Williams agreed, decided to support Katz for re-election, and so informed Chacharis, who in turn agreed to support Katz.

Hatcher subsequently announced his candidacy and put together a team of the strangest political bedfellows ever assembled. White radicals, black nationalists, upper-middle-class blacks, winos, black mothers on welfare, and wealthy Jewish businessmen, they were united in one cause—to defeat the machine and Katz. This could only be done by electing Hatcher.

Also announcing his opposition to Katz for the Democratic nomination was Bernard Konrady, who quickly became tagged as the white backlash candidate. The campaign was one of Gary's most violent in years. The tone was set when a top Hatcher aide, Jesse Bell, a public school teacher, was accused in a story in the *Gary Post-Tribune* on March 30, 1967, of having told an all-black audience in January: "All methods should be used to expose the Uncle Toms in this city and we should use whatever methods possible, including violence, in order to meet our goals."

Bell denied the charges, but they opened the floodgates for a wave of threats, intimidations of black people, and black party officials supporting Katz. Bricks were thrown through windows, tires of Katz supporters were deflated, and businessmen on the main thoroughfare of Broadway in the ghetto were told to put Hatcher signs in their windows or risk possible physical injury. Dr. Williams and his wife were threatened so often with personal violence by telephone calls and late night visitations that it became necessary for Williams to purchase a .38-caliber pistol, which he carried in the last couple of weeks of the campaign as he drove around the city speaking for Katz. April 19, in the early hours of the morning, a Molotov cocktail was thrown through the window of the pro-Katz black weekly newspaper, *The Gary Crusader*.

Katz campaigned hard in both the black and white communities, but he was like a man trying to keep his finger in the dike against white racism while the earthquake of black power was crumbling the earth beneath him. On May 2, 1967, Katz was chopped up between a defecting white vote for Konrady and a defecting black vote for Hatcher. The results were: Hatcher, 20,272; Katz, 17,910; Konrady, 13,133.

The voting was strictly along racial lines. Hatcher received 75 per cent of the black vote; Katz, 24 per cent (his headquarters had estimated that he needed to retain a minimum of 30 per cent of the black vote to defeat Hatcher); and Konrady, 1 per cent. Among the white voters in the predominantly white 1st, 2nd, and 6th districts, Konrady captured 46 per cent, Katz 45 per cent (doing far better than he anticipated among whites), and Hatcher 7 per cent.

Hatcher did almost no campaigning, accurately concluding that Katz and Konrady would decimate each other in the white community, and the near solid black vote would elect him. After the election, Hatcher made no effort to make his peace with the Democratic machine, which then announced it would not support him. Denied funds, Hatcher went on a national campaign and took out a full-page in the *New York Times* headlined, "For God Sakes, Let's Get Ourselves Together," in which he appealed for funds. He became the focus of national publicity, and Senator Robert Kennedy gave a fund-raising party for him in New York City.

In the face of the now-united white vote against him and an informal alliance of the Republicans and white Democrats, he knew he needed a small percentage of the white vote to win. Many white Americans looking for a peaceful antidote to the black violence overrunning American cities saw in Hatcher a chance to stem the revolutionary tide and enthusiastically supported his candidacy with financial contributions.

In Gary, just enough white Democrats remained loyal to the party for Hatcher to win, and he defeated the Republican candidate, Joseph B. Radigan, a very unimpressive businessman whose bland exterior as much as his party affiliation cost him victory.

The final tally was: Hatcher, 39,330; and Radigan, 37,941.

The vote once again divided on racial lines, with Hatcher winning 91 per cent of the black vote and Radigan winning 83 per cent of the white vote. The 6762 white votes Hatcher received were more than sufficient for his 1389-vote margin of victory.

The City Council acquired another black man and is now divided, four blacks, four whites, and one Latin American.

Hatcher's biggest campaign issues were corruption in Gary and "crime in the streets," a phrase that has been useful for white reactionaries. But it paid off, and white voters supported him in the hope that he could, indeed, make the streets safe. Hatcher kept his promise to black voters that he would make more black appointments and appointed as his administrative assistant the firebrand Jesse Bell; as fire chief sixty-year-old Alphonso Holliday, a forty-year veteran of the fire department, who had been appointed assistant fire chief by Katz, but who nevertheless supported Hatcher during the campaign; corporation counsel Hilbert Bradley, replacing a black man, Laurence Anderson, a Katz loyalist; and for the first time in Gary's history, a black controller, forty-eight-year-old businessman Maurice Baptiste, the second-highest ranking city official, who would succeed Hatcher were anything to happen to him.

In line with his anticrime crusade, Hatcher appointed a white police department veteran who had headed the narcotics squad for twelve years, forty-one-year-old Detective Sergeant James Hilton. White men were appointed as city engineer and head of the city planning department. The Gary administration was finally and truly integrated.

Gary's future—and Hatcher's—will depend on the capacity of his administration to solve the rising crime rate, clean up corruption, and bring new urban renewal projects into Gary with Federal money (public housing is desperately needed, but has been vigorously opposed by whites since white areas are the only place such building construction could take place), and on his ability to tap U.S. Steel's till for more tax money (Hatcher claims it is not paying its way for the land it now occupies in Gary).

Problems of air pollution, downtown revitalization and slum eradication are all tied to the other, more pressing problems. It will take months and may take years before the scars of racial bitterness injected into the campaign are healed. Certainly, Hatcher, an early public advocate of black power whose attraction to many black people was based on his forthright advocacy of the new doctrine, was as much to blame for the hostilities engendered in both campaigns as any man. His silence on the violence of his followers and his subtle playing off of white radicals against black militants did not help.

How deeply Gary felt about this election was witnessed by the fact that of 103,077 registered voters, 77,271, or almost 75 per cent, turned out, exceeding the previous high of 72,890 who voted in the 1964 Presidential race.

Perhaps, in an unexpected way, the creative disorder of racial tensions is a revitalizing force for American democracy. When people feel passionately about something, they will get out and vote as they did in Gary. Black people obviously felt more strongly about electing Hatcher than white people did about defeating him, and the proportion of black voters was higher than that of whites.

If Hatcher can channel the black jubilation and the white fears into a workable alliance within the political crucible, it is possible he will have engineered a great experiment in American democracy. Hatcher, a taciturn, unattractive person, eventually will need to go beyond the emotionalism of his skin-black charisma and forge an administration to build Gary and not Hatcher. They go together, and the extent to which Hatcher can submerge his personal ambitions for the good of Gary will determine Gary's survival as a viable American city.

## 12 | The First Year of Black Power in Gary, Indiana*

*Edward Greer*

As Director of the Office of Program Coordination under Mayor Richard Gordon Hatcher of Gary, Indiana, through February 1969, I was able to directly observe black political control of a middle-sized American city. Gary is an exemplary case; both because the sharp delineations of class structure of the city throw into bold relief what is often obscured elsewhere, and because Gary foreshadows a striking new development of our urban life—the achievement of effective black political majorities.

This article confines itself to the effect of black control on the civil bureaucracy of the city. It omits discussion of the role of state coercion (e.g., the police), and the relationship between the civil authorities and the economic structure (i.e., the United States Steel Corporation).[1] Its conclusion is that in the absence of definite types of popular organization, the American social system can absorb and deflect major political insurgencies such as the "black power" movement through concessions by the federal executive branch and by corporate elites.

The practical consequences of this conclusion is that as long as oppressed groups and their political leadership believe that their problems can be solved by parliamentary means (whether in the form advocated by social democrats such as Bayard Rustin, or nationalists such as Stokely Carmichael),[2] they are unlikely to overcome their oppression despite their best efforts. Of more use than pieces of state power (which at the present time such groups are relatively unprepared to utilize effectively) would be mass education and transformation of social relations from below through a "cultural revolution." A discussion of the forms and strategies for popular organizations which could undertake such tasks is outside the scope of this article.[3]

* The author gratefully acknowledges the editorial assistance of Mr. Charles Isenberg of Harvard University in preparing this article.

## THE HISTORICAL SETTING

One would have to be a William Blake to do full justice to the scene Gary, Indiana, presents to the eye. The immense and overwhelming sight of the steel mills of the U.S. Steel Corporation, with their stacks belching ruddy smoke into the sky defies description.[4] Until I adjusted to it, the atmosphere caused my eyes to water and nose to run. Gary has one of the highest air pollution rates in the world. These mills, for a while, the largest steel complex in the world, have produced over a quarter of a trillion tons of steel in their half-century of existence.

After its physical appearance, the most striking feature of Gary is the narrow bounds within which its cultural life occurs. Almost 75 percent of male employment in Gary is in durable goods manufacturing and in the wholesale-retail trades.

With the majority of its male labor force in blue-collar occupations, Gary's 200,000 population is solidly working-class. But it is not poor. Most workers own their own homes and median income in the city is about 10 percent above the national average. The United States Steel Corporation directly employs three-quarters of the total work force.[5]

The life-style of the working population is parochial and circumscribed. With the exception of the ethnic clubs, the union, and the Catholic Church, the outstanding social edifices in Gary are its bars, gambling joints, and whorehouses.

The City of Gary was the largest of all company towns in America. The United States Steel Corporation began its construction in 1905, after assembling the necessary parcel of land on the Lake Michigan shorefront. Within two years, over $40,000,000 had been invested in the project (by now the figure must be well into the billions).

There was extensive dredging of swamps and leveling of dunes; the construction of a belt-line railroad to Chicago; the creation of a port for ore ships; as well as the creation of a vast complex of manufacturing facilities which included coke ovens, blast furnaces, and an independent electrical power plant. The City was laid out by Corporation architects and engineers, and largely developed by the Corporation-owned Gary Land Company. This Company did not own all the land in the City, and controversies arose continually over priorities of development of roads, etc., until the Land Company sold off most of its holdings by the thirties.[6]

In much more than its genesis and choice of name, Gary is indelibly stamped in the mold of its corporate creators. Even though the original city plan included locations for a variety of civic, cultural, and commercial uses (though woefully little for park land), an eminent critic points out that it "failed sadly in its attempt to produce a community pattern noticeably different or better than elsewhere."[7]

The Corporation planned more than the physical nature of the city. It also had agents advertise in Europe and the South to bring in workers from as many different backgrounds as possible to build and work in the mills. Today over fifty ethnic groups are represented in the population.

This imported labor was cheap, and it was hoped that cultural differences and language barriers would curtail the growth of a socialist labor movement. The tough, pioneer character of the city, and the fact that many of the workers were immigrants whose families had not yet joined them in this country, combined to create a lawless and vice-ridden atmosphere which the Corporation did little to curtail.

### The Trade Union Movement

During the course of the First World War, government and vigilante repression broke the back of the Socialist Party in small-town America. Simultaneously, the left grew rapidly as a political force among the foreign-born in large urban centers.[8] As the war continued, a combination of prosperity (full-employment and overtime), pressures for production in the "national interest," and Wilsonian and corporate promises of an extension of democracy in the workplace after the war ended kept labor peace. But immediately after these special conditions ended and the promises for a change of priorities proved empty, the long suppressed grievances of the steel workers broke forth. Especially among the unskilled immigrant workers demands for an industrial union, a reduction of the workday from 12 to 8 hours, and better pay and working conditions sparked a spontaneous movement for an industry-wide strike.

Despite the capable leadership of William Z. Foster, and the illusive appearance for a time of a great victory, the Great Steel Strike of 1919 was broken.[9] The native white skilled labor aristocracy refused to support the strike, and the Corporation imported blacks from the South as strikebreakers.[10] This defeat smashed the prospect of militant industrial trade unionism in America for almost a generation, and allowed the corporate elite to consolidate its control of the state machinery and the popular culture. Racism, a consumer-oriented culture (especially the automobile and relaxed sexual mores), and reforms from above (by the mid-twenties the 8-hour day had been voluntarily granted in the mills) combined to prevent the left from recovering as a significant social force.

It was in this period that a substantial black population came to Gary. Before the war only a handful of black families lived in the City, and few of them worked in the mills. During World War I blacks were encouraged to move to Gary to make up for the labor shortage caused by expanding production and the loss of immigration. After the war the policy was continued, most spectacularly during the Strike, but rather consistently throughout the twenties. In 1920, blacks made up 9.6 percent of the population; in 1930, they were 17.8 percent—and they were proportionately represented in the steel industry workforce.[11]

When the CIO was organized during the Depression, an interracial alliance was absolutely essential to the task. In Gary, a disproportionate number of the union organizers were black; the Communist Party's slogan of "black and white unite and fight" proved a successful strategy for organizing industrial unions. Nevertheless, it was only during World War II (and not as the result of the radicals' efforts) that black workers made a substantial structural advance in the economy. Demography, wartime full employment, and labor shortages proved more important to the lot of black workers than their own efforts and those of their allies.

As after the First World War, the aftermath of the Second was repression to counter the growth of the left. Not only was the communist component of the trade union movement wiped out; but in the general atmosphere of the early Cold War, black people found themselves on the defensive also. The opportunities of wartime emergency were exchanged for those of capitalist normalcy. At the local level in Gary, the remaining trade union leaders made their peace with the Corporation (and the local racketeers and Democratic Party politicians), while efforts at integration in the community foundered.

Finally, in the early fifties, the inherently limited nature of the trade union as a purely defensive organization of the working class—and one moreover which fully accepts capitalist property and legal norms —fully manifested itself. The Steelworkers Union gave up its right to strike over local grievances (which the left had made a key part of its organizing policy) in return for binding arbitration, which better suited the needs and tempers of the emerging labor bureaucrats.[12]

The Corporation thus regained effective full control over the work process. As a result, they could intensify the general rate of exploitation (reflected in their profit per worker). They could also intensify the special oppression of the black workers (e.g., foremen assigning them discriminatorily to the worst tasks; now without real union opposition).

This corporate racism had the additional benefit of weakening the workers' solidarity. As an ancillary development, the union abolished shop stewards, replacing them with one full-time elected "griever." This practice, of course, further attenuated rank-and-file control over the union bureaucracy, aided in depoliticizing the workers, and thus accentuated the union's tendency to mediate the class struggle at the point of production.[13]

The corporate and union elites justified this process by substantial wage increases, together with other benefits such as improved pension and welfare plans, etc. For these gains a price was paid. Higher product prices, inflation,[14] and a rising tax burden on the workers all ensued from the passive acceptance by the unions of the priorities of the corporate dominated political economy.

This last development proved to have the most vital racial consequence, for as that process continued, a large part of the industrial working-class found itself in the novel posture of opposing the needs of the poorest workers for increased social welfare services. A large part of the material basis for white working-class racism originates here. Gary steelworkers struggling to meet their home mortgage payments are loath to permit increased assessments for additional municipal services which will go in large part to black people.

### The United States Steel Corporation

Needless to say, the Corporation helped to develop, promote, and protect the Gary working classes' new ways of viewing themselves and their world.

In the Mill, the Corporation systematically gave the black workers the dirtiest jobs (e.g., coke plant); and bypassed them for promotion— especially for the key skilled jobs and as foremen. Nor has that policy changed. Although about one-third of the employees in the Gary Works are black and many of them have high seniority, and although virtually all the foremen are promoted up directly from the ranks without needing any special qualifications; nevertheless, there are almost no black (or Spanish-speaking) foremen. According to figures submitted by the United States Steel Corporation to the Gary Human Relations Commission, as of 31 March 1968, out of a total of 1,011 First Line Supervisors (i.e., foremen) only 22 were black.[15]

The Corporation not only directly practices racism, but also encourages it indirectly by supporting other institutions in Gary which practice racial discrimination.

If one excepts some free professionals and small businesses, the entire business community is a *de facto* fief of the Corporation. For instance it is well known that the local banks[16] are very reluctant to advance mortgage money in black areas of town, thus assuring their physical decline. White workers then draw the reasonable conclusion that the movement of blacks into their neighborhoods will be at the expense of the value of their homes, and respond accordingly.

The local business community, organized in the Gary Chamber of Commerce, has never to my knowledge differed from the Corporation on any matter of substance, even when it would have been in their direct economic self-interest to do so.[17] This has been true even with regard to raising the Corporation's property assessment, which would directly financially benefit local business. And in their hiring and sales practices, as well as in their social roles, this group is a leading force for both institutional racism and racist attitudes in the community.

The local media, completely dependent financially on the local business community, can fairly be described overtly racist. For instance, I was informed that the publisher of the local newspaper was present when the voting fraud conspiracy to deprive Hatcher of the election was revealed; yet the story was not released by the local media until days after it made the front page of the *New York Times*, and not until it was too late to affect the electorate's choice of candidates.[18]

The newspaper publisher is very close to the national Catholic hierarchy and the local bishop, who in turn is closely linked to the local banks. The Church is rhetorically moderately liberal at the diocesan level, but among the ethnic parishes the clergy are often overtly racist.

### The City Government

While the United States Steel Corporation has an annual budget of $5 billion, the City of Gary operates on some $10 million annually.[19]

And the power of the city government, as is usually the case in this country, is highly fragmented. Its legal and financial powers are inadequate to carry out the public functions for which it bears responsibility. The power of the Mayor, in particular, is limited. State civil service laws insulated school, welfare, fire, and police personnel from the control of City Hall.

Administrative agencies, the hallmark of the modern monopoly capitalist state, control key functions such as urban renewal, the low-income housing authority, the sanitation district, the park system, and the board of health. Appointive boards (with long and staggered terms of tenure) hire the administrators of these agencies, and although over the long run a skillful Mayor can obtain substantial control over their operations, in the immediate situation (especially if there are sharp policy differences) his power may well be marginal.[20]

Two other structural factors set the context in which local government in Gary—and in America generally—is forced to operate. First, increasingly key municipal functions come to depend upon federal aid. This is the case with such activities as the poverty program, urban renewal, low income housing; and to a substantial degree with welfare, education, and even police and sanitation activities. Thus, the priorities of the federal government increasingly shape the alternatives and options open to local officials, and their real independence is attenuated.

Second, the tax resources of local governments—resting for the most part on comparatively static real estate levies—are decreasingly able to meet the sharply rising costs of municipal expenditures. These costs reflect the increased social costs of production and welfare of a modern capitalist civilization. They are costs which corporations are able to pass on to the general public.

This problem is particularly acute in Gary because of the ability of the Corporation to remain grossly underassessed. As a result, there are implacable pressures to resist expansion of municipal services, even if the "need" for them is critical. In particular, since funds go to maintain existing services, it is virtually impossible for a local government to initiate any substantive innovations unless prior funding is assured. In this context, a sustained response to the "urban crisis" is prevented not only by a fragmentation of power, but also by a lack of the economic resources on the scale necessary to obtain significant results.

For the City of Gary, until the election of Mayor Hatcher, such considerations as the limits of local government as an instrument of social change and improvement of the general welfare were academic. The municipal government mediated between the rackets on the one hand, and the ethnic groups and business community on the other.

The Democratic Party, structured through the Lake County machine, was the mechanism for accomplishing the division of spoils, and for maintaining the public legitimation of a government which provided a minimum return to the citizenry. Left alone by the Corporation, which practiced what seemed to be nonintervention in local affairs, this political coalition governed Gary as it saw fit.

In return for the benevolent neutrality of the Corporation toward its junior partner, the governing coalition refrained from attempting to raise the Corporation's tax assessments; or to otherwise insinuate itself into the absolute sovereignty of the Corporation over the Gary Works. Air pollution activities were subjected only to token inspection and control; and in the entire history of the city, the Building Department never sent an inspector into the Mill.[21]

In this setting—particularly in the absence of a large middle-class interested in "good government" reform—politics was little more than a racket, with the city government as the chief spoils. An informal custom grew up that representatives of different ethnic minorities would each hold the Mayor's office for one term. The Mayor then, in association with the county officials, would supervise the organized crime (mostly gambling, liquor, and prostitution) within the community. In effect, the police force and the prosecutor's office were used to erect and centralize a protection racket with the Mayor as its director and organized crime as its client. Very large sums of liquid capital were involved; as indicated by the evidence that one recent Mayor was described by Internal Revenue officials as having an estimated annual income while in office of $1.5 million.

Besides the income from partnership with the criminals, other sources of funds contributed to the large illicit incomes of the city officials. There were almost 1,000 patronage jobs to distribute to supporters, or sell to friends. There were proceeds from a myriad of business transactions and contracts carried out under municipal authority. Every aspect of municipal activity was drawn into the cash nexus.

For instance, by local ordinance, one had to pass an examination and pay a $150 fee for a contractor's license to do repair or construction work within city limits. The licensing statute was enacted to maintain reasonable standards of performance and thus protect the public. In reality, to pass the exam as late as 1967 required few skills, but rather a payment of $1,200 to the relevant officials; or $1,500 if the applicant was unfortunate enough to have black skin.

Gary municipal affairs also had a racist quality. The black population of the city continued to rise until in the early sixties it composed an absolute majority of the population. Yet the benefits of the system just outlined were restricted to the less scrupulous among the white ethnic groups who constituted altogether only 40 percent of the population.[22] The spoils came from all; yet they were distributed only among whites.

And this was true not only for illegal spoils and patronage, but also for legitimate municipal services. As one example, after Hatcher became Mayor, one of the major complaints of the white citizenry was the sharp decline in the frequency of garbage collection. This resulted, not from a drop in efficiency of the General Services division as was often charged; but from the fact that the garbage routes were finally equalized as between white and black areas.

Thus, the city government itself became an additional aspect of the institutionalized structure of racism in Gary. To assure the acquiesence of Gary's blacks to the system, traditional mechanisms of repression were used: bought black politicians and ward leaders, token jobs, the threat of violence against rebels, and the spreading of a sense of impotence and despair. For instance, it was a Gary tradition for the Democratic machine to contribute $1,500 each week to a black ministers' alliance for them to distribute to needy parishioners—with the tacit understanding that when elections came around they would help deliver the vote. The Hatcher insurgents, however, needed armed guards to prevent intimidation of their campaign workers.

### The Hatcher Campaign

The successful insurgency of Richard Gordon Hatcher destroyed the core of this entire relationship.

Hatcher successfully developed what can best be described as a black united front, inasmuch as it embraced all sectors of the black community, by class, occupation, ideology, and temperament. The basis of this united front was a commonly held view that black people as a racial group were discriminated against by the politically dominant forces. This united front involved both an ability to bridge existing gaps in the black community and Hatcher's refusal to be drawn into a disavowal of any sector of the black movement either to his left or right—except those local black politicians who were lackeys of the Democratic machine. Despite immense public pressure, for instance Hatcher refused to condemn Stokely Carmichael even though scurrilous right-wing literature was widely circulated calling him a tool of Carmichael and Fidel Castro. Actually, the rumor which hurt Hatcher the most was the false assertion that he was secretly engaged to a white campaign worker—and it was so damaging in the black community that special pains had to be taken to overcome it.

Muhammad Ali was brought to the city to campaign for Hatcher, but Hubert Humphrey was not invited because of the bitter opposition of white antiwar elements within his campaign committee. It is worth noting that a substantial portion of Hatcher's financial and technical assistance came from a very small group of white liberals and radicals, who both played a role disproportionate to their numbers, and suffered significant social disapprobation for involving themselves openly with Hatcher. Their support, however, made it possible for the campaign to appeal, at least rhetorically, to all the citizens on an interracial basis.

Of course, this support did not translate into votes in the white community.[23] When the count was complete in the general election, only 13 percent of Gary's overwhelmingly Democratic white voters failed to bolt to the Republicans; and if one omits the Jewish professional and business section of town, that percentage falls to 6 percent (in blue-collar Glen Park)—a figure more explicable by polling booth error than good-will.

Even with the support of a large majority of the Spanish-speaking vote, and overwhelming support (over 90 percent) of the black vote, Hatcher barely won the Democratic primary against the incumbent Mayor. This victory was only possible, moreover, because the white vote was split due to the entry of an insurgent and popular "backlash" candidate, who split the white vote almost down the middle.

Hatcher's primary victory was particularly impressive when it is realized under what obstacles he was laboring. First, his entire primary campaign was run on less than $50,000; while the machine spent an estimated $500,000 in cash on buying black votes alone! Second, the media was openly hostile to Hatcher. And third, efforts were made to physically intimidate the candidate and his supporters. Death threats were common, and many beatings occurred. Without a doubt, the unprecedented action of the Hatcher organization in forming its own self-defense squads was essential in preventing mass intimidation. It was even necessary for armed groups to force the opening of polls in black areas on primary day, which would otherwise have remained inoperative.

These extraordinary methods demonstrated both how tenuous are the democratic rights of black people, and what amazing organization and determination are necessary to enforce them when real shifts of power appear to be at stake—for no one really knew what a Hatcher victory would entail. When the primary results came in, thousands of black citizens in Gary literally danced in the streets with joy; and everyone knew that the old Gary was gone forever.

Immediately after the primary victory, the local alignment of forces was to some degree overshadowed by the rapid interposition of national ones. Until Hatcher won the primary, he was left to sink or swim by himself; after he established his own independent base of power, a new and more complex political process began: his reintegration into the national political system.

The county Democratic machine offered Hatcher a bargain: its support and $100,000 for the general election campaign in return for naming the Chief of Police, Corporation Counsel, and Controller. Naturally, Hatcher refused to agree to a bargain which would have made him a puppet of the corrupt elements he was determined to oust from power. Thereupon the county machine (and subdistrict director of the Steelworkers Union) declared itself for, and campaigned for, the Republican.

But the question was not left there. To allow the Democratic Party to desert a candidate solely because he was black would make a shambles of its appeal to black America. And dominant liberal forces within the Democratic Party clearly had other positive interests in seeing Hatcher elected. Most dramatically, the Kennedy wing of the Democratic Party moved rapidly to adopt Hatcher: offering him sorely needed political support, financial backing, and technical assistance, without any strings attached. By doing this, it both solidified its already strong support from the black community, and made it more reasonable for blacks to continue to place their faith in the Democratic Party as a whole and, more generally, in the political system as a whole.

Certainly, as a necessary response to this development (although it might have happened anyway), the Johnson-Humphrey wing of the Democratic Party also offered support. And this meant that the Governor of Indiana and the Indiana State Democratic Party endorsed Hatcher as well, despite the opposition of the powerful Lake County machine. Thus, Hatcher achieved legitimacy within the political system —a legitimacy which was necessary to block a massive voting fraud plot to prevent his winning the election.

Despite clear evidence of what was happening, the Justice Department nevertheless refused to intervene against this plot until Hatcher's campaign committee sent telegrams to key federal officials warning them that failure to do so would result in a massive race riot for which the federal officials would be held publicly responsible. Only by this unorthodox maneuver, whose credibility rested on Hatcher's known independent appeal and constituency, was the Federal Executive branch persuaded to enforce the law. Their intervention, striking 5,000 phony names from the voters rolls, guaranteed a Hatcher victory instead of a Hatcher defeat.

The refusal of the Justice Department to move except under what amounted to blackmail, indicated that the Johnson-Humphrey wing of the Party was not enthusiastic about Hatcher, whose iconoclastic and often radical behavior did not assure that he would behave appropriately after he was in power. But their decision finally to act, together with the readiness of the Kennedy forces to fully back Hatcher, suggests that there was a *national strategy* into which the Hatcher insurgency could perhaps be fitted.

My own view of that national strategy is that the federal government and the Democratic Party were attempting to accommodate themselves to rising black insurgency, and especially electoral insurgency, so as to contain it within the two-party system. This strategy necessitated sacrificing, at least to a degree, vested parochial local interests such as entrenched and corrupt machines.

Furthermore, black insurgency from below is potentially a force to rationalize obsolete local governments. The secular crisis of the city, itself reflecting a contradiction between public gain and private interest, certainly has called forth the best reform efforts of the corporate liberal elite. Centered in the federal government, its penumbra of foundations, law firms, and universities, the political forces associated with this rationalizing process were most clearly predominant in the Kennedy wing of the Democratic Party.

The economic forces whose interests are served by this process are specifically the banks, insurance companies, and other sections of large capital heavily invested in urban property, and more generally, the interests of corporate capital as a whole whose continued long-range profit and security rests on a stable, integrated, and loyal population.

Thus the support given to Hatcher was rational to the system as a whole, and not at all peculiar, even though it potentially implied economic and political loss for the corporation, U.S. Steel, whose operations on the spot might become more difficult. The interests of the governing class as a whole and of particular parts of it often diverge; this gap made it possible for Hatcher to achieve some power within the system. How these national factors would shape the amount and forms of power Hatcher actually obtained became quite evident within his first year of office.

## THE MOSAIC OF BLACK POWER

Decolonization is the best image to describe Gary in the initial months of the Hatcher regime. When I arrived in the city five months after the inauguration, my first task was to aid in the process of bringing a semblance of order out of what can only fairly be described as administrative chaos.

When the new administration arrived at City Hall in January 1968, they found themselves without the keys to offices, with many vital records missing (e.g., the file on the U.S. Steel Corporation in the Controller's Office), and with a large part of the city government's movable equipment stolen. For instance, the police force had so scavenged the patrol cars for tires and batteries that about 90 percent of them were inoperable. Such developments are certainly not part of what are thought of as the normal processes of American government. They seem more appropriate to a bitter ex-colonial power.

There were no funds available. This was because the City Council had sharply cut the municipal budget the previous summer in anticipation of a Hatcher victory. They intended if he lost the election to legislate a supplemental appropriation. His having won without the backing of a Council majority assured that he would be particularly crippled in his efforts to run the city government with a modicum of efficiency. Then whenever something went wrong, the media could and did blame the Mayor for his lack of concern or ability.

Not only did Richard Hatcher find his position sabotaged by the previous administration before he even arrived, but holdovers in office continued to circumvent his authority by design or accident until removed from their positions. And this comparatively unfavorable situation extended to every possible sphere of municipal activities.

Another problem was that the new administrators had to take over the management of a large, unwieldy, and obsolete municipal system without the slightest prior executive experience. That there were no black people in Gary with such experience in spite of the high degree of education and intelligence in the black community is explicable only in terms of institutionalized racism; blacks in Gary were never permitted such experiences and occupational roles. Hatcher staffed his key positions with black men who had been schoolteachers, the professional role most closely analogous to running a government bureaucracy for which he could find black Gary citizens. Although in the author's estimation several of these men were of outstanding capability, they still had to learn everything by trial and error, an arduous and painstaking way to maintain a complex institution.

Furthermore, this learning process was not made any easier by the unusually heavy demands placed on the time of the Mayor and his top aides by the national news media, maneuvering factions of the Democratic Party, a multiplicity of civil rights organizations, universities and voluntary associations, and others, who viewed the Mayor as a celebrity to be importuned, exploited, or displayed. This outpouring of national interest in a small, parochial city was an addition to the already heavy work load of the Mayor of a magnitude almost equal to his local duties.

Nor were there even clerical personnel to answer the mail and phone calls, let alone rationally respond to the deluge. The municipal budget provided the Mayor with a single secretary; it took most of the first summer to make the necessary arrangements to pay for another two secretaries for the Mayor's own needs. One result was that as late as June 1968 there was still a two-month backlog of unanswered personal mail, which was finally answered by much overtime work.

In addition to these sort of problems there were others, not as common to American politics, such as the threat of violence which had to be faced as a direct personal aspect of daily life. The problem of security was debilitating, especially after the King and Kennedy assassinations. In view of the Mayor's aggressive drive against local organized crime, the race hatred whipped up during and after the campaign by the right wing, and the history of violence in the steel town, this concern with security was not excessive. Moreover, maintaining security was a problem. Since the police were closely linked with the local right, it was necessary to provide the Mayor with private bodyguards. And with an armed and foreboding staff efficiency was impaired, especially since the Mayor shrugged off the danger and refused to cooperate with these security efforts.

In addition, the tremendous amounts of aid we were offered by foundations, universities, and federal officials proved to be a mixed blessing.[24] The time which was necessary to oversee existing processes was preempted by the complex negotiations surrounding the development and implementation of a panoply of new federal programs. There had never been a Concentrated Employment Program in Gary, nor a Model Cities Program, nor had the poverty program been locally controlled. Each of these new ventures involved the top municipal administrators in interminable rounds of conferences.

These programs were instituted in a city whose organizational structure, personnel job competences, and management techniques were, to express it generously, archaic. For instance, when Mayor Hatcher took over, each of the more than thirty department heads reported directly to him; nor were there any uniform personnel rules whatsoever. The city bureaucracy had been run for a small-town milieu; it was totally unprepared to utilize the highly sophisticated methods of the large eastern metropolises.

The new administration in Gary was offered, and accepted, new federal programs which in some cases no one in the city had even heard of before. Not only had these modern new methods of allegedly coping with the urban crisis never been used in Gary before, but some of them were so experimental they had never been implemented anywhere else either. The municipal bureaucracy, which under previous administrations had deliberately spared itself the embarrassment of federal audits, did not have the slightest idea as to how to utilize or run these complex federal programs.

Moreover, though they sometimes believed that they did (and even more often convinced the local officials), my opinion is that often the federal and foundation experts themselves did not really have a very clear notion as to what they were creating. None of the experts who brought this largesse to Gary had any clear understanding of how it was to be integrated into the existing municipal system and social structure. These new federal programs sprang up overnight: new bureaucracies, ossified at birth. Their actual purposes and effects bore little relation to the legislative purposes of the Congressional statutes which authorized them.

Needless to say, ordinary municipal employees experienced this process of outside assistance as a source of confusion and additional demoralization, and their efficiency fell even more. And even the new leadership was often overwhelmed by, and defensive before, the sophisticated Eastern federal bureaucrats and private consultants who clearly wanted only to help out America's first black mayor, a situation which made it more difficult to refuse the favors being offered. Of course these gifts carried a fearful price.

### The Municipal Bureaucracy

In Gary, only a small proportion of the muncipal work force was protected by civil service regulations; that part of Progressivism never took root in the city. So except for the uniformed officials, and the schools, which were largely outside the Mayor's control, how to deal with the standing city bureaucracy was a key dilemma for Mayor Hatcher.

The Mayor had run on a reform program. The official campaign platform of the Hatcher election effort placed "Good Government" first, ahead of even tax reform and civil rights.[25] Hatcher was deeply committed to eliminating graft and corruption, improving the efficiency of municipal government—especially the delivery of services to those sectors of the citizenry who had been most deprived—and he did not view his regime as merely the substitution of black faces for white ones in positions of power.

But he also had a particular historic injustice to rectify: the gross underrepresentation of blacks in the city government, and their complete exclusion from policy-making positions. There was also a series of implied campaign promises to reward followers, who were mostly black. (At least most participants in the campaign assumed that there was, although Hatcher never spoke about the matter).

Consequently, there was tremendous pressure from below to kick out everyone not covered by civil service protections, and substitute all black personnel in their places; a decision which would have deepened the hostility of the white population, and probably weakened Hatcher's potential leverage in the national Democratic Party.[26] Hatcher resisted this pressure, asserting that he believed in an interracial administration. However, in addition to this belief (which as far as I could determine was genuinely held by him), there were other circumstances which dictated his course of action in this matter.

To begin with, it was always a premise of the administration that vital municipal services had to be continued (e.g., police and fire protection, garbage collection, education, public health measures), both because the people of Gary absolutely needed them and because the failure to maintain them would represent a setback for black struggles throughout the country.

It also appeared that with a wholesale and abrupt transition to a totally new work force it would be impossible to continue these services, particularly because of a lack of the necessary skills and experiences, especially at the administrative and skilled technical level, among the black population. In this respect, Hatcher faced the classical problem faced by all social revolutions and nationalist movements of recent times: after the seizure of power how is it possible to run a complex society when those who traditionally ran it are now enemies?[27]

The strategy which Hatcher employed to meet this problem was the following: the bulk of the old personnel were retained. At the top level of the administration (e.g., personal staff, Corporation Counsel, Chief of Police, Controller) new, trustworthy, individuals were brought in. Then gradually new department heads were chosen, and new rank-and-file people were brought in; if they had the skill already they came at the beginning. And if they didn't, they were brought in at a rate slow enough to provide for on-the-job training from the holdovers, without disrupting the ongoing functions of the particular department. Conversely, this strategy necessitated retaining old bureaucrats. Therefore, these employees were not dismissed except upon proof of incompetency or dishonesty. Since the number of black and Spanish-speaking persons in Gary with the requisite skills was quite low (for instance, it was impossible to find locally a black civil engineer), this strategy entailed a *gradual process* of personnel and administrative change.

The main weakness with this strategy was that it permitted the old bureaucracy to survive; their institutional base was not destroyed. Consequently, the city government continued to suffer from incompetence, and corruption; it began to suffer from active and passive sabotage (e.g., slowdowns, refusal to implement new policy decisions); and worse, it underwent the subversion of the new personnel by causing them to be trained into the traditional modes of work and authority.

The result was that the new political priorities of the administration could not be implemented with any degree of effectiveness in a new municipal political practice. This practice remained remarkably like it was in the past at least from the perspective of the average citizen in the community. While the political leadership was tied up with the kinds of problems discussed above, the bureaucracy proceeded on its own course.

They engaged in passive resistance to changes in procedures and priorities, hiding behind a veil of customary practice and expertise. This passive resistance had two components: bureaucratic inertia, a sullen rejection of changes in any established routine which minimized conflicts and difficulties for the employees; and active opposition, based on politics and racism, to new methods and goals advocated by the Mayor.

For example, the Mayor decided to give a very high priority to enforcement of the housing codes, which had never been seriously implemented by preceding administrations. After much hard work, the Building Department was revamped to engage in aggressive inspection work. Cases stopped being "lost," and the number of inspections was increased by 4,000 percent while their quality was improved and standardized. Then it was discovered that cases prepared for legal enforcement were being tabled by the Legal Department on grounds of technical defects.

I personally then ascertained that the alleged legal defects were simply untrue.[28] I then assumed that the reason for the legal staff's behavior was that they were overburdened with work, and therefore conferences were held with the staff members to explain the Mayor's priorities so they could rearrange their work schedule. Instead, a series of bitter personal fights resulted, culminating in my removal from that area of work since the staff attorneys threatened to resign if there was continued interference with their professional responsibility. In the course of these disputes both black and white attorneys expressed the opinion that they did not consider themselves a legal aid bureau for Gary's poor, and that furthermore, the root of the city's housing problem was the indolent and malicious behavior of the tenants. In their view, it was therefore unjust to vigorously enforce the existing statutes against the landlords. Thus, despite the administration's pledge, black ghetto residents did not find their lives ameliorated in this respect.

Gradually then, the promise of vast change after the new Mayor took office came to be seen as illusory. Indeed, what actually occurred was much like an African neo-colonial entity: new faces, new rhetoric, and a people whose lives were scarcely affected except in their feelings toward their government.

This condition was neither the result of a failure of good faith on the part of the Hatcher administration, nor the result of the fallacious maximalist proposition that no amelioration of the people's conditions of life is possible prior to a revolution. Instead, it was an outcome consequent upon the decline of the local mass base of the Hatcher administration and the array of national political forces which confronted the administration.

The mass of black people in Gary were neither prepared nor able to take upon themselves the functions performed for them by specialized bureaucracies. They relied upon the government for education, welfare, public health, police and fire protection, enforcement of the building codes and other standards, maintenance of the public roads, etc. Unable to develop alternative popularly based community institutions to carry on these functions by democratic self-government, the new administration was forced to rely upon the city bureaucracy and forced to pursue the option which could only result in minor changes.

## The Decline of Popular Support

The most significant result of the failure of the Hatcher administration to transcend the structural terrain on which it functioned was political. This political outcome consisted in the erosion of popular support after the successful mobilization of energies involved in the campaign for office. The decline of mass participation in the political process contributed in turn to the tendency of the new regime to solve its dilemmas by bureaucratic means, or by relying on outside support from the federal government.

The decline in mass support ought not to be confused with a loss of votes in an election. Indeed, Hatcher is now probably as secure politically as the average big city mayor. The point is that the mass of the black population is not actively involved in helping to run the city. Thus, their political experiences are not enlarged, nor are there great gains in their understanding of the larger society and how it functions, nor are they being trained to better organize for their own interests. In short, the liberating process of the struggle for office was aborted after the initial goal was achieved and before it could even begin to confront the profound problems faced by the mass of urban black Americans.

For example, after the inauguration old supporters found themselves on the outside looking in. For the most part, since there was not any organized effort to continue to involve them (and indeed to do so could not but conflict with the dominant strategy of the administration), they had to be content to remain passive onlookers. The average citizen put a lot of faith in the Mayor, and wanted to give him an opportunity to do his job without intruding on the process.

Even among the most politicized rank-and-file elements there was fear of interfering: for disruption might ensue, especially as they were painfully conscious of their lack of training and experience. Thus, an attitude of benevelent watchfulness characterized the larger part of the black community who had participated in the activities leading to the assumption of power by the Mayor. Moreover, the sense that Hatcher was unique—and was presented by the media of a racist nation as some kind of test of black people as a race—still further inclined black citizens to quietude.

Furthermore, old supporters who did not receive the patronage or other assistance which they had expected were disillusioned, while people who found themselves treated rudely by a bureaucratic hold-over (or merely were unable to reach the ear of a leader who was once accessible as a friend), also lost confidence. All of this manifested itself as relative mass depoliticization.

In particular, this process expressed itself most markedly in the Spanish-speaking community, which could not reassure itself with the symbolic satisfaction of having a member of their group in the national spotlight. With even less education and prior opportunity than the blacks, they found that the qualifications barrier to municipal government left them with even less patronage than they felt to be their due reward. This feeling of betrayal was actively supported by the former machine politicians and criminal elements, who consciously evoked ethnic prejudices to isolate the Mayor and weaken his popular support.

What happened in the first year of the new administration then, was a contradiction between "expertness" and "ethnicity."[29] At each point, the Mayor felt the necessity to rely upon the expert bureaucracy, even at the cost of increasing his distance from his mass base. And this conflict manifested itself in a series of inexorable political events (e.g., the appointment of outside advisors), each of which further contributed to eroding the popular base of the still new leadership.

As Gramsci pointed out, beneath this contradiction lies a deeper one: an historic class deprivation—inflicted on the oppressed by the very structure of the existing society—which barred the underclass from access to the skills necessary for them to directly run the society in their own interests and according to their own standard of civilization.

Unless an oppressed social group is able to constitute itself as what Gramsci characterizes as a counterhegemonic social bloc, its conquest of state power cannot be much more than a change in leaders.[30] Given the overall relation of forces in the country at large such an undertaking was beyond the power of the black community in Gary in 1968. Therefore dominant national political forces were able to quickly reconstitute their overall control of the situation.

### National Power and Its Neo-Colonial Strategy

In its weakened local posture, the Hatcher administration was unable to successfully resist a large degree of cooptation by the national political authorities. Despite a brave vote at the Democratic National Convention for Reverend Channing Philips, Hatcher was essentially forced to cooperate with the national government and Democratic Party—even to the extent of calling on Sheriff Wood of Cook County to send deputies to reinforce the local police when a "mini-riot" occurred in the black ghetto.

Without either a nationally coordinated movement or an autonomous base of local insurgency—one capable of carrying out on a mass scale government functions outside of the official structure[31]—Hatcher's insurgency was contained within the existing national political system. Or, to express it somewhat differently, the attempt by black forces to use the electoral process to further their national liberation was aborted by a countervailing process of neo-colonialism carried out by the federal government. Or to put it differently, the piecemeal achievement of power through parliamentary means is a fraud, at least as far as black Americans are concerned.

The process by which the national power reconstituted itself, and even forced the new administration to aid it in doing so, was relatively simple. As the gap between the popular constituency and the new government widened, it found itself increasingly forced to rely upon its "accomplishments" to maintain its popularity and to fulfill its deeply held obligation to aid the community.

Lacking adequate autonomous financial resources—the Mill remained in private hands, and it even proved impossible to assess it for tax purposes at its true value—accomplishments necessarily were dependent upon the obtaining of outside funds. In this case, the funds had to come from the federal government, preferably in the form of quick performance projects to maintain popular support and enable everyone to do something to improve matters.[32]

These new programs injected a flow of cash into the community, and they created many new jobs. In his first year in office, the Mayor obtained in cash or pledges more federal funds than his entire local budget. Hopes begin to be engendered that these programs were the key to solving local problems,[33] while the time spent on preparing them completed the isolation of the leadership from the people.

Then too, under the stress of this forced and artificial growth, endless opportunities for nepotism and even impeculation were created. Men who had never earned a decent living before found themselves as high-paid executives without the requirement that they produce any tangible results. Indeed, federal authorities seemed glad to dispense the funds without exercising adequate controls over their expenditures. Thus, they created a situation in which those who boasted of how they were hustling the system became completely prisoners of its largesse.

Even the most honest and courageous leader, such as Mayor Hatcher, could not help but be trapped by the aid offered him by the federal authorities. After all, how can any elected local executive turn down millions of dollars to dispense with as he sees fit to help precisely those people he was elected to aid? The acceptance of the help guaranteed the recreation of bonds of dependency. For without any real autonomous power base, and with new vested interests and expectations created by the flow of funds into the community, and with no available alternate path of development, the relation of power between the local leader and the national state was necessarily decisively weighted toward the latter.

In Gary, Indiana, within one year after the most prodigious feat in the history of its black population—the conquest of local political power—their insurgency has been almost totally contained. It is indeed difficult to see how the existing administration can extricate itself from its comparative impasse in the absence of fresh national developments, or of a new, more politically coherent, popular upsurge from below.

There is however, no doubt that the struggle waged by the black people of Gary, Indiana, is a landmark on their road to freedom; for the experiences of life and struggle have become another part of their heritage—and thus a promise for us all.

## NOTES

1. I am presently preparing articles on these topics.
2. Bayard Rustin, "From Protest to Politics: The Future of the Civil Rights Movement," *Commentary* (February 1965): 25–34; Stokeley Carmichael and Charles V. Hamilton, *Black Power: The Politics of Liberation in America* (New York: Random House, 1967).
3. See Andre Gorz, *Strategy For Labor* (Boston: Beacon Press, 1967); and for some proposed American examples, Frank Brodhead, Edward Greer, Amy Kesselman, Karl Klare, and Ruth Meyerowitz, "Toward an American Socialist Strategy," *SACC Newsletter* (Cambridge, Massachusetts, December 3, 1969): 25–31.
4. A good impression of the city is created by Marshall Frady, "Gary, Indiana," *Harper's* (August 1969): 35–45.
5. *Labor Force Study: Gary, Indiana* (Washington, D. C.: City Planning Associates, 1965); *Gary, Indiana Community Renewal Program* (Gary: Gary Redevelopment Commission, 1968), p. 15.
6. The best history of early Gary is Powell A. Moore, *The Calumet Region: Indiana's Last Frontier*, Indiana Historical Collections, Vol. XXXIX (Indiana Historical Bureau, 1959).
7. John W. Reps, *The Making of Urban America: A History of City Planning in the United States* (Princeton: Princeton University Press, 1965), p. 428.
8. James Weinstein, *The Decline of Socialism in America, 1912–1925* (New York: Monthly Review Press, 1967).
9. David Brody, *Labor in Crisis: The Steel Strike of 1919* (Philadelphia, Lippincott, 1965). The post-war anti-union offensive was part of a general domestic reaction which included white-led race riots to smash the insurgent black movement and the Palmer raids to decimate the left. This domestic reaction was itself part of a general response to international social turmoil and the rise of Bolshevism. Arno Mayer, *Politics and Diplomacy of Peacemaking: Containment and Counterrevolution at Versailles, 1918–1919* (New York: Alfred A. Knopf, 1967).
10. Moore, "The Calumet Region," pp. 505–524. Also see Dolly Millender, *Yesterday in Gary: A History of the Negro in Gary* (n.p., 1967), p. 31.
11. Moore, "The Calumet Region," pp. 386–390.

12. Cf. C. Wright Mills, *The New Men of Power: America's Labor Leaders* (New York: Harcourt, Brace, 1948).

13. Staughton Lynd, "Guerrilla History in Gary," *Liberation* (October 1969): 17–20.

14. Although national corporate profits after taxes rose 80 percent between 1960 and 1967, the real wages of employees in manufacturing increased by only 13.5 percent. Since then, their real wages have actually declined.

15. Charles H. King, Jr., "Gary Human Relations Commission vs. U.S. Steel Gary Works," mimeographed (confidential document in possession of author, 1968), p. 3.

16. The Gary National Bank, the city's largest, "was organized in 1908 under the direction of George Campbell, a son-in-law of Judge Gary." Close ties have been maintained since. Moore, *The Calumet Region*, p. 340.

17. It is easy to conceptualize this group as a *compradore bourgeoisie*. Rather than unleash new social forces to their political left, they prefer to take an economic loss to outside capital. Cf. Jean Chesneaux, *The Chinese Labor Movement, 1919–1927* (Stanford: Stanford University Press, 1968).

18. There is a brief discussion of this event in the lead editorial of the *Calumet Voice* (March 1969).

19. *City of Gary Annual Report for Fiscal Year Ending December 31, 1968.* This figure applies only to municipal government functions; it excludes expenditures by the schools, welfare authorities, the Sanitary Board, and the Redevelopment Commission.

20. These restrictions on municipal officials are a product of the Progressive movement, in particular the corporate liberal concept of the government as a neutral technical administrator. James Weinstein, *The Corporate Ideal in the Liberal State, 1900–1918* (Boston: Beacon Press, 1968). See also, Gabriel Kolko, *The Triumph of Conservatism* (New York: Free Press, 1963); and Reich, "The New Property," *Yale Law Journal* 73: 733–777, for the immediate economic causes and ultimate legal consequences of this phenomena.

21. Personal investigation by author. (Assertions throughout on illegal activities are based upon reliable informants; usually verified by a second source).

22. About 5 percent of Gary's inhabitants are of Mexican and Puerto Rican origins.

23. Jeffrey K. Hadden, Louis H. Masotti, and Victor Thiessen are incorrect in asserting that racist attacks on Hatcher won him "some white votes he wouldn't have received otherwise." "The Making of the Negro Mayors, 1967," *Trans-action* (January/February, 1968): 21–30. At

least no one active in the campaign interviewed by me believed that that occurred.

24. In this regard, the author has a more ascerbic view than most of his former colleagues. In a document for HUD prepared under his supervision, the problem was summarized as "the imposition of several complex federal programs on an administrative system not designed to implement them." *1969 Gary Workable Program for Community Improvement* (Form HUD-1082), p. 16B2.

25. Platform of Richard Gordon Hatcher, 1967.

26. Local white radicals were not given jobs despite their campaign activities, and were passed over for more conservative whites who had often opposed him before the election. The author heard from an unusually reliable source that Hatcher had been warned "by high Washington authorities" to do this, but was unable to obtain details or confirmation.

27. This problem was first discussed by Karl Marx with respect to the Paris Commune. Its resolution was basic to shaping the outcome of the Russian Revolution. See Moshe Lewin, *Lenin's Last Struggle* (New York: Pantheon Books, 1968). And it remains a pressing problem to this day. For instance, in regard to China see, Franz Schurmann, *Ideology and Organization in Communist China* (Berkeley and Los Angeles: The University of California Press, 1966); and cf., Barry M. Richman, *Industrial Society in Communist China* (New York: Random House, 1969).

28. No one else (other than the Mayor) in the Gary city administration had the knowledge—the author holds a law degree from Yale—to openly challenge the Legal Department's "expert opinion" in this matter.

29. An explanation of this contradiction in the context of post-revolutionary Chinese society is developed by Schurmann, especially pp. 90–101.

30. Antonio Gramsci, *The Modern Prince and Other Writings* (New York: International Publishers; London: Lawrence and Wishart, 1957).

31. Examples of such organizations would be the Russian "soviets" or the Turin, Italy "workers councils" of 1919.

32. Thus the neo-colonial model is closely followed: after independence, the masses lapse into passivity and the new regime (regardless of its former ardor in fighting the imperialists) finds itself subordinated to international finance to pay for its "modernization" program.

33. I once heard a top administration official remark enthusiastically to a personal friend that, "if even one of these programs clicks, we've got it made."

# V | The Struggle for Black Political Power

Most black Americans believe that autonomous political power is the only basis on which the black nation in America will be able to destroy the institutional structure of racism which presently oppresses them. However, within the black community, and among outside observers of its plight, there exists a wide range of views as to precisely what kinds of power are needed by the black community to effect its liberation.

In part, the plurality of views is the result of a continuing debate concerning the content and meaning of black liberation in the context of the present world situation. In part, it is also the result of a debate whether the power necessary for liberation can be achieved within the American political system.

A significant minority of black Americans have come to the conclusion that the political system of America, and the economic and social system on which the political system rests, is structured to prevent the reforms which black liberation requires. Those who have arrived at this conclusion argue that it is necessary to challenge the political economy as a whole in the name of a global alternative, though there are many differences as to what that alternative should be (e.g., a separate black republic, emigration to Africa, a socialist revolution, etc.).

In many ways then, the fundamental political debate about black political power is the ancient one between reform and revolution. This debate has an alien ring about it to many Americans, since our political culture does not have much of a revolutionary component to it:

most Americans believe that their problems are soluble
by Constitutional processes.

Among black Americans, however, experience has been
such that the ideological notion that the system can
solve their problems has come increasingly in recent
years to be perceived as false. Despite all the efforts of
blacks to bring change within the system, the liberation
of blacks seems little closer than it did in former
times. Consequently, black Americans are more drawn
toward viewing themselves as members of an oppressed
*domestic colony*, for whom some type of revolution is
the only realistic course of self-help.

As yet, this process has not gone far enough to
predominate in black America, although the trend in that
direction has both deepened and speeded up considerably
over the past few years, indicating to many that its
ultimate hegemony among black Americans is inevitable.
But at present, the American political tradition of
pragmatic, reformist, pluralistic politics still predominates.
Harold Cruse has argued, in his monumental *The Crisis
of the Negro Intellectual* (New York: William Morrow,
1967), that such is still the case because black leaders
in the past failed to build an autonomous mass black
movement with a clear strategic direction.

Whether Cruse's analysis is correct or not, the fact
is that today the most intense debate is going on as to
what *strategic options* for political action ought to be
employed by the black community. And the debate can be
roughly categorized as between those who believe in
*electoral politics* as the main strategy for black liberation,
and those who see it as either useless or of only
minor value.

In reality, few individuals take pure positions on
either side. Many, if not most, practicing black
politicians—men who make their living by running for
elected office—agree that profound structural changes
are needed in American society. They often believe that
extra-parliamentary means (such as boycotts, strikes,
etc.) are useful or even essential. But their main emphasis
tends to be on voting and consequent legal actions
(e.g., FEPC legislation, ghetto business subsidies, etc.)

carried out by the state apparatus as a means of social change.

Conversely, many, if not most, black protest activists accept the ballot as a legitimate tool for achieving gains for black America. Very few black activists argue that blacks should systematically boycott all elections. Even if the "lesser evil" theory is rejected, usually such individuals favor voting for black politicians, or at least participating in other elections set up by the government, such as community school board elections.

The activist group tends to argue that the ballot is inadequate to meet the problems; and that it is necessary to change the basis on which elections are held—that is, to alter the social structure of the society (e.g., control of the mass media which helps determine voting patterns). This posture argues for disruption of existing social processes (whether by boycotts, strikes, or even riots and armed insurrection) to engender the possibility of creating new institutions which will better serve the needs of the people (e.g., community ownership of the property in the ghetto).

Two important additional points must be made here. The first is that the distinction is not, as the popular press tends to present it, between nonviolence and violence. For the violence of enforcing a particular law (e.g., legislation ending school segregation) may be far greater than what ensues if a highly organized and political community group occupies an institution which it has no legal "right" to, and begins to run it for the benefit of the entire community. The question really turns far more on whether blacks are morally obliged to accept the legitimacy of the American political system (e.g., the Constitution); a positive argument would be difficult for a white person to make in good faith.

Second, and closely related to the first point, is the question of whether there is a scale of tactics which separate into either reform or revolutionary politics. The answer is clearly negative, for it is the context which determines whether, for instance, a strike is revolutionary or reformist in character. Thus in actual practice, there is no *formal* way to determine whether a free breakfast

program for children, such as the one run by the Black
Panther Party; or a demand for black ghetto cooperatives,
lies within the camp of reform or the camp of revolution.*
A judgment in this matter depends on an overall
strategic vision of the course of the black liberation
struggle, for the meaning of an activity is often quite
different from what its initiators intend. Ultimately, a
sure answer depends upon the historical hindsight of a
successful political practice.

It is in this context that the selections which follow
should be approached. The classical argument for a
parliamentary path to black liberation was articulated
by Bayard Rustin, (a close associate of Reverend Martin
Luther King, Jr. and A. Philip Randolph, a social
democrat, pacifist, and the chief organizer of the 1963
March on Washington), in "From Protest to Politics:
The Future of the Civil Rights Movement." Rustin's
argument, which is implicitly accepted by virtually all
black politicians, is that blacks as a minority cannot
transform their situation by themselves, that they need
white allies, and that the way to find them is by creating
a progressive coalition within the Democratic Party.
Therefore, the main emphasis of the black struggle must
be to create the conditions for realigning the Democratic
Party and for turning it into an effective instrument
of social change.

Chuck Stone (the former legislative aide of
Representative Adam Clayton Powell, Jr., and vice-
chairman of the 1967 National Conference on Black
Power) presents a sober evaluation of what the results
of that strategic approach were during the Johnson
Administration. He demonstrates that blacks achieved
little power in any of the branches of the federal
government, and, moreover, that the situation was no
better at the state level.

Defenders of this progressive-Democrat approach
usually explain the underrepresentation of blacks on the

---

* On distinguishing reformist from revolutionary political strategies
in advanced capitalist countries, see Andre Gorz, *Strategy for Labor*
(Boston: Beacon Press, 1967).

basis of a lower level of black political participation in comparison with whites, thus placing the burden of blame on the blacks themselves. The reader is, therefore, referred to the very important article by Anthony M. Orum, "A Reappraisal of the Social and Political Participation of Negroes," *American Journal of Sociology*, July 1966, pp. 32–46, which makes it quite clear that by equivalent class status, black Americans have a significantly *higher* level of participation in voluntary associations than whites.

The two selections which follow indicate that the content and style of black political activity within the parliamentary framework is increasingly determined by the activities of those who reject a reformist strategy. The article by Professor Richard Young, "The Impact of Protest Leadership on Negro Politicians in San Francisco," demonstrates that as early as 1965 the activities of black radicals influenced black politicians in the Democratic Party. The article by black writer Joyce Ladner, "What Black Power Means to Negroes in Mississippi," indicates that with the failure of the civil rights movement to resolve the pressing economic and political needs of the mass of black southerners, activist strategic notions— rejecting more moderate goals within the system— begin to predominate.

Focus is then shifted to the black ghetto as the underlying cultural context of revolutionary consciousness. The importance of this setting is particularly apparent when seen through the eyes of Ulf Hannerz, a Swedish anthropologist. In an excerpt from his monograph, *Soulside*, which treats a Washington, D.C. black community, Hannerz with quiet understatement, portrays daily ghetto life, including the overpricing of goods and police brutality which accompany it.

Although Hannerz states merely the residents' beliefs about these matters, it is worth noting for readers who have not personally experienced them that there is overwhelming evidence that the perception of ghetto residents is basically correct. See for instance, David Caplovitz, *The Poor Pay More: Consumer Practices of*

*Low-Income Families* (New York: Free Press, 1963); and
Paul Chevigny, *Police Power: Police Abuses in New York
City* (New York: Pantheon Books, 1969).

The theoretical implications of this cultural and
economic context for the development of revolutionary
black consciousness are outlined by Berkeley sociologist
Robert Blauner. In an important article, "Internal
Colonialism and Ghetto Revolt," Blauner attempts a
theoretical explanation of the rise of black nationalism
as a mass force, the growth of black caucuses, and the
development of the Black Panther Party by means of
understanding black America as a domestic colony.

Black trade union activist Charles Denby, in "Black
Caucuses in the Unions," discusses one of the most
significant aspects of the emerging black movement—the
elaboration of black caucuses in the workplace. These
caucuses, independent of the trade union bureaucracies,
often highly political and always closely tied to the
immediate needs of the mass of black workers, are
potentially the single most vital and powerful expression
of black liberation politics. They are still in an embryonic
stage, and little has been reported about them. Yet the
caucuses represent an immense reservoir of strength,
for they tie together the national and class components of
the black liberation struggle—and, moreover, they
foreshadow the new basis for working-class solidarity.

*The Black Panther Party Platform and Program* is
self-explanatory. The Black Panther Party represents a
historically decisive tendency within the black movement;
although its organizational future is threatened by
massive state repression. As the leader of the revolutionary
left in America, both black and white, its political legacy
is already assured. The Party has demonstarted by its
teachings and practice that the national liberation of
black America requires a socialist revolution, led by
the working class—whose vanguard in turn will be the
black workers, organized in a political party.

Precisely because the editor's sympathies lie so closely
with the Panthers, he felt it necessary to conclude with
an essay of thoughtful criticism of the Panthers by black
intellectual Harold Cruse. In "The Fire This Time?," a

review of a collection of essays by Panther Minister of Information Eldridge Cleaver, Cruse as a nationalist argues that the prerequisite for a successful black liberation struggle in America is the full unfolding of a genuine revolutionary black culture; and that the Panthers, by engaging directly in revolutionary struggle are skipping over the necessary *precedent* step of a "cultural revolution."

Thus, while Cruse is in political disagreement with the Panthers, he agrees with their underlying analysis of black America as a domestic colony. Cautioning that a genuine liberation movement involves the flourishing of a distinct, self-conscious cultural identity among the oppressed, he avers that premature engagement in armed struggle would be disastrous. He, therefore, calls upon black intellectuals to elaborate this black culture as performance of their primary task.

The questions which Cruse raises are indeed vital. One wonders, however, whether his implicit stage theory of the black revolution makes sense. Perhaps the black "cultural revolution" can only occur *simultaneously* and as a part of the national liberation struggle as a political movement. Moreover, can Cruse's genuine objections be met without recognizing that the black liberation struggle is a part of the international anti-imperialist movement of the twentieth century, a movement which revolutionaries as diverse as Franz Fanon and Mao-tse Tung insist is an integral part of the world socialist movement?

| 13 | **From Protest to Politics: The Future of the Civil Rights Movement** |
|---|---|

*Bayard Rustin*

ONE

The decade spanned by the 1954 Supreme Court decision on school desegregation and the Civil Rights Act of 1964 will undoubtedly be recorded as the period in which the legal foundations of racism in America were destroyed. To be sure, pockets of resistance remained; but it would be hard to quarrel with the assertion that the elaborate legal structure of segregation and discrimination, particularly in relation to public accommodations, has virtually collapsed. On the other hand, without making light of the human sacrifices involved in the direct-action tactics (sit-ins, freedom rides, and the rest) that were so instrumental to this achievement, we must recognize that in desegregating public accommodations, we affected institutions which are relatively peripheral both to the American socio-economic order and to the fundamental conditions of life of the Negro people. In a highly industrialized, 20th-century civilization, we hit Jim Crow precisely where it was most anachronistic, dispensable, and vulnerable—in hotels, lunch counters, terminals, libraries, swimming pools, and the like. For in these forms, Jim Crow does impede the flow of commerce in the broadest sense: it is a nuisance in a society on the move (and on the make). Not surprisingly, therefore, it was the most mobility-conscious and relatively liberated group in the Negro community— lower-middle-class college students—who launched the attack that brought down this imposing but hollow structure.

The term "classical" appears especially apt for this phase of the civil rights movement. But in the few years that have passed since the

Reprinted from *Commentary* (February 1965): 25–31. Copyright © 1965 by the American Jewish Committee. By permission of the American Jewish Committee and the author.

first flush of sit-ins, several developments have taken place that have complicated matters enormously. One is the shifting focus of the movement in the South, symbolized by Birmingham; another is the spread of the revolution to the North; and the third, common to the other two, is the expansion of the movement's base in the Negro community. To attempt to disentangle these three strands is to do violence to reality. David Danzig's perceptive article, "The Meaning of Negro Strategy,"* correctly saw in the Birmingham events the victory of the concept of collective struggle over individual achievement as the road to Negro freedom. And Birmingham remains the unmatched symbol of grass-roots protest involving all strata of the black community. It was also in this most industrialized of Southern cities that the single-issue demands of the movement's classical stage gave way to the "package deal." No longer were Negroes satisfied with integrating lunch counters. They now sought advances in employment, housing, school integration, police protection, and so forth.

Thus, the movement in the South began to attack areas of discrimination which were not so remote from the Northern experience as were Jim Crow lunch counters. At the same time, the interrelationship of these apparently distinct areas became increasingly evident. What is the value of winning access to public accommodations for those who lack money to use them? The minute the movement faced this question, it was compelled to expand its vision beyond race relations to economic relations, including the role of education in modern society. And what also became clear is that all these interrelated problems, by their very nature, are not soluble by private, voluntary efforts but require government action—or politics. Already Southern demonstrators had recognized that the most effective way to strike at the police brutality they suffered from was by getting rid of the local sheriff—and that meant political action, which in turn meant, and still means, political action within the Democratic party where the only meaningful primary contests in the South are fought.

And so, in Mississippi, thanks largely to the leadership of Bob Moses, a turn toward political action has been taken. More than voter registration is involved here. A conscious bid for *political power* is being made, and in the course of that effort a tactical shift is being effected: direct-action techniques are being subordinated to a strategy calling for the building of community institutions or power bases. Clearly, the implications of this shift reach far beyond Mississippi. What began

* *Commentary*, February 1964.

as a protest movement is being challenged to translate itself into a political movement. Is this the right course? And if it is, can the transformation be accomplished?

## TWO

The very decade which has witnessed the decline of legal Jim Crow has also seen the rise of *de facto* segregation in our most fundamental socio-economic institutions. More Negroes are unemployed today than in 1954, and the unemployment gap between the races is wider. The median income of Negroes has dropped from 57 per cent to 54 per cent of that of whites. A higher percentage of Negro workers is now concentrated in jobs vulnerable to automation than was the case ten years ago. More Negroes attend *de facto* segregated schools today than when the Supreme Court handed down its famous decision; while school integration proceeds at a snail's pace in the South, the number of Northern schools with an excessive proportion of minority youth proliferates. And behind this is the continuing growth of racial slums, spreading over our central cities and trapping Negro youth in a milieu which, whatever its legal definition, sows an unimaginable demoralization. Again, legal niceties aside, a resident of a racial ghetto lives in segregated housing, and more Negroes fall into this category than ever before.

These are the facts of life which generate frustration in the Negro community and challenge the civil rights movement. At issue, after all, is not *civil rights*, strictly speaking, but social and economic conditions. Last summer's riots were not race riots; they were outbursts of class aggression in a society where class and color definitions are converging disastrously. How can the (perhaps misnamed) civil rights movement deal with this problem?

Before trying to answer, let me first insist that the task of the movement is vastly complicated by the failure of many whites of good will to understand the nature of our problem. There is a widespread assumption that the removal of artificial racial barriers should result in the automatic integration of the Negro into all aspects of American life. This myth is fostered by facile analogies with the experience of various ethnic immigrant groups, particularly the Jews. But the analogies with the Jews do not hold for three simple but profound reasons. First, Jews have a long history as a literate people, a resource which has afforded them opportunities to advance in the academic and

professional worlds, to achieve intellectual status even in the midst
of economic hardship, and to evolve sustaining value systems in the
context of ghetto life. Negroes, for the greater part of their presence
in this country, were forbidden by law to read or write. Second, Jews
have a long history of family stability, the importance of which in
terms of aspiration and self-image is obvious. The Negro family structure was totally destroyed by slavery and with it the possibility of
cultural transmission (the right of Negroes to marry and rear children
is barely a century old). Third, Jews are white and have the *option*
of relinquishing their cultural-religious identity, intermarrying, passing,
etc. Negroes, or at least the overwhelming majority of them, do not
have this option. There is also a fourth, vulgar reason. If the Jewish
and Negro communities are not comparable in terms of education,
family structure, and color, it is also true that their respective economic roles bear little resemblance.

This matter of economic role brings us to the greater problem—the
fact that we are moving into an era in which the natural functioning
of the market does not by itself ensure every man with will and ambition a place in the productive process. The immigrant who came to
this country during the late 19th and early 20th centuries entered a
society which was expanding territorially and/or economically. It was
then possible to start at the bottom, as an unskilled or semi-skilled
worker, and move up the ladder, acquiring new skills along the way.
Especially was this true when industrial unionism was burgeoning,
giving new dignity and higher wages to organized workers. Today the
situation has changed. We are not expanding territorially, the western
frontier is settled, labor organizing has leveled off, our rate of economic
growth has been stagnant for a decade. And we are in the midst of a
technological revolution which is altering the fundamental structure
of the labor force, destroying unskilled and semi-skilled jobs—jobs in
which Negroes are disproportionately concentrated.

Whatever the pace of this technological revolution may be, the
*direction* is clear: the lower rungs of the economic ladder are being
lopped off. This means that an individual will no longer be able to
start at the bottom and work his way up; he will have to start in the
middle or on top, and hold on tight. It will not even be enough to have
certain specific skills, for many skilled jobs are also vulnerable to automation. A broad educational background, permitting vocational adapt-
ability and flexibility, seems more imperative than ever. We live in a
society where, as Secretary of Labor Willard Wirtz puts it, machines
have the equivalent of a high school diploma. Yet the average educational attainment of American Negroes is 8.2 years.

Negroes, of course, are not the only people being affected by these developments. It is reported that there are now 50 percent fewer unskilled and semi-skilled jobs than there are high school dropouts. Almost one-third of the 26 million young people entering the labor market in the 1960's will be dropouts. But the percentage of Negro dropouts nationally is 57 per cent, and in New York City, among Negroes 25 years of age or over, it is 68 per cent. They are without a future.

To what extent can the kind of self-help campaign recently prescribed by Eric Hoffer in the *New York Times Magazine* cope with such a situation? I would advise those who think that self-help is the answer to familiarize themselves with the long history of such efforts in the Negro community, and to consider why so many foundered on the shoals of ghetto life. It goes without saying that any effort to combat demoralization and apathy is desirable, but we must understand that demoralization in the Negro community is largely a common-sense response to an objective reality. Negro youths have no need of statistics to perceive, fairly accurately, what their odds are in American society. Indeed, from the point of view of motivation, some of the healthiest Negro youngsters I know are juvenile delinquents: vigorously pursuing the American Dream of material acquisition and status, yet finding the conventional means of attaining it blocked off, they do not yield to defeatism but resort to illegal (and often ingenious) methods. They are not alien to American culture. They are, in Gunnar Myrdal's phrase, "exaggerated Americans." To want a Cadillac is not un-American; to push a cart in the garment center is. If Negroes are to be persuaded that the conventional path (school, work, etc.) is superior, we had better provide evidence which is now sorely lacking. It is a double cruelty to harangue Negro youth about education and training when we do not know what jobs will be available for them. When a Negro youth can reasonably foresee a future free of slums, when the prospect of gainful employment is realistic, we will see motivation and self-help in abundant enough qualities.

Meanwhile, there is an ironic similarity between the self-help advocated by many liberals and the doctrines of the Black Muslims. Professional sociologists, psychiatrists, and social workers have expressed amazement at the Muslims' success in transforming prostitutes and dope addicts into respectable citizens. But every prostitute the Muslims convert to a model of Calvinist virtue is replaced by the ghetto with two more. Dedicated as they are to maintenance of the ghetto, the Muslims are powerless to affect substantial moral reform. So too with every other group or program which is not aimed at the destruction of slums, their causes and effects. Self-help efforts, directly or indirectly, must be geared to mobilizing people into power units capable of effecting social change. That is, their goal must be genuine self-help, not merely self-improvement. Obviously, where self-improvement activities succeed in imparting to their participants a feeling of some control over their environment, those involved may find their appetites for change whetted; they may move into the political arena.

## THREE

Let me sum up what I have thus far been trying to say: the civil rights movement is evolving from a protest movement into a full-fledged *social movement*—an evolution calling its very name into question. It is now concerned not merely with removing the barriers to full *opportunity* but with achieving the fact of *equality*. From sit-ins and freedom rides we have gone into rent strikes, boycotts, community organization, and political action. As a consequence of this natural evolution, the Negro today finds himself stymied by obstacles of far greater magnitude than the legal barriers he was attacking before: automation, urban decay, *de facto* school segregation. These are problems which, while conditioned by Jim Crow, do not vanish upon its demise. They are more deeply rooted in our socio-economic order; they are the result of the total society's failure to meet not only the Negro's needs, but human needs generally.

These propositions have won increasing recognition and acceptance, but with a curious twist. They have formed the common premise of two apparently contradictory lines of thought which simultaneously nourish and antagonize each other. On the one hand, there is the reasoning of the New York *Times* moderate who says that the problems are so enormous and complicated that Negro militancy is a futile irritation, and that the need is for "intelligent moderation." Thus, during the first New York school boycott, the *Times* editorialized that Negro demands, while abstractly just, would necessitate massive reforms, the funds for which could not realistically be anticipated; therefore the just demands were also foolish demands and would only antagonize white people. Moderates of this stripe are often correct in perceiving the difficulty or impossibility of racial progress in the context of present social and economic policies. But they accept the context as fixed. They ignore (or perhaps see all too well) the potentialities inherent in linking Negro demands to broader pressures for radical revision of existing policies. They apparently see nothing strange in the fact that in the last twenty-five years we have spent nearly a trillion dollars fighting or preparing for wars, yet throw up our hands before the need for overhauling our schools, clearing the slums, and really abolishing poverty. My quarrel with these moderates is that they do not even envision radical changes; their admonitions of moderation are, for all practical purposes, admonitions to the Negro to adjust to the status quo, and are therefore immoral.

The more effectively the moderates argue their case, the more they convince Negroes that American society will not or cannot be reorganized for full racial equality. Michael Harrington has said that a successful war on poverty might well require the expenditure of a $100 billion. Where, the Negro wonders, are the forces now in motion to compel such a commitment? If the voices of the moderates were raised in an insistence upon a reallocation of national resources at levels that could not be confused with tokenism (that is, if the moderates stopped being moderates), Negroes would have greater grounds for hope. Meanwhile, the Negro movement cannot escape a sense of isolation.

It is precisely this sense of isolation that gives rise to the second line of thought I want to examine—the tendency within the civil rights movement which, despite its militancy, pursues what I call a "no-win" policy. Sharing with many moderates a recognition of the magnitude of the obstacles to freedom, spokesmen for this tendency survey the American scene and find no forces prepared to move toward radical solutions. From this they conclude that the only viable strategy is shock; above all, the hypocrisy of white liberals must be exposed. These spokesmen are often described as the radicals of the movement, but they are really its moralists. They seek to change white hearts—by traumatizing them. Frequently abetted by white self-flagellants, they may gleefully applaud (though not really agreeing with) Malcolm X because, while they admit he has no program, they think he can frighten white people into doing the right thing. To believe this, of course, you must be convinced, even if unconsciously, that at the core of the white man's heart lies a buried affection for Negroes—a proposition one may be permitted to doubt. But in any case, hearts are not relevant to the issue; neither racial affinities nor racial hostilities are rooted there. It is institutions—social, political, and economic institutions—which are the ultimate molders of collective sentiments. Let these institutions be reconstructed *today*, and let the ineluctable gradualism of history govern the formation of a new psychology.

My quarrel with the "no-win" tendency in the civil rights movement (and the reason I have so designated it) parallels my quarrel with the moderates outside the movement. As the latter lack the vision or will for fundamental change, the former lack a realistic strategy for achieving it. For such a strategy they substitute militancy. But militancy is a matter of posture and volume and not of effect.

I believe that the Negro's struggle for equality in America is essentially revolutionary. While most Negroes—in their hearts—unquestionably seek only to enjoy the fruits of American society as it now exists, their quest cannot *objectively* be satisfied within the framework of existing political and economic relations. The young Negro who would demonstrate his way into the labor market may be motivated by a thoroughly bourgeois ambition and thoroughly "capitalist" considerations, but he will end up having to favor a great expansion of the public sector of the economy. At any rate, that is the position the movement will be forced to take as it looks at the number of jobs being generated by the private economy, and if it is to remain true to the masses of Negroes.

The revolutionary character of the Negro's struggle is manifest in the fact that this struggle may have done more to democratize life for whites than for Negroes. Clearly, it was the sit-in movement of young Southern Negroes which, as it galvanized white students, banished the ugliest features of McCarthyism from the American campus and resurrected political debate. It was not until Negroes assaulted *de facto* school segregation in the urban centers that the issue of quality education for *all* children stirred into motion. Finally, it seems reasonably clear that the civil rights movement, directly and through the resurgence of social conscience it kindled, did more to initiate the war on poverty than any other single force.

It will be—it has been—argued that these by-products of the Negro struggle are not revolutionary. But the term revolutionary, as I am using it, does not connote violence; it refers to the qualitative transformation of fundamental institutions, more or less rapidly, to the point where the social and economic structure which they comprised can no longer be said to be the same. The Negro struggle has hardly run its course; and it will not stop moving until it has been utterly defeated or won substantial equality. But I fail to see how the movement can be victorious in the absence of radical programs for full employment, abolition of slums, the reconstruction of our educational system, new definitions of work and leisure. Adding up the cost of such programs, we can only conclude that we are talking about a refashioning of our political economy. It has been estimated, for example, that the price of replacing New York City's slums with public housing would be $17 billion. Again, a multi-billion dollar federal public-works program, dwarfing the currently proposed $2 billion program, is required to reabsorb unskilled and semi-skilled workers into the labor market—and this must be done if Negro workers in these categories are to be employed. "Preferential treatment" cannot help them.

I am not trying here to delineate a total program, only to suggest the scope of economic reforms which are most immediately related to the plight of the Negro community. One could speculate on their political implications—whether, for example, they do not indicate the obsolescence of state government and the superiority of regional structures as viable units of planning. Such speculations aside, it is clear that Negro needs cannot be satisfied unless we go beyond what has so far been placed on the agenda. How are these radical objectives to be achieved? The answer is simple, deceptively so: *through political power.*

There is a strong moralistic strain in the civil rights movement which would remind us that power corrupts, forgetting that the absence of power also corrupts. But this is not the view I want to debate here, for it is waning. Our problem is posed by those who accept the need for political power but do not understand the nature of the object and therefore lack sound strategies for achieving it; they tend to confuse political institutions with lunch counters.

A handful of Negroes, acting alone, could integrate a lunch counter by strategically locating their bodies so as *directly* to interrupt the operation of the proprietor's will; their numbers were relatively unimportant. In politics, however, such a confrontation is difficult because the interests involved are merely *represented.* In the execution of a political decision a direct confrontation may ensue (as when federal marshals escorted James Meredith into the University of Mississippi—to turn from an example of non-violent coercion to one of force backed up with the threat of violence). But in arriving at a political decision, numbers and organizations are crucial, especially for the economically disenfranchised. (Needless to say, I am assuming that the forms of political democracy exist in America, however imperfectly, that they are valued, and that elitist or putschist conceptions of exercising power are beyond the pale of discussion for the civil right movement.)

Neither that movement nor the country's twenty million black people can win political power alone. We need allies. The future of the Negro struggle depends on whether the contradictions of this society can be resolved by a coalition of progressive forces which becomes the *effective* political majority in the United States. I speak of the coalition which staged the March on Washington, passed the Civil Rights Act, and laid the basis for the Johnson landslide—Negroes, trade unionists, liberals, and religious groups.

There are those who argue that a coalition strategy would force the Negro to surrender his political independence to white liberals, that he would be neutralized, deprived of his cutting edge, absorbed into the Establishment. Some who take this position urged last year that votes be withheld from the Johnson-Humphrey ticket as a demonstration of the Negro's political power. Curiously enough, these people who sought to demonstrate power through the non-exercise of it, also point to the Negro "swing vote" in crucial urban areas as the source of the Negro's independent political power. But here they are closer to being right: the urban Negro vote will grow in importance in the coming years. If there is anything positive in the spead of the ghetto, it is the potential political power base thus created, and to realize this potential is one of the most challenging and urgent tasks before the civil rights movement. If the movement can wrest leadership of the ghetto vote from the machines, it will have acquired an organized constituency such as other major groups in our society now have.

But we must also remember that the effectiveness of a swing vote depends solely on "other" votes. It derives its power from them. In that sense, it can never be "independent," but must opt for one candidate or the other, even if by default. Thus coalitions are inescapable, however tentative they may be. And this is the case in all but those few situations in which Negroes running on an independent ticket might conceivably win. "Independence," in other words, is not a value in itself. The issue is which coalition to join and how to make it responsive to your program. Necessarily there will be compromise. But the difference between expediency and morality in politics is the difference between selling out a principle and making smaller concessions to win larger ones. The leader who shrinks from this task reveals not his purity but his lack of political sense.

The task of molding a political movement out of the March on Washington coalition is not simple, but no alternatives have been advanced. We need to choose our allies on the basis of common political objectives. It has become fashionable in some no-win Negro circles to decry the white liberal as the main enemy (his hypocrisy is what sustains racism); by virtue of this reverse recitation of the reactionary's litany (liberalism leads to socialism, which leads to Communism) the Negro is left in majestic isolation, except for a tiny band of fervent white initiates. But the objective fact is that *Eastland and Goldwater* are the main enemies—they and the opponents of civil rights, of the war on poverty, of medicare, of social security, of federal aid to education, of unions, and so forth. The labor movement, despite its obvious faults, has been the largest single organized force in this country pushing for progressive social legislation. And where the Negro-labor-liberal axis is weak, as in the farm belt, it was the religious groups that were most influential in rallying support for the Civil Rights Bill.

The durability of the coalition was interestingly tested during the election. I do not believe that the Johnson landslide proved the "white backlash" to be a myth. It proved, rather, that economic interests are more fundamental than prejudice: the backlashers decided that loss of social security was, after all, too high a price to pay for a slap at the Negro. This lesson was a valuable first step in re-educating such people, and it must be kept alive, for the civil rights movement will be advanced only to the degree that social and economic welfare gets to be inextricably entangled with civil rights.

The 1964 elections marked a turning point in American politics. The Democratic landslide was not merely the result of a negative reaction to Goldwaterism; it was also the expression of a majority liberal concensus. The near unanimity with which Negro voters joined in that expression was, I am convinced, a vindication of the July 25th statement by Negro leaders calling for a strategic turn toward political action and a temporary curtailment of mass demonstrations. Despite the controversy surrounding the statement, the instinctive response it met with in the community is suggested by the fact that demonstrations were down 75 per cent as compared with the same period in 1963. But should so high a percentage of Negro voters have gone to Johnson, or should they have held back to narrow his margin of victory and thus give greater visibility to our swing vote? How has our loyalty changed things? Certainly the Negro vote had higher visibility in 1960, when a switch of only 7 per cent from the Republican column of 1956 elected President Kennedy. But the slimness of Kennedy's victory—of his "mandate"—dictated a go-slow approach on civil rights, at least until the Birmingham upheaval.

Although Johnson's popular majority was so large that he could have won without such overwhelming Negro support, that support was important from several angles. Beyond adding to Johnson's total national margin, it was specifically responsible for his victories in

Virginia, Florida, Tennessee, and Arkansas. Goldwater took only those states where fewer than 45 per cent of eligible Negroes were registered. That Johnson would have won those states had Negro voting rights been enforced is a lesson not likely to be lost on a man who would have been happy with a unanimous electoral college. In any case, the 1.6 million Southern Negroes who voted have had a shattering impact on the Southern political party structure, as illustrated in the changed composition of the Southern congressional delegation. The "backlash" gave the Republicans five House seats in Alabama, one in Georgia, and one in Mississippi. But on the Democratic side, seven segregationists were defeated while all nine Southerners who voted for the Civil Rights Act were re-elected. It may be premature to predict a Southern Democratic party of Negroes and white moderates and a Republican Party of refugee racists and economic conservatives, but there certainly is a strong tendency toward such a realignment; and an additional 3.6 million Negroes of voting age in the eleven Southern states are still to be heard from. Even the *tendency* toward disintegration of the Democratic party's racist wing defines a new context for Presidential and liberal strategy in the congressional battles ahead. Thus the Negro vote (North as well as South), while not *decisive* in the Presidential race, was enormously effective. It was a dramatic element of a historic mandate which contains vast possibilities and dangers that will fundamentally affect the future course of the civil rights movement.

The liberal congressional sweep raises hope for an assault on the seniority system, Rule Twenty-two, and other citadels of Dixiecrat-Republican power. The overwhelming of this conservative coalition should also mean progress on much bottlenecked legislation of profound interest to the movement (e.g., bills by Senators Clark and Nelson on planning, manpower, and employment). Moreover, the irrelevance of the South to Johnson's victory gives the President more freedom to act than his predecessor had and more leverage to the movement to pressure for executive action in Mississippi and other racist strongholds.

None of this *guarantees* vigorous executive or legislative action, for the other side of the Johnson landslide is that it has a Gaullist quality. Goldwater's capture of the Republican party forced into the Democratic camp many disparate elements which do not belong there, Big Business being the major example. Johnson, who wants to be President "of all people," may try to keep his new coalition together by sticking close to the political center. But if he decides to do this, it is unlikely that even his political genius will be able to hold together a coalition so inherently unstable and rife with contraditions. It must come apart. Should it do so while Johnson is pursuing a centrist course, then the mandate will have been wastefully dissipated. However, if the mandate is seized upon to set fundamental changes in motion, then the basis can be laid for a new mandate, a new coalition including hitherto inert and dispossessed strata of the population.

Here is where the cutting edge of the civil rights movement can be applied. We must see to it that the reorganization of the "consensus party" proceeds along lines which will make it an effective vehicle for social reconstruction, a role it cannot play so long as it furnishes Southern racism with its national political power. (One of Barry Goldwater's few attractive ideas was that the Dixiecrats belong with him in the same party.) And nowhere has the civil rights movement's political cutting edge been more magnificently demonstrated than at Atlantic City, where the Mississippi Freedom Democratic Party not only secured recognition as a bona fide components of the national party, but in the process routed the representatives of the most rabid racists —the white Mississippi and Alabama delegations. While I still believe that the FDP made a tactical error in spurning the compromise, there is no question that they launched a political revolution whose logic is the displacement of Dixiecrat power. They launched that revolution within a major political institution and as part of a coalition effort.

The role of the civil rights movement in the reorganization of American political life is programmatic as well as strategic. We are challenged now to broaden our social vision, to develop functional programs with concrete objectives. We need to propose alternatives to technological unemployment, urban decay, and the rest. We need to be calling for public works and training, for national economic planning, for federal aid to education, for attractive public housing— all this on a sufficiently massive scale to make a difference. We need to protest the notion that our integration into American life, so long delayed, must now proceed in an atmosphere of competitive scarcity instead of in the security of abundance which technology makes possible. We cannot claim to have answers to all the complex problems of modern society. That is too much to ask of a movement still battling barbarism in Mississippi. But we can agitate the right questions by probing at the contradictions which still stand in the way of the "Great Society." The questions having been asked, motion must begin in the larger society, for there is a limit to what Negroes can do alone.

# 14 Measuring Black Political Power

*Chuck Stone*

> In general, we understand by "power," the chance of a man or of a number of men to realize their own will in a communal action against the resistance of others who are participating in the action.
>
> —Max Weber

In the American political system, organizations and interest groups wield power, individuals don't. Individuals can affect power outside organizations only if they possess charisma, that undefinable quality of body and spirit reserved for a few "world historical individuals." Such charismatic leaders must still, however, rely on followers, and eventually these followers become institutionalized into some form of organizational structure.

If organizations are the true power brokers in society, then political parties represent summit political power. Their power is measurable by the number of elections they win, the number of public officials they elect, and the amount of control they can exercise over the administration of government. Because the state is the supreme power in any society, that organization which controls the government controls the state. Political parties control governments. The power of political parties is measured by the degree of sovereignty they exercise over the heads of government, its appointees, its domestic and foreign policies, and its dispensation of patronage.

The measurement of the political power of an ethnic group, an economic class, or another interest group is far more difficult. Such a group's claim of political achievements are usually exaggerated and extravagantly publicized. On occasion, they have been able to estab-

Reprinted from *Black Political Power in America*, pp. 58–81. Copyright © 1968 by C. Sumner Stone. By permission of the publishers, The Bobbs-Merrill Company, Inc.

lish a direct connection between the defeat or election of a candidate inimical or responsive to their wishes. But this group's ability to deliver the vote of its members is not always subject to scientific verification. Their leaders may fervently endorse a particular candidate or policy. But the group's members, by their decision at the polls, will vote diametrically opposite to the official position of the interest group. For example, in the Gary mayorality election of November 1967, the labor union leaders in Gary publicly endorsed the Democratic candidate, a negro. In a political race governed by strong racial overtones, white steel workers from the Gary steel mills ignored the official posture of their labor leaders and instead gave 89 per cent of their vote to the white Republican candidate.

This is a classic example of the social variables that impinge on the consciousness of individuals, forcing them to structure a priority of loyalties and then decide which loyalty will determine their political decisions. As the distinguished Lebanese philosopher and statesman Charles Malik has written: ". . . man has other loyalties than his loyalty to the state. He has his loyalty to his family, to his religion, to his profession; he has his loyalty to science and to truth. These loyalties are equally exacting as the loyalty to the state."*

Thus, a white Roman Catholic living in an integrated city neighborhood whose children attend integrated schools is not likely to respond as antagonistically to his church's call for more integrated schools as is a white Roman Catholic living in a wealthy suburb where no negroes live or attend school. Nor are union members of an industrial union with a large percentage of negroes likely to be as determined to bar union participation of negroes as the racially exclusive crafts unions.

Throughout the history of American politics, various interest groups have tended to follow rather than reject the advice of their leaders in tacit fealty to the pragmatic doctrine that to do otherwise would dilute the group's credibility and power. Interest groups have sought political power through five methods:

1. Political oscillation—threatening to take their votes to another candidate or party.
2. Proportionate control of policy-making jobs in government— placing its members in sensitive positions in order to influence public policy favorably toward their interests.
3. Retribution—punishing politicians through a "backlash vote" for opposing the group's interests.

* Extracts from the Proceedings of the United Nations Commission on Human Rights, 1947.

4. Educational propaganda—influencing other members of the electorate to a sympathetic adoption of the group's point of view
   through the use of pamphlets, meetings, and public statements.
5. Lobbying in Congress and state legislatures for legislation which
   promotes the group's interest or against legislation which
   threatens the group's survival and political power.

Of these five methods, the first and second have tended to dominate
the activities of most interest groups. The possibility of other groups
determining the outcome of an election as the result of a "backlash"
and the confluence of other groups also lobbying with equal effectiveness for a piece of legislation decrease one group's ability to claim sole
credit for such accomplishments. With very infrequent exceptions,
negroes have been unsuccessful in all five methods.

Occasionally, they have managed to rally friends to their cause—the
passage of civil-rights laws, the creation of the open society—but their
success has stemmed more from their activities outside politics (demonstrations, marches, sit-ins) rather than within the framework of the
political system. One of the greatest tragedies of the civil-rights movement has been its inability—or maybe its lack of understanding—to
transmit the fervor of civil-rights activities into political activity.

Civil-rights demonstrators make good marchers, but poor politicians.

Civil-rights leaders can get up a good boycott, but they can never
get out a good vote.

Civil-rights laws provide for equality of opportunity, but do not
ensure equality of results.

Equality of results is what the science of politics is concerned with.

Because they have never concerned themselves with real power in
society, civil-rights leaders have danced on the fringes of the political
and economic apparatuses that control society.

As already stated, they have feared that any diligent seeking of real
political power, resulting in the possible displacement of sympathetic
politicians, might in turn alienate those politicians. But politicians are
not primarily concerned with any ethnic group's rights as much as
they are concerned with their own right to survive.

In one of the most perceptive columns ever written about this
paradox, Mike Royko, a white columnist for the *Chicago Daily News*,
commented in his April 5, 1967, column the day after a Chicago
primary:

> . . . black power was available in sizable quantities in Chicago Tuesday.
> And a person didn't have to march, sing, riot or boycott to get it.

It was inside the voting machine. By pulling a lever or using a pencil, the Negro could have thrown a scare into City Hall.

Instead Chicago Negroes went out and gave something like 80 to 85% of their vote to Mayor Richard J. Daley; about 10% to John Waner and just a dib and a dab to Dick Gregory. And Daley didn't even campaign in the Negro areas.

I'm not saying they shouldn't have voted for Mayor Daley. If he is their man—fine. But is he their man? If so, they show it in strange ways.

They should remember that the city was in an uproar most of last summer because the civil rights wing of the Negro population was marching to protest the way the Negro was being treated by the mayor's administration.

It was the mayor's house that was being picketed for the last couple of summers. It was the administration's school system that they boycotted and raged against.

It was the mayor's police department that was accused of being unkind to Negroes. The mayor's firemen were the ones shot at and stoned. And it was his fire department that was accused of being segregated.

. . . The inconsistency mounts when you consider that the poorest Negro areas—the most riot-inclined areas—were where Daley got his best support. He didn't do much better in his own neighborhood than he did in some West Side wards. . . .

And finally, if there is a leader of Chicago's Negroes, he is Richard J. Daley, that rosy-cheeked Irishman from the Back of the Yards. . . .

So this summer, don't sing me that old refrain of "black power." The voting machine was listening Tuesday, but he couldn't hear you even humming.

While Royko's analysis defines the peculiarity of the Chicago political machine with its tyrannical control over the electorate because of the crime syndicate's enforcement powers, it is a fact that the black vote has not always predictably followed its best civil-rights interests. Black voters have invariably been more slavishly loyal to a political machine with its built-in hostility to their best interests than other ethnic groups. Nevertheless, the classical myth—and fear—of the black vote as a balance of power in close elections has persisted.

In some quarters, recognition has been given to the appointment of negroes to high office for the first time (member of a Federal agency, the Cabinet, the U.S. Supreme Court, etc.) as an example of the potency of the black vote.

High-level negro appointments are still rare, and, because they are, they must be categorized as symbolic appointments. Symbolic negro appointments do not control power. Usually, they are more honorific than substantial and are extremely impressive to black people. The appointment of a negro does not guarantee any improvements in the economic, educational, or political conditions of the black masses, however. Not a single additional negro receives an increase in his wages because one negro is appointed to the Supreme Court.

Worse still, the symbolic negro appointment is ofttimes a promotion to a higher position. In such an instance, the promotion is valueless because negroes have gained no new political power.

When Carl Rowan was promoted from Ambassador to Finland to the directorship of the United States Information Agency, a negro was not appointed Ambassador to succeed him. Negroes thus lost that appointment. They gained no power. This has occurred repeatedly in government, particularly under the Johnson administration. The appointment of Thurgood Marshall to Solicitor General and then to the U.S. Supreme Court does not mean an accretion of political power because one negro has simply been rotated between jobs.

The only way in which black people can develop political power in government is to be able to control the hiring processes. This they have never been able to do. When negroes have been placed in top-level positions, they have usually refused to hire other negroes.

As other ethnic groups have achieved political power, they have expanded their power base by bringing members of their own group into the bureaucratic mainstream of government. Certain departments, certain job classifications have become the exclusive province of certain ethnic groups. In certain agencies, an Irish Catholic has been expected to head that department, just as certain specialties have been reserved for Jews. The success of an ethnic group in maintaining exclusive dominion over certain policy-making jobs as well as reserving an unspecified percentage of jobs for their group is the true exercise of ethnic political power.

Once they have been appointed to high positions, negroes have shied away from hiring other negroes in the belief that a quick and perceived upswing in the number of negro employees would tend to increase the possibilities for resegregation. The civil-rights movement's philosophical emphasis on integration has taken its psychic toll of negro office-holders.

Moreover, negro office-holders have usually been appointed either to positions that control little patronage or with an understanding that their hiring policies would be governed by other ethnic and political considerations.

There is also the elation many black people have felt in being a "first" or even an only negro within a department. For them to encourage the employment of other negroes within their departments or the appointment of negroes to similarly high positions would be to diminish the honorific distinction of their achievement.

Given the paucity, then, of black appointments to high office, analyses of negro political power have been confined to measuring the black vote. Because of their high visibility and physical confinement to ghettos, negro voting strength has been more easily measured than that of other ethnic groups.

The vast majority of black people in any city live in definable areas —in New York City, Harlem; in Chicago, the South Side and the West Side; in Philadelphia, the North Side; in Los Angeles, Watts. To rely on the vote as the sole standard of measurement of negro political power is sterile. The electoral process is merely one step in the acquisition of power, and votes do more than simply elect officials. Votes guarantee a favorable disposition of an ethnic group's aspiration and demands. Votes should ensure that the members of a particular group will be appointed in significant numbers in the policy-making councils of government. Votes are promissory notes on the dispensation of jobs. Votes are judgeships, commissionerships, governorships, mayorships, Congressional seats, aldermanships, superintendencies, political party chairmanships, government contracts, Federal aid, construction projects, and political contributions. Consequently, discussion of any group's voting strength as the sole measurement of its political power neglects the realities of politics and misunderstands the relationship of government to pressure groups.

## PROPORTIONAL POLITICAL PATRONAGE

The most important indices of a group's political power are its numerical percentage of the population and its percentage of the vote during an election. For example, an ethnic group might comprise 20 per cent of the population in a city but regularly deliver, on the average, only 10 per cent of the vote. Somewhere between these two percentages should lie the accommodation by the party organization and its control of the government to the demands of the particular ethnic group.

Nationally, black people comprise approximately 12 per cent of the population. In America's thirty largest cities, the proportion of negroes

*Proportion of Negroes in Each of the 30 Largest Cities,[a]*
*1960 and 1965 Estimated*

| City | 1960 | 1965 | City | 1960 | 1965 |
|------|------|------|------|------|------|
| New York, N.Y. | 14 | 18 | Pittsburgh, Pa. | 17 | 21 |
| Chicago, Ill. | 23 | 28 | San Antonio, Texas | 7 | 8 |
| Los Angeles, Calif. | 14 | 17 | San Diego, Calif. | 6 | 7 |
| Philadelphia, Pa. | 26 | 31 | Seattle, Wash. | 5 | 7 |
| Detroit, Mich. | 29 | 34 | Buffalo, N. Y. | 13 | 17 |
| Baltimore, Md. | 35 | 38 | Cincinnati, Ohio | 22 | 24 |
| Houston, Texas | 23 | 23 | Memphis, Tenn. | 37 | 44 |
| Cleveland, Ohio | 29 | 34 | Denver, Colorado | 6 | 9 |
| Washington, D.C. | 54 | 66 | Atlanta, Ga. | 38 | 44 |
| St. Louis, Mo. | 29 | 36 | Minneapolis, Minn. | 2 | 4 |
| Milwaukee, Wis. | 8 | 11 | Indianapolis, Ind. | 21 | 23 |
| San Francisco, Calif. | 10 | 12 | Kansas City, Mo. | 18 | 22 |
| Boston, Mass. | 9 | 13 | Columbus, Ohio | 16 | 18 |
| Dallas, Texas | 19 | 21 | Phoenix, Ariz. | 5 | 5 |
| New Orleans, La. | 37 | 41 | Newark, N.J. | 34 | 47 |

[a] As of 1967, the six black U.S. Congressmen (including Adam Clayton Powell, who was excluded from the Ninetieth Congress on March 10, 1967) came from the five largest cities, New York City (Powell), Chicago (William L. Dawson), Los Angeles, Calif. (Augustus Hawkins), Philadelphia (Robert N.C. Nix), and Detroit (Charles C. Diggs, Jr., and John Conyers). All six are Democrats.

in the population ranged from a low of 4 per cent in Minneapolis, Minn., and 5 per cent in Phoenix, Ariz., to a high of 66 per cent in Washington, D.C., and 47 per cent in Newark, N.J.*

Two unanswered questions about black political power are: 1) What are the political circumstances that in 1965 enabled New York City, with an 18 per cent black proportion, and Los Angeles, with 17 per cent, to have one black Congressman each among its Congressional delegation, while twelve other cities, all with proportionally larger black populations, have none? (Baltimore, 38 per cent; Cincinnati, 24 per cent; Cleveland, 34 per cent; Dallas, 21 per cent; Houston, 23 per cent; Indianapolis, 23 per cent; Kansas City, 22 per cent; Memphis, 44 per cent; Newark, 47 per cent; New Orleans, 41 per cent; Pittsburgh, 21 per cent; and St. Louis, 36 per cent.)

* Although these figures are from a joint report prepared by the Bureau of the Census and the Bureau of Labor Statistics in October 1967, titled "Social and Economic Conditions of Negroes in the United States," they are for the year 1965. Newark officials and various city agencies concerned directly with urban renewal and race relations agree that in 1967 Newark had a majority of negroes in its population—52 percent for 1967.

2) What combination of racial cohesion and political organization enabled the Detroit black electorate to elect *two* black Congressmen in 1964 with a black proportion of 34 per cent, while five cities with larger black proportions were unable to elect even one?

Part of the explanation for the absence of black Congressmen from Memphis, New Orleans, St. Louis, Baltimore and Kansas City are the Southern traditions and orientations of these cities. Black voters have yet to exhibit the fierce independence and black pride that would unleash a black leader who could whip ambition together into a phalanx of bloc voting in exchange for black spoils—i.e., a Congressional seat.

But the election of black Congressmen is only one facet of black political power in a city. Black state senators and representatives, black city councilmen or aldermen, black city and state judges, black heads of city departments (commissioners, etc.), black members of boards of education, black key figures in the state and city political organizations, and other honorary appointments that recognize the individual power and importance of black community leaders comprise a more accurate measurement of the ethnic group's political power.

The first law for measuring the political power of an ethnic group is that there must be a direct relationship between the proportion of its vote in an election or its proportion of the population—whichever is higher—and its proportion of all political jobs and elective offices.

This is the theory of proportional equality, and, as will be demonstrated in the chapter "The Irish, the Italians, the Jews, and the Poles," practically every other ethnic group in America has been able to develop political power at the national, state, and local levels commensurate with its proportion of the population.

## STONE'S INDEX OF PROPORTIONAL EQUALITY

Political power can be qualified and measured by the proportion of elective offices and jobs in specific areas. Stone's Index of Proportional Equality establishes minimum standards for measuring the political power of an ethnic group. There are six factors, which include the proportion of the ethnic group within a city in the following areas of political activity: 1) U.S. Congressmen; 2) city councilmen and aldermen; 3) state representatives; 4) heads of municipal departments; 5) judges (at the city, state, and national levels); and 6) members of the board of education.

Again, as will be proved in the chapter on the four ethnic groups, the Irish, the Italians, the Jews, and the Poles have all developed political control in several cities where they are numerically strong by dominating in all six areas. A political canon of the Irish when they first became active in politics was: "It is better to know the judge than the law."

The reason all city departments are included in this standard of measurement is the tendency for black appointments of department heads to be concentrated in the weaker, or "human relations" and "welfare," departments. Black people are rarely appointed as heads of the departments that control finance, real estate, construction, city contracts, public works, buildings, and taxes. Instead they saturate the departments of welfare, human relations, and education. There is little political power in these departments.

Thus, if black people constitute 10 per cent of the vote or 10 per cent of the population and are given 10 per cent of the jobs and elective offices in a city and state administration, and if this 10 per cent is concentrated in the lower-paying positions or unimportant elective offices, then black people in that situation do not have political power.

As of 1967, negro political power at the Federal level was insignificant, with the exception of two appointments, Housing and Urban Development Secretary Robert C. Weaver, one of the twelve members of the President's Cabinet, and U.S. Supreme Court Justice Thurgood Marshall, one of nine Associate Justices.

But using the black national proportion of 12 per cent for 1966 as a base index, the relationship of this proportion to negroes' total political participation in the Federal legislative, executive, and judiciary branches of government can be assessed. It is important to keep in mind the national proportion of 11 per cent in any kind of analysis of black political activity.


## U.S. CONGRESS, 1966


Of 435 U.S. Representatives elected to the 89th Congress in 1966, only six, or 1.3 per cent, were black. (Compare this proportion, for example, to the number of Jewish Congressmen. In 1966, Jews comprised 3 per cent of the population—5,600,000 out of 200,000,000—and also constituted 3 per cent (15 Jewish Congressmen) of the Congress.

Of one hundred Senators, one, or 1 per cent, was black (the first to be elected since 1881).

Thus, nationally, it is mournfully obvious that negroes can exert very little influence as legislators in the U.S. Congress. Rather, they must rely on a tenuous alliance with committed white liberals or white Congressmen with significant black constituencies to secure the passage of legislation designed to elevate the economic and educational standards of black people.

White Congressmen with substantial black constituencies are not going to be influenced unless their districts are politically unstable and tend to swing back and forth between the two parties. Only in such instances, if the negro vote cohesively acted as a balance of power to guarantee the election of a Congressman, and if he, in turn, recognized this fact, would he be responsive to negro demands.

But, of the ninety-six Congressmen who have a 20 per cent or greater black constituency, sixty-five are Southerners. Because of a traditional pattern of massive racial intimidation and oppression through murders, bombings, and economic reprisals, negroes still have not registered or voted in numbers approximating their proportion. Even where they have voted, they still have tended to simplistically (lazily) accept the lesser of two white evils rather than cut the umbilical cord of white subordination by voting for a strong black challenger. This happened in the Memphis, Tenn., October 5, 1967, primary. In a seven-man race for mayor, one of the candidates was black state representative A. W. Willis. Although the registered black vote was exactly one-third of the total number of Memphis votes (80,033 out of 235,303), a united vote behind one negro candidate could have placed him in the final run-off, assuming a split white vote among the other six candidates. Memphis negroes instead voted for the incumbent white mayor, and even gave a substantial proportion of their votes to a former white mayor. Willis ran a poor fourth. He subsequently charged that Memphis negroes had been brainwashed all their lives. During his campaign, he declared that the campaign was raising for the first time "the real problems of racial inferiority. The Negro has been taught to be inferior. He thinks the white man's ice is colder, his sugar is sweeter, his medicine is better."

In most Southern communities, black people will also support a racist Congressman who, despite his consistent antinegro votes in Congress, looks after his black constituents with the same benevolent paternalism of the old plantation owner. Negroes in South Carolina's Sixth Congressional District have continued to vote for Representative John L. McMillan, even though he was known as one of the staunchest opponents of home rule for the District of Columbia because of its black majority. In Tampa, Fla., not one Negro publicly criticized Tampa's Representative Sam M. Gibbons for leading the move to strip Representative Adam Clayton Powell of his powers as Chairman of the Education and Labor Committee in September 1966.

If Congress is a microcosm of the white racism that continues to dominate the United States, Congressional staffs show the same loving affection for this pattern. Of the five black Congressmen, four have negro women as administrative assistants. Representative John Conyers has a white administrative assistant, as does Senator Edward W. Brooke. Until his exclusion from the Congress, Adam Clayton Powell was the only man in either the House or the Senate to have a black man as an administrative assistant. He had two. His first was Livingston Wingate, who later became executive director of Harlem's antipoverty program HARYOU-ACT. The second was myself. Powell was also the only Congressman to employ black people in several capacities as professional staff members. Not only was his special assistant a black, but the chief clerk of the committee, Miss Louise Maxienne Dargans, and the education chief, Dr. Eunice Matthews, were black.

None of the other 535 Representatives and Senators has black legislative assistants. One Indiana Congressman assigned such a title to one aide, but on closer investigation, it was revealed that the aide was, in fact, a very intelligent office boy who performed routine office chores instead of drafting bills and doing legislative research.

There is a plethora of negro secretaries on Capitol Hill, but only because there is a shortage of secretaries. Although the average Congressman is a racial bigot, he is also a pragmatist. So, negro secretaries are hired, if for no other reason than to keep the office running.

Of the sixteen Senate committees and the twenty House committees, only one committee in the House, as of 1967, had a professional negro staff member. She is Mrs. Christine Ray Davis, staff director of the House Government Operations Committee, whose chairman is William L. Dawson. Mrs. Davis was the first negro to become a staff director of a Congressional committee. She has served as the top staff member of that committee since 1949, when Dawson became its chairman and she was appointed chief clerk. During 1952–53, when the Republicans were in control of the House, she was a minority staff consultant, and in 1954, when Democrats resumed control of the House, she was appointed staff director.

The unwritten law against black pages in the House and Senate was broken in the first half of the Eighty-ninth Congress, in 1965, when

Lawrence W. Bradford, Jr., of New York City, became the first black page in the Senate and Frank V. Mitchell, Jr., of Detroit, Mich., became the first black page in the House. Oddly enough, both boys were sponsored by Republicans, who secured their appointments.

## U.S. CONGRESS, 1968

For the Ninety-first Congress beginning in January 1969, there will be a new high of eight black Congressmen and possibly nine, depending upon what happens in the Third Congressional District in Chicago, where a white Congressman is being seriously challenged for the first time by a black man.

Adam Clayton Powell has announced his intention to run again and, barring a most cataclysmic unforeseen event, will be re-elected, as will the other five black Congressmen. Two new black Congressmen will come from Cleveland's newly formed Twenty-first Congressional District, and Brooklyn's newly formed Twelfth Congressional District representing that community's black ghetto, Bedford-Stuyvesant.

The Democratic candidate for Cleveland's new Congressional District is Louis Stokes, brother of that city's black mayor, Carl B. Stokes. While the Democratic candidate for Brooklyn's Twelfth Congressional District had not been nominated as of this writing, that race portends excitement with the entry of former C.O.R.E. executive director, James Farmer, who has been endorsed by both the Liberal and Republican Parties. Although not a Brooklyn resident, Farmer is expected to wage a strong race because of his famed civil rights role.

## U.S. EXECUTIVE

Of the many public exercises that have seemed to delight the Southern heart of President Lyndon Baines Johnson, none has been carried off with more P. T. Barnum fanfare than the announcement of a "first negro appointment." So much carnival hoopla has attended these sessions that the impression has been gained that this President, who, as a Congressman, vigorously fought against civil rights for negroes, "has done more for the cause of civil rights" than any other President "in our history."*

* From the brochure "This President . . . Is Doing More," published in 1967 by the Democratic National Committee.

The spectacular appointments of the first negro Cabinet member, Robert C. Weaver, as Secretary of the Department of Housing and Urban Development on January 18, 1967, Andrew F. Brimmer as the first black Governor of the Federal Reserve Board, Thurgood Marshall as the first black Solicitor General in the Department of Justice and the first black Supreme Court Justice, and Mrs. Patricia Harris as the first black woman ambassador (to Luxembourg) have created the external appearance of a government where black people are taking giant steps forward in helping to run their country.†

In the history of American politics, no greater charade has been played by any President. The fact is that these showcase appointments have not substantially changed the administrative and policy-making patterns of government.

Again, bearing in mind that blacks comprise 11 per cent of the national population, the progress of negro employment in the higher councils of the Federal government can be measured. In the Executive Office of the President, the following is the breakdown of black positions, as of 1967, among the top positions listed in the Congressional Directory of the Ninetieth Congress, First Session, but revised for subsequent changes in the latter part of the year:

| Office | Number of Top Positions | Number of Negroes |
|---|---|---|
| White House Office | 25 | 0 |
| Bureau of the Budget | 26 | 0 |
| Council of Economic Advisers | 4 | 0 |
| National Security Office | 7 | 0 |
| Central Intelligence Agency | 5 | 0 |
| National Aeronautics and Space Agency | 6 | 0 |
| Office of Economic Opportunity | 16 | 1 |
| Office of Emergency Planning | 16 | 0 |
| Office of Science and Technology | 5 | 0 |
| Office of Special Representative for Trade Negotiations | 15 | 0 |
| Total: | 125 | 1 (1 per cent) |

† The author had lunch with Louis Martin, Deputy Chairman of the Democratic National Committee, a few days after Secretary of Defense Robert S. McNamara's appointment to the presidency of the World Bank had been announced. Martin said that he received a telephone call from a very prominent Southern white politician, who growled into the phone, half-jokingly but with just enough rancor to indicate his belief in the possibility: "What nigger have you got lined up for the Secretary of Defense job now?"

Were it not for the one black executive in the Office of Economic Opportunity, the eleven offices within the Executive Office of the President would be lily-white.

Of the forty-four largest Federal independent agencies, only one—the Equal Employment Opportunity Commission—is headed by a "*Negro*," Clifford Alexander, Jr., a colorless and mediocre lawyer who was previously a Deputy Special Counsel to the President with no precise administrative responsibilities. Typical of the excessively cautious Federal civil servant, Alexander climbed slowly through the ranks by becoming a faceless negro who neither made controversial comments nor militantly condemned the injustices against negroes in American society.

Of the 183 Commissioners, members of the boards and the executive directors or administrators of these forty-four independent agencies, only seven, or 3 per cent, were negroes: Mrs. Frankie Muse Freeman, of the U.S. Commission on Civil Rights; Clifford L. Alexander, Jr., Chairman, and Samuel C. Jackson, member, of the Equal Employment Opportunity Commission; Dr. G. Franklin Edwards, member of the National Capital Planning Commission; Howard Jenkins, Jr., member of the National Labor Relations Board; Dr. Kenneth W. Clement, member of the National Selective Service Appeal Board; and Dr. Andrew F. Brimmer, governor of the Federal Reserve Board. No independent agency in the Federal government is headed by a black staff member.

A third index of the exclusion of negroes from the policy-making and executive positions of government is indicated by the number of negro assistant secretaries and deputy assistant secretaries. This is the administrative level at which Cabinet departments are compartmentalized into operational units of responsibility.

Of the 220 assistant secretaries and deputy assistant secretaries in the twelve Cabinet departments and the Army, Navy and Air Force, only five, or 2 per cent, are negroes. These five negroes are concentrated in only four departments: State, Labor, Health, Education and Welfare, and Agriculture: Samuel Z. Westerfield, Jr., Deputy Assistant Secretary of State for African Affairs; Mrs. Charlotte M. Hubbard, Deputy Assistant Secretary of State for Public Affairs; George L. P. Weaver, Assistant Secretary for International Affairs in the Department of Labor; Shelton B. Granger, Deputy Assistant Secretary of HEW for Education, International Affairs; and Alfred L. Edwards, Deputy Assistant Secretary of Agriculture for Rural Development and Conservation.

Thus, there is not a single negro among the 130 Assistant or Deputy Assistant Secretaries in the Departments of the Treasury, Defense, Army, Navy, Air Force, Justice, Post Office, Interior, Commerce, Housing and Urban Development, and Transportation.

Two of the Federal government's most powerful negroes who do not have Assistant Secretary or Deputy Assistant Secretary status are Miss Barbara Watson, Acting Administrator of the State Department's Bureau of Security and Consular Affairs, and Edward C. Sylvester, Jr., Director of the Labor Department's Office of Federal Contract Compliance. Both make critical decisions which respectively shape America's foreign and domestic policies. Miss Watson has been the target of intensive lobbying by white industrialists with heavy investments in Africa and Mr. Sylvester has been the constant target of the various construction trades unions which have resented his rulings requiring nondiscriminatory union practices in order to work on Federal projects.

This pattern of "white-out" for negroes, however, is far more entrenched than the obvious executive levels would indicate.

Within the twelve Cabinet departments, there are no black staff executives or appointees in the eleven top positions of the U.S. Mission to the United Nations, the twenty-six top positions in the Agency for International Development, the twenty-three top positions in the Peace Corps, the eleven top positions in the Internal Revenue Services, the eleven top positions in the Bureau of Customs, the fifteen top positions of the Office of the Comptroller of the Currency, and the seven top positions of the Secret Service.

In the twelve Cabinet Departments, there are *no negroes* in any of the policy-making or responsible administrative positions in the Coast Guard, Office of Merchant Marine Safety, Director of Defense Research and Engineering, the Joint Chiefs of Staff, Defense Atomic Support Agency, Defense Communications Center, Defense Contract Audit Agency, Defense Intelligence Agency, Defense Supply Agency, Office of Civil Defense, the Army Staff, the Navy Administrative Staff, Naval Office of Civilian Manpower, Naval Office of the Comptroller, Naval Office of Information, Office of Naval Research, Naval Office of Program Appraisal, Office of the Judge Advocate of the Navy, Navy Appellate Review Activity, the U.S. Marine Corps, Naval Bureau of Medicine and Surgery, National Naval Medical Center, Office of the Chief of Naval Operations, Bureau of Naval Personnel, Naval Air Systems Command, Naval Ordnance Systems Command, Naval Ship Systems Command, Naval Electronic Systems Command, Naval Supply

Systems Command, Naval Facilities Engineering Command, U.S. Naval Station, Air Force Office of Information, the Air Staff, Comptroller of the Air Force, Deputy Chief of Staff for Personnel, Deputy Chief of Staff for Plans and Operations, Deputy Chief of Staff for Programs and Resources, Deputy Chief of Staff for Systems and Logistics, Deputy Chief of Staff for Research and Development, the Immigration and Naturalization Service, Bureau of Prisons, Board of Parole, the Federal Prison Industries, Inc., the Post Office's Bureau of Personnel (*despite the fact that negroes comprise an estimated 40 per cent of Post Office employees*), the Post Office's Office of General Counsel, Bureau of the Chief Postal Inspector, Bureau of Research and Engineering, the *Interior Department's* Fish and Wildlife Service, Geological Survey, Bureau of Indian Affairs, Bureau of Land Management, Bureau of Mines, National Park Service, Bureau of Reclamation, Office of Territories, Bureau of Outdoor Recreation, Federal Water Pollution Control Administration, the *Agricultural* Stabilization and Conservation Service, Commodity Credit Corporation, Federal Extension Service, Foreign Agricultural Service, International Agricultural Development Service, Consumer and Marketing Services, Commodity Exchange Authority, Rural Development and Farmers Home Administration, Forest Service, Rural Electrification Administration, Soil Conservation Service, Economic Research Service, Statistical Reporting Service, Office of Budget and Finance, Office of Information, Office of Management Services, Office of Personnel, Office of Plant and Operations, Office of the General Counsel, Office of the Inspector General, *Commerce Department's* Office of Business Economics, Bureau of International Commerce, Office of Foreign Commerce Activities, Business and Defense Services Administration, Bureau of the Census, Maritime Administration, National Bureau of Standards, Patent Office, Bureau of Public Roads, National Highway Safety Agency, *Labor Department's* Labor-Management Services Administration, Office of the Solicitor, the Wage and Labor Standards' Bureaus and Divisions, the Food and Drug Administration, Vocational Rehabilitation Administration, the Public Health Service, Bureau of Disease Prevention and Environmental Control, Bureau of Health Manpower, Bureau of Health Services, National Institutes of Health, National Institutes of Mental Health, Social Security Administration, Welfare Administration (this is a particularly ironic form of racial discrimination since such a large portion of Negroes are on public welfare), the Housing and Urban Development's Federal National Mortgage Association, and the HUD Regional Offices.

The appointment of a black assistant secretary, or Cabinet official, or member of a commission makes front-page news. The nonappointment of black people as administrators, assistant administrators, deputies, office managers, and to the thousands of administrative categories that make policy for the U.S. government is not news. And the exclusion pattern of black people from the apparatus of policy-making and re- sponsible positions in the Federal government, with the exceptions already listed, is as rigid and as racially determined as ever. Racial bigotry in America begins at the White House.

## THE FEDERAL COURTS

There are 480 Federal judgeships.* These include the nine in the U.S. Supreme Court, Eighty-eight in the eleven Judicial Circuits of the U.S. Court of Appeals, 342 in the U.S. District Courts, and forty-one in the five Special Courts (U.S. Court of Claims, U.S. Court of Customs and Patent Appeals, U.S. Customs Court, Tax Court of the United States, and the U.S. Court of Military Appeals).

Of these 480 Federal judgeships, eleven, or 2 per cent, are held by black people:

| | |
|---|---|
| U.S. Supreme Court | Thurgood Marshall |
| U.S. Court of Appeals | |
|     District of Columbia Circuit | Spottswood W. Robinson, III |
|     Third Judicial Circuit | William Henry Hastie |
|     Sixth Judicial Circuit | Wade Hampton McCree, Jr. |
| U.S. District Courts | |
|     District of Columbia | William B. Bryant |
|     Illinois (Northern) | James B. Parsons |
|     New York (Northern) | Mrs. Constance Baker Motley |
|     Pennsylvania (Eastern) | Leon Higginbotham |
|     Virgin Islands | Walter A. Gordon |
| U.S. Customs Court | |
| | Scovel Richardson |
| | James L. Watson |

Judge Hastie was the first negro in the history of the United States to be appointed to a Federal court. President Roosevelt appointed him in 1937. Judge Parsons became the first negro in 1961 to be appointed to a Federal District Court. President Kennedy made the appointment.

* Administrative Office of the United States Court, Washington, D.C.

The generally conservative orientation of the Federal courts, compounded by the dual standards of justice for blacks and whites of Southern judges, has been one of the factors most acutely inhibiting the negro's quest for racial equality. Invariably, the burden of proof of discrimination, intimidation, denial of Constitutional rights, or simple denial of the most elementary exercise of his rights rested on the negro.

In making Federal appointments, Presidents, as a matter of political courtesy or to minimize the risk of disapproval, clear their prospective choices with Senators, Congressmen, or state officials in a region, depending upon which wields the most power. Naturally, Southern officials will seek to influence the appointments of Southerners. And 99 per cent of all white Southerners, even in 1967, are hard-core racists.

This historical pattern of justice dispensed firmly, but unequally, for negroes in the South can be traced to the racial orientations of the judges appointed. Only with rare exceptions have Southern judges been able to break through their Southern backgrounds and render decisions which guarantee the Constitutional rights of negroes. One such rare exception, which electrified the black community, was the ruling by a South Carolina U.S. District Judge, J. Waites Waring, on July 12, 1947, that South Carolina's exclusion of negroes from Democratic primaries was a de facto denial of the right to vote. Judge Waite's decision was upheld by the U.S. Circuit Court of Appeals, and the lily-white primaries of South Carolina's Democratic Party were dead forever. After his ruling, Judge Waring was acclaimed as one of the negro community's new heroes and was honored and feted by a variety of negro and interracial organizations throughout America.

## THE REVOLVING-DOOR NEGRO

The thesis can be advanced, of course, that negroes have made phenomenal progress in government and politics in the Kennedy and Johnson administrations, compared to previous gains. There is a persuasiveness to the argument that negro political power measured at 3 per cent is a three-hundredfold increase over 1 per cent. Yet, a close examination of many Federal appointments reveals that frequently the same negro has been appointed to two or even three history-making positions during the course of his career. While the historical value of the racial breakthroughs has been acclaimed for their favorable impact on the state of race relations, the rotation of two or three appointments within the career of one negro means that negroes have not acquired any additional political power, nor has there been an accretion of policy-making positions for black people in government.

Those negroes who have been appointed to a series of high-level Federal appointments by a President are what are known as "revolving-door negroes." They are used by the President to initiate a racial breakthrough in several areas. After they have been appointed to their new position, a negro is never appointed to their previous position. The "revolving-door negroes" do not add more negroes to the policy-making positions in government. Instead, they add more status to the individual achievements of that particular negro appointee. His personal pride is increased, not the political power of his race.

This is not an indictment of the negro accepting a series of such appointments or even an indictment of the negro's personal ambitions. Rather, the inability of a President to find an additional black man for a high-level Federal appointment is the harshest indictment of that President's limited approach to the solution of the racial problem. It is the President who makes the decision that he has sufficient respect for only one or two negroes to fill the various positions to which they are appointed. The "revolving-door negro" is simply another manifestation of the racism inherent in the office of the President of the United States. While the "revolving-door negro" is utilized most successfully and exploited with the greatest fanfare by one President, it is nonetheless possible for two or three Presidents to appoint the same negro to a variety of prestigious positions because this particular "negro leader" has established impeccable credentials to national leadership or personal achievement.

Historically, a "revolving-door negro" could be a militant, or he could be one who was forthright and uncompromising in his fight for equality. More often than not, however, he was usually the safest the Congressional traffic could bear without provoking a united opposition to the appointment. In the Johnson administration, the "revolving-door negro" has either been an "Uncle Tom" or one who could be counted upon not to cause any serious emotional dislocation of the body politic. Still a Southerner by temperament and in his relations with negroes, President Johnson has gravitated toward those negroes who did not make him feel personally uncomfortable and who could assure him that everything he was doing in the area of race relations was right, good, and proper. Thus, one of Johnson's favorite negroes, to whom he often turned for advice, was the moderate-conservative executive secretary of the NAACP, Roy Wilkins.

Probably the first "revolving-door negro" in the Federal appointive
process was that brilliant and legendary "father of the protest move-
ment" and the intellectual forerunner of the Black Power philosophy,
Frederick Douglass. Douglass was appointed first by President Grant
in 1871 to be the secretary of the Santo Domingo Commission. In 1877,
President Hayes appointed Douglass as Federal Marshal for the District of Columbia, and in 1881, President Garfield appointed him
Recorder of Deeds for the District of Columbia. In 1889, President
Harrison named him Minister Resident and Consul General to Haiti.
In Douglass' case, not only were his appointments well deserved, but
there was a paucity of men of his incredible intellect and personal
charisma. There were other negroes on the national scene who could
have held these jobs and administered them with the same degree of
competence as Douglass. But Douglass was unquestionably one of the
most distinguished black men of his day, and his appointments were
a justifiable recognition by the Federal government of his contributions
to progress. What the series of Douglass appointments did do, however, was to lay a kind of prior claim by negroes to that office and to
endow the office with new respectability and remove it from the
category of "for whites only."

The second nationally prominent revolving-door negro was William
H. Hastie, a scholarly lawyer and former dean of Howard University
Law School. In 1940, President Roosevelt appointed him a civilian aide
and race-relations adviser to Secretary of the Army Henry Stimson.
In 1943, Hastie did something that very few negro Federal appointees
have ever had the courage to do—he resigned in protest against an
Army decision to establish a segregated technical training school at
Jefferson Barracks, Mo. His unusual display of personal courage appar-
ently did not injure his promising career, and in 1946 Hastie was named
Governor of the Virgin Islands by President Truman. In 1949, President
Truman nominated Hastie to be the first black member of the U.S.
Circuit Court of Appeals, where he now serves with distinction.

While President Kennedy was the first President to make many
historic appointments for negroes within one administration, he appointed few "revolving-door negroes" because of his determination to
avail himself of a quantity of competent negro appointees.

On the other hand, President Johnson has shown a propensity for
keeping the black revolving door whirling constantly. Of the twenty-
eight major appointments during the first four years of his administration (including the first negro to the U.S. Supreme Court, the first

negro member of the Federal Reserve Board of Governors, the first negro director of the U.S. Information Agency, the first negro Cabinet member, and the first negro woman ambassador), six were "revolving-door negroes," Thurgood Marshall, Robert C. Weaver, Carl T. Rowan, Clifford L. Alexander, Andrew F. Brimmer and Hobart Taylor.

The "revolving-door negro" process may knock down racial barriers, but it does not build up racial political power. Thus, the proportion of negroes in policy-making positions in government is increased at an agonizingly sluggish pace. Had black people recognized earlier the built-in element of political retardation in the "revolving-door negro" process and complained about its efficiency in relaying a true accretion of black political power, they might have been able to move rapidly into the higher councils of Federal power.

## THE STATES

Negro political power as reflected by state representatives, elected and appointed state officials, and judicial appointees varies with individual states. For the most part, however, negroes have not been successful at the state level in striking any remote balance between the proportion of negro elective offices or appointments and their proportion in the population.

As of the November 1967 elections, thirty states had black state legislators in either the lower house or the senate.

As of 1967, only Connecticut had an elected official among the five top state offices of governor, lieutenant governor, secretary, treasurer or controller, and attorney general. He is Gerald A. Lamb of Waterbury, the state treasurer, who was nominated in 1962 on the Democratic ticket after the Republicans had already nominated a negro attorney from Hartford, William Graham. Lamb defeated Graham in a Democratic sweep and was subsequently re-elected for a second term in 1966.

As of 1967, only three states had negroes in the state cabinet—New York, California, and Ohio. At the time of these appointments, all three states had Republican governors (Nelson A. Rockefeller, New York; Ronald Regan, California; and James A. Rhodes, Ohio).

As the following table indicates, negro membership in thirty state legislatures was 127 out of a total of 657 or 4.4 per cent in 1967. Illinois led with the largest number of negro legislators (thirteen) in the lower house, but Missouri negroes should be regarded as possessing more

Extent of Negro Representation in State Legislative Bodies in U.S. (1966-67)*

| | In State Lower Houses | | | In State Senates | | | |
|---|---|---|---|---|---|---|---|
| State | Total Members | Negro Members | Negro Per Cent of Total | Total Members | Negro Members | Negro Per Cent of Total | Negro Per Cent of Total Population |
| Michigan | 110 | 9 | 8.1 | 34 | 3 | 8.8 | 9.2 |
| Illinois | 177 | 13 | 7.3 | 58 | 4 | 6.8 | 10.3 |
| Missouri | 163 | 12 | 7.3 | 34 | 1 | 2.9 | 9.0 |
| Ohio | 127 | 9 | 6.5 | 33 | 2 | 6.0 | 8.1 |
| California | 80 | 5 | 6.2 | 40 | 2 | 5.0 | 5.6 |
| Tennessee | 99 | 6 | 6.0 | | | | 16.5 |
| Georgia | 205 | 12 | 5.8 | 54 | 2 | 3.7 | 28.5 |
| Delaware | 35 | 2 | 5.7 | 17 | 1 | 5.8 | 13.6 |
| Maryland | 123 | 7 | 5.6 | 29 | 2 | 6.9 | 16.7 |
| New York | 150 | 8 | 5.3 | 58 | 3 | 5.1 | 8.4 |
| Pennsylvania | 210 | 10 | 4.7 | 50 | 1 | 2.0 | 7.5 |
| Indiana | 100 | 4 | 4.0 | 40 | 1 | 2.5 | 5.8 |
| New Jersey | 50 | 3 | 6.0 | 21 | 1 | 4.7 | 8.5 |
| Colorado | 65 | 2 | 3.0 | 35 | 1 | 2.8 | 2.3 |
| Nevada | 37 | 1 | 2.7 | | | | |
| Oklahoma | 119 | 3 | 2.5 | 44 | 1 | 2.2 | 6.6 |
| Arizona | 80 | 1 | 2.5 | | 1 | | 3.3 |
| Nebraska | 43 | 1 | 2.3 | Unicameral Body | | | |
| Kentucky | 100 | 2 | 2.0 | | | | 7.1 |
| Iowa | 108 | 2 | 1.8 | | | | 0.9 |
| Connecticut | 294 | 4 | 1.3 | 36 | 1 | 2.7 | 4.2 |
| Texas | 150 | 3 | 1.3 | 31 | 1 | 3.2 | |
| Massachusetts | 240 | 3 | 1.2 | | | | 2.2 |
| West Virginia | 100 | 1 | 1.0 | | | | 4.8 |
| Washington | 99 | 1 | 1.0 | | | | 1.7 |
| Wisconsin | 100 | 1 | 1.0 | | | | 1.9 |
| Kansas | 125 | 1 | 0.8 | 40 | 3 | 7.5 | 4.2 |
| Totals | 3281 | 126 | 3.8 | 657 | 31 | 4.4 | |

* Statistics were compiled by Ernest Calloway and published in the November 25, 1966, issue of the *Missouri Teamster*. It is one of the most comprehensive studies ever undertaken of negro state representation. As has been already indicated earlier, three Deep South states—Virginia, Louisiana, and Mississippi—elected negroes to state legislatures in 1967, thus bringing the total of the states that have negro state representatives to 30.

political power in the state legislature since their twelve negro members constituted 11.1 per cent of the total in the lower house, compared to Illinois's negro legislators, who constituted only 7.3 per cent. When these two percentages are related to the percentage of the two states' negro population—Missouri, 9.0 per cent and Illinois, 10.3 per cent—we see that the legislative power of Missouri negroes is appreciably greater.

As the electoral patterns in the loyalties of negroes in the last twenty years have indicated, the overwhelming majority of elective offices have been held by Democrats.

Progress in the short span of seven years in the state legislatures has kept pace with the strident urgency of the civil-rights movement. As of 1960, there were only an estimated thirty state representatives and six state senators.

There is still a political blackout of negro state legislators in the Southern states of Alabama, Arkansas, Florida, and South Carolina, even though negroes are respectively 30 per cent, 22 per cent, 18 per cent, and 35 per cent of the population. As of 1967, the Bureau of the Census estimated that 55 per cent of the country's black people still lived in the South.

As is true for the Federal judiciary, the judiciary of most states have traditionally barred negroes from their higher courts. As of 1967, there were no negroes in any of the state supreme courts or highest courts. The negro judge occupying the highest state judicial position is Harold A. Stevens, a Justice of the Appellate Division of the Supreme Court of New York State. (The highest court in New York State is the Court of Appeals, which hears cases from the Appellate Division of the Supreme Court.)

According to a study made by California State Senator Mervyn M. Dymally in 1967, published in the *Christian Science Monitor* on November 4, 1967, there were eight negroes serving on state college governing boards.

In summary, the pattern of negro political power in the state executive, legislative, and judicial branches is one of weakness. The greatest power is exhibited in the legislatures and there is a near absence of any negro representation in the state courts. As will be demonstrated in the case studies of the cities, negro political power has been most successfully orchestrated in the cities. Here, the black vote, as a balance of power and as a cohesive bloc to elect black officials, has realized its fullest expression.

Rarely, however, has the negro vote been organized by negro politicians or been responsive to their leadership as a punitive force. Blindly loyal and as affectionately faithful as an overgrown sheep dog, the black vote has lain at its white master's feet, lapping up the small bones of patronage tossed its way. When the master has commanded the vote to exhibit its fidelity, it has stirred itself from the fireplace of its second-class status, risen slowly, and lumbered to the polls to vote without question or discrimination. After the vote, it has returned to its preferred place by the smoldering coals of contentment and lazily waited for a few more tiny bones of patronage to keep it amused as a substitute for the large delights enjoyed by other ethnic groups.

There are two classic examples of the black vote defying the expected pattern of behavior. In one instance, it successfully switched parties to elect a mayor. In another instance, it supported a negro candidate at the risk of causing the defeat of a liberal white candidate, but did so deliberately to teach the white politician a lesson.

The first instance, one of the very few remarkable displays of outright Machiavellian maneuvering by a negro politician, occurred in 1928 in Memphis, Tenn., under the astute and shrewd generalship of Robert R. Church, one of America's most brilliant black politicians.

The incumbent Democratic mayor, Rowlett Paine, had been elected in 1923 with the help of negro votes by promising certain improvements in the black community and a cessation of police brutality against negroes. Subsequently, these promises were not fulfilled to the satisfaction of negroes. Compounding their disappointment was the construction of a garbage incinerator only a few hundred yards away from a negro high school and a negro amusement park, despite their organized protests. Negroes angrily struck back. Church threw the full weight of his organization and political skills to the support of Watkins Overton, the Democratic nominee for mayor, against the Republican nominee supported by Paine. Church led a voter-registration drive among negroes and it was this expanded vote that was credited with the election of the Democratic candidate, Overton.[*]

The political ingredients of this particular election are a fascinating study in power politics. A powerful Republican negro politician turned his back on the nominee of his own party in a Southern city, crossed over to the Democratic Party to support its nominee, organized a vote drive, and brought the black vote with him to defeat the nominee of

[*] Paul Lewinson, *Race, Class and Party*, p. 141.

his own party! That is a classic example of black political power in the most splendid exercise of its retributive energies to make a point.

A second instance of black political power operating for a different purpose—the recognition of demands in an election or the deliberate scuttling by negroes of an entire slate to cause its defeat—occurred in Houston in 1956. Samuel Lubell describes what happened:

> In Houston, Texas . . . a loose sort of understanding existed under which Negroes joined with labor unions and other "progressive" groups in supporting "liberal" candidates. When the 1956 campaign for the school board started, the liberal leaders wanted to avoid the segregation issue, believing that raising it meant certain defeat. When this view was presented to Carter Wesley, who published a string of Negro newspapers in the Houston area, he insisted the segregation question be met head on. Declaring "it's time to stand up and be counted," Wesley demanded the coalition run a Negro as one of its candidates. When the coalition refused, a Negro entered the race independently. He was defeated, along with the entire liberal slate.
>
> "We knew he couldn't win without liberal support," explained Wesley, "but we showed them they could not win without us either.†

That commitment to "us" among black politicians has been as much a political rarity as attendance by Alabama's George Wallace at a meeting of the Student Nonviolent Coordinating Committees.

Black voters have not yet developed the political sophistication of retribution to the extent other ethnic groups have. A politician voting against the state of Israel will lose 95 per cent of the Jewish vote. A legislator voting to sever diplomatic relations with Italy would lose 95 per cent of the Italian vote. A politician who is an uncompromising advocate of birth control would be treated just as uncompromisingly at the polls by Irish Catholic voters. Yet, at the 1964 Democratic National Convention in Atlantic City, very few black delegates protested when the segregated Mississippi delegation was seated and the Mississippi Freedom Democratic Party's predominantly negro delegation was rejected. Despite the tense emotionalism of this issue and the fact that the MFDP voted unanimously to reject the so-called compromise plan offered by the Credentials Subcommittee, there was little black delegate support for the Mississippi negroes. Racial loyalties were overcome by political chains.

---

† Samuel Lubell, *Black and White* (New York: Harper & Row, 1964), p. 70.

An almost shocking example of the black voters' lack of ability to discern loyalty to the cause of advancing the interests of his ethnic group occurred in the April 1964 Democratic primary in Chicago.

Running for re-election in the Sixth Congressional District was Representative Thomas J. O'Brien, an elderly fourteen-term Congressman. Ill for several months prior to the primary, O'Brien had been unable to campaign in the predominantly black district on the West Side. Running against him was a young black woman who had long been active in civic and civil-rights programs. On primary day, Congressman O'Brien died. But that did not matter to the black voters in his district. They went out anyway and voted for a dead white man over a live colored woman, re-electing O'Brien.

Loyalty, whether it derives from a religious or a racial background, is the most important element in building a powerful bloc vote. After loyalty, the ability to punish enemies is next. The four most important elements in building a powerful voting bloc are: 1) ethnic loyalty at any cost; 2) the ability to promise punishment and make good on the promise; 3) the capacity to switch political loyalties at any given time on any issue; and 4) the ability to secure jobs and important policy-making appointments for members of that voting bloc.

Political switching involves ticket-splitting, a habit that not only has eluded black voters, but has evaded the intelligence of most white voters. Thus, while it was logical for negroes to vote for Kennedy in 1960, it was not equally consistent for them to vote for Democratic Southern racists. Had the black vote, critical in Texas, South Carolina, and Illinois, which provided the margin of victory in those three states and thus Kennedy's election, voted for the local or state Republicans who were not so antagonistic to black ambitions as their Democratic opponents, the white political bosses would have acquired a new respect for—and fear of—black voters.

The last element, the ability to secure jobs for its members, has been the area of greatest weakness among negroes. This is because black voters have been brainwashed with the sterile value of their vote as a balance of power.

The voting process must relate to the governmental process. Unless the black vote has been able to guarantee a significant increase in jobs, better housing, high-level appointments, and more modern educational facilities, then the vote is useless as a force for negro progress.

Although the black vote in the South has increased from a 1940 low of approximately 85,000 to a 1966 comparative high of 2,700,000, there has been no comparable increase in black political strength in the legislatures, the courts, and the state policy-making positions. With the exception of Georgia and Texas (and in 1967, Virginia, Louisiana, and Mississippi, which each elected the first negro to their state legislatures since Reconstruction), Southern negroes have been unable to make the political impact of their vote felt at the state level. Thus, the mere announcement of a dramatic increase in negro voter registrations is meaningless unless it is juxtaposed with a comparable increase of black judicial and executive appointments and elective offices.

Nor is there evidence to date that this increase in the Southern black vote has influenced the Southern white vote toward a more liberal posture on equal rights for negroes. Thus, in 1966, the two most segregationist candidates in the race for governor of Georgia, Republican Howard H. Callaway and Democrat Lester G. Maddox, polled the largest number of votes in their respective primaries. Any candidate for office in the Deep South who has dared to take a remotely liberal position on the race question has been defeated and will continue to be defeated unless there is a sufficiently large black voting bloc that can ensure his victory in combination with a small number of liberal white votes. This has happened in Atlanta, where the liberal Democrat Charles Weltner was elected to the House of Representatives in 1962 with nearly solid support of Atlanta's black voters, who comprised 38 per cent of the electorate.

Until black voters begin to demand more jobs and appointments for their support, politicians will continue to seek the black vote only as a necessary balance of power to guarantee the margin of victory. Until black voters develop the kind of sophistication that the Memphis negroes exhibited in 1928, when they switched political parties to punish an official who had reneged on his promises, white political bosses will have no respect for the black vote. Until black voters are secure enough and militant enough to demand that white politicians take a strong liberal stand on the racial issue, even at the risk of defeat, the white politicians will continue to compromise and postpone the inevitable day of full black participation in the administration of American democracy.

15 | # The Impact of Protest Leadership on Negro Politicians in San Francisco*

## Richard Young

Although a decade ago it seemed to many that America's race problem was confined to her Southern states, the events of the 1960's have made it clear that the "Negro problem" is national in scope. In fact, it seems not unlikely that the gravest chapter in American race relations may be written in the Negro ghettoes of the large cities of the North. Negro protest groups have proliferated throughout the North giving emphasis to the severe socioeconomic problems which plague Northern Negroes; Negro riots are now regarded as a seasonal occurrence.

While Negro protest (and Negro protest organizations) in the North have been widely studied and discussed, little serious attention has been given to the impact of Negro protest on Negro political behavior. This is surprising in light of the commonly held assumption in our society that political and governmental action is the key to solving the problems facing Negro Americans and the fact that Northern Negro protest is strongest in those areas where, because of the density and size of the Negro population, Negro political influence is greatest. In order to gain a better understanding of the interrelation between Negro protest and politics, I have studied the relationship between Negro protest leaders and Negro politicians in one Northern city, San Francisco. The results of that study are presented in this paper. In addition, I have attempted in this paper's conclusion to relate the findings of this study to some of the conclusions regarding Negro political and protest behavior which were made by Edward Banfield and James Q. Wilson in *City Politics.*

Reprinted from *Western Political Quarterly* XXII, no. 1 (March 1969): 94–111. By permission of the University of Utah, copyright holders.

* I wish to thank Alan Saltzstein and Professor Raymond Wolfinger for their critical readings of an earlier version of this paper. This article was written in 1966.

What has been the effect of Negro protest on Northern Negro politicians who are a steadily growing group because of the growing (and
concentrated) Northern Negro population? Have Negro politicians
played a leadership role in the protest groups or have they regarded
these organizations as a threat to their power? Have the leaders of the
new or revitalized protest groups attempted to enter politics? Have the
mass protest groups forced the traditional Negro political leaders to
become more militant in their demands for greater justice and opportunities for their Negro constituents?

## SETTING AND RESEARCH DESIGN

The setting for this study is San Francisco. It is the twelfth largest
city in the United States, and is representative of the type of city in
which the bulk of America's Northern Negroes live. Although San
Francisco's Negro population is not as large proportionately as the
Negro populations of many Eastern cities, it has grown considerably
since World War II and today comprises over 10 percent of the city's
total population.[1] Most of San Francisco's Negroes live in the city's
Negro ghettoes, the Fillmore District and Hunter's Point. The Fillmore
District is the larger and more cohesive of the two ghetto areas and is
the scene of virtually all of San Francisco's Negro political and protest
activity. In general socioeconomic terms, the Negro population of San
Francisco is comparable to Negroes in other urban areas; a significant
gap exists between San Francisco whites and Negroes in respect to income, education, employment, and so forth.[2]

San Francisco's Negroes have gained substantial political representation. When this study was made in 1965, the city-county board of
supervisors had a Negro member. Another Negro had been recently
elected to the California Assembly, representing the 18th assembly district which includes the Fillmore area. In addition, Negro politicians
are playing leadership roles in a number of political clubs, and some of
them have received lucrative political appointments. San Francisco's
Negroes, like most American Negroes, vote overwhelmingly Democratic.

San Francisco has seen a great deal of Negro protest activity in recent years. The NAACP, CORE, the Urban League, and the Black
Muslims are all active. A number of local ad hoc protest groups have
also been formed. Massive and often chaotic demonstrations have
shown that the protest groups enjoy substantial support from the Negro
community.

This study was conducted during the first five months of 1965. Eight Negro protest leaders and seven Negro politicians were interviewed by the author.[3] For the purpose of this study, Negro protest leaders are defined as de facto executive officers of Negro protest groups. In other words, the term "leader" is used in a functional sense, and, as Daniel C. Thompson used the term in another study of Negro leadership, it applies to "those individuals who by their efforts are able to initiate, stimulate, coordinate, and direct the activities of others in the solution of common problems or the achievement of specific social goals."[4] For the purposes of this study, Negro protest groups are organizations with a predominantly Negro membership and leadership whose primary function is to achieve "race" ends. Race ends are ends which benefit the Negro race in general *and* the Negro community of San Francisco in particular. Race ends may include either welfare ends or status ends (such as integration).[5] The protest groups vary considerably in their definitions of proper race ends. For example, the Black Muslims feel that racial segregation is a valid race end. The protest groups of San Francisco are: the local chapter of the NAACP, the local chapter of CORE, the local office of the Urban League, the local mosque of the Black Muslims, Freedom House, and the Ad Hoc Committee to End Racial Discrimination. Leaders of all six of these protest groups were interviewed.[6]

Negro politicians are operationally defined as Negroes holding elective or paid appointive posts in government or in partisan political organizations. The seven Negro politicians interviewed represent the cream of San Francisco's Negro political leadership: one member of the city's board of supervisors, one member of the state legislature, two former or present members of the Democratic county central committee, one member of the Republican county central committee, three former or current presidents of Democratic clubs, and a state inheritance tax appraiser.[7] Six of the politicians were Democrats; only one was a Republican.

The interviews of the Negro protest leaders and politicians were loosely structured and open-ended. They ranged in length from thirty minutes to more than two hours. Each respondent was asked about his own background, education and occupation; the nature of his organization or constituency; his involvement in local protest groups; his involvement in local politics; his attitude towards local "race" issues; the goals he seeks; the means he favors to achieve these goals; his attitudes towards other protest and political leaders; his attitudes towards white leaders; and so on.[8]

The purpose of these interviews was twofold: (1) to construct pro-
files of San Francisco's Negro political and protest leadership, and (2)
to discover the relationship between Negro protest leaders (and their
groups) and Negro politicians in San Francisco.

## NEGRO POLITICIANS

In terms of socioeconomic status, the seven Negro politicians interviewed are a rather homogeneous group. All seven are members of the
middle or upper-middle classes; five are lawyers. Of those remaining,
one is a dentist, and the other holds a managerial position in a department store. Professionally and socially, most of the politicians, especially
the lawyers, seem to be oriented outside of the Negro ghetto. One politician, who considers himself atypical, stated that the Negro politicians
of San Francisco have lost contact with the Negro masses: "Willie
[Brown] and Terry [Francois] are not sufficiently aware of the needs
of the average Negro. The old Irish politicians lived in their communities, even after they had bettered themselves economically. . . . Francois
and Brown have moved out of the ghetto; Brown has moved as far
away from the Fillmore District as possible without leaving his assembly district. . . ."

Whether or not they are actually fleeing the ghetto, either physically
or psychologically, these politicians, as a group, are ambitious, pragmatic men whose political careers and vocations (in the case of the
lawyers) take them into frequent contact with influential whites. The
center of power is outside the ghetto, and if they are to be successful,
they must learn to master an environment which requires them to perceive problems in a citywide, or possibly even statewide, context. It
does not necessarily follow that these politicians are unconcerned about
the Negro masses and are dedicated only to self-advancement. Like all
politicians, the Negro politician of San Francisco must interact successfully with two disparate groups, his constituents and his peers. The
racial factor adds to the complexity of this task.

One dimension of the Negro politician's relationship with his constituency is the role he plays in the protest groups organized by his constituents. With the important exception of the NAACP, the Negro
politicians interviewed are inactive in local protest groups; they often
neglect even to purchase memberships in protest organizations, or are
unaware if they have or not. They also display surprisingly little interest
in the more radical protest groups such as CORE, Freedom House, the

Ad Hoc Committee, and the Black Muslims, even though these organizations have made significant contact with the lower-class Negroes of the Fillmore District.

NAACP membership seems to be a necessary prerequisite for a Negro to enter politics in San Francisco. All seven politicians interviewed are NAACP members. More significantly, two of the politicians are past presidents of the NAACP, and two more have been board members.[9] Terry Francois' presidency of the NAACP from 1960 to 1963 was probably of crucial importance to his appointment to the San Francisco board of supervisors. The NAACP is virtually the sole protest group in which Negro politicians are active. Three politicians said that they belonged to CORE, but all admitted they were inactive members. Only one politician, John Dearman, a young lawyer, was active in the Ad Hoc Committee demonstrations and even though he is nominally a member of the NAACP and CORE, he gives almost none of his time to protest organizations.

The NAACP is the traditional Negro protest organization in San Francisco. Not only has it had long and strong support in the Negro community, but it is also the most respectable of the Negro protest groups. It is not surprising that white politicians prefer to deal with NAACP leaders rather than with the lower-class and often extremist leaders of the newer protest groups. The fact that a number of NAACP leaders have received political appointments (Francois' being the most important) has opened them to the charge that they are token leaders. While NAACP leaders who go into politics are definitely not "Uncle Toms" or old-style token leaders, they do draw their support from an organization that is clearly under the control of middle- and upper-middle-class Negroes.

Despite their lack of activity in the other Negro protest organizations, Negro politicians display, in general, positive attitudes toward all the protest groups. One politician termed the Ad Hoc Committee a "dangerous extremist group" and stated that "the sit-in trials killed the movement in San Francisco," and another compared the Black Muslims to the Ku Klux Klan, but those responses were exceptional. Five of the seven politicians interviewed said that they are in favor of direct action mass protest, a tactic used by the more radical protest groups in San Francisco. Only one politician said that he disapproves of the Black Muslims; all the others felt that the Black Muslims accomplish far more good than ill despite their rather negative image in the white community. However, rather than being "true believers" in the "movement," most Negro politicians endorse the tactics of the more militant protest groups from pragmatic or even cynical views toward the effects of Negro protest. Most of the politicians seem to agree with the observation of Willie Brown, assemblyman from California's 18th district, that "all civil rights groups make positive contributions, including thé Black Muslims." As another politician put it, ". . . even the Black Muslims help because of their scare value." Only one politician, Herman Griffin, displayed the sort of enthusiasm for the newer protest groups that is held by the activists of these organizations: "CORE and SNCC represent the mainstream of Negro thought; they represent best the interests of the Negro. . . . Politicians have not organized a base among the masses. CORE, SNCC, the NAACP, and the Urban League have." Griffin considers himself a political outsider, unique in his desire to maintain contact with the masses in the Fillmore District. Despite his high esteem for the protest groups of San Francisco, he has not been active in any of them.

Most of the Negro politicians disagree with Griffin's contention that the protest groups have been more successful than the politicians in organizing the Negro masses. Most of the politicians consider the protest leaders to be inefficient and unsophisticated; not surprisingly, almost all the politicians view politics as the most effective tool for bettering the Negro's lot. Willie Brown, probably the most successful Negro politician interviewed, emphatically stated that Negro politicians are not responsible to the civil rights movement. In assessing the contribution of various groups to his successful campaign for election to the California Assembly, he ranked in order of importance: first, the Democratic clubs; second, the Negro churches; and third, the protest groups. Brown has great confidence in his own political organization. Terry Francois' views are similar; political action is the best way to solve the problems of the Negro community. Francois stated that Negro politicians have strong grass roots support. He feels that he must be responsible to his entire constituency (San Francisco), not just to Negro protest groups. The views of the other Negro politicians are similar (with the exception of Griffin); this confidence in Negro political organization was best expressed by a young politician: "Negroes are better organized than whites politically. We can turn out a hell of a Negro vote." However, while these other politicians consider Negro political activity of basic importance, they are more favorably impressed by the accomplishments of the protest groups than are Brown and Francois. Perhaps because they hold far less political power than the Assemblyman and the Supervisor, they have less faith in Negro political efficacy.

The charge is often heard within the Negro community that certain Negro politicians are "Uncle Tom's"; outside the ghetto, other Negro politicians are labeled "dangerous extremists" or demagogues by their white critics. However, all the Negro politicians interviewed display a high regard for one another and seem to have sincere respect for their colleagues. Terry Francois, perhaps the most frequent target of the "Uncle Tom" charge, was consistently defended. The politicians, as a group, feel strongly that politics involves compromise and that a politician's image as a protester does not necessarily measure his accomplishments for the Negro community. One politician, in assessing Francois' public performance, stated the importance of being pragmatic in politics: "You cannot be as militant as you want to be in public office. Francois is accomplishing something. In politics, you must choose between something or nothing; militants accomplish nothing." The politicians feel that Francois is indeed accomplishing "something." They feel that he is severely constrained in what he can do. Francois is an appointed member of the board of supervisors; he has not yet demonstrated any independent political power. His constituency is the entire city of San Francisco where Negroes are only one-tenth of the electorate. Thus, for Francois, militancy would be political suicide and the end of any effectiveness that he might have as a Negro leader.

Willie Brown, San Francisco's only Negro member of the California legislature, is generally respected by San Francisco's other Negro politicians. Although a few of the more conservative men expressed some doubts about him, the more common reaction was favorable. A number of politicians emphasized that they did not consider Brown an extremist: "He's learned that he can't be too militant; he's become more pragmatic."

On the basis of this writer's interview with Brown, he seems far more pragmatic than one would assume from his reputation as a young Negro militant, a reputation that does him great service in the Negro ghetto and great disservice outside it. According to Brown, he differs from Francois not on principle but in the constituencies they represent. Twenty-five percent of the inhabitants of Brown's constituency are Negroes. In addition, his district votes 69.1 percent Democratic and 24.8 percent Republican.[10] Thus, when Brown wins the nomination in the Democratic primary, his election is assured. The Negroes in his district vote almost unanimously Democratic. As a result, the effectiveness of the Negro vote is maximized, and Brown is well on his way toward winning the nomination with Negro votes alone. To win the Democratic nomination, Brown has only to gain the support of an additional 10 percent of the voters in his district. This is not difficult because Brown has sizable white support which is symbolized by his close alliance with the Burton brothers, the liberal white congressman from the

5th congressional district (which includes Brown's assembly district) and the equally liberal assemblyman from a neighboring district.

On the other hand, Brown points out that Francois has only a 10 percent Negro political base because his constituency is the entire city of San Francisco. Francois must be very sensitive to views of the white majority. "It's easier for me to act on principle than it is for Terry. For me, good principle is good politics." Brown feels that the district system should replace San Francisco's present system in which members of the board of supervisors are chosen in at-large elections. He feels that this would give the Negro community more representation and would enable the Negroes on the board to be responsible only to the Negro community. Brown's analysis is very similar to that of James Q. Wilson who has suggested that "other things being equal, Negro political strength in city organizations tends to be directly proportional to the size and density of the Negro population, and inversely proportional to the size of the basic political unit."[11] Wilson and Edward Banfield have argued that Negroes hoping to win at-large elections must be more "reasonable" on racial questions than Negroes campaigning in a predominantly Negro ward.[12]

The disparate styles of Francois and Brown seem to be explained by the dramatically different natures of their constituencies. Both men have said as much. In addition, both men are remarkably similar in outlook; they are both hard-headed ambitious politicians who are sincerely concerned about Negro problems, but feel that politics involves compromise. They are on good personal terms. The two men have shared the same law offices and secretaries. However, there are important differences between them. It does not seem likely that their political styles were completely shaped by their constituencies. It appears more likely that their political styles determined to which constituencies they would be attracted. Francois is more at home in an environment of consensus politics while Brown is happier competing in the more strifeful politics of a ghetto district.

## NEGRO PROTEST LEADERS

In terms of socioeconomic status, the Negro protest leaders of San Francisco are a heterogeneous group. The NAACP leaders interviewed are middle- or upper-middle-class: a doctor of medicine and member of the faculty of the University of California, a newspaper publisher, and a lawyer. The Urban League director is a middle-class professional social worker. On the other hand, the leaders of the more "radical" protest groups (CORE, Freedom House, the Ad Hoc Committee and the Black Muslims) are lower-class Negroes.[13] They are all young and virtually full-time activists. Two of the four lower-class leaders spent some time attending public college but did not graduate.

As a group, the protest leaders seem to be restricted in their orientation to the San Francisco ghetto. The NAACP leaders are, however, an important exception to this pattern: they appear to be even more integrated into the surrounding white community than are the Negro politicians. A number of factors explain this phenomenon: the occupational and educational backgrounds of the NAACP leaders, the high level of integration within San Francisco's NAACP, and the strong national nature of the organization. The leaders of the Urban League, CORE, Freedom House, and the Black Muslims are, in different ways, immersed in the problems of the Negro community. This parochialism seems to result from the backgrounds of these leaders and the natures of their organizations. Another possible exception to this pattern is the leadership of the Ad Hoc Committee to End Racial Discrimination. The Ad Hoc Committee contains many radical students, and the Negroes active in the organization seem to be more concerned with San Francisco (and national) radical politics than with the problems of the Negroes of San Francisco.

The protest group which seems to have the greatest influence on the Negro protest leaders of San Francisco is CORE. Of the eight protest leaders interviewed, only two did not claim membership in CORE, and these two were from the Urban League and the Black Muslims, organizations at opposite extremes from the consensus area of Negro protest. Only one leader, a Black Muslim minister, expressed negative sentiments about CORE. Not only can CORE's impact be measured by the fact that it enjoys greater membership among protest leaders than does any other protest group (the NAACP was second with four members out of eight), but, of greater importance, it seems to exert a powerful influence on most of the other protest groups.

CORE's relationship to the NAACP is an especially controversial subject among both Negro politicians and protest leaders. Shortly before I interviewed San Francisco's Negro protest leaders, the San Francisco NAACP held a bitter election (December 20, 1964) which, according to one newspaper account, "swept its traditional leaders out of office and handed the power to a reform administration dedicated to more vigorous action."[14] Supervisor Terry Francois, who had supported the repudiated conservative slate, charged that the election was a

"CORE takeover." Francois' charge was denied by the victorious NAACP militants. Dr. Thomas Burbridge who was elected vice-president in this election, told the San Francisco press that Francois' allegation was "a completely dishonest position."[15]

I could find no evidence to support Francois' charge. There does not seem to have been any plot on the part of the CORE leadership to grab control of the NAACP. Beverly Axelrod was the only CORE leader to win election at the December 1964 meeting. However, membership in the two groups is not exclusive. Many Negroes strongly feel that the NAACP should honestly represent the aspirations of the Negro community, and many CORE members probably did become involved in the bitter campaign for NAACP office because they felt that the organization was in too conservative hands. The CORE influence on the NAACP election was indirect and primarily ideological. The militant point of view espoused by CORE was the viewpoint of the majority of the nearly 300 NAACP members (out of a total membership of over 2,300) who bothered to vote for NAACP officials.

CORE has attempted to keep in close touch with the Negro masses of the Fillmore District; the NAACP, on the other hand, has usually been almost solely a middle- or upper-middle-class organization. However, the militant victory described above also resulted in the election of at least two lower-class Negro militants to the NAACP executive board. Thus, both in approach and in the composition of its leadership, the NAACP in San Francisco is tending to come closer to the nature of CORE.

CORE's influence is even greater among the more militant protest groups, the Ad Hoc Committee and Freedom House. Only three protest groups are visible to the thousands of Negroes who walk the busy "downtown" streets of the Fillmore District. They are CORE, Freedom House, and the Black Muslims. These organizations all have store front offices (or a temple in the case of the Black Muslims) which are open to the public and which are often filled with inhabitants of the ghetto. The influence of these groups is not restricted to those Negroes who have formally joined them. These organizations have a dynamic nature which results partly from their constant communication with the inhabitants of the Negro ghetto. The Black Muslims proceed in lonely isolation: CORE and Freedom House cooperate with each other. Pleasant Carson, the coordinator of Freedom House, is a member of CORE. He strongly supports CORE and the Ad Hoc Committee "because they favor direct action"; he is critical of the NAACP which he considers "too moderate."

In general, the protest leaders have favorable attitudes towards all of San Francisco's protest groups. However, two important exceptions should be noted here because the attitudes of two protest leaders, Bernard Cushmeer of the Black Muslims and Percy Steele of the Urban League, frequently differ from the views held by the other six leaders studied. Cushmeer is a dogmatic spokesman of his faith; he regards Elijah Muhammad as the source for all his views on the Negro and his problems. Cushmeer considers other Negro protest groups to be appeasers of the white man. The Black Muslims are opposed to direct action protest and are more concerned with organizing Negroes for self-improvement than with taking to the streets in order to gain rights which can never be achieved in a white land. Thus, the Black Muslims have isolated themselves from all the other protest groups in terms of style as well as membership.

Percy Steele is at the other end of the ideological spectrum, but many of his specific attitudes are similar to those of Cushmeer. Steele is a professional Urban League staff worker with an M.A. in social work. He is an integrationist. He confines his civil rights activity to a non-active membership in the NAACP, because he feels that his presence in a demonstration would be bad for the image of the Urban League. Steele is very disturbed by what he considers to be irresponsible leadership in San Francisco's civil rights movement, and is very doubtful about the wisdom of direct action protest. [However, since 1965, Steele has adopted a much more militant position in regards to black protests.]

The other six protest leaders all regard aggressive direct action protest as an effective means for improving Negro conditions. None of them disapproves of the Black Muslims. On the other hand, some of the lower-class leaders expressed some doubts about the effectiveness of the NAACP, because they fear that the NAACP's support for mass action is not complete.[16] This strong commitment to direct action protest by the bulk of San Francisco's Negro protest leaders represents more than a pragmatic assessment of mass action as a productive tactic. As James Q. Wilson has observed, it also involves moral and ideological considerations: "The militant leader values protest over access. Since protest is usually on behalf of ends which are felt to have a moral justification, this statement could be enlarged to argue that the protester values principle over position."[17] With the exception of the Urban League and the Black Muslims, the protest groups of San Francisco have adopted mass action as their principal means and ends. As a result, it is possible, and often even necessary, for the various protest groups to cooperate in order to make their demonstrations successful. In many of the turbulent demonstrations in San Francisco, CORE, the NAACP, the Ad Hoc Committee, and Freedom House have been allies.

With the exception of the executive director of the Urban League, San Francisco's Negro protest leaders consider direct action protest to be a far more effective tool for bettering the Negro's lot than political activity. In fact, four of the eight leaders interviewed feel that Negro political activity (in the sense of electing Negroes and liberals to public office who will attempt to bring about political solutions to the problems of the ghetto) is actually harmful to the Negro. Only three protest leaders (all members of the NAACP) have been active in partisan politics, and in two of these cases this activity was confined to the precinct level.[18]

In part, this hostility to political activity results from the low esteem in which Negro politicians are held by many Negro protest leaders. The following statements are representative of the attitudes four of the protest leaders interviewed have towards Negro politicians: "Politics and civil rights activity do not mix. . . . Politicians are a serious obstacle to the civil rights movement." "Negro politicians are opportunists. . . . Politicians are no good; they're all out for themselves." While the other four leaders did not express such negative attitudes, they definitely tend to feel that Negro politicians have little or no efficacy.

These attitudes towards Negro political activity and politicians do not seem to be the result of personal animosity towards the Negro politicians of San Francisco. Rather, the protest leaders tend to feel that Negro politicians are hopelessly vulnerable to the demands of the "white power structure." To the leaders of the Ad Hoc Committee and Freedom House and to the militant leaders of CORE and the NAACP, election or appointment to political office means entry into the white world. Government, like business, labor, and the press, is part of the white power structure and is by definition hostile to the interests of the Negro.[19] Just as a factory worker who enters management can no longer lead his union, a Negro who becomes part of the governmental policy-making process can no longer lead the Negro movement. He becomes someone to influence or to threaten, not someone to follow.

The proper role of political activity in the Negro protest movement was a major issue in the NAACP election discussed earlier in this article. On October 14, 1964, two months before the election was held, NAACP president Dr. Thomas Burbridge resigned his office because of a dispute with the NAACP executive board. The specific issues involved were Burbridge's charge that the Board was acting with "gross insincerity" in fighting a redevelopment program in the Negro ghetto and the Board's refusal to fire a part-time secretary as requested by Burbridge. However, according to Dr. Burbridge, these were not the real issues: ". . . underlying these incidents is a deep philosophical rift. Those of us who resigned feel that the more a civil rights organization can divorce itself from politics, the better off it is. Those opposing us feel the branch should be involved in the political arena."[20] Five other NAACP leaders resigned with Dr. Burbridge.

When the election for NAACP offices was held on December 20, Burbridge's point of view was vindicated. Burbridge was elected vicepresident and his fellow militants won most of the offices which were contested.[21] The San Francisco Chronicle concluded that the election "showed strong support for the branch dissidents' arguments that high NAACP office holders should not also hold high political office in the community."[22] United States Attorney Cecil Poole, regarded by many militants as an "Uncle Tom," was denied a seat on the board of directors. Supervisor Terry Francois was elected by only a ten-vote majority and resigned in protest.

We have seen that most Negro protest leaders endorse mass action protests while tending to reject political activity or Negro political leadership. One could argue that this strategy is determined by the nature of the protest organizations. The following argument could be developed in support of this hypothesis: Protest leaders lack both the temperament and the personnel to create political organizations. Militant activists, cut off from the mainstream of Negro thought, choose the only strategy that can maximize their effectiveness, direct action protest. A mass demonstration camouflages the fact that those demonstrating lack support in the Negro community. In addition, a day or two on the picket line is easier than the months and years of steady labor necessary to build a political organization. Unfortunately, this line of thought cannot be fully examined on the basis of the data contained in this article. However, some of the data indicate that serious doubts can be raised about the above hypothesis. First of all, the leaders of protest groups are not dilettantes; their investment of time is probably equal to that required by a political career. CORE, Freedom House, the Ad Hoc Committee, the Black Muslims, and the Urban League require full-time commitments on the part of their leaderships. Only the NAACP requires merely part-time attention from its executives. In addition, CORE and Freedom House have developed mass organizations with strong support among the Negro masses of San Francisco. Freedom House deserves particular attention.

Although Freedom House was established in March 1964 to organize the inhabitants of the Fillmore District to combat a proposed urban renewal program, it quickly aquired other functions. By 1965, it was involved in rent strikes, job training, political education, and community organization. Young white college students, many of them from San Francisco State College, originally organized the Fillmore area on a block-by-block basis. The area was divided into 35 blocks, and the inhabitants of each block were given instruction in electing a block captain. At the time of this research, there were between 15 and 20 block captains; most of them were Negroes. All the block captains lived in the Fillmore area. Almost all the white college students have departed from the scene leaving Freedom House under the control of its new grass-roots leadership.

The chief executive at Freedom House is Pleasant Carson, who was elected staff coordinator by his fellow block captains. Carson's background is similar to the backgrounds of many urban Negro youths. [Nevertheless, in spite of poverty he attended San Francisco City College for almost two years.] He has often been unemployed. At one time he was a black nationalist. While he has rejected racism, he still is a very militant leader. At the age of twenty-three, Carson is a community leader who has extensive contacts in the Fillmore District; his prime goal is to organize the Negro masses in the ghetto. Carson is completely unconcerned about the image he conveys to whites and moderate (usually middle-class) Negroes: "I don't mind being called a Communist. . . . That's a good sign that I'm effective. I'll worry when they don't call me one."

Carson has a small but dedicated full-time staff; they man a storefront office on Fillmore Street which is open to the public. Carson is also the editor of a mimeographed newspaper, the "Fillmore Stand." Through these means and the block captain system, Carson and his organization have contact with thousands of Negroes in the Fillmore District. Freedom House has been able to organize hundreds of Negroes on short notice for various protest purposes. In short, Freedom House has an organization in many ways stronger and healthier than that of any Negro politician in San Francisco. However, Carson has no use for conventional politics and politicians. In the case of Freedom House, the decision to avoid political activity is a conscious one, not a decision dictated by organizational weaknesses. To Carson, politicians are simply "bad." New laws are useless. Only through direct action protest can the Negro solve his problems.

Carson feels direct action protests can be used to deal with the most pressing problems of the ghetto. Freedom House has been very active in using rent strikes as a means of gaining improved services from land-lords and to see that the city building and health codes are obeyed. Such diverse problems as police brutality, discrimination in employ-ment, urban renewal, segregated and poorly equipped schools, and poor housing can all be attacked through mass protests. In order to carry out successful demonstrations, the entire Negro community must be organized; this is the goal of Freedom House. Carson's attitudes represent in an extreme form the views held by the leaders of CORE, the Ad Hoc Committee, and (in the more militant cases) the NAACP. This line of thought is based on the assumption that the interests of the Negro and the white power structure are incompatible and antagonistic. Only through mass protest can the power structure be forced to grant the Negro his political, social, and economic rights.

## CONCLUSIONS AND OBSERVATIONS

At first glance, the data contained in this article seem to indicate that the relationship between Negro politicians and protest leaders in San Francisco is similar to the pattern James Q. Wilson found in Chi-cago six years before. In *Negro Politics*, Wilson concluded that Negro politicians and Negro civic leaders tend to be antagonistic. This is especially true regarding the relationship between Negro politicians and the leaders of Negro protest groups. Wilson terms this pattern one of "diverging elites."[23]

Can the pattern of Negro leadership in San Francisco be described as one of "diverging elites"? The differences between Negro politicians and protest leaders are numerous and pronounced. There is virtually no overlapping of personnel between the two groups. Negro politicians devote little time or energy to protest groups, and even their member-ships are usually restricted to the NAACP. On the other hand, protest leaders tend to avoid formal politics. The socioeconomic differences between the two groups are clear and dramatic. The Negro politicians are a homogeneous group; most of them are successful lawyers. The protest leaders are a very heterogeneous group whose composition ranges from upper-middle-class to lower-class. Differences in "world view" seem equally important. The politicians are oriented outside the ghetto, while the protest leaders (with the important exception of the

NAACP leaders) tend to be far more provincial in their outlooks. Finally, a low level of communication seems to exist between these groups. Whether protest leaders are hostile or friendly to Negro politicians, they display little knowledge about San Francisco politics. Negro politicians display a surprising lack of interest in the more radical protest organizations of San Francisco, even though these groups have made significant contact with the Negro lower class of the Fillmore District.

As Wilson has shown, the Negro politician obviously must respond to different demands from those influencing the protest leader.[24] In San Francisco, both politicians and protest leaders show a high degree of loyalty toward their respective groups. Negro politicians think highly of one another and believe that their fellow politicians are very efficacious. Most Negro protest leaders think well of all other protest groups and have great faith in the effectiveness of protest. Relations between the two groups are not the best. Negro politicians tend to minimize the effectiveness of the protest groups, while the protest leaders are often openly hostile to Negro politicians and consider political activity to be of little or no value.

In many respects, the Negro political and protest elites in San Francisco seem quite "divergent." However, I think there is an essential difference between the relationship between these two groups in San Francisco and the pattern described by Wilson in *Negro Politics*. Unlike the Negro protest leaders of Chicago in the late 1950's, the protest leaders of San Francisco and their organizations seem to influence significantly the political behavior of many Negro politicians. When Wilson made his study, the Negro protest organizations of Chicago were limited exclusively to the NAACP and the Urban League, and these organizations were under the complete control of middle-class professional staffs. These organizations were not interested in organizing the Negro rank-and-file for purposes of protest and had little active mass support.[25] Wilson considered the NAACP and Urban League "ill-equipped to respond to issues which require mass protest tactics,"[26] and he found no evidence to indicate that this pattern would change: "The new Negro leadership is distinctly middle class. The direct action protest groups of the old order are no longer found for the most part, or they survive only in attenuated and sometimes discredited form."[27]

Since these words were written, the situation has changed radically. Throughout the United States, protest organizations have been formed (or resurrected) which have been very successful in organizing large numbers of Negroes in mass protest. CORE and SNCC are the most prominent of these groups. As a result of the appeal of the radical protest groups, the NAACP has been forced to take a more militant stance in order to keep its position of Negro leadership.[28] In San Francisco, there is much evidence, such as the size and frequency of mass demonstrations, the membership lists of the protest groups, and the turn-out at their meetings, to suggest that most of San Francisco's Negro protest groups have mass support within the Negro community. The Ad Hoc Committee, CORE, Freedom House, and the Black Muslims command significant support among lower-class Negroes and have even absorbed lower-class Negroes into their leadership. While the NAACP remains primarily middle-class in terms of support and leadership, it has attempted to expand its base by placing a few lower-class Negroes on its executive board and by initiating programs in some of the poorer Negro neighborhoods. Only the Urban League remains aloof from the masses and conforms to Wilson's description of Negro "voluntary associations."

In San Francisco, most Negro protest leaders feel that their protest groups should affect politics without directly entering the political arena. (Some of the protest leaders talked of entering formal politics in the future, but it was clear that their plans are vague and that their stance would be uncompromising.) Most of the protest leaders feel that direct action protest against elements of the white power structure (government, business, labor, etc.) accomplishes far more for the Negro than would a political alliance with more moderate forces. The protest leaders regard themselves as the true leaders of the Negro community in that they are responsive to the desires of the community while playing the most influential role in its thinking. Thus, it is the task of the Negro protest groups to make the will of the Negro community known to the white power structure and (to many protest leaders) to its subservient Negro politicians.

The Negro politicians seem to react to the demands of the Negro protest organizations; the protest groups are clearly on the offensive. Although the politicians tend to minimize the effectiveness of the protest groups, most of the politicians speak favorably about them and endorse direct action. (Of those politicians facing Negro electorates, *all* speak highly of the protest groups of San Francisco, and *all* endorse direct action.) The Negro politicians tend not to perceive the relationship between the politicians and the protest groups as being antagonistic. In the eyes of the politicians, both groups are working together (usually under the leadership of the politicians) to advance the cause of the Negro in San Francisco.

Because of the limited nature of this study, only limited conclusions can be made, but a tentative general hypothesis can be offered. All the Negro politicians interviewed in this study appear to have independent support within the Negro community. This support has probably been far more important to their political careers than has been backing from the protest groups or the white politicians and business interests (the so-called white power structure). The Negro protest groups, with the exception of the Urban League, also command a large following in the Negro community. In fact, this support is probably greater than that enjoyed by the Negro politicians, with the probable exception of Willie Brown. The strength of the protest groups in the Negro community could enable them to exert a powerful influence over those politicians who represent Negro districts. Many of these conclusions must remain tentative.[29] However, it is clear from the data gathered in this study that either because of the extent of support for the protest groups in the Negro community or merely because the protest groups are vocal and (sometimes) well organized, they have a significant effect on the behavior of the Negro politicians. The Negro politicians, in turn, fail to exert much influence on the protest groups.

The above findings conflict with a number of observations made by Edward Banfield and James Q. Wilson in *City Politics*. Banfield and Wilson argue that Negro protest groups are led and supported primarily by underemployed middle-class Negroes, and that "lower-class Negroes play little part" in these organizations.[30] Banfield and Wilson include no data to support these assertions, and the only sources cited are studies made in the 1950's or earlier. However, journalistic studies published within a year after the publication of *City Politics* (and, in one case, one year earlier) indicate that the situation in San Francisco is not unique: Negro protest groups seem to be gaining sizable lower-class support throughout the nation.[31] A survey of Negro opinion made by *Newsweek* in 1963 revealed majority support among the Negro masses for the prime tactic of the protest groups, direct action. Fifty-nine percent of the non-Southern Negroes polled said that they would be willing to take part in a sit-in. Fifty-two percent expressed a willingness to go to jail. The percentages in these categories were *higher* for lower-class non-Southern Negroes.[32] Similarly, *Newsweek's* opinion studies in 1963 and 1966 indicate that, with the exception of the Black Muslims, Negroes express positive, rather than negative, attitudes towards all the Negro protest groups, and that the more militant protest groups are gaining in popularity.[33]

Banfield and Wilson cite six features of Negro social structure which affect Negro civic action:[34] (1) the predominance of a lower-class lacking a strong sense of community; (2) the relative inability, or unwillingness, of the middle class to identify with the lower class and to provide leadership for it; (3) the fairly large and growing number of young people who have more education than the job market enables them to use; (4) the relative fewness of entrepreneurs and the consequent importance of professionals; (5) many important individuals and institutions have a vested interest in the maintenance of discrimination and segregation; and (6) Negro civic organizations are small in size and short on resources. These factors, with the important exception of the third feature, act as constraints on Negro civic action.

I have already suggested that the sixth feature does not apply to San Francisco, or, if the sources cited above are reliable, to much of the nation, even though Banfield and Wilson argue that this feature "is to a large extent explained by the other five."[35]

Serious questions can also be raised about the conclusions Banfield and Wilson draw from features (1) and (2). Drawing upon Essien-Udom's perceptive study *Black Nationalism*, they point out that relations between the Negro middle and lower classes tend to be antagonistic,[36] and they argue that the existence of a large Negro lower class and the hostility between the Negro lower and middle classes act as constraints on Negro civic action. This may often be the case, as Wilson's study of Negro politics in Chicago in the late 1950's and my own observations of Negro politics in Saginaw, Michigan, in 1966–67 indicate. However, in San Francisco, a different phenomenon exists despite the presence of these same factors. The existence of a large Negro lower class, hostile to the Negro middle class and the white power structure, could (and in San Francisco did) provide the right environment for the creation of radical protest movements under lower-class or militant middle-class leadership which rejects the styles and goals of conventional "middle-class" politics.[37]

To Banfield and Wilson it is axiomatic that Negro political leadership must come from the middle class: "In any community, of course, it is the middle and upper classes who provide most of the civic and political leadership."[38] While this truism may be applicable to American society in general, it is not necessarily correct when applied to the Negro community of San Francisco. If the concept "lower-class leadership" could be expanded to include leaders of middle-class backgrounds who have turned to lower-class Negroes for support and have articulated programs which appeal primarily to lower-class Negroes, then this statement is completely inapplicable to San Francisco's protest leadership. However, Banfield and Wilson argue that even alienated "underemployed" middle-class Negroes will behave in a definitely middle-class manner: ". . . Because of the nature of these activists, the goals sought and methods employed are often of a special kind—status rather than welfare goals, protest rather than bargaining tactics, and with middle-class rather than lower-class backing."[39]

It seems likely that in light of the great impact which the civil rights movement has made on Northern Negroes in the 1960's, many of the conclusions in *City Politics* regarding the nature of Negro protest groups are no longer valid. In San Francisco, both lower-class and militant middle-class protest leaders have appealed to the Negro lower class for support and have received it.

This change in the nature and support of Negro protest groups has in turn led to a change in the relationship between these groups and Negro politicians. As the membership of these organizations expands from a narrow middle-class base to include significant mass support, and as these organizations succeed in involving a significant number of the Negro rank-and-file in protest activities, it would seem that the strength of these organizations becomes too great for them to be ignored by Negro politicians. This appears to be the case in San Francisco. Negro politicians are faced with the strong possibility that if they ignore the demands of the protest groups, they will endanger their own chances for election. Thus, Negro politicians in San Francisco have become responsive not only to the political system of the city as a whole, but also to the demands of the Negro masses as articulated by the Negro protest groups. In my opinion, future research will find similar patterns emerging in other Northern cities.


APPENDIX

Negro Leaders Interviewed

I. *Negro Politicians*:
   Willie Brown: assemblyman (D), California's 18th assembly district
   Dr. Daniel Collins: former president, Fillmore Democratic Club
   John Dearman: former president, San Francisco Young Democrats
   Terry Francois: member (D), San Francisco board of supervisors

Herman Griffin: member, Democratic county central committee; president, 18th Assembly Democratic Club

Solomon Johnson: member, Republican county central committee

Joseph Williams: state inheritance tax appraiser; vice-president, Bay View Democratic Club; former member, Democratic county central committee

II. *Negro Protest Leaders*:

Beverly Axelrod:* board member, San Francisco CORE; board member, San Francisco branch of the NAACP

Dr. Thomas Burbridge: vice-president, San Francisco branch of the NAACP

Pleasant Carson, Jr.: staff coordinator, Freedom House, San Francisco

Bernard Cushmeer: minister, Black Muslim mosque, San Francisco

Joe Goncalves: vice-chairman, San Francisco CORE

Dr. Carlton Goodlett: editor and publisher, *Sun-Reporter*, former board member and president, San Francisco branch of the NAACP

Tracy Sims: chairman, The Ad Hoc Committee to End Racial Discrimination

Percy Steele, Jr.: executive director, Bay Area Urban League

## NOTES

1. In 1960, San Francisco's Negro population was 74,383 out of a total population of 740,316. United States Bureau of the Census, *Census of Population: 1960. Characteristics of the Population*, Vol. I, Part 6, California (Washington: Government Printing Office), p. 141.

2. See "The Economic Status of Negroes in the San Francisco-Oakland Bay Area" (San Francisco: California State Employment Service, 1963). (Mimeographed.)

3. See the Appendix for a list of those interviewed.

4. Daniel C. Thompson, *The Negro Leadership Class* (Englewood Cliffs: Prentice-Hall, 1963), p. 4.

5. James Q. Wilson, *Negro Politics* (Glencoe: Free Press, 1960), p. 185.

6. In addition, in the cases of CORE and the NAACP, influential board members were interviewed as well as the executive officers of these

* The basis for Miss Axelrod's selection as a respondent was not her skin color but the role she played in the San Francisco Negro protest movement in 1964 and 1965.

organizations, because in these groups some board members were playing significant executive roles.

7. This list totals more than seven because two of the politicians held two posts.

8. An attempt was made to utilize two concepts developed by James Q. Wilson, "militant" and "moderate" styles of leadership; but contrary to Wilson's findings, it was impossible to place those interviewed in Wilson's categories. (See *Negro Politics*, pp. 214–254.) Wilson argues that many real Negro leaders closely resemble his ideal types, and he lists approximately twenty attitudes on questions of issues, values, ends, means, and other factors which would be displayed by each type of leader. All of the leaders interviewed in this study displayed both "militant" and "moderate" attitudes; only five (out of fifteen) displayed any real tendency to exhibit either a "militant" or "moderate" style. No significant pattern in terms of Wilson's categories could be discerned from the responses of the other ten.

9. Dr. Carlton Goodlett, the only protest leader interviewed who is active in politics, has been a president and board member of the NAACP. (Dr. Goodlett was an unsuccessful candidate for governor in the 1966 Democratic primary.)

10. All figures are Brown's.

11. Wilson, *op. cit,*. p. 27.

12. Edward C. Banfield and James Q. Wilson, *City Politics* (Cambridge: Harvard U. Press, 1965), pp. 303–308.

13. The one exception is Beverly Axelrod, a lawyer who serves on the boards of both CORE and the NAACP. See Appendix.

14. *San Francisco Chronicle*, December 21, 1964, p. 1.

15. *Ibid.*, pp. 1 and 15.

16. Miss Sims refused to comment on other protest groups.

17. *Negro Politics*, p. 224.

18. However, the third leader, Dr. Carlton Goodlett, has been deeply involved in San Francisco politics and even ran for governor in the 1966 Democratic primary.

19. Again, the leaders of the Black Muslims and Urban League are atypical. Cushmeer, of course, rejects all involvement with the white world and even refrains from voting. Percy Steele, unlike all the other protest leaders interviewed, feels that politics accomplishes more than protest.

20. *San Francisco Chronicle*, October 23, 1964, p. 6.

21. The president-elect, attorney Richard Bancroft, was supported by both factions.

22. December 21, 1964, p. 1.

23. Pp. 313–314.

24. *Ibid.*, p. 113.

25. *Ibid.*, p. 283.

26. *Ibid.*, p. 302.

27. *Ibid.*, p. 299.

28. See Louis E. Lomax, *The Negro Revolt* (New York: New American Library of World Literature, 1963); and Charles E. Silberman, *Crisis in Black and White* (New York: Random House, 1964), pp. 123–161.

29. It is beyond the scope of this study to compare with any precision the support in the Negro community of San Francisco for the Negro politicians and the Negro protest groups.

30. Banfield and Wilson, *op. cit.*, pp. 299–301.

31. See Lomax, Silberman, and Nat Hentoff, *The New Equality* (New York: Viking, 1964).

32. William Brink and Louis Harris, *The Negro Revolution in America* (New York: Simon and Schuster, 1964), p. 203.

33. *Ibid.*, p. 117; *Newsweek*, August 22, 1966, p. 34.

34. Banfield and Wilson, *op. cit.*, pp. 297–300.

35. *Ibid.*, p. 300.

36. E.U. Essien-Udom, *Black Nationalism* (New York: Dell, 1962), pp. 355–356. My own research in San Francisco tends to support the findings of Essien-Udom regarding class polarity in Negro society.

37. Lower-class Negroes may be more prone to civic and political activity than is generally assumed. Anthony M. Orum has convincingly argued that despite the high correlation between socio-economic status and organizational activity in America society as a whole, "the relationship between class and membership is much less pronounced for Negroes." ("A Reappraisal of the Social and Political Participation of Negroes," *American Journal of Sociology*, 72 (July 1966), 42.) Lower-class Negroes are more likely to join organizations than lower-class whites, and once members, the lower-class Negroes tend to be more active than their white counterparts. (*Ibid.*, pp. 32–46.)

38. Banfield and Wilson, *op. cit.*, p. 297.

39. *Ibid.*, p. 303. In his numerous writings on Negro politics, Wilson seems to consider it axiomatic that Negro leadership must be middle-class. In his study of Negro politics in Chicago, this assumption may have prevented him from seriously examining lower-class Negro leadership. He chose his "leaders" not by finding men who had mass support in the Negro community (one possible definition of leadership) but by applying instead the following standards: "We shall not begin with definitions, as the leaders selected for research in Chicago were not chosen by the application to the Negro community of a single concept of leadership. Rather, a list was compiled which started with those

Negroes who were reputed to be civic leaders as *indicated by newspaper accounts* and the roster of officers of *various* Negro voluntary associations and political organizations. The list was built up by adding to it names of Negroes who were participating in specific civic issues in some capacity, as well as Negroes *who were named by other Negro leaders as being leaders in some sense.* . . . The haphazard manner in which it was compiled appears to have presented no serious problems. . . ." Emphasis added. (P. 10.) Relevant to Wilson's research procedure is the comment of a Negro politician in San Francisco that "the day is gone when newspapers can make Negro leaders." Although Wilson included the NAACP and Urban League, he excluded the Black Muslims from his study, though he was studying "leaders who acted as if the interests of the race and the community were their goals." (*Ibid.*) In my opinion Wilson's research designated an important factor in leading him to the conclusion that "the new Negro leaders were distinctly middle class." (*Ibid.*, p. 299.)

## 16 What "Black Power" Means to Negroes in Mississippi

*Joyce Ladner*

For three months during the summer of last year, I conducted a study aimed at finding out how Mississippi Negroes who endorsed "black power" interpreted this new concept. I learned that even those civil-rights activists who welcomed the concept attached curiously different meanings to it. My research also helped me understand why the black-power slogan proved so welcome to these activists, and why its acceptance was accompanied by the expulsion of whites from positions of leadership. Finally, my investigation provided some hints on the usefulness of the black-power slogan in helping Mississippi Negroes achieve their goals.

The black-power concept that emerged during the past year created fierce controversy, not only among white liberals but among Negro activists and conservatives. Most of the nation's top civil-rights leaders denounced the slogan—or vigorously embraced it. Instead of "black power," Martin Luther King Jr. advocated the acquisition of "power for all people." The N.A.A.C.P.'s Roy Wilkins, in condemning the slogan, used such terms as "anti-white power . . . a reverse Hitler . . . a reverse Ku Klux Klan and . . . can only mean black death." On the other hand, Stokely Carmichael, former head of SNCC, was the chief advocate of the slogan, which he defined as "the ability of black people to politically get together and organize themselves so that they can speak from a position of strength rather than a position of weakness." CORE's Floyd McKissick agreed.

But though Negro civil-rights leaders were divided about black power, the slogan was welcomed by many disenchanted Negroes living in Northern ghettos. These Negroes tended to view black power as a tangible goal that, when acquired, would lift them from their inferior

Reprinted from *TRANS-action* V, no. 1 (November 1967): 7–15. Copyright © 1967 by *TRANS-action* Magazine, New Brunswick, New Jersey.

positions in the social structure. Still, despite the positive identification that Negroes in the Northern ghettos had with the rhetoric of black power, SNCC and CORE made no massive attempts to involve these Negroes in black-power programs.

But what about the South? How did Negroes in Mississippi, and civil-rights organizations in Mississippi, interpret the new slogan? This was what I wanted to find out.

I used two methods of study. The first was *participant-observation*—in informal, small meetings of civil-rights activists; in civil-rights rallies; and in protest demonstrations, including the historic Meredith march. The second was the *focused interview*. I chose to interview 30 Negroes who, I had found, were in favor of black power. All were friends or acquaintances of mine, and all had had long experience in Southern civil-rights work. They represented about two-thirds of the black-power leaders in the state. (My personal involvement with the civil-rights movement helped provide the rapport needed to acquire the observational data, as well as the interview data.)

Among other things, I learned that many Negro activists in Mississippi had immediately embraced the black-power slogan—because of the already widely-held belief that power *was* an effective tool for obtaining demands from the ruling elite in Mississippi. Since 1960, civil-rights organizations have been playing a major role in involving Mississippi Negroes in the fight for equality. As a result, these Negroes became more and more dissatisfied with their impoverished, powerless positions in the social structure. The 1960 census reports that the median family income for Mississippi Negroes (who constitute 42.3 percent of Mississippi's population) was $1168, as opposed to $3565 for whites. Until fewer than five years ago, only 6 percent of the eligible Negroes were registered to vote. Today, the traditional all-white primary still exists—in almost the same form as it did 25 years ago. Since many of the efforts Mississippi Negroes made to change the social structure—through integration—were futile, they began to reconceptualize their fight for equality from a different perspective, one designed to acquire long-sought goals through building bases of power.

The black-power concept was, then, successfully communicated to Mississippi Negroes because of the failure of integration. But it was also communicated to them by the shooting of James Meredith on his march through Mississippi. This act of violence made Negro activists feel justified in calling for "audacious black power." For only with black power, they contended, would black people be able to prevent events like the shooting.

## LOCALS AND COSMOPOLITANS

But there were varying degrees of acceptance of the slogan among Mississippi Negroes. Some, of course, did not accept the slogan at all—those who were never part of the civil-rights movement. Despite the fact that Mississippi has been one of the centers of civil-rights activity in the United States for the past six or seven years, no more than half the Negro population (I would surmise) has ever been actively involved in the movement. In such areas as Sunflower County, a very high percentage of Negroes have participated; but in many other areas, like Laurel, only a small percentage of the Negroes have taken part.

As for those Negroes active in the movement, they can be broadly classified into two groups. The first: the traditional, moderate, N.A.A.C.P.-style activists, who boast of having been "freedom fighters" before the "new movement" came into existence. They include ministers; small-businessmen; professionals; a sizable following of middle-class people; and a small number of the rank and file. Frequently the white ruling elite calls these activists the "responsible" leaders. The primary activities of this group include selling N.A.A.C.P. memberships; initiating legal action against segregation and discriminatory practices; negotiating with the ruling elite; and conducting limited boycotts and voter-registration campaigns.

The second group of activists are the less economically advantaged. Although a small number were once members of the N.A.A.C.P., most of them joined the movement only since 1960. They are readily identified with such organizations as the Freedom Democratic Party, CORE, SNCC, the Delta Ministry, and the Southern Christian Leadership Conference. Members of this group include plantation workers, students, the average lower-class Negro, and a small number of ministers, professionals, and businessmen. More militant than the first group, these activists conduct mass marches, large-scale boycotts, sit-ins, dramatic voter-registration campaigns, and so forth.

Members of the traditional organizations, in sum, are still committed to working for integration. It is the militants who are oriented toward a black-power ideology, who consider integration irrelevant to what they see as the major task at hand—uniting black people to build black institutions. I suspect that a larger number of activists identify with traditional organizations like the N.A.A.C.P. than with the more militant ones.

The 30 black-power advocates I interviewed were, of course, the

militant activists. Even so, I found that even these 30 could be further
classified—into categories that Robert K. Merton has called *local* and
*cosmopolitan*:

> The localite largely confines his interest to this [town of Rovere]
> community. Devoting little thought or energy to the Great Society
> he is preoccupied with local problems, to the virtual exclusion of the
> national and international scene. He is, strictly speaking, parochial.
>    Contrariwise with the cosmopolitan type. He has some interest in
> Rovere and must of course maintain a minimum of relations within
> the community since he, too, exerts influence there. But he is also
> oriented significantly to the world outside Rovere and regards him-
> self as an integral part of that world. . . . The cosmopolitan is
> ecumenical.

In this paper, I shall use "local" to refer to those long-term residents
of Mississippi—usually uneducated, unskilled adults—whose strong
commitment to civil-rights activity stemmed primarily from their desire
to produce massive changes in the "home-front," the area they call
home.

I shall use "cosmopolitan" to refer to the urbane, educated, highly
skilled young civil-rights activists who are usually newcomers to Mississippi. Because they went to the state to work in the civil-rights
movement only temporarily, their identification with the area tends to
be weak.


### THE MOVEMENT'S PHILOSOPHERS

One-third of my respondents, I found, hold the cosmopolitan view.
The majority are Negro men, but there are a small group of Negro
women and a very small group of white sympathizers. The mean age
is about 23 or 24. About half are from the North; the remainder are
from Mississippi and other southern states. Most of the cosmopolitans
are formally educated and many have come from middle-class Northern
families and gone to the better universities. They are widely read and
widely traveled. They are also artistic: Writers, painters, photogra-
phers, musicians, and the like are often found in the cosmopolitan
group. Their general orientation toward life is an intellectual one. They
are associated with SNCC, the Freedom Democratic Party, and CORE.
Although a few are actively engaged in organizing black people in the

various counties, much of their work in the state is centered on philosophical discussions, writing, and so forth. All of the cosmopolitans
have had wide associations with white people. Some grew up and
attended school with whites; others had contact with whites in the civil-
rights movement. The cosmopolitans maintain that black people in
American society must redefine the term "black" and all that it symbolizes, and that black pride and dignity must be implanted in all Negro
Americans. The cosmopolitan position embraces the belief that the
plight of Negro Americans is comparable to neocolonialized "colored
peoples" of the world.

The cosmopolitans' participation in the Southern civil-rights scene,
by and large, dates back to 1960 and the beginning of the student
movement in the South. Their present ideology has to be viewed in the
framework of the history of their involvement in the movement, with
special emphasis on the negative experiences they encountered.

Some six years ago, black Americans began to seek their long-desired
civil rights with a new sense of urgency. The N.A.A.C.P.'s painstaking
effort to obtain legal, theoretical rights for Negroes was challenged.
Groups of Negro college students in the South decided to fight the
gradualism that had become traditional and to substitute radical action
aimed at bringing about rapid social change. These students began
their drive for equal rights with lunch-counter demonstrations. After
much immediate success, they spread their drive to the political arena.
Their only hope for the future, they felt, lay in the ballot. Much to
their disappointment, acquiring political power was not so easy as integrating lunch counters. The students met their strongest resistance
from whites in full possession of the sought-after political power. To
deal with this resistance, the Federal Government passed two civil-
rights laws: public accommodation and voting rights. But the Government did little to implement these laws. Still, in the early 1960s, student
civil-rights workers had an almost unrelenting faith in the Federal
Government and believed that changes in the laws would rapidly pave
the way for sweeping changes in the social structure. This was the era
when students were much involved in hard-core organizing. They paid
little attention to abstract philosophizing. Instead they occupied themselves with such pressing problems as the mass arrests of Negroes in
Greenwood, Miss.

As time went on, the cosmopolitans became more and more discouraged about their organizing efforts. They began to seriously question the feasibility of their strategies and tactics. By the end of 1964,
after the historic Mississippi Summer Project, the cosmopolitans began

to feel that their organizational methods were just not effective. For roughly a year and a half, they groped and searched for more effective strategies. Frequently they felt frustrated; sometimes they despaired. A number of them returned to the North and got well-paying jobs or went to graduate and professional schools. Others were alienated from some of the basic values of American society. Some students developed a strong interest in Africa and began to look to various African states as possible havens. Still others, after deciding that they had accomplished all that was possible through organizations such as SNCC, associated themselves with radical leftist groups.

It was during the tail end of this six-year period that two position papers were written by the cosmopolitans. One was by a group that insisted that Negroes expel whites from leadership roles in civil-rights organizations, and that Negroes develop "black consciousness" and "black nationalism." "Black consciousness" refers to a set of ideas and behavior patterns affirming the beauty of blackness and dispelling any negative images that black people may have incorporated about blackness. "Black nationalism" is a kind of patriotic devotion to the development of the Negro's own political, economic, and social institutions. Black nationalism is *not* a racist ideology with separatist overtones, however, but simply a move toward independence from the dominant group, the whites. This paper states:

> If we are to proceed toward true liberation, we must cut ourselves off from white people. We must form our own institutions, credit unions, co-ops, political parties, write our own histories. . . . SNCC, by allowing whites to remain in the organization, can have its effort subverted. . . . Indigenous leadership cannot be built with whites in the positions they now hold. They [whites] can participate on a voluntary basis . . . but in no way can they participate on a policy-making level.

In response, one white civil-rights worker—Pat McGauley—wrote a paper acceding to the demands of the black-consciousness group:

> The time has indeed come for blacks and whites in the movement to separate; however, it must always be kept in mind that the final goal of the revolution we are all working for is a multi-racial society.

The cosmopolitans I interviewed conceived of black power in highly philosophical terms—as an ideology that would unite black people as never before. To most of them, black power was intricately bound up with black consciousness. To a long-time SNCC worker, black consciousness was:

. . . an awareness of oneself as a removed nation of black people who are capable of running and developing their own governments and who have pride in their blackness to the extent that they won't sell out. . . . To the extent that he can say, "I'm no longer ashamed of my blackness." The individual redefines the society's rules in terms of his own being. There is a new kind of awakening of the individual, a new kind of realization of self, a type of security, and a type of self-confidence.

Another cosmopolitan equated black consciousness with community loyalty:

Black consciousness is not the question but rather [the question is] from which community one comes from. If you know that, you can identify with black people anywhere in the world then. That is all that is necessary.

These young people firmly believe that even the term "black" has to be redefined. To one of them, "Black has never had any favorable expression in the English language." To another, "American society has characterized black as the symbol for strength, evil, potency and malignancy. . . . People are afraid of the night, of blackness."

Most cosmopolitans feel that black people must acquire black consciousness before they can successfully develop the tools and techniques for acquiring black power. As one of them put it:

Black consciousness is the developmental stage of black power. Black power will be incomplete without black consciousness. Black consciousness is basically the search for identity; or working out one's own identity. . . . There must be a long process of learning and unlearning in between and a period of self-questing.

In short, by developing black consciousness, a Negro can appreciate his blackness and thus develop a kind of community loyalty to other colored peoples of the world.

Most of the cosmopolitans felt that the redefinition of blackness must take place in the black community *on the black man's terms.* When such a redefinition has taken place, black men who feel psychologically castrated because of their blackness will be able to compete with whites as psychological equals. ("Psychologically castrated" is a popular term among cosmopolitans, and refers to Negroes whose beliefs and behavior have become so warped by the values of white American society that they have come to regard themselves as inferior.)

## HEROES OF THE BLACK REVOLUTION

Cosmopolitans are familiar with the works of Marcus Garvey, Malcolm X, Franz Fanon, Kwame Nkrumah, and other revolutionary nationalists. Some can quote passages from their works. To the cosmopolitans, Marcus Garvey, (1887–1940), who tried to instill racial pride in Negroes, was a pioneer of black nationalism and black consciousness in America. The greatest impact on the cosmopolitans, however, comes from the contemporary Malcolm X, whose philosophy—toward the latter period of his life—reflected a revolutionary spirit and a total dissatisfaction with the plight of Negroes in this country. One of the cosmopolitans had this to say about Malcolm X:

> Malcolm was very much together. . . . He was a man who knew what he was doing and would have eventually showed everyone what he was capable of doing. . . . Malcolm had history behind him and was with the cat on the block.

To another:

> Malcolm X . . . was able to relate to people and to the press. The press is your right arm. . . . In order to be a real militant, you have to use the man [press] and that is what Malcolm did. They [the press] didn't create Malcolm. . . . The press was attuned to Malcolm. . . . Malcolm was not attuned to the press.

Some cosmopolitans call themselves students of Malcolm X and express the hope that another such leader will soon emerge.

Another symbolic leader is the late Algerian revolutionary, Franz Fanon, whose *The Wretched of the Earth* has become a veritable Bible to the cosmopolitans. Fanon tried to justify the use of violence by the oppressed against the oppressor, and to relate the neocolonialization of the black man in Algeria to the plight of colored peoples everywhere. Similarly, the cosmopolitans have great admiration for Stokely Carmichael, one of their associates, whose philosophy is highlighted in this passage:

> The colonies of the United States—and this includes the black ghettos within its borders, north and south—must be liberated. For a century this nation has been like an octopus of exploitation, its tenacles stretching from Mississippi and Harlem to South America, the Middle East, southern

Africa, and Vietnam; the form of exploitation varies from area to area but the essential result has been the same—a powerful few have been maintained and enriched at the expense of the poor and voiceless colored masses. This pattern must be broken. As its grip loosens here and there around the world, the hopes of black Americans become more realistic. For racism to die, a totally different America must be born.

Embodied within the philosophy of the cosmopolitans is an essential proposition that American society is inherently racist, that the majority of the white Americans harbor prejudice against black people. Few make any distinction between whites—for example, the white Southerner as opposed to the Northern liberal. Whites are considered symbolic of the black man's oppression, and therefore one should not differentiate between sympathetic whites and unsympathetic whites. The conclusion of the cosmopolitans is that any sweeping structural changes in American society can come about only through the black man's taking an aggressive role in organizing his political, economic, and social institutions. The black man must control his destiny.

## THE PRACTICAL ORIENTATION

I have categorized the remaining two-thirds of my 30 respondents as locals. (Of what significance these ratios are, by the way, I am not sure.) The locals are almost as committed to solving the pressing problems of inadequate income, education, housing, and second-class citizenship *practically* as the cosmopolitans are committed to solving them *philosophically*. Most of the locals are life-long residents of the communities or other Mississippi communities. Most of them, like the cosmopolitans, have been drawn into the movement only since 1960. Unlike the generally youthful cosmopolitans, the age range of the locals is from young adult to elderly. Many locals are indigenous leaders in their communities and in state-wide organizations. Whereas cosmopolitans tend to be middle-class, locals are members of the lower-class black communities and they range from plantation workers to a few who have acquired modest homes and a somewhat comfortable style of life. Many are leaders in the Mississippi Freedom Democratic Party, which in 1964 challenged the legality of the all-white Mississippi delegation to the national Democratic convention and in 1965 challenged the constitutionality of the elected white Representatives to serve in the U.S. House of Representatives. (Both challenges were based upon the fact that Negroes did not participate in the election of the delegates and Representatives.)

Although most of the locals are native Mississippians who have always been victimized by segregation and discrimination, I have also placed a number of middle-class students in this category—because of their very practical orientation to black power. The backgrounds of these students are somewhat similar to those of the cosmopolitans, except that the majority come from the South and are perhaps from lower-status families than the cosmopolitans are. These students are deeply involved in attempts to organize black-power programs.

Because of segregation and discrimination, the locals are largely uneducated; they subsist on a totally inadequate income; and they are denied the privileges of first-class citizenship. They have had a lot of experience with the usual forms of harassment and intimidation from local whites. Their entire existence can be perceived in terms of their constant groping for a better way of life. Because of many factors—like their low level of income and education and their Southern, rural, small-town mentality (which to some extent prevents one from acquiring an intellectualized world view)—the definition they have given to black power is a very practical one.

The black-power locals can be considered militants to much the same degree as the cosmopolitans, but on a different level. In essence, the nature and kind of activities in which they are willing to participate (voter registration, running for political office, boycotts, etc.) are indeed militant and are not surpassed by the nature and kind to which the cosmopolitans orient themselves. Indeed, in some cases the locals are deeply involved in realizing black-power programs: In certain counties, women have organized leathercraft and dress-making cooperatives. And in Senator Eastland's home county of Sunflower, an unsuccessful effort was even made to elect an all-black slate of public officials.

The great difference between cosmopolitans and locals is that the locals are committed to concrete economic and political programs, while the cosmopolitans—to varying degrees—endorse such programs but actually have made little effort to realize them.

Most locals perceived black power as a more effective, alternate method of organizing and acquiring those rights they had been seeking. In the past they had been committed to integration. Power had not originally been considered important in and of itself, for it was hoped that America would voluntary give Negroes civil rights. Therefore the locals sought coalition politics—they aligned themselves with Northern labor groups, liberals, national church groups, and so forth. During their several years of involvement, they—like the cosmopolitans— suffered many defeats. For example, many were involved with the Mississippi Summer Project, which brought hundreds of Northerners into the state in 1964. At that time the locals were convinced that such a program would bring about the wide structural changes they desired. But, to their disappointment, once the volunteers returned to the North the old patterns of segregation and discrimination returned. Some of the locals had gone to the Democratic Convention in Atlantic City, N.J., in 1964 hoping to unseat the all-white slate of delegates from Mississippi. When this failed, they invested further moral and physical resources into challenging the legality of the all-white slate of Mississippi Representatives in the U.S. House. Another set-back came when a large contingent pitched their tents on the White House lawn in a last-ditch effort to obtain poverty funds to aid in building adequate housing. All were sharecroppers, evicted because their participation in voter-registration programs was contrary to the desires of their plantation landlords. These evicted sharecroppers later set up residence in the buildings of the inactive Air Force base in Greenville, Miss. They were deeply depressed when officials of the Air Force ordered military police to remove them. One of the leaders of this group remarked, "If the United States Government cares so little about its citizens that it will not allow them to live in its abandoned buildings rather than in unheated tents [this occurred during winter], then that government can't be for real."

I submit that the events outlined above, among many others, caused a large number of the locals—like the cosmopolitans—to pause and question the effectiveness of their traditional organizational tactics and goals. Indeed, many even came to seriously question the Federal Government's sincerity about alleviating the problems of the Negro. A number of the participants in these events stopped being active in the movement. Others began to express strong anti-white sentiments.

## THE ATTRACTIONS OF BLACK POWER

Black power was embraced by many of the locals from the very beginning, and they began to reconceptualize their activities within the new framework. To the locals, black power was defined in various ways, some of which follow:

> Voter registration is black power. Power is invested in the ballot and that's why the white man worked like hell to keep you away from it. . . . We were even taught that it was not right to register [to vote]. The civil-

rights movement in this state started around the issue of voting—we shouldn't forget that.

Black power is political power held by Negroes. It means political control in places where they comprise a majority. . . . Black power is legitimate because any time people are in a majority, they should be able to decide what will and will not happen to them.

Black power was further viewed as a means of combining Negroes into a bond of solidarity. It was seen as a rallying cry, a symbol of identification, and a very concrete tool for action. Many said that former slogans and concepts such as "Freedom Now" were ambiguous. One could easily ask, "Freedom for what and from what?" One local said:

First we wanted Freedom Now. I ran around for six years trying to get my freedom. I really didn't know what it was.

Black power, they felt, was more concrete, for it had as its central thesis the acquisition of power. (Actually, the locals have also defined black power in various ways, and to some the slogan is as ambiguous as "Freedom Now.") The locals felt that Negroes would be able to acquire certain rights only through the control of their economic and political institutions, which—in some cases—also involves the eventual control of the black community. One black-power advocate put it succinctly when he said:

Black power means controlling the Negro community. It means that if the Negro community doesn't want white cops coming in, they can't come in. It means political, economic, and social control.

Asked how this control could be obtained, he replied:

We will have to start putting our money together to organize cooperatives, and other kinds of businesses. We can get political power by putting Negroes into public offices. . . . We will have to tell them to vote only for Negro candidates.

To others, control over the black community was not the goal, but rather a *share* in the existing power:

All we're saying to the white man is we want some power. Black power is just plain power. . . . It just means that Negroes are tired of being without power and want to share in it.

Thus, we can observe that there are several variations of the concept, all revolving around a central theme: the acquisition of power by Negroes for their own use, both offensively and defensively.

Despite the obvious practical orientation of the locals, there can also be found traces of black consciousness and black nationalism in their thought patterns. Most have never read Garvy, Fanon, Malcolm X, and other nationalists, but they tend to readily identify with the content of speeches made by Stokely Carmichael bearing the message of black nationalism. They are prone to agree with the cosmopolitans who speak to them about ridding themselves of their "oppressors." When the chairman of the Mississippi Freedom Democratic Party speaks of overthrowing neocolonialism in Mississippi, shouts of "Amen!" can be heard from the audience. There is also a tendency in this group to oppose the current war in Vietnam on the grounds that America should first concentrate on liberating Negroes within the United States' borders. The locals also believe that the war is indeed an unjust one. Perhaps the following statement is typical:

> Black men have been stripped of everything. If it takes black power to do something about this, let us have it. Black power has got the country moving and white people don't like it. We marched into Dominica, we marched into Vietnam. Now if we [black people] can conquer this country, we will conquer the world.

There is a growing feeling among both locals and cosmopolitans of kinship with the colored peoples of the world, including the Vietnamese. To engage in warfare against other colored people is regarded as a contradiction of this bond of solidarity.

For both the Mississippi cosmopolitans and locals, then, it was mainly frustration that drew them to the concept of black power.

## WHY WHITES WERE EXPELLED

The black-power slogan should be viewed in the perspective of the overall civil-rights movement, one of the most popular social movements in the history of this country. Now, there are some scholars who maintain that, by viewing a particular social movement over a period of time, one can discern a typical sequence: the movement's crystallization of social unrest; its phase of active agitation and proselytism; its organized phase; and the achievement of its objectives. The civil-rights movement, with much success, achieved each of these phases—except the final one, the achievement of objectives. Despite the great amount of effort and resources expended by black people and their allies to obtain civil rights, there was a disproportionate lack of gains. Indeed, in much of Mississippi and the South, conditions have barely changed from 10 or even 20 years ago. Many black people are still earning their livelihood from sharecropping and tenant farming; many household heads are still unable to earn more than $500 a year; many black children are still deprived of adequate education because of the lack of facilities and adequately trained teachers. To date, only 42.1 percent of Negroes of voting age are registered as opposed to 78.9 percent of whites. We still hear of lynchings and other forms of violence of which Negroes are the victims.

The black-power thrust is thus an inevitable outgrowth of the disillusionment that black people have experienced in their intense efforts to become integrated into the mainstream of American society. Thwarted by traditional formulas and organizational restrictions, some Mississippi Negroes have responded to the black-power concept in a sometimes semirational, emotionally charged manner—because it seemed the only available resource with which they could confront white American society.

How was the black-power concept related to the expulsion of whites from leadership positions in the movement? The fact is that the alienation and disaffection found throughout the entire black-power group also resulted from strained interpersonal relations with white civil-rights workers. During the past two years, there has been a growing belief among black people in Mississippi that white civil-rights workers should go into the *white* communities of that state to work. Only then, they contended, could the "inherent racism" in American society, with particular reference to the "Southern racist," begin to be dealt with. Even the seriousness of white civil-rights workers was questioned. Many Negroes felt that a sizable number of them had come South mainly to resolve their very personal emotional difficulties, and not to help impoverished black Mississippians. Rather, they were considered rebellious youth who wanted only to act out their rebellion in the most unconventional ways, Stokely Carmichael stated:

> Too many young, middle-class Americans, like some sort of Pepsi generation, have wanted to come alive through the black community; they've wanted to be where the action was—and the action has been in the black community. . . .

It's important to note that those white people who feel alienated from white society and run into the black society are incapable of confronting the white society with its racism where it really does exist.

Much strain also resulted from the inability of many black civil-rights activists—skilled organizers but lacking the formal education and other technical skills white workers possessed—to deal with the increased bureaucratization of the civil-rights movement (writing proposals for foundation grants, for example). Black activists, in addition, constantly complained about the focus of the mass media on white "all-American" volunteers who had come South to work in the movement. The media never paid attention to the thousands of black people who frequently took far greater risks. These factors played a major role in destroying the bond of solidarity that had once existed between whites and blacks in the movement. Before the emergence of the black-power concept, it is true, many young black civil-rights workers had cast white civil-rights workers in the same category as all other white people. The new slogan was, to some extent, a form of justification for their own prejudice against whites.

In terms of practical considerations, however, urging the white volunteers to leave the black communities has had negative effects. SNCC and CORE, which at one time directed most of the grass-roots organizing, have always depended upon the economic and volunteer resources of liberal white individuals and groups. These resources are scarce nowadays.

On another level, there have been positive results from removing whites from black communities. Black activists—all cosmopolitans and some locals—contend that, now that the whites have gone, they feel more self-confident and capable of running their own programs. They tend to view the earlier period of the movement, when whites played active roles in executing the programs, as having been a necessary phase; but they maintain that the time has arrived when black people must launch and execute their own programs.

## COSMOPOLITANS VS. LOCALS

Clearly, the long-range aims of the locals and cosmopolitans are basically the same. Unlike Negroes in such traditional organizations as the N.A.A.C.P., locals and cosmopolitans have turned away from integration. Both groups want to unite black people and build political, economic, and social institutions that will render a certain amount of control to the black community. For some time, however, the two groups have been operating on different levels. The cosmopolitans focus on developing black consciousness among black people, which they consider a necessary step to developing black power; the locals concentrate on solving the immediate problems resulting from segregation and discrimination.

While it may seem that the locals are more prudent and realistic than the cosmopolitans, it should be said that there are many positive features to black nationalism and black consciousness. It *is* important to establish a positive black identity in a great many sectors of the black communities, both North and South, rural and urban, lower and middle class. Indeed, it is both important and legitimate to teach black people (or any other ethnic minority) about their history, placing special emphasis upon the positive contributions of other black people. Thus black consciousness has the potential to create unity and solidarity among black people and to give them hope and self-confidence. Perhaps it fulfills certain needs in black people that society, on the whole, cannot. Martin Luther King has made the following statement about black consciousness:

> One must not overlook the positive value in calling the Negro to a new sense of manhood, to a deep feeling of racial pride and to an audacious appreciation of his heritage. The Negro must be grasped by a new realization of his dignity and worth. He must stand up amid a system that still oppresses him and develop an unassailable and majestic sense of his own value. *He must no longer be ashamed of being black.* (Emphasis Ladner's.)

Moreover, the task of getting blacks to act *as blacks, by* themselves and *for* themselves, is necessary for developing black consciousness, or psychological equality. Thus one is led to the conclusion that black consciousness does *necessarily* call for the expulsion of whites from leadership roles in the black communities.

The locals, on the other hand, have adopted concrete strategies that, in reality, involve the same kind of techniques that existed in the integration era. Specifically, when they refer to developing black-power programs, they speak of registering to vote, running for political office, and building independent political parties. As for the economic situation, they have begun to concentrate on building cooperatives and small businesses, and on almost-exclusively patronizing black-merchants in an effort to "keep the money in the black community." If we turn back two years, however, we find that the same strategies, though somewhat modified, were being used then. In the past, the locals concentrated on registering large numbers of black people to vote, in an effort to be able to have a voice in the decision-making apparatus. The emphasis is now on registering to vote so that the Negro can have control over his community and eventual control over his political destiny. Cooperatives were organized at least a year before the black-power concept emerged, but—ever since emphasis was put on economic control—there has been an expansion and intensification in certain sectors of this area. At present, cooperatives are still operating on a small-scale, though, considering the masses of people whose lives could be immensely improved by cooperatives.

The differences in the emphasis on priorities of achieving black power between locals and cosmopolitans can be viewed as complementary rather than oppositional, because each level of emphasis is vital for the achievement of their goals. This is becoming increasingly true since, within the last year, black-power advocates have taken a far more aggressive and militant stance toward the realization of such aims. Locals who a year ago might have questioned the importance and feasibility of "Black Liberation" schools, which teach black history and culture, are less likely to do so now. This is an indication that there is a trend toward unity between the groups. Because of the strong emphasis among some sectors of the black-power movement on drawing the parallels of the plight of the black Americans with that of the inhabitants of the Third World, locals are quite likely to become more cosmopolitan through time.

Through the development of such unity, there is a great possibility that black-power advocates in Mississippi will again turn to creative, large-scale organizing that would incorporate the major emphasis of each group: black consciousness and immediate gains.

## THE FUTURE OF BLACK POWER

The key question, of course, is, what are the prospects for Mississippi Negroes' developing black-power institutions in the near future? Clearly, this will depend to a great extent upon the number of organizers in the field, on adequate economic resources, and on commitments from major civil-rights organizations to the Mississippi scene. Certainly the presence of a local charismatic leader also would aid in the development of pervasive black-power institutions. Indeed, a black-power "prophet" whose task was to keep the message before all the advocates would give them immeasurable support and strength for their undertakings.

Where black-power institutions have a good chance of developing at present are in the small number of Mississippi counties where there are strong black-power organizations with large Negro voting populations. Since the cosmopolitans are reentering the field and beginning to organize (and some of the most skilled organizers are in this group), the prospects—here at least—seem favorable. On the other hand, it seems highly doubtful at this point that the needed resources can be obtained from the traditional sources (Northern students, white liberals, church and labor organizations). So these resources (inadequate as they may be) may have to be obtained from the black community. CORE and SNCC have already begun to establish financial bases in the black communities throughout the country. Should this tactic fail, perhaps there will be a revaluation of the strategies employed in the acquisition of black power.

# 17 Waiting for the Burning to Begin

*Ulf Hannerz*

Harlem 1964, Watts 1965, Chicago and Cleveland 1966 . . . The list of black ghetto risings in Northern cities was growing as the study of the Winston Street neighborhood began. The events of Harlem and Watts had already been incorporated into the history of black America, the newspaper headlines about Cleveland and Chicago were only a few weeks old. More was to follow, including Newark and Detroit 1967 and—toward the end of the study—Washington, D.C., itself, in the days following the assassination of Martin Luther King in April, 1968. But by then an eruption of this kind could hardly come as a surprise. The circumstances understood to be at the basis of earlier risings had clearly been at work in Washington as well; besides, as the nation's attention moved from one violent ghetto crisis to another, people like those in the Winston Street neighborhood had also become concerned with the prospect of turmoil in their own community, its causes and its possible consequences. Although not an everyday subject of conversation for most ghetto dwellers, it seemed continuously present as a background understanding; when a verbal exchange concerning it occurred, practically everybody seemed to have pertinent experiences and opinions. There were also a number of incidents which pointed forward to more tumultuous times. The climate of large-scale trouble thus existed long before the outbreak became a fact. Here we will attempt to throw some light at grassroots conditions and events along the road to a ghetto rebellion, with an emphasis on the ghetto dwellers' own perspective toward it.

Reprinted from *Soulside: Inquiries into Ghetto Culture and Community* (New York: Columbia University Press, 1969), pp. 159–176. By permission of the author.

## THE SHARING OF DISCONTENT

Ghetto dwellers have much to resent about the way the outside world treats them: poor jobs, unemployment, unfair practices on the part of many employers, high rents for unsatisfactory housing, inadequate schools and health and welfare services, arbitrary, inefficient, and sometimes brutal police work, the poor performance and sharp practices of many businesses aiming at ghetto customers, as well as a host of major and minor expressions of prejudice and discrimination which may confront a member of the black minority as he goes about his everyday social traffic in American society. Although such circumstances do not hit every member of the community with equal force, they provide each ghetto dweller with some basis for discontent, and probably they all play some role in the accumulation of grievances which may finally result in a rising. However, they do not seem to be equally prominent in the collective articulation of resentment which occurs spontaneously in the ghetto, and some of them are obviously of greater significance than others for the understanding of the form of ghetto rebellion. Some of the grievances are discontinuous and more private in their character, and one may perhaps only diffusely conceive of who is responsible for them. Thus complaints may be aired now and then about the insufficiency of garbage collection, about hours spent in waiting rooms, about a job a no better qualified white person got, or about a landlord who refuses to make repairs. But there are fewer of these, and they tend to be assimilated to the general body of knowledge about the hostile, distant white world. In the Winston Street neighborhood, at least, many more conversations about grievances dwell on white-owned businesses and the police; probably this is so because these are continuously present, represented by "real people," on ghetto territory. This may make it easier for ghetto dwellers to share experiences directly and to see the relevance of one's own experience to that of others. Since merchants and policemen are also those outsiders who become most directly involved in the insurrection itself, we will pay particular attention to how ghetto dwellers define their discontent with respect to these. This obviously does not mean that they are the only objects of "real" grievances; rather, they seem to become the foci of concern toward which discontent is channeled also from other sources. Thus they are particularly important in interpreting the insurrectionary mood of the ghetto in terms of social processes within the community.

As we have noted before, a great many of the business establishments in the ghetto are white-owned. Although some of these are quite modest enterprises—streetcorner groceries, carry-outs, variety stores and the like—most of the larger establishments are also among them, such as liquor stores, record stores, clothing stores, dry-cleaning operations, appliance and furniture stores, and auto dealers. Furthermore, there are the ghetto links of large supermarket and drugstore chains. The getto dwellers' attitude toward this white dominance behind the store fronts in their community is often one of bitterness. First of all this is based simply on the categorical relationship between blacks and whites. The people of the ghetto see that the meager resources allotted to them flow straight back to white people. It is very obvious to them that businessmen who are dependent on them for a living are doing much better than they. "See, there goes our bread, but he'll be back for more tomorrow," a streetcorner man says to his friends as they watch the owner of the liquor store across the street lock up his store and drive off in his car toward the suburb. But there is more to the resentment than this.

There is the question of prices, important all the way down the line from cars and TV sets to groceries. Since the ghetto dwellers are largely a low-income population, their desire for expensive goods—supported by TV and radio commercials, but also by the general affluence of the society surrounding them—creates a demand for credit, and the businesses catering specifically to a ghetto public thus specialize in instalment-plan sales. These often make items more expensive than they would ordinarily be. Quite often high-pressure sales tactics are used, and advertising and information about sales conditions—on black radio stations and elsewhere—are frequently incomplete and misleading, so that the customers in due time find out that they will have to pay much more than they originally thought. Of course, few ghetto dwellers are so aware of the technicalities of instalment buying that they can protect themselves fully against unpleasant surprises. Thus they have personal or vicarious experiences of how they or friends or neighbors have been pursued by creditors or their agents, claiming debts which the dwellers feel are morally non-existent. And such questionable debts are incurred not only by those in the community who are least well off but also by mainstreamers with steady and reasonably satisfactory incomes whose wishes for a comfortable and respectable life may lead them, for example, to acquire expensive furniture from one of the stores advertising their credit plans on ghetto radio.

Whether he knew what he was doing or not when he entered into debt, there are times when the ghetto dweller simply cannot make the payment which is due. The creditor may then have the debt attached through a routine court action to the debtor's salary, so that the latter's income is channeled straight to the creditor. This, of course, can cause great hardship on a poverty-stricken ghetto dweller, and it can also poison his relationship to his employer. When this method of claiming debts cannot be used or for some other reason is not used, the merchandise in question may be reclaimed—and whether or not this is done in a justifiable manner, it is not likely to enhance the ghetto dweller's love for the merchants in his community. Freddy, living with his girl friend in a basement apartment, only had occasional income of his own but wanted the signs of success in street life. He made the down payment on an old Ford Thunderbird, and he and a friend of his spent days going over its engine, painting over its scratches, and cleaning it thoroughly—all a labor of love. At this time he was doing a little business in bootlegging, and as the time approached for the next instalment on the car, his apartment was raided by detectives. He was fined heavily, could not pay the car dealer, and lost the Thunderbird which was his pride. Rather understandably, he turned a little bitter. A girl swinger had a coat laid away for her in a store and had made a sizeable part of the payment as she lost her job and could not pay any more. She did not get the coat, nor was she given her money back, and she was not allowed to take something else and cheaper for what she had already paid. While she was sure the store had maltreated her, she felt she could do nothing about it.

The feeling that unfair business practices are involved is also directed toward the supermarkets and streetcorner stores catering to the ghetto dwellers' daily shopping needs. The opinion is widespread that chain stores charge more for an item in a ghetto branch than they do in more affluent areas, and that the food stuffs on sale in the ghetto are often of inferior quality. When it was reported that at least one supermarket chain hiked its prices on those days when welfare payments were made, this seemed rather generally accepted as the truth by people in the Winston Street neighborhood, although business officials denied it. One community organization posted pickets outside the stores involved, but business continued much as usual. One man had this to say:

> Sure I can stop buying my groceries in those stores. But you know, then I have to buy everything from the old man up here at the corner, and he'll charge me even more. So I'll just have to go to the one who cheats me less.

It is undoubtedly true that it is generally more expensive to shop at the streetcorner groceries. It is not very difficult to give a couple of acceptable partial reasons why this is so: the small shopkeepers must make up for their limited turnover, and the small scale of their businesses also makes it difficult for them to stock up in an economical way. Yet it is not difficult for a ghetto dweller to believe that the streetcorner grocer is simply charging as much as he can possibly get away with.

The quality of the interaction between businessmen and ghetto dwellers is also often tense in a more personal way. Probably this is partially due to simple racial prejudice on the part of the white merchants; at least many ghetto dwellers complain about unjustified rudeness on the part of store owners. However, when shopkeepers appear to behave unnecessarily brusquely they may also be influenced by their fear of pilfering and even robbery which they understand to be common problems of ghetto business. This is certainly particularly likely to hit those customers whose outward appearance is not altogether "respectable": children, teenagers, or streetcorner men. But even if there is some basis for this fear it will anger a great many innocent people who find yet another reason to dislike white businessmen. This is evident as streetcorner men try to convince each other to make the visit to the liquor store with their collected funds; several of them hesitate to go because they "don't like the man in there." And when they send a child on an errand to the grocery store although they are idle themselves, one may also suspect that they want to avoid a confrontation with a disliked shopkeeper.

With the businessmen, the police are the representatives of the wider society who are most strongly in evidence on ghetto streets. According to the President's Commission on Crime in the District of Columbia (1966:165), Washington's police force is about four-fifths white, despite the large black majority in the city. Thus most of the policemen patrolling the ghetto are also white. The relationship of the people of the ghetto to these policemen is markedly ambivalent and often tinged with more hostility than respect. True, as ghetto dwellers sometimes point out, "You got to say this about them, they got a job to do." As we have noted before, the people of the ghetto feel that theirs is a dangerous environment; they are almost constantly conscious of the potential of trouble. For this reason they are highly aware of the need for law enforcement, and they have nobody but the police to turn to. If there is a violent fight in the house next door some ghetto dwellers will indeed call the police, and occasionally a streetcorner man may report an enemy just to settle a score. Thus there is no consistent policy of non-cooperation. But one of the complaints ghetto dwellers have against the police is that to a great extent it fails to protect them against the violence of the urban jungle. This laxity, they feel, is itself evidence of racial discrimination:

> The police say, "Let the niggers cut each other up." They don't care as long as it is not in a white neighborhood. They're just watching out for the stores.

However, the kinds of actions the police do take is probably more important in causing ghetto resentment than what they do not do. Teenagers and streetcorner men feel they are being harassed quite unnecessarily in their everyday lives at the hangouts. As we have seen, for instance, public drinking and drunkenness are among the offenses for which most arrests are made. The men who are drinking at the corner or in the back alley are constantly on guard against policemen and patrol cars; since they consider their drinking quite harmless to everybody else, they do not consider it any business of the police. It may indeed be impossible for them to find more privacy for their sociability than they do at their hangouts in public places; wives, mothers, sisters, or landladies may object to their getting together at home, and it is too expensive to drink at bars all the time. In fact, some policemen look the other way most of the time to avoid unnecessary arrests in such cases, but others seem to want to enforce the law to the letter, and the outcome is a feeling that the policemen act quite arbitrarily.

There are certainly a great many ghetto dwellers who take a much dimmer view of public drinking and drunkenness than these men do, and who would not mind if the police could actually enforce the law even more firmly in this field. Even so, they may concur in seeing the police as a source of trouble in their lives. A great many men can recall being arrested some time in their lives—if not recently, then quite often when they were young. In many of these cases they still consider the arrest to have been unjustified, and whether they do or not, they may reminisce about harsh treatment. One middle-aged man recounted a recent experience of his as follows:

> I just got out of bed and had breakfast, and then I stood here on the stairs and thought about what I should do next, you know, and I had just decided to go over across the street and see some buddies when this police car came up, and the policemen called me. "Hey boy," he said.

So I said, "Yeah." And then he said, "Get into the car." "What for?" I said. "Just get into the car." And then when we got down to the precinct I was booked as a drunk. So I said, "Shi-it, I'm no more drunk than you are." So they had to let me go, and I said I'd bring charges against them. Yeah, I really think I should, you know, but I won't, 'cause, see, if I do that he'll be bugging me every time he sees me, and charging me with one thing or another, and I don't want none of that. Would have been another thing if I had lived in another precinct.

Another man complaining about his lack of exercise, said that he really should take to running around a few blocks each morning.

But I can't, 'cause if I do that I'll probably get busted. The police won't believe that you're up to any good if they see you running, see.

Only slightly later, it did indeed happen that a man was arrested while running toward the hospital where his mother lay dying.

Some such actions on the part of the police may well be simple harassment. The use of disliked epithets—"boy," "nigger," and so forth —shows that many policemen do not bother to hide their prejudice, and some excessive use of force cannot be understood as anything but police brutality. However, it seems that the police may also behave in ways unacceptable to the ghetto dwellers—or any public—because of the understandings they have of what the ghetto situation calls for from them as professionals. To the police the ghetto is a high-crime district where the dangers of police work are great and where the public is generally suspect. Any strange behavior—and what is "strange" to an outsider like a policeman need not at all be so to someone with a greater knowledge of the community—should be investigated, and if an infraction against the law has occurred, anybody who happens to be seen close to the scene of the crime soon afterwards is liable to be treated as a suspect, especially if he is young or if he does not look quite "respectable." Since a person who gets arrested in a high-crime community is thought to be potentially dangerous—he may resist arrest or even carry a weapon—the policeman may anxiously show a little extra strength just in case it should be necessary. With such rather primitive and categorical notions of how to treat ghetto dwellers, the policemen are apt to make arrests which should never have been made and to leave themselves yet more open to allegations of racism and police brutality. And since their actions may hit any member of the ghetto community, even its most law-abiding people may come to resent the police, not only for what they fail to do but also what they do. One is not always ready to give the police the benefit of a doubt; the following notes from a street incident in the Winston Street neighborhood show how quickly the tensions between police and ghetto dwellers may escalate.

It was a rather cold Friday night in November, about 8 p.m. I was talking with Carl, George, Sonny, and Lee, one of the mainstreamer men in the neighborhood, outside Rubin's grocery. Outside the carry-out across the intersection a group of teenagers were talking and laughing loudly, with a couple of them engaging in a boxing bout. Two policemen walked up to the police telephone at the corner with a young man under arrest— apparently for drunkenness, as he had some difficulty walking. Another policeman came just after them. They called the precinct station for a car, then started searching the arrestee. To the bystanders they seemed to shake him with more force than necessary; he reacted with a jerk and shouted, "Leave me alone, mother-fucker." They found no weapon on him and continued to hold him in a firm grip. More people were coming by, and many of them stopped to watch. Before the police car arrived, there were people watching from each corner of the intersection. The teenagers outside the carry-out were shouting insults at the police; a number of friends of the arrestee arrived in cars, and some got out. "We'll make sure they don't do nothing to you," one of them said. The people in my group began speculating whether this was the start of a major clash. They felt the policemen would not dare beat the man while everybody was watching but that he would probably be brutalized in the car on the way to the precinct station, then sentenced for "resisting arrest" which would serve to explain any marks on him. A couple of teen-agers were threatening the policemen as daringly as was possible without yet coming to blows. Lee went over to them and said that policemen are dangerous and do not know what they are doing, so they had better not provoke them. Finally, after one of the policemen had made a new hurried call to the station, a patrol car came to take two of them and the arrestee to the station. Immediately afterwards, three police buses rushed in with lights flashing, coming to a halt at the intersection where each parked at a different corner. A number of policemen jumped out and shouted to people to leave, so as not to "hinder traffic on the sidewalks." Faced with this massive show of concern with the problems of pedes-trians, everyone left.

This was obviously a routine arrest. It just so happened, however, that there were unusually many people outside for a late fall evening, and the policemen and the arrestee were highly visible to them for a rather long time. Both the policemen and the spectators seemed to overreact to each other. The ghetto people were quickly ready to interpret what they saw in terms of police brutality; the policemen feared a riot and brought in a force which may have stopped any further escalation but which to the ghetto dwellers constituted strong evidence that the police saw them all as an enemy. Thus a minor event became a basis for symmetrically schismogenetic interaction between the police and the ghetto as they progressively strengthened their showing and understanding of animosity. As the spectators walked off from the scene they were talking about what might be happening at the precinct station; it was generally held that the police have turned to beating prisoners over their heads through telephone books. It is said to hurt just as badly but to leave no marks.

As the ghetto dwellers experience the behavior of white businessmen and policemen and work out interpretations of it together, they arrive at a collective definition of their grievances. They chuckle as they see a good friend and neighbor leave by the back door as the bill collector enters through the front door. They find themselves under constant surveillance from slow-moving patrol cars and feel they know what the policemen inside are thinking about them. They note that the "fresh greens" at the grocery look like they have been around for some time, and that the children they send to the store on an errand often seem to get too little change in return. And they know of instances when policemen "accidentally" shot those suspected of only minor offenses— something they can only see as gross disregard for black lives. Of course, a great deal of the interaction between the ghetto dwellers and these white outsiders in their territory flows quite smoothly. Quite possibly, too, the outsiders may be able to explain satisfactorily some of that behavior of theirs which from the ghetto dwellers' point of view is only evil. But what matters is that the people of the ghetto do in fact accumulate and share among themselves so much evidence of injuries to their interests and honor, and that they find little or no reason not to see the merchants as exploiters and the police as oppressors. Thus there is a withdrawal of legitimacy from these as community institutions; for they seem to be working against the community rather than for it. With the ghetto dwellers continuously strengthening this interpretation with new data, the foundations for rebellion against these outside powers exist long before the eruption comes.

## THE TRADITION OF BEING OPPRESSED

One should not, however, understand the ghetto view of the police and the ghetto merchants only in terms of their own ability to cause resentment. They have the additional burden of being the most accessible representatives of the white world as a whole, a world by which black people have a tradition of being exploited and oppressed. It is indeed a tradition; to many ghetto dwellers the relationship to whites does not seem to have changed much in recent times, and the white problem is still defined in terms reminiscent of the racist politics of the Deep South. The typical black-and-white joke at the Howard Theatre is still about the Ku Klux Klan. Whether or not the understanding of white people's racial attitudes which this reflects remains correct today, the institutionalized segregation of ghetto dwellers prevents many of them from finding out much about the current state of white opinion at first hand. Just as black people are taught about the meaning of blackness by other blacks, they learn about white people and race relations within the ghetto community rather than in face-to-face contacts with whites. White people are being typed by black people, as "crackers," "grays," "Whitey," "Mr. Charlie," "ofays," "PWT" (poor white trash), "honkies," or "blue-eyed blond devils" (a Muslim term), just as white people among themselves are typing black people. In both cases the vocabulary becomes a cultural storehouse for hostility, a part of the community's own information about its external affairs which is seldom contradicted by other sources. Perhaps the white suburbs do not all share the views of the Klan, but the unemployed streetcorner man who hardly knows any white people personally does not necessarily know. As far as he is concerned, the machinery of the society may still seem like a Klan device to keep him down, and it is not impossible to fit ghetto merchants, the police, and many fleeting contacts with other whites into such an interpretation. In his state of isolation from mainstream society, a ghetto dweller may well view institutionalized segregation as a direct expression of average white personal prejudice. Whether he is correct in this or not, the impact of this is such that he will take any not obviously prejudiced white person with whom he comes in contact to be an exception to the rule. There are shopkeepers in the ghetto who can hardly be said to be "liberals on the race question" but are yet hailed by neighborhood people as "good white people," and the moderator of one TV talk show whom a fair number of white people would certainly consider strongly conservative was believed by many Winston Street people to be a "typical white liberal."

   The ghetto community can thus keep alive its traditional representation of the relationship between white and black America without being confronted with much contrary evidence. To the notion of racism as a dominant force in the wider society is added that of racketeering—this understanding is probably a Northern ghetto innovation. Many ghetto men hint in conversations to "the Syndicate" as one of the great powers in society, if not even the greatest. Some of the facts of ghetto life which cannot be easily explained in terms of racism may be blamed on large-scale white racketeering, with influences extending into government—"the Syndicate" is said to have its own congressmen. One former alcoholic threw light on his conception of the power of racketeers in this statement:

> I'd rather smoke pot than be a juicehead, you know, you can stay cool, you don't piss in your clothes, you don't get into fights with your friends, and you can have some whenever you want it and you can afford it. Look, it's these ordinary cigarettes that give you cancer and you get addicted to, and they're legal, but pot which only makes you feel good is outlawed. You know why? Because if pot was legal, all those racketeers couldn't make so much money—that's why they keep pot illegal.

Most of the talk about these racketeers is independent of most ghetto dwellers' personal experiences, and their ideas about big crime are very hazy. If the imagery about "the Syndicate" is not entirely without foundation, it certainly seems rather exaggerated. Even so, it must be taken into account as a part of many ghetto dwellers' model of black-white relations. The power imputed to racketeers constitutes a further reason for the ghetto dwellers to deny the morality of white dominance in their community.

## THE YOUNG AND THE OLD

If there is continuity in the tradition of oppression, its impact on the oppressed may yet be changing. There is a growing feeling that white dominance need not be accepted. A strong generational cleavage is noticeable at this point, for the younger people are clearly much more militant than the older. In the Winston Street neighborhood this shows up in how people regard the idea of black power. Hardly anyone feels that more power for black people to manage their own affairs would be a bad thing, but particularly the middle-aged and the elderly are worried that any kind of action against white dominance would hurt nobody more than it would hurt the ghetto dwellers themselves. They feel that "black power" may be taken as a licence for unruly teenagers to go around knocking down people, black and white, thus starting a white avalanche which would come to destroy ghetto lives and homes. That is, the older people still believe much more in white power than in black, and they feel that the less noise they make about the latter, the less risk is there that the former will engage in retaliation. When a well-known spokesman of a black power organization paid a visit to the neighborhood some of these older people were afraid that he would start trouble there. Afterwards they expressed their support of a bootlegger's wife who went out into the street to tell him in no uncertain terms that although she surely had no more love for white people than he did, she wanted him out of there. It may be, of course, that her action was partially motivated by her particular concern for the family business which could be harmed if police attention were drawn to the neighborhood; this was the view of some of her more cynical young neighbors.

Among the younger people, on the other hand, many more are willing to listen to the black power message and acknowledge that "it makes a lot of sense." Many of them know little or nothing about the older civil rights organizations; they are familiar with the Nation of Islam (the "Black Muslims") with which some of the streetcorner men in the neighborhood sympathize, but they are rather skeptical of it. The Muslim ideology seems notoriously unhip with its bans on pork, liquor, tobacco, dancing, flirtation, and so forth, and there is a feeling that the Muslims who were once in the front line of militant protest are accommodating themselves to co-existence with white power, despite their continuing rhetoric. Besides, Elijah Muhammad gets his share of the suspicion that religious leaders are con-men. Thus for the younger generation at least, black power seems more in line with their own thinking. Although they usually continue to stay away from organized political participation, they can accept it as a rallying concept; this does not necessarily mean that they are aware of all its implications. But the black power movement gives some coherence to their own notions of what is wrong with the ghetto condition, and particularly to the discontent with white power. In so doing, it serves as a catalyst for ghetto change.

While the older people are concerned with the rebelliousness of the younger men and women, the latter feel that the preceding generations have too often been "conned by the white man" into a complacency which has taken them nowhere. The middle-aged and the elderly have been "Uncle Toms," "handkerchief heads." If there is some truth to this, there may be a good reason for it in that the generations have to a great extent lived their lives under different circumstances. More of the older people are still to a great extent black Southerners. They have had their own experiences of being under constant white scrutiny in a much more personal way than is possible in the large Northern ghetto. What this meant not too long ago was made clear by John Dollard in *Caste and Class in a Southern Town* (1937); for instance, it was possible to punish by whipping those black persons who had been found to subscribe to Northern Negro newspapers. Perhaps the older ghetto generation of migrants are still more prone to "watch their steps" as they begin new lives in the North. One of the streetcorner men at Winston Street clearly had this opinion about his neighbors:

> Those people around here ain't gonna do nothing they'd think a cracker wouldn't like. They're all from the Carolinas, you know—North Carolina and South Carolina. They just say "Yes sir," "no sir." They gonna shuffle forever.

The younger people "ain't gonna shuffle no more." In fact, it is questionable whether they, as born ghetto dwellers, ever had reason to shuffle very much. Harsh as the circumstances of life may be in the ghetto, black-white relationships in the North are seldom so close that the white party needs constantly to reassert its dominance, and the anonymity of the large ghetto also provides greater personal freedom for black people. It is, at least, a freedom to be relatively more militant in one's views and to be more daring in one's behavior.

## THE LACK OF POLITICS

As we have noted, grievances were strongly felt and openly articulated in the Washington ghetto before the April rising. Yet most ghetto dwellers took no part in those organized political expressions which occurred. Civil rights groups and others carried on their work but seemed to draw little interest from most people in the community who agreed with what the groups did but paid little or no attention to them. The black power groups were to some extent an exception, both because they made some attempts to take their message to the streets and because mass media took a noticeable interest in them. Generally, however, there was no concerted political activity. Many people, of course, still felt it could be dangerous. They continued to look to the South for examples and had no trouble finding them. The weekend before Martin Luther King was killed a few men at a Winston Street corner were telling about the Poor People's March he was planning for Washington, D.C.; King had just participated in a march in Memphis in connection with the sanitation workers' strike, and the march had broken up in disorder. Reinhardt Ross, one of the men, was skeptical of marching:

> They don't get me to walk in one of those marches and get my head busted. So where was King when all those people were beaten up by the police? On his way to the airport! You see? On his way to the airport! That's what happens every time with those protests, the leaders run off and the people who have been dumb enough to follow them get busted. No, he ain't gonna have no march here, King ain't gonna have no march here.

More often, however, the organized political activities were simply not of a kind which most ghetto dwellers would regard as any of their business, such as public meetings. When asked if they planned to go to some meeting coming up, most people in the Winston Street neighborhood were obviously surprised at the idea, and in this they seemed to represent well the ghetto as a whole. Attendance at public meetings tended to confirm the ghetto dwellers' lack of concern with this kind of organized activity. In the fall of 1966, when the black power concept was fairly new and widely debated, in the ghetto as well as outside, the local branch of the NAACP held a public meeting to discuss it. The meeting was held at the YMCA in the middle of the ghetto and included the local SNCC representative as a main speaker, but although the meeting was well advertised, few other than the predominantly middle-class, outer-city NAACP supporters showed up. More people came to a meeting on police brutality, called by all the better-known militant black groups and personalities, centrally located in a black church and again widely publicized. The ghetto population was also clearly better represented; plainclothes policemen in the audience were pointed out and asked to leave. Yet considering the size of the Washington ghetto, attendance was still small. At neither of these two meetings was anybody from the Winston Street neighborhood present. A third meeting was held by a civic group in order to discuss urban renewal plans for a large area including Winston Street. It was advertised through leaflets distributed to all households in the area, but only one resident of the Winston Street neighborhood attended, a preacher from a storefront church who took a greater than ordinary interest in community affairs.

Another test case for ghetto activism was a plan for a May Day boycott of public schools, to protest against conditions in ghetto schools and against the reappointment of an unpopular school superintendent. This boycott was largely a failure. Few children, on Winston Street or elsewhere in the community, stayed home. In this case, however, black groups were not united behind the boycott.

Although school conditions were not talked about a great deal in everyday ghetto conversations, at least in the Winston Street neighborhood, black power and police injustice certainly were recurrent topics, and neighborhood renewal was certainly a matter of concern. The very limited number of people who went to meetings such as these seems to show, then, that organized political activity did not reach the majority of ghetto dwellers. Although groups and meetings were involved in articulating ghetto grievances, their work had very little noticeable impact on the everyday lives of the majority of ghetto dwellers. Successes which could dramatize their activity were largely lacking. Meanwhile, other ghettos showed a radical way out of muteness.

## THE STATE OF READINESS

It did not escape the ghetto dwellers of Washington that the characteristics of other Northern ghettos were similar to those of their own community, and as Watts, Detroit and others burned, this was easily seen as a forecast for Washington. The mass media certainly strengthened this view as they detailed the conditions likely to lead to an eruption and spoke grimly of long hot summers to come. Over the afternoon paper Bee Jay could comment that if there were a rising in Washington it would be really bad; he thought there were firearms in practically every house. (This was probably greatly exaggerated.) But he would go along with it, for he would always be with his people. His friend disagreed. They could not win, and there was too much to lose. "If anything happens here I'll go and hide in the basement till it's over," he said. But although opinions were divided about what to do in case of an eruption, few doubted that there might be one coming. Now and then as someone felt poorly treated by a ghetto business, he could mutter that "a place like that ought to be burned to the ground." Mass media showed quite clearly what goes on in a rising, and further information was supplied by friends who came to visit from cities where rising had already occurred—or who were visited there by Washingtonians. While some of this evidence was clearly unfavorable, there were visitors who evinced enthusiasm about their own rebellions. Sonny ran into an old musician acquaintance who had just returned to

Washington from Detroit and who told him the ghettos of the two cities were a lot alike; "you ought to do it here, too." And at the meeting against police brutality mentioned above, a young man stood up to say that he had recently arrived from Watts—"the brothers back there wonder what's going on in Washington, if you're all a bunch of Toms or something." Obviously visitors such as these gave risings a political interpretation. These were rebellions, acts of black self-assertion—not just riots, outbreaks of selfish plundering, lawnessness, and irrational violence. Although the terminology varied, the general idea was clear. It was obviously one which many ghetto dwellers could develop on their own; but if they were so inclined, ideological support from experienced outsiders would do nothing to diminish their readiness for rebellion.

The Washington ghetto dwellers did not only take note of turmoil at a distance. There were also a number of incidents involving their own community. During the 1966 Easter holidays there was a disturbance caused by black teenagers in an amusement park outside the city; reportedly those in the Winston Street neighborhood knew of it in advance. In late summer that year there was a considerable rise of tension and some violence between the police and the inhabitants of a distant ghetto area in Southeast Washington. For some time afterwards Washington newspapers focused their attention on the "breakdown of law and order" in this area, particularly on the problems of shop-keepers. Ghetto dwellers in other areas also acknowledged that there was "a lot of trouble" going on there. The next major period of crisis came the following summer. As the risings of Newark and Detroit had followed closely on each other many asked the question whether Washington was next in line. Some younger men in the Winston Street neighborhood alleged that there were newcomers to the city who were propagating the opinion that a rising would be a good thing; with the high death figures in Detroit and Newark in mind, they were themselves among those who were worried by the prospect of a repetition in their city. Therefore they very consistently argued strongly against a rising when conversations turned to this topic. During this period a number of rumors about agitators and incidents were flying and given varying credence. One very real incident occurred in the North-western corner of the ghetto where a young man left in charge of a delicatessen shot two youths who were allegedly trying to rob the store. Other young men in the area reputedly felt that there was something odd about the circumstances of the shooting. For some time people in this neighborhood were brooding over what had occurred, and at one point an angry crowd assembled close to the store. Apparently it was dissolved by a leader of a local civil rights group who dissuaded the people present from taking violent action. The situation was generally understood as one which could have been the starting point of general turmoil.

There came an outburst of looting and burning a rainy summer night, largely concentrated to the lower ghetto end of Seventh Street in the Northwest section of the city where there were a number of used furniture stores. Comparatively few stores were damaged, however, and there were not many arrests. Compared to what people expected could have happened, this was only a minor outbreak involving mainly a rather small number of teenage boys—it was generally believed that the rain had contributed strongly in keeping people off the streets. Those in the Winston Street neighborhood who had feared a large-scale rebellion with police and military reprisals on the model of Newark and Detroit seemed almost relieved. Many saw only a temporary respite, however; this was certainly not the expression of pent-up feelings which they thought would be as natural in Washington as it had been elsewhere. One swinger with a far-ranging network who usually appeared to have a good idea of what was going on in the community had this to say:

> I think maybe that's it for this summer, but a lot of people I know would be in that kind of thing didn't even hear about this one till it was over. The rain did a lot, you know. And then a lot of people are a little scared right now, with all those people who got killed in Newark and Detroit, and they might be ready again when they've forgot about that. Next year they could start all over again.

In late October there was a tumultuous ending to a rock-and-roll show at the Washington Coliseum which was crowded to more than capacity with an audience of 6,000 to 8,000 people, most of them young; there was a noticeable amount of gatecrashing. It was an attractive bill including the popular duo Peaches and Herb and the comedian Clay Tyson as emcee; the stars of the show and thus last to appear were the Temptations, one of the leading Motown groups. Since there had been few major musical events in the community this fall even the Coliseum which usually has many empty seats was not large enough. People were standing in the aisles, and anybody who left his seat during the show—and there are always people moving around—could not be sure to get it back. Thus there was considerable commotion throughout the show. Finally, soon after the Temptations came on stage, a crowd surged forward toward it, dancing, walking, and pushing. This is not unusual at such shows, although it is discouraged by the management. In this case, however, the people who were moving ahead pushed one of the special policemen guarding the stage area to the ground. He apparently panicked as he felt he might get trampled to death; thus he reached for his gun and fired in the air. With the kind of expectation of violence prevalent among ghetto dwellers, this started a panic. People in the hall cried in alarm, one young woman could be heard shouting, "They're shooting! No, No!" and while many fled, others joined those pushing toward the stage which was quickly vacated by the Temptations. Several people were hurt in the throng. Rufus "Catfish" Mayfield, the well-known leader of a recently formed ghetto work corps, went on stage to ask people to return to order but was greeted with hostility or indifference. Chairs and other objects were flying as it was announced that the show would not be resumed. In the next hours there was rock throwing, window breaking, and looting in the area around the Coliseum; a few policemen were injured but not many arrests were made.

The years and months preceding the insurrection of April were thus far from uneventful to the ghetto dwellers. Again and again they were reminded of the possibility of violent conflict. Apart from the incidents which became more generally known there were such neighborhood happenings as the Friday night streetcorner arrest described earlier in this chapter. If the quick response of part fear, part violence by the Coliseum audience at the Temptations show gave a glimpse of how ready many ghetto dwellers were to see danger and violence in a situation, such an incident as this fall evening arrest showed the ghetto dwellers that the police were thinking in similar terms. As the next spring approached, it was a very obvious question whether there was another long, hot, violent ghetto summer beyond it.

## THE INSURRECTION

Like most people those in the Winston Street neighborhood were used to thinking of ghetto rising as phenomena of the summer; the street scene is more lively then, so escalation comes quicker, and the summer unemployment of high school students may add to the unrest. Among young people with a higher degree of political awareness it was pointed out now and then that turmoil could very well occur any time of the year, but as April came there was no widespread expectation that anything would happen very soon. One of the first evenings of the month there was an incident at a drug store at the always restless corner of Fourteenth and U Street, but it was reportedly calmed through the intervention of black power militants. Only two days later Martin Luther King was assassinated in Memphis, and the same street corner was soon again in the midst of the action.

As the news of the Memphis shooting—and somewhat later, of King's death—came over radio and television, neighbors on Winston Street quickly told each other about it, and many of those who had telephones called friends and relatives to see if they had heard about it. They speculated about what might happen. As the black radio stations turned to religious music the disc jockeys counseled their listeners to be calm. On WOL Nighthawk asked everybody to stay off the streets; King would not have wanted anybody to take to arms. But it could hardly be avoided that crowds formed to vent their united anger. Apparently there were more of them at the corner of Fourteenth and U Streets than anywhere else. As Stokely Carmichael appeared from the SNCC office on Fourteenth Street just north of the corner, a crowd gathered around him. He went around to those businesses which were still open, asking them to close in honor of Dr. King, and they did so. In a couple of instances he advised those around him against violence, pointing to the overwhelming power of the adversary. Yet he could not contain the anger of the people on the streets whose number grew as the news of the assassination spread. Store windows started breaking and looting followed. After a while Carmichael gave up his attempt to keep the protest orderly and left the area. While he may have influenced the ghetto's contemporary ideology of discontent, he had little power over its ultimate expression. One young man who had been out on the streets this night commented a few days later:

> You know, this thing had been building up for a long time, and so when something like this happens you can't just say, "Hey, cool it, it's dangerous." People felt they just got to do something, you know, and I guess most people don't believe too much in marching and that kind of stuff any more.

There were few policemen in the area as looting began, and the looters apparently did not feel very constrained by their presence. (According to one report, the police were told when crowds started to assemble that a conspicuous presence on their part could only exacerbate feelings.) Soon there were also attacks on stores on other main business streets in the ghetto. According to eye witnesses euphoria was added to anger as people felt they were finally striking back. When more police arrived on the scene bottles, bricks, and other objects were thrown at them; they were still too few to confront the larger groups involved in ransacking the stores, but a heavy rain began to fall during which the number of people on the streets decreased. However, looting did not stop. One young man on upper Fourteenth Street apparently shouted a few words out of a popular James Brown hit: "We all get together, in any kind of weather . . ." Fires began to burn along the street, but with fewer people around, the police were slowly regaining control, partly with the use of teargas. Toward the early morning hours the community seemed largely quiet again.

This was Thursday night. On Friday morning people on Winston Street were debating what would happen that evening; ghetto streets are always lively on weekend nights, with more people than usual moving about, and people were still angry. "This ain't over yet," one of the mainstreamer men said. "It could go on a couple of more days."

He was quite right; already that morning people were throwing bricks at cars passing through the ghetto, and looting and burning began again. Some groups went downtown but looting there was rather limited—as we have noted once before, it was particularly men's fashion stores that were hit—and there was hardly any burning outside the ghetto, where most of it continued to be concentrated on the main shopping streets. Some groups seemed to concentrate on going around "opening up" stores which had closed early—that is, they broke doors and windows to leave the way in open to looters. This made it possible for a great many to join in who had qualms about taking the first step themselves. One young mother said afterwards:

> Well, you could see all the stuff lying there and all those people going in and out, and somebody was gonna take it, so I thought I could as well get some for myself.

Of course, a great many ghetto dwellers took no part in the looting. There were those who felt it safest to stay home, perhaps following what was happening on radio and television. One young man on Winston Street accounted for his weekend this way:

> I got myself a bottle of gin on Friday morning when the stores were still open, and then when I came home and saw all those people running around I just sat down and switched on the television. And that's what

I did all the time, drinking and watching those crazy people taking care of business.

Some older people disapproved more directly of what was going on, seeing it not as a rising but as theft and destruction. This was the view a middle-aged woman expressed a few days later:

> I was really sorry to see it. Some of the people I saw should have a lot better sense. They was just stealing, that's what I think. Some of the people in them stores hadn't done nothing wrong.

As far as most of the people on the streets were concerned, however, they did not appear to think that they were doing anything immoral; rather, they were affirming an emergent community morality. It was as if goods hoarded by somebody who had no right to it were suddenly released for general consumption. Although profits were derived from looting, it could be easily understood as a political act against white oppression and exploitation. At the very least, there was little question of "theft" on the part of any individual participant, as previous ownership became simply irrelevant when the stores came temporarily under generous community control. Furthermore, the burning which often followed on looting was obviously to be seen within the framework of black-white conflict; nobody could profit directly from throwing Molotov cocktails. Even more important, the participants abided quite strictly by their definition of the ghetto moral community and generally did not harm businesses with "soul brother" or "soul sister" signs. (There were at least one "sole brother" and one "sold brother" sign— ghetto-specific culture is largely non-literate.) Any harm to ghetto dwellers' lives and properties was thus unintentional; yet it was rather extensive, as fires spread to black-owned businesses as well as to the apartments where ghetto dwellers lived above white business establishments. To the residents on the large business streets, then, the fire-bombing was a great danger. Fats, who had recently moved from Winston Street to a building just off Fourteenth Street where the fires were heaviest, said afterwards that if he had seen anybody trying to set fire to his building he would have shot him.

During much of the Friday the police were alone in trying to halt the rising. However, they were much too few to do so successfully. Their presence in small numbers had little effect, as their authority was not recognized. There were acts of hostility against them as well as against firemen; however, they were under orders to use their weapons only with the greatest restraint, so direct violence between ghetto dwellers and police was limited. Very few sniping incidents were reported; afterwards there were many comments to the effect that ghetto dwellers could well have responded in kind had the police started shooting. As it was, the police often seemed simply irrelevant as the looting and burning continued.

Those who went on radio and television to ask people to leave the streets did not seem to have a great influence either. On Saturday, as the rising was drawing toward an end, they were joined by "soul brother number one," James Brown; this must have been one of the few times when many young ghetto dwellers reacted to him only with derision. Otherwise the black radio stations had a very restrained coverage of what was going on in the city, as it had been claimed that the news media had helped intensify earlier risings through their reporting. One station returned repeatedly to a gospel hit by the Violinaires, "I don't know what this world is coming to," with this bewildered beginning:

> Demonstration and protest
> putting brother 'gainst brother
> juvenile delinquency
> putting child against mother

While this responded to the sentiments of some ghetto dwellers, others found it simply ridiculous.

In the Winston Street neighborhood, a few blocks away from ghetto business centers, there was no burning, but some of the businesses at neighborhood street corners were raided. Liquor stores were particularly heavily hurt as people swarmed in and around them on Friday afternoon. However, those neighborhood people who took part in the looting did so mainly on the principal shopping streets. Most of them were swingers and teenagers, but there were also streetcorner men and younger children.

## AFTER THE TURMOIL

On Friday evening the National Guard and federal troops were called into action in Washington, and through their massive presence, rather than through much use of force, they put an end to the rising. During Saturday looting and burning gradually ceased. Soldiers were standing guard outside the stores that were left, but along long stretches of the main business streets only ruins remained. While white radio stations reported that the soldiers' guns were unloaded, black radio stations said nothing about this. In the Winston Street neighborhood small boys who had been to see the military encampment at a nearby school were practicing marching, while adults stood in small groups gossiping and joking about the last few days' events. On Sunday things were returning to normal. People hurried to do their shopping at those chain stores which were still in existence and which opened for a little while to meet the needs of those customers who had not been able to do any shopping in the past days. Some neighborhood people went over to the large shopping streets to see what they looked like; there they could mix with sightseeing white suburbanites whose movie cameras, steadily aimed at the ruins, were spinning out of the windows of slow-moving cars.

First people wondered what would happen on Tuesday when Martin Luther King was buried in Atlanta; then the question arose if something might not happen again the following weekend, which was Easter holiday. Fires were set to several ghetto business establishments in the days which followed, and acute tenseness remained for some time as many were not yet convinced that the turmoil was over. There was a good laugh as somebody appeared in a new outfit he had not had before the rising, and one could hear of exchanges as well as goods for sale—some had gotten the wrong size, and there were obviously those who had taken booty not only for their own consumption. In the Winston Street neighborhood there appeared to be rather few who strongly resented the rising. Nobody there had been greatly harmed by it, while those ghetto dwellers who had lost homes, belongings, and jobs may well have had another opinion. Fats, coming back to see his friends from his new home, complained that there was nowhere to go shopping in the area of upper Fourteenth Street, but even so he was only rather slightly inconvenienced. Even those, particularly among the mainstreamers, who did not approve of what had happened were usually ready to explain it in terms of ghetto grievances, although some of them then continued to propose rather superficial remedies, such as more youth workers on the recreation department payroll. (However, they thought of this as a black power program.) Others looked at the rising from a more humorous angle—looting was made to resemble trickster behavior, a familiar ghetto theme. The illegality of taking from the oppressor could be recognized, but it was a wickedness it was easy to empathize with. Younger people, in particular, looked at the rising in the most strictly political terms, expressing the hope that "they gotta do something now." Thus for some, participation in the rising, if only a matter of momentary anger at first, or fun and convenience later, may have become an act of political commitment—at least public meetings held in the months after the rising seemed to draw larger audiences than most earlier meetings.

However, what would actually happen continued to be uncertain. It would probably take long before ghetto business streets were rebuilt, and it was very likely that many of the white merchants would not come back even then. A considerable number probably did not want to, and with insurance rates in black ghettos soaring, even more of them could not afford to. Perhaps this could leave niches open for black enterprises, since only their "soul brother" signs seemed to be as valuable as a lot of insurance.

As far as the police is concerned, the other focus of discontent which we discussed above, its relationship to the community continued to deteriorate in the months following the April rising. A number of incidents were quite widely talked about, and black power groups emphasized the demand for some kind of community control of the police. Undoubtedly it would help to have more black policemen, recruited from the ghetto. After all, a policeman's role is to a great extent that of an officer of the peace; if the goal of keeping the peace is best pursued by his staying off the streets, as it seems to have been in many recent critical ghetto situations, he is obviously a failure. Black officers might be better able to calm feelings in the community by virtue of their skill in the interaction idiom of the ghetto dwellers, even if it is true that they are no less harsh than others if violence does erupt. It is also likely that their common-sense knowledge of ghetto life would make them more sure of themselves and thus much less vulnerable to accusations of arbitrariness and brutality. But in the current situation of conflict between the police and the community, it may not be easy to recruit ghetto dwellers to the force, as they could well come to be seen as renegades. Even if it were possible, there could come a reaction on the part of ghetto militants against attempts to manipulate the community by putting a black man on the beat. So perhaps there is no other way of restoring confidence in the police than granting some form of community control.

But after all, if demands for greater black participation in ghetto business and law enforcement were met, the problems of the relationship between the ghetto and mainstream society would still have been dealt with only in a marginal way. The questions of income and employment, for instance, would probably not be greatly influenced. Because they are based within ghetto territory, shopkeepers and policemen are particularly easily touched by ghetto protest, but they are only the most accessible symbols of the whole body of ghetto grievances against the wider society. And, we must conclude, for the wider society to try to deal only with the symbols may be an unrealistic solution, since symbols could possibly be exchanged.

# 18 Internal Colonialism and Ghetto Revolt[1]

*Robert Blauner*

It is becoming almost fashionable to analyze American racial conflict today in terms of the colonial analogy. I shall argue in this paper that the utility of this perspective depends upon a distinction between colonization as a process and colonialism as a social, economic, and political system. It is the experience of colonization that Afro-Americans share with many of the nonwhite people of the world. But this subjugation has taken place in a societal context that differs in important respects from the situation of "classical colonialism." In the body of this essay I shall look at some major developments in Black protest—the urban riots, cultural nationalism, and the movement for ghetto control—as collective responses to colonized status. Viewing our domestic situation as a special form of colonization outside a context of a colonial system will help explain some of the dilemmas and ambiguities within these movements.

The present crisis in American life has brought about changes in social perspectives and the questioning of long accepted frameworks. Intellectuals and social scientists have been forced by the pressure of events to look at old definitions of the character of our society, the role of racism, and the workings of basic institutions. The depth and volatility of contemporary racial conflict challenge sociologists in particular to question the adequacy of theoretical models by which we have explained American race relations in the past.

For a long time the distinctiveness of the Negro situation among the ethnic minorities was placed in terms of color, and the systematic discrimination that follows from our deep-seated racial prejudices. This was sometimes called the caste theory, and while provocative, it missed essential and dynamic features of American race relations. In the past

Reprinted from *Social Problems* XVI, no. 4 (Spring 1969): 393–408. By permission of The Society for the Study of Social Problems and the author.

ten years there has been a tendency to view Afro-Americans as another ethnic group not basically different in experience from previous ethnics and whose "immigration" condition in the North would in time follow their upward course. The inadequacy of this model is now clear—even the Kerner Report devotes a chapter to criticizing this analogy. A more recent (though hardly new) approach views the essence of racial subordination in economic class terms: Black people as an underclass are to a degree specially exploited and to a degree economically dispensable in an automating society. Important as are economic factors, the power of race and racism in America cannot be sufficiently explained through class analysis. Into this theory vacuum steps the model of internal colonialism. Problematic and imprecise as it is, it gives hope of becoming a framework that can integrate the insights of caste and racism, ethnicity, culture, and economic exploitation into an overall conceptual scheme. At the same time, the danger of the colonial model is the imposition of an artificial analogy which might keep us from facing up to the fact (to quote Harold Cruse) that "the American black and white social phenomenon is a uniquely new world thing."[2]

During the late 1950's, identification with African nations and other colonial or formerly colonized peoples grew in importance among Black militants.[3] As a result the U.S. was increasingly seen as a colonial power and the concept of domestic colonialism was introduced into the political analysis and rhetoric of militant nationalists. During the same period Black social theorists began developing this frame of reference for explaining American realities. As early as 1962, Cruse characterized race relations in this country as "domestic colonialism."[4] Three years later in *Dark Ghetto*, Kenneth Clark demonstrated how the political, economic, and social structure of Harlem was essentially that of a colony.[5] Finally in 1967, a full-blown elaboration of "internal colonialism" provided the theoretical framework for Carmichael and Hamilton's widely read *Black Power*.[6] The following year the colonial analogy gained currency and new "respectability" when Senator McCarthy habitually referred to Black Americans as a colonized people during his campaign. While the rhetoric of internal colonialism was catching on, other social scientists began to raise questions about its appropriateness as a scheme of analysis.

The colonial analysis has been rejected as obscurantist and misleading by scholars who point to the significant differences in history and social-political conditions between our domestic patterns and what took place in Africa and India. Colonialism traditionally refers to the establishment of domination over a geographically external political unit, most often inhabited by people of a different race and culture, where this domination is political and economic, and the colony exists subordinated to and dependent upon the mother country. Typically the colonizers exploit the land, the raw materials, the labor, and other resources of the colonized nation; in addition a formal recognition is given to the difference in power, autonomy, and political status, and various agencies are set up to maintain this subordination. Seemingly the analogy must be stretched beyond usefulness if the American version is to be forced into this model. For here we are talking about group relations within a society; the mother country—colony separation in geography is absent. Though whites certainly colonized the territory of the original Americans, internal colonization of Afro-Americans did not involve the settlement of whites in any land that was unequivocably Black. And unlike the colonial situation, there has been no formal recognition of differing power since slavery was abolished outside the South. Classic colonialism involved the control and exploitation of the majority of a nation by a minority of outsiders. Whereas in America the people who are oppressed were themselves originally outsiders and are a numerical minority.

This conventional critique of "internal colonialism" is useful in pointing to the differences between our domestic patterns and the overseas situation. But in its bold attack it tends to lose sight of common experiences that have been historically shared by the most subjugated racial minorities in America and non-white peoples in some other parts of the world. For understanding the most dramatic recent developments on the race scene, this common core element—which I shall call colonization—may be more important than the undeniable divergences between the two contexts.

The common features ultimately relate to the fact that the classical colonialism of the imperialist era and American racism developed out of the same historical situation and reflected a common world economic and power stratification. The slave trade for the most part preceded the imperialist partition and economic exploitation of Africa, and in fact may have been a necessary prerequisite for colonial conquest—since it helped deplete and pacify Africa, undermining the resistance to direct occupation. Slavery contributed one of the basic raw materials for the textile industry which provided much of the capital for the West's industrial development and need for economic expansionism. The essential condition for both American slavery and European colonialism was the power domination and the technological superiority of the Western world in its relation to peoples of non-Western and non-white origins. This objective supremacy in technology and military power buttressed the West's sense of cultural superiority, laying the basis for racist ideologies that were elaborated to justify control and exploitation of non-white people. Thus because classical colonialism and America's internal version developed out of a similar balance of technological, cultural, and power relations, a common *process* of social oppression characterized the racial patterns in the two contexts—despite the variations in political and social structure.

There appear to be four basic components of the colonization complex. The first refers to how the racial group enters into the dominant society (whether colonial power or not). Colonization begins with a forced, involuntary entry. Second, there is an impact on the culture and social organization of the colonized people which is more than just a result of such "natural" processes as contact and acculturation. The colonizing power carries out a policy which constrains, transforms, or destroys indigenous values, orientations, and ways of life. Third, colonization involves a relationship by which members of the colonized group tend to be administered by representatives of the dominant power. There is an experience of being managed and manipulated by outsiders in terms of ethnic status.

A final fundament of colonization is racism. Racism is a principle of social domination by which a group seen as inferior or different in terms of alleged biological characteristics is exploited, controlled, and oppressed socially and psychically by a superordinate group. Except for the marginal case of Japanese imperialism, the major examples of colonialism have involved the subjugation of non-white Asian, African, and Latin American peoples by white European powers. Thus racism has generally accompanied colonialism. Race prejudice can exist without colonization—the experience of Asian-American minorities is a case in point—but racism as a system of domination is part of the complex of colonization.

The concept of colonization stresses the enormous fatefulness of the historical factor, namely the manner in which a minority group becomes a part of the dominant society.[7] The crucial difference between the colonized Americans and the ethnic immigrant minorities is that the latter have always been able to operate fairly competitively within that relatively open section of the social and economic order because these groups came voluntarily in search of a better life, because their movements in society were not adminstratively controlled, and because they transformed their culture at their own pace—giving up ethnic values and institutions when it was seen as a desirable exchange for improvements in social position.

In present-day America, a major device of Black colonization is the powerless ghetto. As Kenneth Clark describes the situation:

> Ghettoes are the consequence of the imposition of external power and the institutionalization of powerlessness. In this respect, they are in fact social, political, educational, and above all—economic colonies. Those confined within the ghetto walls are subject peoples. They are victims of the greed, cruelty, insensitivity, guilt and fear of their masters. . . .
>
> The community can best be described in terms of the analogy of a powerless colony. Its political leadership is divided, and all but one or two of its political leaders are shortsighted and dependent upon the larger political power structure. Its social agencies are financially precarious and dependent upon sources of support outside the community. Its churches are isolated or dependent. Its economy is dominated by small businesses which are largely owned by absentee owners, and its tenements and other real property are also owned by absentee landlords.
>
> Under a system of centralization, Harlem's schools are controlled by forces outside of the community. Programs and policies are supervised and determined by individuals who do not live in the community . . .[8]

Of course many ethnic groups in America have lived in ghettoes. What make the Black ghettoes an expression of colonized status are three special features. First, the ethnic ghettoes arose more from voluntary choice, both in the sense of the choice to immigrate to America and the decision to live among one's fellow ethnics. Second, the immigrant ghettoes tended to be a one and two generation phenomenon; they were actually way-stations in the process of acculturation and assimilation. When they continue to persist as in the case of San Francisco's Chinatown, it is because they are big business for the ethnics themselves and there is a new stream of immigrants. The Black ghetto on the other hand has been a more permanent phenomenon, although some individuals do escape it. But most relevant is the third point. European ethnic groups like the Poles, Italians, and Jews generally only experienced a brief period, often less than a generation, during which their residential buildings, commercial stores, and other enterprises were owned by outsiders. The Chinese and Japanese faced handicaps of color prejudice that were almost as strong as the Blacks faced, but very soon gained control of their internal communities, because their traditional ethnic culture and social organization had not been destroyed by slavery and internal colonization. But Afro-Americans are distinct in the extent to which their segregated communities have remained controlled economically, politically, and administratively from the outside. One indicator of this difference is the estimate that the "income of Chinese-Americans from Chinese-owned businesses is in proportion to their numbers 45 times as great as the income of Negroes from Negro owned businesses."⁹ But what is true of business is also true for the other social institutions that operate within the ghetto. The educators, policemen, social workers, politicians, and others who administer the affairs of ghetto residents are typically whites who live outside the Black community. Thus the ghetto plays a strategic role as the focus for the administration by outsiders which is also essential to the structure of overseas colonialism.¹⁰

The colonial status of the Negro community goes beyond the issue of ownership and decision-making within Black neighborhoods. The Afro-American population in most cities has very little influence on the power structure and institutions of the larger metropolis, despite the fact that in numerical terms, Blacks tend to be the most sizeable of the various interest groups. A recent analysis of policy-making in Chicago estimates that "Negroes really hold less than 1 percent of the effective power in the Chicago metropolitan area. [Negroes are 20 percent of Cook County's population.] Realistically the power structure of Chicago is hardly less white than that of Mississippi."¹¹

Colonization outside of a traditional colonial structure has its own special conditions. The group culture and social structure of the colonized in America is less developed; it is also less autonomous. In addition, the colonized are a numerical minority, and furthermore they are ghettoized more totally and are more dispersed than people under classic colonialism. Though these realities affect the magnitude and direction of response, it is my basic thesis that the most important expressions of protest in the Black community during the recent years reflect the colonized status of Afro-America. Riots, programs of separation, politics of community control, the Black revolutionary movements, and cultural nationalism each represent a different strategy of attack on domestic colonialism in America. Let us now examine some of these movements.

## RIOT OR REVOLT?

The so-called riots are being increasingly recognized as a preliminary if primitive form of mass rebellion against a colonial status. There is still a tendency to absorb their meaning within the conventional scope of assimilation-integration politics: some commentators stress the material motives involved in looting as a sign that the rioters want to join America's middle-class affluence just like everyone else. That motives are mixed and often unconscious, that Black people want good furniture and television sets like whites is beside the point. The guiding impulse in most major outbreaks has not been integration with American society, but an attempt to stake out a sphere of control by moving against that society and destroying the symbols of its oppression.

In my critique of the McCone report I observed that the rioters were asserting a claim to territoriality, an unorganized and rather inchoate attempt to gain control over their community or "turf."[12] In succeeding disorders also the thrust of the action has been the attempt to clear out an alien presence, white men and officials, rather than a drive to kill whites as in a conventional race riot. The main attacks have been directed at the property of white business men and at the police who operate in the Black community "like an army of occupation" protecting the interests of outside exploiters and maintaining the domination over the ghetto by the central metropolitan power structure.[13] The Kerner report misleads when it attempts to explain riots in terms of integration: "What the rioters appear to be seeking was fuller participation in the social order and the material benefits enjoyed by the majority of American citizens. Rather than rejecting the American system, they were anxious to obtain a place for themselves in it."[14] More accurately, the revolts pointed to alienation from this system on the part of many poor and also not-so-poor Blacks. The sacredness of private property, that unconsciously accepted bulwark of our social arrangements, was rejected; people who looted apparently without guilt generally remarked that they were taking things that "really belonged" to them anyway.[15] Obviously the society's bases of legitimacy and authority have been attacked. Law and order has long been viewed as the white man's law and order by Afro-Americans; but now this perspective characteristic of a colonized people is out in the open. And the Kerner Report's own data question how well ghetto rebels are buying the system: In Newark only 33 percent of self-reported rioters said they thought this country was worth fighting for in the event of a major war; in the Detroit sample the figure was 55 percent.[16]

One of the most significant consequences of the process of colonization is a weakening of the colonized's individual and collective will to resist his oppression. It has been easier to contain and control Black ghettoes because communal bonds and group solidarity have been weakened through divisions among leadership, failures of organization, and a general disspiritment that accompanies social oppression. The riots are a signal that the will to resist has broken the mold of accommodation. In some cities as in Watts they also represented nascent movements toward community identity. In several riot-torn ghettoes the outbursts have stimulated new organizations and movements. If it is true that the riot phenomenon of 1964–68 has passed its peak, its historical import may be more for the "internal" organizing momentum generated than for any profound "external" response of the larger society facing up to underlying causes.

Despite the appeal of Frantz Fanon to young Black revolutionaries, America is not Algeria. It is difficult to foresee how riots in our cities can play a role equivalent to rioting in the colonial situation as an integral phase in a movement for national liberation. In 1968 some militant groups (for example, the Black Panther Party in Oakland) had concluded that ghetto riots were self-defeating of the lives and interests of Black people in the present balance of organization and gunpowder, though they had served a role to stimulate both Black consciousness and white awareness of the depths of racial crisis. Such militants have been influential in "cooling" their communities during periods of high riot potential. Theoretically oriented Black radicals see riots as spontaneous mass behavior which must be replaced by a revolutionary organization and consciousness. But despite the differences in objective conditions, the violence of the 1960's seems to serve the same psychic function, assertions of dignity and manhood for young Blacks in urban ghettoes, as it did for the colonized of North Africa described by Fanon and Memmi.[17]

## CULTURAL NATIONALISM

Cultural conflict is generic to the colonial relation because colonization involves the domination of Western technological values over the more communal cultures of non-Western peoples. Colonialism played havoc with the national integrity of the peoples it brought under its sway. Of course, all traditional cultures are threatened by industrialism, the city, and modernization in communication, transportation, health, and education. What is special are the political and administrative decisions of colonizers in managing and controlling colonized peoples.

The boundaries of African colonies, for example, were drawn to suit the political conveniences of the European nations without regard to the social organization and cultures of African tribes and kingdoms. Thus Nigeria as blocked out by the British included the Yorubas and the Ibos, whose civil war today is a residuum of the colonialist's disrespect for the integrity of indigenous cultures.

The most total destruction of culture in the colonization process took place not in traditional colonialism but in America. As Frazier stressed, the integral cultures of the diverse African peoples who furnished the slave trade were destroyed because slaves from different tribes, kingdoms, and linguistic groups were purposely separated to maximize domination and control. Thus language, religion, and national loyalties were lost in North America much more completely than in the Caribbean and Brazil where slavery developed somewhat differently. Thus on this key point America's internal colonization has been more total and extreme than situations of classic colonialism. For the British in India and the European powers in Africa were not able—as outnumbered minorities—to destroy the national and tribal cultures of the colonized. Recall that American slavery lasted 250 years and its racist aftermath another 100. Colonial dependency in the case of British Kenya and French Algeria lasted only 77 and 125 years respectively. In the wake of this more drastic uprooting and destruction of culture and social organization, much more powerful agencies of social, political and sociological domination developed in the American case.

> Colonial control of many peoples inhabiting the colonies was more a goal than a fact, and at Independence there were undoubtedly fairly large numbers of Africans who had never seen a colonial administrator. The gradual process of extension of control from the administrative center on the African coast contrasts sharply with the total uprooting involved in the slave trade and the totalitarian aspects of slavery in the United States. Whether or not Elkins is correct in treating slavery as a total institution, it undoubtedly had a far more radical and pervasive impact on American slaves than did colonialism on the vast majority of Africans.[18]

Yet a similar cultural process unfolds in both contexts of colonialism. To the extent that they are involved in the larger society and economy, the colonized are caught up in a conflict between two cultures. Fanon has described how the assimilation-oriented schools of Martinique taught him to reject his own culture and Blackness in favor of Westernized, French, and white values.[19] Both the colonized elites under traditional colonialism and perhaps the majority of Afro-Americans today experience a parallel split in identity, cultural loyalty, and political orientation.[20]

The colonizers use their culture to socialize the colonized elites (intellectuals, politicians, and middle class) into an identification with the colonial system. Because Western culture has the prestige, the power, and the key to open the limited opportunity that a minority of the colonized may achieve, the first reaction seems to be an acceptance of the dominant values. Call it brainwashing as the Black Muslims put it; call it identifying with the aggressor if you prefer Freudian terminology; call it a natural response to the hope and belief that integration and democratization can really take place if you favor a more commonsense explanation, this initial acceptance in time crumbles on the realities of racism and colonialism. The colonized, seeing that his success with colonialism is at the expense of his group and his own inner identity, moves radically toward a rejection of the Western culture and develops a nationalistic outlook that celebrates his people and their traditions. As Memmi describes it:

> Assimilation being abandoned, the colonized's liberation must be carried out through a recovery of self and of autonomous dignity. Attempts at imitating the colonizer required self-denial; the colonizer's rejection is the indispensable prelude to self-discovery. That accusing and annihilating image must be shaken off; oppression must be attacked boldly since it is impossible to go around it. After having been rejected for so long by the colonizer, the day has come when it is the colonized who must refuse the colonizer.[21]

Memmi's book, *The Colonizer and the Colonized*, is based on his experience as a Tunisian Jew in a marginal position between the French and the colonized Arab majority. The uncanny parallels between the North African situation he describes and the course of Black-white relations in our society is the best impressionist argument I know for the thesis that we have a colonized group and a colonizing system in America. His discussion of why even the most radical French anti-colonialist cannot participate in the struggle of the colonized is directly applicable to the situation of the white liberal and radical vis-à-vis the Black movement. His portrait of the colonized is as good an analysis of the psychology behind Black Power and Black nationalism as anything that has been written in the U.S. Consider for example:

> Considered *en bloc* as *them, they,* or *those,* different from every point of view, homogeneous in a radical heterogeneity, the colonized reacts by

rejecting all the colonizers *en bloc*. The distinction between deed and intent has no great significance in the colonial situation. In the eyes of the colonized, all Europeans in the colonies are de facto colonizers, and whether they want to be or not, they are colonizers in some ways. By their privileged economic position, by belonging to the political system of oppression, or by participating in an effectively negative complex toward the colonized, they are colonizers. . . . They are supporters or at least unconscious accomplices of that great collective aggression of Europe.[22]

The same passion which made him admire and absorb Europe shall make him assert his differences; since those differences, after all, are within him and correctly constitute his true self.[23]

The important thing now is to rebuild his people, whatever be their authentic nature; to reforge their unity, communicate with it, and to feel that they belong.[24]

Cultural revitalization movements play a key role in anti-colonial movements. They follow an inner necessity and logic of their own that comes from the consequences of colonialism on groups and personal identities; they are also essential to provide the solidarity which the political or military phase of the anti-colonial revolution requires. In the U.S. an Afro-American culture has been developing since slavery out of the ingredients of African world-views, the experience of bondage, Southern values and customs, migration and the Northern lower-class ghettoes, and most importantly, the political history of the Black population in its struggle against racism.[25] That Afro-Americans are moving toward cultural nationalism in a period when ethnic loyalties tend to be weak (and perhaps on the decline) in this country is another confirmation of the unique colonized position of the Black group. (A similar nationalism seems to be growing among American Indians and Mexican-Americans.)

## THE MOVEMENT FOR GHETTO CONTROL

The call for Black Power unites a number of varied movements and tendencies.[26] Though no clear-cut program has yet emerged, the most important emphasis seems to be the movement for control of the ghetto. Black leaders and organizations are increasingly concerned with owning and controlling those institutions that exist within or impinge upon their community. The colonial model provides a key to the understanding of this movement, and indeed ghetto control advocates have increasingly invoked the language of colonialism in pressing for local home rule. The framework of anti-colonialism explains why the struggle for poor people's or community control of poverty programs has been more central in many cities than the content of these programs and why it has been crucial to exclude whites from leadership positions in Black organizations.

The key institutions that anti-colonialists want to take over or control are business, social services, schools, and the police. Though many spokesmen have advocated the exclusion of white landlords and small businessmen from the ghetto, this program has evidently not struck fire with the Black population and little concrete movement toward economic expropriation has yet developed. Welfare recipients have organized in many cities to protect their rights and gain a greater voice in the decisions that affect them, but whole communities have not yet been able to mount direct action against welfare colonialism. Thus schools and the police seem now to be the burning issues of ghetto control politics.

During the past few years there has been a dramatic shift from educational integration as the primary goal to that of community control of the schools. Afro-Americans are demanding their own school boards, with the power to hire and fire principals and teachers and to construct a curriculum which would be relevant to the special needs and culture style of ghetto youth. Especially active in high schools and colleges have been Black students, whose protests have centered on the incorporation of Black Power and Black culture into the educational system. Consider how similar is the spirit behind these developments to the attitude of the colonized North African toward European education:

> He will prefer a long period of educational mistakes to the continuance of the colonizer's school organization. He will choose institutional disorder in order to destroy the institutions built by the colonizer as soon as possible. There we will see, indeed a reactive drive of profound protest. He will no longer owe anything to the colonizer and will have definitely broken with him.[27]

Protest and institutional disorder over the issue of school control came to a head in 1968 in New York City. The procrastination in the Albany State legislature, the several crippling strikes called by the teachers union, and the almost frenzied response of Jewish organizations makes it clear that decolonization of education faces the resistance of powerful vested interests.[28] The situation is too dynamic at present to assess probable future results. However, it can be safely predicted that some form of school decentralization will be institutionalized in New York, and the movement for community control of education will spread to more cities.

This movement reflects some of the problems and ambiguities that stem from the situation of colonization outside an immediate colonial context. The Afro-American community is not parallel in structure to the communities of colonized nations under traditional colonialism. The significant difference here is the lack of fully developed indigenous institutions besides the church. Outside of some areas of the South there is really no Black economy, and most Afro-Americans are inevitably caught up in the larger society's structure of occupations, education, and mass communication. Thus the ethnic nationalist orientation which reflects the reality of colonization exists alongside an integrationist orientation which corresponds to the reality that the institutions of the larger society are much more developed than those of the incipient nation.[29] As would be expected the movement for school control reflects both tendencies. The militant leaders who spearhead such local movements may be primarily motivated by the desire to gain control over the community's institutions—they are anticolonialists first and foremost. Many parents who support them may share this goal also, but the majority are probably more concerned about creating a new education that will enable their children to "make it" in the society and the economy as a whole—they know that the present school system fails ghetto children and does not prepare them for participation in American life.

There is a growing recognition that the police are the most crucial institution maintaining the colonized status of Black Americans. And of all establishment institutions, police departments probably include the highest proportion of individual racists. This is no accident since central to the workings of racism (an essential component of colonization) are attacks on the humanity and dignity of the subject group. Through their normal routines the police constrict Afro-Americans to Black neighborhoods by harassing and questioning them when found outside the ghetto; they break up groups of youth congregating on corners or in cars without any provocation; and they continue to use offensive and racist language no matter how many intergroup understanding seminars have been built into the police academy. They also shoot to kill ghetto residents for alleged crimes such as car thefts and running from police officers.[30]

Police are key agents in the power equation as well as the drama of dehumanization. In the final analysis they do the dirty work for the larger system by restricting the striking back of Black rebels to skirmishes inside the ghetto, thus deflecting energies and attacks from the communities and institutions of the larger power structure. In a historical review, Gary Marx notes that since the French revolution, police and other authorities have killed large numbers of demonstrators and rioters; the rebellious "rabble" rarely destroys human life. The same pattern has been repeated in America's recent revolts.[31] Journalistic accounts appearing in the press recently suggest that police see themselves as defending the interests of white people against a tide of Black insurgence; furthermore the majority of whites appear to view "blue power" in this light. There is probably no other opinion on which the races are as far apart today as they are on the question of attitudes toward the police.

In many cases set off by a confrontation between a policeman and a Black citizen, the ghetto uprisings have dramatized the role of law enforcement and the issue of police brutality. In their aftermath, movements have arisen to contain police activity. One of the first was the Community Alert Patrol in Los Angeles, a method of policing the police in order to keep them honest and constrain their violations of personal dignity. This was the first tactic of the Black Panther Party which originated in Oakland, perhaps the most significant group to challenge the police role in maintaining the ghetto as a colony. The Panther's later policy of openly carrying guns (a legally protected right) and their intention of defending themselves against police aggression has brought on a series of confrontations with the Oakland police department. All indications are that the authorities intend to destroy the Panthers by shooting, framing up, or legally harassing their leadership—diverting the group's energies away from its primary purpose of self-defense and organization of the Black community to that of legal defense and gaining support in the white community.

There are three major approaches to "police colonialism" that correspond to reformist and revolutionary readings of the situation. The most elementary and also superficial sees colonialism in the fact that ghettoes are overwhelmingly patrolled by white rather than by Black officers. The proposal—supported today by many police departments —to increase the number of Blacks on local forces to something like their distribution in the city would then make it possible to reduce the use of white cops in the ghetto. This reform should be supported, for a variety of obvious reasons, but it does not get to the heart of the police role as agents of colonization.

The Kerner Report documents the fact that in some cases Black policemen can be as brutal as their white counterparts. The Report does not tell us who polices the ghetto, but they have compiled the proportion of Negroes on the forces of the major cities. In some cities the disparity is so striking that white police inevitably dominate ghetto patrols. (In Oakland 31 percent of the population and only 4 percent of the police are Black; in Detroit the figures are 39 percent and 5 percent; and in New Orleans 41 and 4.) In other cities, however, the proportion of Black cops is approaching the distribution in the city: Philadelphia 29 percent and 20 percent; Chicago 27 percent and 17 percent.[32] These figures also suggest that both the extent and the pattern of colonization may vary from one city to another. It would be useful to study how Black comunities differ in degree of control over internal institutions as well as in economic and political power in the metropolitan area.

A second demand which gets more to the issue is that police should live in the communities they patrol. The idea here is that Black cops who lived in the ghetto would have to be accountable to the community; if they came on like white cops then "the brothers would take care of business" and make their lives miserable. The third or maximalist position is based on the premise that the police play no positive role in the ghettoes. It calls for the withdrawal of metropolitan officers from Black communities and the substitution of an autonomous indigenous force that would maintain order without oppressing the population. The precise relationship between such an independent police, the city and county law enforcement agencies, a ghetto governing body that would supervise and finance it, and especially the law itself is yet unclear. It is unlikely that we will soon face these problems directly as they have arisen in the case of New York's schools. Of all the programs of decolonization, police autonomy will be most resisted. It gets to the heart of how the state functions to control and contain the Black community through delegating the legitimate use of violence to police authority.

The various "Black Power" programs that are aimed at gaining control of individual ghettoes—buying up property and businesses, running the schools through community boards, taking over anti-poverty programs and other social agencies, diminishing the arbitrary power of the police—can serve to revitalize the institutions of the ghetto and build up an economic, professional, and political power base. These programs seem limited; we do not know at present if they are enough in themselves to end colonized status.[33] But they are certainly a necessary first step.

## THE ROLE OF WHITES

What makes the Kerner Report a less-than-radical document is its superficial treatment of racism and its reluctance to confront the colonized relationship between Black people and the larger society. The Report emphasizes the attitudes and feelings that make up white racism, rather than the system of privilege and control which is the heart of the matter.[34] With all its discussion of the ghetto and its problems, it never faces the question of the stake that white Americans have in racism and ghettoization.

This is not a simple question, but this paper should not end with the impression that police are the major villains. All white Americans gain some privileges and advantage from the colonization of Black communities.[35] The majority of whites also lose something from this oppression and division in society. Serious research should be directed to the ways in which white individuals and institutions are tied into the ghetto. In closing let me suggest some possible parameters.

1. It is my guess that only a small minority of whites make a direct economic profit from ghetto colonization. This is hopeful in that the ouster of white businessmen may become politically feasible. Much more significant, however, are the private and corporate interests in the land and residential property of the Black community; their holdings and influence on urban decision-making must be exposed and combated.

2. A much larger minority have occupational and professional interests in the present arrangements. The Kerner Commission reports that 1.3 million non-white men would have to be upgraded occupationally in order to make the Black job distribution roughly similar to the white. They advocate this without mentioning that 1.3 million specially privileged white workers would lose in the bargain.[36] In addition there are those professionals who carry out what Lee Rainwater has called the "dirty work" of administering the lives of the ghetto poor: the social workers, the school teachers, the urban development people, and of course the police.[37] The social problems of the Black community will ultimately be solved only by people and organizations from that community; thus the emphasis within these profes-

sions must shift toward training such a cadre of minority personnel. Social scientists who teach and study problems of race and poverty likewise have an obligation to replace themselves by bringing into the graduate schools and college faculties men of color who will become the future experts in these areas. For cultural and intellectual imperialism is as real as welfare colonialism, though it is currently screened behind such unassailable shibboleths as universalism and the objectivity of scientific inquiry.

3. Without downgrading the vested interests of profit and profession, the real nitty-gritty elements of the white stake are political power and bureaucratic security. Whereas few whites have much understanding of the realities of race relations and ghetto life, I think most give tacit or a least subconscious support for the containment and control of the Black population. Whereas most whites have extremely distorted images of Black Power, many—if not most—would still be frightened by actual Black political power. Racial groups and identities are real in American life; white Americans sense they are on top, and they fear possible reprisals or disruptions were power to be more equalized. There seems to be a paranoid fear in the white psyche of Black dominance; the belief that Black autonomy would mean unbridled license is so ingrained that such reasonable outcomes as Black political majorities and independent Black police forces will be bitterly resisted.

On this level the major mass bulwark of colonization is the administrative need for bureaucratic security so that the middle classes can go about their life and business in peace and quiet. The Black militant movement is a threat to the orderly procedures by which bureaucracies and suburbs manage their existence, and I think today there are more people who feel a stake in conventional procedures than there are those who gain directly from racism. For in their fight for institutional control, the colonized will not play by the white rules of the game. These administrative rules have kept them down and out of the system; therefore they have no necessary intention of running institutions in the image of the white middle class.

The liberal, humanist value that violence is the worst sin cannot be defended today if one is commited squarely against racism and for self-determination. For some violence is almost inevitable in the decolonization process; unfortunately racism in America has been so effective that the greatest power Afro-Americans (and perhaps also Mexican-Americans) wield today is the power to disrupt. If we are going to swing with these revolutionary times and at least respond positively to the anti-colonial movement, we will have to learn to live with conflict, confrontation, constant change, and what may be real or apparent chaos and disorder.

A positive response from the white majority needs to be in two major directions at the same time. First, community liberation movements should be supported in every way by pulling out white instruments of direct control and exploitation and substituting technical assistance to the community when this is asked for. But it is not enough to relate affirmatively to the nationalist movement for ghetto control without at the same time radically opening doors for full participation in the institutions of the mainstream. Otherwise the liberal and radical position is little different than the traditional segregationist. Freedom in the special conditions of American colonization means that the colonized must have the choice between participation in the larger society and in their own independent structures.

## NOTES

1. This is a revised version of a paper delivered at the University of California Centennial Program, "Studies in Violence," Los Angeles, June 1, 1968. For criticisms and ideas that have improved an earlier draft, I am indebted to Robert Wood, Lincoln Bergman, and Gary Marx. As a good colonialist I have probably restated (read: stolen) more ideas from the writings of Kenneth Clark, Stokely Carmichael, Frantz Fanon, and especially such contributors to the Black Panther Party (Oakland) newspaper as Huey Newton, Bobby Seale, Eldridge Cleaver, and Kathleen Cleaver than I have appropriately credited or generated myself. In self-defense I should state that I began working somewhat independently on a colonial analysis of American race relations in the fall of 1965; see my "Whitewash Over Watts: The Failure of the McCone Report," *Trans-action*, 3 (March-April, 1966), pp. 3–9, 54.

2. Harold Cruse, *Rebellion or Revolution*, New York: 1968, p. 214.

3. Nationalism, including an orientation toward Africa, is no new development. It has been a constant tendency within Afro-American politics. See Cruse, *ibid*, esp. chaps. 5–7.

4. This was six years before the publication of *The Crisis of the Negro Intellectual*, New York: Morrow, 1968, which brought Cruse into prominence. Thus the 1962 article was not widely read until its reprinting in Cruse's essays, *Rebellion or Revolution, op. cit.*

5. Kenneth Clark, *Dark Ghetto*, New York: Harper and Row, 1965. Clark's analysis first appeared a year earlier in *Youth in the Ghetto*, New York: Haryou Associates, 1964.

6.  Stokely Carmichael and Charles Hamilton, *Black Power*, New York: Random, 1967.

7.  As Eldridge Cleaver reminds us, "Black people are a stolen people held in a colonial status on stolen land, and any analysis which does not acknowledge the colonial status of black people cannot hope to deal with the real problem." "The Land Question," *Ramparts*, 6 (May, 1968), p. 51.

8.  *Youth in the Ghetto, op. cit.*, pp. 10–11; 79–80.

9.  N. Glazer and D. P. Moynihan, *Beyond the Melting Pot*, Cambridge, Mass.: M.I.T., 1963, p. 37.

10. "When we speak of Negro social disabilities under capitalism, . . . we refer to the fact that he does not own anything—*even what is ownable in his own community.* Thus to fight for black liberation *is to fight for his right to own.* The Negro is politically compromised today because he owns nothing. He has little voice in the affairs of state because he owns nothing. The fundamental reason why the Negro bourgeois-democratic revolution has been aborted is because American capitalism has prevented the development of a black class of capitalist owners of institutions and economic tools. To take one crucial example, Negro radicals today are severely hampered in their tasks of educating the black masses on political issues because Negroes do not own any of the necessary means of propaganda and communication. The Negro owns no printing presses, he has no stake in the networks of the means of communication. Inside his own communities he does not own the house he lives in, the property he lives on, nor the wholesale and retail sources from which he buys his commodities. He does not own the edifices in which he enjoys culture and entertainment or in which he socializes. In capitalist society, an individual or group that does not own anything is powerless." H. Cruse, "Behind the Black Power Slogan," in Cruse, *Rebellion or Revolution, op. cit.*, pp. 238–239.

11. Harold M. Baron, "Black Powerlessness in Chicago," *Trans-action*, 6 (Nov., 1968), pp. 27–33.

12. R. Blauner, "Whitewash Over Watts," *op. cit.*

13. "The police function to support and enforce the interests of the dominant political, social, and economic interests of the town" is a statement made by a former police scholar and official, according to A. Neiderhoffer, *Behind the Shield*, New York: Doubleday, 1967 as cited by Gary T. Marx, "Civil Disorder and the Agents of Control," *Journal of Social Issues*, forthcoming.

14. Report of the National Advisory Commission on Civil Disorders, N.Y.: Bantam, March, 1968, p. 7.

15. This kind of attitude has a long history among American Negroes. During slavery, Blacks used the same rationalization to justify stealing

from their masters. Appropriating things from the master was viewed as "*taking* part of his property for the benefit of another part; whereas *stealing* referred to appropriating something from another slave, an offense that was not condoned." Kenneth Stampp, *The Peculiar Institution*, Vintage, 1956, p. 127.

16. Report of the National Advisory Commission on Civil Disorders, *op. cit.*, p. 178.

17. Frantz Fanon, *Wretched of the Earth*, New York: Grove, 1963; Albert Memmi, *The Colonizer and the Colonized*, Boston: Beacon, 1967.

18. Robert Wood, "Colonialism in Africa and America: Some Conceptual Considerations," December, 1967, unpublished paper.

19. F. Fanon, *Black Skins, White Masks*, New York: Grove, 1967.

20. Harold Cruse has described how these two themes of integration with the larger society and identification with ethnic nationality have struggled within the political and cultural movements of Negro Americans. *The Crisis of the Negro Intellectual, op. cit.*

21. Memmi, *op. cit.*, p. 128.

22. *Ibid.*, p. 130.

23. *Ibid.*, p. 132.

24. *Ibid.*, p. 134.

25. In another essay, I argue against the standard sociological position that denies the existence of an ethnic Afro-American culture and I expand on the above themes. The concept of "Soul" is astonishingly parallel in content to the mystique of "Negritude" in Africa; the Pan-African culture movement has its parallel in the burgeoning Black culture mood in Afro-American communities. See "Black Culture: Myth or Reality" in Peter Rose, editor, *Americans From Africa*, Atherton, 1969.

26. Scholars and social commentators, Black and white alike, disagree in interpreting the contemporary Black Power movement. The issues concern whether this is a new development in Black protest or an old tendency revised; whether the movement is radical, revolutionary, reformist, or conservative; and whether this orientation is unique to Afro-Americans or essentially a Black parallel to other ethnic group strategies for collective mobility. For an interesting discussion of Black Power as a modernized version of Booker T. Washington's separatism and economism, see Harold Cruse, *Rebellion or Revolution, op. cit.*, pp. 193–258.

27. Memmi, *op. cit.*, pp. 137–138.

28. For the New York school conflict see Jason Epstein, "The Politics of School Decentralization," *New York Review of Books*, June 6, 1968, pp. 26–32; and "The New York City School Revolt," *ibid.*, 11, no. 6, pp. 37–41.

29. This dual split in the politics and psyche of the Black American was poetically described by Du Bois in his *Souls of Black Folk*, and more recently has been insightfully analyzed by Harold Cruse in *The Crisis of the Negro Intellectual, op. cit.* Cruse has also characterized the problem of the Black community as that of underdevelopment.

30. A recent survey of police finds "that in the predominantly Negro areas of several large cities, many of the police perceive the residents as basically hostile, especially the youth and adolescents. A lack of public support—from citizens, from courts, and from laws—is the policeman's major complaint. But some of the public criticism can be traced to the activities in which he engages day by day, and perhaps to the tone in which he enforces the "law" in the Negro neighborhoods. Most frequently he is "called upon" to intervene in domestic quarrels and break up loitering groups. He stops and frisks two or three times as many people as are carrying dangerous weapons or are actual criminals, and almost half of these don't wish to cooperate with the policeman's efforts." Peter Rossi *et al.*, "Between Black and White—The Faces of American Institutions and the Ghetto," in Supplemental Studies for The National Advisory Commission on Civil Disorders, July 1968, p. 114.

31. "In the Gordon Riots of 1780 demonstrators destroyed property and freed prisoners, but did not seem to kill anyone, while authorities killed several hundred rioters and hung an additional 25. In the Rebellion Riots of the French Revolution, though several hundred rioters were killed, they killed no one. Up to the end of the Summer of 1967, this pattern had clearly been repeated, as police, not rioters, were responsible for most of the more than 100 deaths that have occurred. Similarly, in a related context, the more than 100 civil rights murders of recent years have been matched by almost no murders of racist whites." G. Marx, "Civil Disorders and the Agents of Social Control," *op. cit.*

32. Report of the National Advisory Commission on Civil Disorders, *op. cit.*, p. 321. That Black officers nevertheless would make a difference is suggested by data from one of the supplemental studies to the Kerner Report. They found Negro policemen working in the ghettoes considerably more sympathetic to the community and its social problems than their white counterparts. Peter Rossi *et al.*, "Between Black and White—The Faces of American Institutions in the Ghetto," *op. cit.*, chap. 6.

33. Eldridge Cleaver has called this first stage of the anti-colonial movement *community* liberation in contrast to a more long-range goal of *national* liberation. E. Cleaver, "Community Imperialism," Black Panther Party newspaper, 2 (May 18, 1968).

34. For a discussion of this failure to deal with racism, see Gary T. Marx, "Report of the National Commission: The Analysis of Disorder or Disorderly Analysis," 1968, unpublished paper.

35. Such a statement is easier to assert than to document but I am attempting the latter in a forthcoming book tentatively titled *White Racism, Black Culture,* to be published by Little Brown, 1970.

36. Report of the National Advisory Commission on Civil Disorders, *op. cit.,* pp. 253–256.

37. Lee Rainwater, "The Revolt of the Dirty-Workers," *Trans-action,* 5 (Nov., 1967), pp. 2, 64.

## 19 | Black Caucuses in the Unions

*Charles Denby*

The whole new stage of black revolt that has now moved directly into the factories has to be seen as part of the long, long history of black caucuses. To understand both today and tomorrow, you first have to know what the black caucuses were yesterday, when they sprang up spontaneously at the end of World War II.

I remember the first strike I ever led. It was over the discrimination against black women workers in our shop. It was during World War II, when I was at Briggs and I was so new in the shop that I didn't even know what a strike was. I was working in the dope room, where you put glue on the airplane wing. You had to paint on so many coats of glue and then it was baked and painted again. The room was sealed and ventilated through some kind of fans in the ceiling. The fumes and odor were so bad we had no appetite left by lunchtime.

When I was first hired, there were all white men in the room. But as they hired blacks, the whites were transferred to better jobs. One day they brought in the first black woman. By the end of that week they had brought in about five black women, and there were only one or two white men left. That's when we decided to get those girls out of there. The women had been talking about their husbands who were in the service in Germany—and here they couldn't even get a job in the sewing room next door. That was for white women only. These things just burned us up.

None of us knew anything about the union, but I finally got to talk to our white Chief Steward, who told me the reason there were only white women in the sewing room was because they had so much

Reprinted from *New Politics* vol. VII, no. 3 (Summer 1968): 10–17. © New Politics Publishing Co. By permission of *New Politics: A Journal of Socialist Thought.*

seniority, 10 or 15 years. We knew they were lying, because some of those girls were just out of high school. So we told the Steward that if he didn't do something about it we were all going to quit at the same time, on the same day. We didn't know it would be called a strike. All we knew was that every factory had "Help Wanted" signs up and if we quit and went together to some other factory, we'd be working the next day.

On the day we walked out, they locked the gates on us. (That was the first we knew that the huge fence around the shop wasn't so much to keep saboteurs out, as to keep us in.) By that time, other workers inside the factory were coming out with us. We didn't even know what they were coming out for. I thought maybe they just had a problem like we did. It wasn't until the company sent for me as the "strike leader" that I realized what we had actually done.

We learned a lot in that strike, including what to expect from the union leaders. It was a Negro committeeman who, after the company had agreed to transfer the black women to the sewing room, talked them into going to Mack plant where they would make 15¢ an hour more—but be separated from the rest of us. They didn't know until the fifth day they were there that Mack didn't even have a sewing room and that they were going to work on a press.

## THE TULC AND THE "GENTLEMEN'S AGREEMENT"

One stage in the black workers' revolt, in fact, arose because workers began to realize that we would have to fight the union bureaucracy as much as we had fought management up to then. This unrest was what led A. Philip Randolph to organize the Trade Union Leadership Council (TULC) ten years ago. What workers didn't know was that there was some sort of "Gentlemen's Agreement" between Reuther and Randolph.

UAW members all over the country were attacking the bureaucrats —much as the black caucuses are doing today, except that there was no exclusion of whites such as you find in some of the current black caucuses. Randolph came to Detroit to hold his little convention and ran it just like the UAW conventions, "from the top," evading all the questions the rank and file wanted to discuss.

After the convention, we kept pressing Randolph about the question of discrimination in the shop and he told us plainly that this was not going to be an organization to take up grievances of black workers on the shop level. All TULC was going to do, he said, was to raise the question of discrimination but writing grievances would have to be done through regular channels. A lot of the workers said, "Hell, this is what we've been doing all the time and nothing has ever happened." But, because they made a big splash in the papers, many black rank and filers came around, in the beginning.

The leaders always emphasized that it was *not* a "black organization." Yet that is just what the black workers wanted to make it—not by excluding whites but by *blacks controlling it*, for themselves, not for the UAW. As TULC developed, it played around more with community problems than shop problems and when it did raise shop questions, it was more concerned with the building trades or things outside of the UAW than inside it. Reuther has always been a master of substitution—and he managed to teach Randolph the same trick.

After two years there was a tremendous drop in membership, and today, no matter how urgently a meeting is called, you seldom see a rank and filer around. Recently they called a meeting, and sent letters to every older black "activist" they could think of. They said they called it to discuss how they could protect themselves from the "vicious racist extremists"—like the Dodge Revolutionary Union Movement (DRUM). But there were more young black workers outside picketing the meeting than older blacks inside attending it.

The whole situation was summed up pretty well when 26 young black workers were fired after a wildcat strike at the Eldon Axel plant and went down to picket Solidarity House, early this year. The UAW sent a black official, Sheldon Tappes, to meet with them. Tappes had to admit that if TULC had done what it was organized for, there wouldn't have been any such development as DRUM. And one of the young black pickets answered "And if Reuther and the other bureaucrats had done what the *union* was organized for, there wouldn't have been any need for TULC."

## A NEW STAGE TODAY

An entirely new stage was born with the appearance of groups like DRUM within the auto shops. The Dodge Revolutionary Union Movement was organized after Chrysler fired seven of the black workers who had struck the Dodge Main plant last year to protest a speed up on the line, while the UAW Convention was being held in Atlantic City. In

July, when DRUM called for a strike to support a list of demands against racism, both by Chrysler and the UAW, the call brought thousands of workers out of the plant and shut down production for two days.

In February of last year, several months *before* the Dodge strike in Detroit, 500 workers at the Mahwah, New Jersey, Ford plant had shut down production for three days after a racist foreman called a production worker a "black bastard." Out of that spontaneous wildcat, the United Black Brothers of Mahwah Ford was organized. This caucus has just led another wildcat strike over continued racism at that plant.

What is new about these caucuses is that they represent a much more basic opposition than any Reuther has ever before faced. The UAW had, until the appearance of these new caucuses, pretty much eliminated any organized opposition—by any means, ethical or unethical. The bureaucracy has not really had to give a damn about rank and file problems in the shop for years. Now they are facing some real opposition, *from below.*

In the early stages of the black caucus at Dodge, DRUM raised a proposal that amounted to "dual unionism." They proposed in their paper that all black workers stop paying dues to the UAW and pay them  instead to DRUM, to be used in the black communities. Many black workers I spoke with, who were very sympathetic to DRUM's activities *in the plant*, were opposed to this idea completely. They were all for a black caucus that would fight racism and inhuman working conditions in the plants. They were all for militant black workers taking over leadership in the unions for the purpose of making a complete change at the point of production. But they became skeptical of the objectives behind a proposal like this.

Black workers at Sparrow's Point, at Bethlehem Steel mill in Baltimore, on the other hand, formed a group outside the union, called the Committee for Equality, rather than forming a caucus within the union. They had a specific situation there, in which they could apply pressure on the government to end its multi-million dollar contracts with the company unless the company stopped discriminating. These workers created a "dual union" of a sort but it was tactical in their case. They felt they had to find some way to shake everything up—the racist company, as well as their racist union. And it worked.

The opposition of the black workers is part of the opposition of black people as a whole to white racist America, a movement that has been gaining in momentum ever since 1961.

In 1964, a mass picket line of about 500 got world headlines by surrounding the GM building in Detroit with signs saying "Racism Hurts All Labor," "Automation Layoffs—Lily White Departments— Slow Upgrading—What is my job future?" The demonstration had been called by the NAACP and was distinguished from traditional labor picket lines by the presence of student youth and the singing of Freedom songs. GM agreed to negotiate and even without the threat of a demonstration, Chrysler and Ford did the same. What happened after the talks is another question.

In 1965, SNCC helped to organize a Mississippi Freedom Union and later a Tennessee Freedom Union. They had found, while trying to work on voter registration, that what black people in the South wanted most was to do something about their $3 a day wages and miserable working conditions. From organized labor all they got was evasiveness.

Later that same year, the grape workers in California began their strike for a farm workers organization with the help of CORE and other civil rights groups. By March of the next year, 1966, the Freedom Union idea moved North to the cities when CORE organized a pilot project in Baltimore—and the Maryland Freedom Union was born. The greatest victory there was the manner in which the unorganized black workers of Baltimore took matters into their own hands when nursing home workers walked out first and then called to tell the "organizers."

That same year, *organized* black workers were also taking matters into their own hands. When the UAW convention delegates met in Long Beach, California in the summer of 1966, they found black workers from Local 887 of the North American Aviation plant picketing the convention to protest discrimination by their local union against Negroes, women and Mexican Americans. They said, simply: "We've written lots of letters to Reuther. We even sent them return receipt requested. We have a pocketful of receipts. But no answers."

By September, these same NAA workers held the first "civil rights strike" of its kind to protest the discriminatory practices of the company. They wrote me that "One Negro worker who had been trying to be a drill press operator for two years was finally accepted the day after the strike. Another worker who had been told a few months earlier that he had failed (by one point) the test for machine operator's apprentice was told he had been accepted. Another was promoted to assistant foreman, whatever that means. And the company even announced that a Negro top brass was promoted to a $30,000 a year job. Long live tokenism!"

## SHOP PAPERS APPEAR AS DIVERSITY GROWS

One of the most significant developments out of that NAA situation was the appearance of a mimeographed shop paper, edited by these black workers themselves, which they called *The Protester*.

In Detroit, a group of auto workers at the Highland Park Chrysler Plant had come out that same year with a mimeographed shop paper called *The Stinger*. Another *Stinger* has just appeared this year at the Mack Avenue Chrysler plant.

The richness and diversity of the black workers' groups is constantly growing. Moreover, there are significant *differences* between the various black workers' groups that are springing up everywhere. The Mack Avenue "Stinger," for example, though it is edited by black workers, makes a distinction between the "whitey" who is a rank and file worker, and the "whitey" who is either a company representative or a union bureaucrat. The black editor puts it this way: "It's true that we are fighting discrimination against black workers in the shop as one of the most important questions of our lives. But that isn't the only question. The reason many of the white workers in our shop also read —and even support—*The Stinger*, is that we are raising the question of the *inhuman conditions* of all workers in production. Automation speed-up and the inhumanity of the company and union bureaucrats is against workers as a whole. That is what *The Stinger* is fighting, and why white workers have told us they are glad we are distributing it."

There is nothing more stupid than to think that all black workers think alike, or that there is only one face to the whole new phenomenon of the black caucuses. This was one of the most important points discussed at a conference sponsored by News & Letters in Detroit in January of this year, where black youth, workers, women and intellectuals had a chance for the first time to discuss with each other.

One black auto worker at the Detroit Conference felt that "too much of the activity of some black caucuses is pointed to getting on supervision rather than elevating labor on the line. The company doesn't care whether it's a white man or a black man as long as they get the production out. The company is getting very expert at using black supervisors to fight black workers."

Some younger auto workers felt that "trying to get a coalition with white workers is impossible because they are hung up in their racist bag." But a steel worker from the East described the black workers' organization in his mill which was so effective in ending some of the racist practices there that it was recognized by white workers who had their own problems with the union. When the black workers invited a group of white workers to come with them on one of their marches, the same white workers who hadn't wanted to associate with "those raving black militants out to destroy everything" suddenly decided maybe it wasn't such a bad idea, after all, and couldn't wait for the next march.

The United Black Brothers at Mahwah have also made it a point to appeal to all the workers in the shop. A leaflet issued in their wildcat two months ago put it this way:

> Why We Ask Your Support?—Because the same thing can happen to you. The company has been laying off men by the dozens, but the lines have not slowed up a bit. You have been given more work, and if you can't do it, you lose your job or get time off. The supervisors are harrassing the men and calling them all kinds of names such as "Dirty Guinea Bastard," "Black SOB," and "Stinking Spick," to name a few . . . We, the United Black Brothers, demand an end to this now and those guilty of these charges be removed . . . We ask all of you to stay out and support us in this fight!

## WHAT IS NEW IS REVOLUTION

The greatest difference between the new caucuses emerging today and those that appeared before is that most of us who were in black opposition groups up to now thought that the most important thing to do was to throw out the leadership, or change the union structure, or something of that nature. The young people today aren't thinking that way. They are thinking in terms of a complete change—of revolution.

They are just filled up to their necks with racism. And with the war. One professor from Cornell, during the recent revolt there, reported talking to one of the black students about their use of guns. He had sympathized with their demands but he had been trying to point out to them how powerful this country is and to warn them that they were facing tremendous oppression if they continued using such tactics. The black student had just laughed in his face: "You're talking about oppression coming upon me? I've been oppressed all my life. It's you and the people who call themselves liberals who are going to feel the oppression that's coming." It shocked the professor, because he knew the black student was right.

Young blacks today aren't joking about the complete change they are out to get. When the group at Dodge named themselves the Revolutionary Union Movement, it was very significant. Years ago if workers called themselves "revolutionaries," other workers would have shied away from them. Today the very word can attract workers.

It is too early to draw any sweeping conclusions about what will happen next with many black groups that exist independently and spontaneously in shops throughout the country. No national caucus is on the horizon yet and to give the impression that one already exists, much less to imply that DRUM is it—as the *Guardian* did in its March 8 special supplement on the black workers' revolt—is futile self deception.

In the recent shop elections, DRUM lost badly at Dodge Local 3, despite the fact that the membership there is overwhelmingly black. It is true that the union bureaucracy is not telling the whole truth when they claim that *they* won everywhere. At the Eldon Axel plant, for example, where 65 percent of the workers are black, ELDRUM ran candidates for only a few positions and, although they lost, black workers are in complete control of the local for the first time. Doug Fraser, Executive Board Member-at-Large for the Chrysler Division, claims that these workers are the "moderates" he was supporting. But ELDRUM supported them, too. And, most important of all, workers know that black workers have never controlled that local before.

The most honest way to judge the response of black workers is to compare the manner in which thousands responded to DRUM's call for a wildcat last year and the way they reacted at a mass meeting called after the 26 workers were fired at the Eldon Axel plant. The meeting was held in a large church and about five or six hundred workers crowded inside. The majority were younger workers but there were many older workers, too. The first thing that struck me was that those in control of the meeting were not workers in the plant or in any plant.

The speakers went on at great length attacking white racism—with the most vulgar name-calling possible. They spent a lot of time clowning and trying to be comedians. Once in a great while they touched on the vital issue of shop problems. Finally, the principal speaker was called. As soon as he got up, he raised his little red book above his head and said, "My Comrades of the Black Revolutionary Movement, how many of you have this book?" He had to ask several times before four or five raised their books in reply. The speaker told the audience that this was what the movement was all about and gave the address where everyone should go after the meeting to get his copy of "Comrade Mao's Thoughts." When he went on to call Mao "our closest ally" many of the workers in the audience began squirming and I felt that this sort of meeting was what labor bureaucrats need to destroy the movement.

It is clear that the labor bureaucracy will try either to crush it or to kill it by "joining" it. It has done that with every spontaneous movement that ever arose, including the unemployed movement of 1959. Many workers are already sure that Reuther's activity with the black hospital workers in Charleston, S.C., was forced on him by what has been happening in his own union. DRUM has not only attacked Reuther and called him a "racist pig"—but has told *why* they call him that. He has to try to remove that stigma from his "image."

He has not fooled black workers. Of course, they are only too happy to see him give $10,000 to the hospital strikers. But when they see him marching on a picket line in Charleston or Selma or anywhere else, they know that he hasn't been on a picket line with his own UAW workers for so many years he's forgotten what it's like. Reuther is always glad to integrate anything—outside of his own UAW.

The one thing the young black workers may not fully realize is that every time a black independent movement has appeared, the "politicos" who have rushed in to take it over, have helped reactionaries like Reuther to kill it before it can get off the ground. It was true in the first black organization within the union that I was involved with, as early as the '40s. There were about 200 of us, and we "stormed" Lansing and every black worker I knew was enthusiastic about where we were going. But the Communists and the Trotskysists moved in and began a naked fight over control of our organization. It is not so much that the so-called "radicals" come rushing in but every time they come rushing in *they want to take control and direct it.* The same thing is happening today. The only thing the Maoist do differently is to send blacks instead of whites to take control.

The question at this point is: Will the momentum of the movement be great enough to see the black caucuses become a national force separated from the labor bureaucracy and strong enough to keep control in the hands of the rank and file? Or will the bureaucrats and the Maoists succeed in nipping it in the bud?

Everyone in the shop is laughing at the Alliance for Labor Action, which they consider just some more of Reuther's power politics against Meany. They know that Reuther is hoping the black workers in the South will save his neck. Reuther forgets that they have brothers in the North who insist he has to prove his Labor Action at home, in his own union. The black workers have made it clear that they want to stick to shop problems, not get diverted to Reuther's latest schemes for "community organization." That is the message of the wildcats and the shop papers that have appeared in such diverse forms.

# Black Panther Party Platform and Program: What We Want, What We Believe (October, 1966)

1. *We want Freedom. We want power to determine the destiny of our Black Community.*

We believe that black people will not be free until we are able to determine our destiny.

2. *We want full employment for our people.*

We believe that the federal government is responsible and obligated to give every man employment or a guaranteed income. We believe that if the white American businessman will not give full employment, then the means of production should be taken from the businessmen and placed in the community so that the people of the community can organize and employ all of its people and give a high standard of living.

3. *We want an end to the robbery by the white man of our Black Community.*

We believe that this racist government has robbed us and now we are demanding the overdue debt of forty acres and two mules. Forty acres and two mules was promised 100 years ago as restitution for slave labor and mass murder of black people. We will accept the payment in currency which will be distributed to our many communities. The Germans are now aiding the Jews in Israel for the genocide of the Jewish people. The Germans murdered over six million Jews. The American racist has taken part in the slaughter of over fifty million black people; therefore we feel that this is a modest demand that we make.

4. *We want decent housing, fit for shelter of human beings.*

We believe that if the white landlords will not give decent housing to our black community, then the housing and the land should be